WHAT IS IT LIKE TO BE DEAD?

OXFORD STUDIES IN WESTERN ESOTERICISM

Series Editor
Henrik Bogdan, University of Gothenburg

CHILDREN OF LUCIFER
The Origins of Modern Religious Satanism
Ruben van Luijk

SATANIC FEMINISM
Lucifer as the Liberator of Woman in Nineteenth-Century Culture
Per Faxneld

THE SIBLYS OF LONDON
A Family on the Esoteric Fringes of Gregorian England
Susan Sommers

WHAT IS IT LIKE TO BE DEAD?
Near-Death Experiences, Christianity, and the Occult
Jens Schlieter

AMONG THE SCIENTOLOGISTS
History, Theology, and Praxis
Donald A. Westbrook

What Is It Like to Be Dead?

NEAR-DEATH EXPERIENCES, CHRISTIANITY,
AND THE OCCULT

Jens Schlieter

OXFORD
UNIVERSITY PRESS

OXFORD
UNIVERSITY PRESS

Oxford University Press is a department of the University of Oxford. It furthers
the University's objective of excellence in research, scholarship, and education
by publishing worldwide. Oxford is a registered trade mark of Oxford University
Press in the UK and certain other countries.

Published in the United States of America by Oxford University Press
198 Madison Avenue, New York, NY 10016, United States of America.

© Oxford University Press 2018

CIP data is on file at the Library of Congress
ISBN 978–0–19–088884–8

9 8 7 6 5 4 3 2 1
Printed by Sheridan Books, Inc., United States of America

Contents

Preface

AN OVERWHELMING MAJORITY of recent reports or studies on near-death experiences argue that—in one way or the other—the "experience" provides a foothold for the belief that there is survival of death. Having experienced the proximity of death transforms, it seems, both the view of "death" and of "life" as expressed by Augustinian monk Abraham a Sancta Clara: "Who dies before he dies, does not die when he dies."[1] Consequently, "the experience" amounts not only to a new certainty of postmortem survival—it is a call for fundamental change in life itself. For a substantial group of persons concerned, but also for academics studying near-death experiences, the life-changing potential is crucial. Reported aftereffects encompass fundamental changes in attitudes, beliefs, and life orientation. Communicated through various channels, it is claimed that persons who experienced states near or after death lost their fear of death, found their purpose in life, or became "more spiritual" (and either less "religious" or less "materialistic"). The experience itself—often declared to be indescribable, inexplicable, or ineffable—is held by many to be the most important in their lives, and, moreover, as such the best proof available for matters transcendent.

For the study of recent religiosity, near-death experiences and their narrative embeddings are of crucial importance, but, from that perspective, still an understudied phenomenon. Beyond question, experiences near death can be emotionally extremely

---

[1] "*Denn wer stirbt, ehe er stirbt, der stirbt nicht, wann er stirbt*" (Abraham a Sancta Clara 1710, 244).

intense, disruptive, irritating, but also ecstatic and overwhelming. Especially in the late decades of the 20th century, the institutionalization of self-help groups and networks such as the "International Association for Near-Death Studies, Inc." (IANDS) founded in 1977, shows that "experiencers," as they are now called, feel the need to share their enlightening or disturbing experiences in these secure milieus, and, not to forget, to endorse each other in handling the spiritual and social aftereffects. At the same time, the at times depreciative and disenchanting reactions, or psychopathological explanations of medical doctors, psychologists, priests, or society at large, have led some "experiencers" to become cautious in disclosing their experience.

Near-death experiences are, for sure, in many cases dramatic and existential. At the same time, descriptions of these experiences are instrumental in articulating "spiritual" life orientations—especially in modern, secular societies. Memoirs of such experiences may, however, encounter a fundamental paradox: to re-present an experience that was nothing less but "pure presence." Sometimes, it may be a pure presence that is later felt intensely as absence: A crucial element of some reports consists of a praise of the "experience" and the unwillingness to return to the body and into the life lived. In sum, personal memoirs of what the individual experienced while being (or expecting to be) close to death form a structural compound, together with narratives of how the experience has changed the respective individual's life, and, finally, of how the experiences were often rejected, medicalized, or even ridiculed. It is the latter quality, the experiences near death as "rejected knowledge" (Hanegraaff), that fits very well to their often esoteric content.

These testimonies of near-death experiences, their aftereffects, and the appearance of organized groups of witnesses and believers, such as the IANDS chapters, deserve serious attention as a significant development of recent, late modern society. Nevertheless, for a broader understanding of recent testimonies of near-death experiences, it is essential to become aware of the historical tradition in which reports of near-death experiences and their religious corollaries were communicated and handed down in scores of newspapers, journals, and books. Astonishingly, no study published so far covered the last four centuries, and especially the "long 19th century" (Hobsbawm), in which almost innumerable individuals reported such experiences. Only occasionally mentioned in recent studies of near-death experiences, collections of such testimonies have been published for more than 150 years, accompanied by attempts of how to classify and interpret such experiences.

Two major obstacles in current research were especially inhibitive for a historical survey. On the one hand, it is the opinion of transcultural and transhistorical universals expressed in near-death experiences often to be found in near-death research. Such an essentialism of assumed transcultural constants disposes of any incentives to analyze the phenomena more thoroughly. Usually, substantialist presuppositions undermine attempts to outline phenomena in their historical development. More specifically, extant studies were more engaged in uncovering the "common core" of modern near-death experiences and, say, ancient Greek, Egyptian, or Early Christian and medieval accounts of journeys into the beyond and afterlife conceptions, respectively. On the other hand, and in close interaction with the aforementioned, the majority of scholars were above all interested in establishing near-death experiences as authentic visions of, or into, an afterlife—spontaneously generated, authentic, and unconditional. For that matter, neither these experiences nor their reports will be in any way dependent on tradition. As these studies were especially eager to campaign for the acceptance of these experiences as veridical testimonies in the medical system (and other branches of modern society), they saw no need to uncover the pivotal strands of Western spiritualism, occultism, and esotericism that, for the historian of religion, obviously influenced—together with Christian metaculture—a large number of more recent accounts of near-death experiences. To put it more sharply: Since the invention of the generic term "near-death experiences" in the 1970s, we can witness a strong avoidance of disclosing the prominent precursors in the 19th and 20th centuries. Actually, the latter had already reported a large number of visionary and ecstatic experiences "near death," yet, simply as only one of several situations in which those experiences may emerge. In other words, these forerunners could still, and straightforwardly, testify and communicate experiences near death as homogeneously embedded in larger religious and spiritual cosmovisions. In consequence, they saw no need to bundle various different experiences under a new umbrella term of "near-death experiences."

Viewed in this way, it is the changing environment that contributed its share to the coming-together of near-death experiences: the largely successful institutionalization of biomedicine and the process of functional differentiation in modern societies that led to an increasingly autonomous subsystem of "religion" with clear demarcations. Modern biomedicine, secular and empirical psychology, psychoanalysis, positivist philosophy, behaviorism, and other voices joined the polyphonic chorus praising scientific explanations of religion in general, and the brain's "hallucinations near death" in particular. Exactly this environment, together with a decline of church-based religiosity and the ongoing trend toward privatized dying in hospitals, led to an even stronger emphasis of *individual personal experience*, of which experiences near death, "glimpses into the afterlife," may probably be the most meaningful.

Yet, to repeat, the experiences offered as suggestive evidence for a convincing answer to the question "what is it like to be dead?" are still an integral part of Western religious history. Although this study will confine itself to documenting and analyzing the genesis and genealogy of near-death experiences up to the 1970s, here I will provide only one more recent example. After having been comatose for several days and in very critical health in 2008, neurosurgeon Eben Alexander published a highly successful book-length treatise of his near-death experience, "Proof of Heaven" (2012).[2] A central element

---

[2] On Alexander's narrative, cf. Fischer and Mitchell-Yellin 2016, 34–7, 75–7, 174–5; quoting the reluctant reception by the current Dalai Lama (cf. 177–8).

in his highly stylized narrative pertains to a vision of a butterfly, depicted also on the cover the book—a symbol that has now become almost emblematic in circles dealing with near-death experiences. Alexander reports that after experiencing an almost hellish state of being a worm in a giant, dark, and muddy earthen "womb"—a state he called "Realm of the Earthworm's-Eye View," he passed through a gate into the light. "Born" (and not: "born again," or "reborn") into a paradisiacal environment, he flew over a green, lush, earthlike summerland, and finally realized himself as sitting on a large butterfly, with millions of other butterflies all around him (see Alexander 2013, 40–1). Next to him on the butterfly wing, Alexander disclosed, there was a girl, a guardian angel, communicating to him without words that he is loved, can do no wrong, has nothing to fear, and will finally "go back."

Having recovered, however, he realizes a month later, looking at a photo of his deceased sister Betsy whom he had "never met in this world," that it was exactly her whom he had seen on the butterfly. Without being able to interpret the narrative of Alexander and its religious significance (being, of course, avowedly "beyond religion") more in depth here, I may, for the time being, only pick the worm—that is, the butterfly imagery. The butterfly has a long-standing history serving as a metaphor, or allegory, for the metamorphosis of the soul. By saying "I had sloughed off that earthly style of thought like a butterfly breaking from a chrysalis" (82), Alexander connects to a rich narrative tradition. A programmatic framing is provided in William Blake's famous poem "The Marriage of Heaven and Hell" (1793),[3] where he writes, "If the doors of perception were cleansed everything would appear to man as it is, Infinite. For man has closed himself up, till he sees all things thro' narrow chinks of his cavern." In the same year, he had illustrated a picture book for children, *The Gates of Paradise*, showing on the frontispiece a caterpillar and, below that, a chrysalis with a human face, signifying the transformation of the human soul at death. Building on the metamorphosis of the butterfly, Alexander does not only sit on the butterfly wing in his after-death vision—he also sits, I may say, on the wings of religious tradition. It is worth mentioning in passing that such traditions include not only European ones, but also the Western reception of Asian traditions, as a closer look at Alexander's book will quickly reveal. Of the innumerable instances in which the butterfly illustrates, especially in occult and esoteric literature, the human potential for transformation at the moment of death, and the postmortem life of the soul, we quote a beautiful example from the work *Is Spiritualism True?* (1871), written by American Spiritualist William Denton. He invites us to imagine two worms, folded in their cocoons, and debating whether there is to be any future life for them: "'I have an idea,' says one, 'that I shall fly when I have eaten my way out of this case in which I am enclosed.'—'You fly!' says the other: 'that is all nonsense [. . .]. Whoever saw worms fly? Worms we are, and worms we must ever be, and are now shut up in what must, in the nature of things, be our

---

[3] Cf. http://www.gailgastfield.com/mhh/mhh14.jpg (accessed Feb. 28, 2018).

grave.'—'But what are these wings for? I can feel wings that are growing on my sides; and I am persuaded that they are to be used. I shall fly, and, in the summer's sun of another year, flit from flower to flower, and enjoy the beauty of the bright world'" (Denton 1874, 23).[4] Of course, Denton adds, the visionary worm will after all be right. Significantly, he provides this parable while discussing the "spiritual body" that, for him, is evident in cases in which it finds itself "out of the body"—be it "close to death" or be it in cases in which the soul travels in "magnetic" states at will to distant locations.

With the previous remarks, I do not aim to establish a direct connection of Eben Alexander and the 19th-century occult. It will suffice to note that the imagery, metaphors, and other topoi of modern near-death experiences share essential features with the occultism of the 19th century, which, however, found an uninterrupted continuation in the spiritualism and esotericism of the 20th century. And indeed, Alexander himself mentions that his interest was raised for further spiritual guidance—of course, *after* the experience had transformed him. So he read, in the aftermath of his experience, extensively esoteric literature, or took part in exploring "deep conscious states" at the Monroe Institute. Founding father Robert A. Monroe, whose works are referenced in Alexander's work, had written the influential book *Journeys Out of the Body* (1971). As will be shown, Monroe's work portrayed and transmitted an important spiritualist and esoteric practice to a receptive 20th-century audience, namely, the "astral projection," developed already in occult and theosophical circles of the 19th century (cf. Deveney 1997). Astral projection, for its part, shares an essential feature of many modern near-death experiences, namely, being an out-of-body experience, as it will be called in the 20th century. This comes, however, with one significant and characteristic difference: In contrast to being forced out of the body while near death, astral projection, embedded in a system of spiritual goals, will usually be brought forth willingly and intentionally.

Although I must admit that Alexander's report leaves several questions open, particularly about its credibility, it is, to repeat, not the aim of this study to drive unnecessary nails into the coffin of near-death experiences. Any unilinear, causal explanation of this complex phenomenon will surely end in a blind alley. However, presenting here for the first time the exciting historical genealogy of such experiences as they were reported—and how the term near-death experience became their common designation—I hope to contribute to our understanding of the experiences themselves. In addition, analyzing their specific functions within the religious metacultures of Western modernity will demonstrate how these reports and experiences are relevant to the study of religion more generally. Finally, our study may also be of interest to individuals who underwent experiences near death and still feel a need to search for a historical contextualization of how such experiences have been articulated.

---

[4] Cf. the cognate parable on larvae "speculating as to their destinies" in Myers 1893, 38, or the butterfly-imagery in John C. Lilly's *Center of the Cyclone* (1972, 14), the first work to introduce the term "near-death experiences."

Acknowledgments

———————————————————————————

BEING A PROJECT of several years, I may try to imagine the genesis of this book in the form of a retrograde "life review" to which many have contributed. I am deeply grateful for all the occasions I could discuss aspects relevant to the study presented here, and I do have to apologize that I will mention only a few by name. For inspiring discussions and for bringing relevant publications or unpublished papers to my attention, I want to thank especially my colleagues Karl Baier (Vienna), Wouter Hanegraaff and Marco Pasi (Amsterdam), Arindam Chakrabarti (Manoa, Hawaii), Michael Stausberg (Bergen), and Helmut Zander (Fribourg). Günter Blamberger (Cologne) and Sudhir Kakar (Goa) kindly invited me to present my thoughts at an inspiring conference on "Figurations of Afterlife/Afterdeath and the Afterlife in East and West" in New Delhi; for an equal occasion, I want to thank Enno E. Popkes (Kiel), Stephanie Gripentrog (Greifswald) and Jens Kugele (Giessen), and the "Western Esotericism Study Group" at the AAR Annual Meeting in San Antonio (2016).

On various long evenings, I could discuss relevant philosophical aspects with Gero Schmidt, Andreas Hirschberg, Jens Eyding, and Thomas D. Gotthilf, whose long-lasting friendship means a lot to me. Furthermore, I want to thank Waylon Weber, Andrea Rota, and Moritz Klenk, who offered valuable comments. I am deeply indebted to Victoria Danahy for her careful and dedicated copyediting, and to Cynthia Read (OUP) for her effort in making this book a reality.

Going further back in time, I wish to extend my gratitude to my philosophical teacher Josef Simon (Bonn) and to Jason W. Brown (New York). Finally, I want to express my thankfulness for several valuable talks with neuroscientist Detlef B. Linke, who passed away much too early. All of them shared their views on the significance of the so-called wake-up dreams with me, which ignited my initial interest in near-death experiences 20 years ago. As I will suggest, these dreams are of special hermeneutical value for the "life-review" phenomenon that reportedly takes place in certain situations either near death or in fear of death.

Finally, my fullest gratitude is reserved for my family, my wife Natassa and my two daughters Hannah Zoe and Julie Alexia, for their love, support, and patience.

Introduction

IN THE FOLLOWING, I provide evidence for a central observation: From the outset, near-death discourse is a religious discourse. Even stronger, the introduction of the new umbrella term "near-death experience" in the 1970s followed almost exclusively a religious agenda. Namely, it was the aim to declare that visionary and ecstatic experiences, ascribed to the soul's glimpse into afterlife realms, can, in scientific discourse, be legitimately addressed as experiences that emerge in situations near death. The introduction of the new term was incredibly successful, and even a growing number of substantial arguments questioning the evidence of the very definition of near-death experiences[1] could not undo its use.

Significantly, no examination has been published so far that offers an intellectual and social history of near-death discourse as religious discourse. Closing this desideratum in research, I aim to show that the reports of near-death experiences are essentially a continuation of Christian (especially Protestant), Mystic, Spiritualist–Occult, Theosophical, and Esoteric discourses—enriched and enlarged by Parapsychology, Analytic Psychology, and the reception of Eastern traditions, namely, Hindu traditions and Buddhism. Undeniably, near-death discourse has become firmly established in modern culture. Personal testimonies of near-death experiences and their interpretation as reports of a

---

[1] In the following, I use the term "near-death experience" in cases that presuppose the meaning of the generic term as outlined in Moody's study. If reported experiences in broader contexts are meant, I speak of "experiences near death."

death-surviving soul—as a "proof of heaven" (Alexander)—are thriving and attract an extraordinary attention. For almost five decades, "believers" and "skeptics" emphatically claim either credibility for the reports or offer a plentitude of causal explanations for the "phenomenon." The first to coin the expression "near-death experience" was Raymond A. Moody, who published *Life After Life* in 1975, though, as we will subsequently see, it was actually John C. Lilly who had introduced the term already in 1972—in a book that Moody knew. Moody, however, offered a "standard set" of these experiences that prepared the ground for several other books to be published shortly thereafter (e.g., Osis and Haraldsson 1977; Ring 1980; Sabom 1982). As of 2001, over 13 million copies of Moody's first book had been sold. Although, however, the literature on near-death experiences is abundant, the large majority of scientific elaborations confine themselves to an analysis either of the significance of the experiences, or a scientific, that is, psychological or neurophysiological, explanation of their origination. Only a small number of studies dealt with their cross-cultural prevalence or with possible ancient or medieval "parallels" of these experiences (e.g. Zaleski 1987; Dinzelbacher 1989; or Shushan 2009). A still smaller minority of studies explored the meaningfulness of these experiences for theology (Fox 2003; Marsh 2010), or its prevalence as a social phenomenon (Kellehear 1996; Knoblauch 1999). The highly controversial truth claims that come along with their interpretation, being far less than a settled dispute, have hindered the academic study of the circumstances that led to the origination of systematic descriptions. Authors delved into defending the truth claims of reported experiences, or offered sober physiological, psychological, and psychoanalytic explanations of these accounts. In general, popular as well as scientific contributions usually followed Moody, who presented the recent near-death accounts first, and offered, in a second step, "parallels" to these accounts in religious sources from various cultures. Being "parallels," they offered more plausibility to accounts of present reporters who were only occasionally asked if they had any knowledge of these "forerunners." Therefore, the influence of esoteric, but also of Protestant, beliefs on the near-death narratives has been largely underestimated. To give an example: Allan Kellehear (1996, 46), one of the few sociologists in the research field, mentions these "unfamiliar" sources while discussing Glaser and Strauss's theory of death as a status passage: "There is usually no social custom and institutional prescription for the NDE. There are isolated exceptions to this in the *Tibetan Book of the Dead* and in similar esoteric and unfamiliar sources." Unfamiliar—really? Far from that, as I subsequently show.

Convinced of certain perennial and transcultural traits of near-death narrations, Carol Zaleski (1987, 100) argued that near-death discourse may essentially emerge in times of crisis: "Although it addresses persistent hopes and fears concerning death, otherworld journey narration is a 'wave' phenomenon rather than a constant. It seems to recur when it is needed most, that is, when the way society pictures itself and its surrounding universe is so changed as to threaten to dislocate the human being." Although Zaleski could trace some important cultural influences, she is still interested in what near-death experiences may reveal—on human nature, postmortem states, and spiritual transformation: "If near-death literature is to have any prophetic value or evidential weight, it will be because it communicates insights capable of being verified—not in medical charts, but in our own experience. We may find no difficulty in respecting the testimony of those, whose lives have been transformed by a near-death vision, but we can verify their discoveries only if, in some sense, we experience them for ourselves" (205). Because of the dominance of her personal quest and involvement, she obviously pushed specific social circumstances that had helped the concept of near-death experiences to emerge into the background. Therefore, we will have to tackle two still insufficiently answered questions: Which factors enabled authors (most interestingly, in the 1970s often medical professionals and psychologists) to direct their attention to the respective phenomena, and what were—apart from scientific curiosity—their motives in collecting and analyzing these experiences? So far, these questions seem not to have been pursued more thoroughly. Combining two conceptual fields—namely, the history of medicine (including institutional practices and medical ethics) and the history of Western spirituality—I aim to show how not only certain elements of near-death experiences, but also the term itself could emerge. The systematic cluster of near-death experiences owes, I will argue, its origination to the following six conditions: (a) the institutionalization of certain biomedical practices, for example, hospitalization of dying, diagnosis of coma and brain death, and the increase of successful reanimation; (b) experimentation with LSD, mescaline, and other means aiming at psychedelic experiences—in addition to the soaring distribution of general anesthesia; (c) the imperative of individual religious experience, especially in the Protestant Christian metaculture of modernity—that is, the need for expressing individual testimonies of deathbed visions—including Jesus, a Being of Light, but also unconventional, individual visions of the "beyond"; (d) the continuous current of Spiritualist, Esoteric, Occult, and Parapsychological metacultures and their revival in the "New Age Spirituality" of the 1960s and 1970s; (e), the study and practice of Indian yogic "ecstatic techniques," catalyzed, quite often, by theosophy; and finally (f) the reception of the so-called *Tibetan Book of the Dead*.

Obviously, the single factors belong to quite different classes. One may certainly subsume (e) and (f) among (d)—yet it seems helpful to separate the two reception processes (e) and (f) from (d) because these factors contributed to the formulation of the "universal" phenomenon of near-death experiences in their own right. For the study pursued here, I designate those factors that are grounded in the cultural transmission of ideas of the beyond, a death-surviving soul, or the postmoral encounter of deceased, and so forth, as "cultural currents." Taken together, the cultural current—factors (c), (d), (e), and (f)—formed the individual social expectations in respect to the assumed higher meaning of these experiences. In contrast, the remaining factors, (a) and (b), build on specific medical and pharmacological inventions and institutions within modern society. In a way, these factors can be conceptualized as "triggers" of those experiences, or, to put it more cautiously, they seem to have enabled the reporting of those experiences as a broader phenomenon—for example, by increasing the survival rate of heart failure. In that respect, I denote these two factors as "triggers," assuming that both—the use of psychotropic substances and the institutionalization of biomedicine—led to an increase of near-death reports.

We may imagine the different currents as a broad river—with (c) as the main stream, (d) as a continuous undercurrent, and (e) and (f) as comparatively late inflows. The two triggers, (a) and (b), on the other hand, can be envisioned as a dam, forcing the water level to rise rapidly.

Only the coming together of these factors, I will argue, could lead to a critical intellectual situation in which a larger number of testimonies of near-death experiences could originate. This was, in consequence, the basis on which the concept itself, and its systematic elaboration, could appear. Therefore, I will only occasionally deal with the *meaning* of death, keeping in mind the maxim of François La Rochefoucault: "Neither the sun nor death can be looked at steadily."[2]

More precisely, I will argue that among the two most influential factors there is one trigger, namely, the large-scale institutionalization of biomedical practices such as artificial respiration and other life-supportive technologies, extending the end of life in newly established intensive care units. As is well known, this development was accompanied by the growing number of individuals dying—quite often alone—in hospitals, which fueled the fear of dying a silent "social death." The documented reluctance of doctors to disclose prognostic information also triggered fear. In this situation, which, moreover, saw a significant rise of organ donation from "brain-dead" patients (ca. 1960–1970), it became a prominent issue to redefine the former criteria of death. Death is now "brain death." Artificial life support was, in other words, the crucial technique that not only produced "comatose" and "brain-dead" persons but also "human material" for "harvesting" organs. These new practices and the considerable ethical discussion that went with their introduction intensified the fear of many to be declared "brain dead." The century-old residual fear of being buried alive in a state of "apparent death" soared again. It is the fear of becoming a powerless, yet still animated, being, if not the fear of being completely and utterly at somebody's mercy—be the latter driven by egoism, scientific curiosity, or medical demand. On the other hand, with the introduction of "coma" and "brain death" it became possible to argue that there is a state of "postdeath," and that those affected, who could "return" from such a state, would return from "postdeath" into life. In concord, it became possible to argue that those people, who, returning from "death," offered accounts of their near-death experiences, were in fact presenting experiences of their "unbound," "nonempirical soul," or "consciousness" after "death."

Of a second group of factors for the emergence of the systematic description of near-death experiences, the probably most important is the broad interest in "altered states of

---

[2] "Le soleil ni la mort ne se peuvent regarder en face" (maxim 26); cf., arguing against the maxim, Yalom 2008, 275.

consciousness" (cf. Tart 1969). Individuals reached ecstatic states beyond the "immanent frame"—if I may use an expression by Charles Taylor (2007) here. For such "paranormal" experiences, induced by psychoactive substances such as LSD, by "trance," or by "sensory deprivation" as offered by John C. Lilly's "isolation tanks," the neologism "psychedelic" as introduced by psychiatrist Humphrey Osmond and the influential writer Aldous Huxley flourished. In close interaction with this interest, the practice of spiritual techniques drawn from various religious traditions such as Buddhism (e.g., the "Tibetan Book of the Dead"), Hindu traditions (e.g., "Transcendental Meditation"), or "Shamanism" (e.g., Carlos Castañeda's appropriation) became widely popular. Moreover, as early as 1935, Carl Gustav Jung wrote an important psychological commentary to the *Tibetan Book of the Dead*, which became most crucial in the 1960s. Well versed in these teachings, Jung (1963) could relate to this imagery in his own near-death experience *avant la lettre*.

This background discourse was especially important for introducing "out-of-[the] body experiences"—a technical term coined in the wake of the 20th century (Hill 1918)—emerging with the theosophical reception of Indian doctrines of yoga in the second half of the 19th century (cf. Albanese 2007, 357–64). Yet again, the term became popular in the early 1970s by the works of "consciousness researcher" Robert A. Monroe in the context of esoteric "second body" and "astral travels" of the soul; it attracted attention in parapsychological research (e.g. Charles Tart), and finally found its place in the systematic description of near-death experiences by Raymond Moody in 1975. The emergence of his all-encompassing concept allowed the fusion of narrative elements that had until then been reported and discussed in different, largely unconnected settings—either within the traditional religious, predominantly Christian metaculture (e.g., the postmortal vision of Jesus or final judgment), or in Spiritualistic, Parapsychological, and Theosophical settings (e.g., out-of-body experiences). At that time, naturalist circles were only occasionally occupied with some elements of these experiences, for example, the "life-review" feature, laying the foundation of a biological and psychological theory of dreams, illusions, and hallucinations. If the preconditions of intellectual history and the introduction of new medical techniques are taken into consideration, it may lead us to new conclusions in respect to the experiences, too. According to the perspective put forward here, these phenomena are primarily phenomena of consciousness, approachable only through individual reporting that can build, in principle, on various different sources (e.g., other literary reports). The individual consciousness, formed in social interaction, is confronted with death from early on. A famous example of this confrontation is the autobiographical narrative of the young Siddhārtha Gautama, the Buddha-to-be. Consciousness is always threatened by the idea of its own nonexistence (the "fear-of-death experience"). The radical contingency of what may happen in the next moment (e.g., a cardiac infarction, a stroke, an aneurysm, or a fatal accident) is, therefore, always a possibility to contend with. In philosophical terms, Martin Heidegger coined the phrase of *Vorlaufen zum Tode* [running forward toward death] as a general description of human existence ("being-toward-death").

For the experiences near death, I propose, therefore, the following interpretative framework: Although triggered in certain fear-of-death or near-death situations, the content of these experiences—which are brought to light only through the respective individual's communication—cannot be separated from the individual's former conscious (or unconscious) reflection on death, the afterlife, and the soul. Essentially, it is the whole life lived before and even after the experience, that frames and configures personal expectations and reports of "what it is like to be dead." This includes, of course, the individual religious background. In fact, Franz Splittgerber, a Protestant minister of the 19th century, had already concluded in his treatment of the "psychological meaning of apparent death" that

> those visions describe the afterlife and the exhilarating or shattering procedures of it in essentially the same pictures and symbols, which were used by the seers for representing them while *awake*—in other words: precisely according to the *religious standpoint* which was taken by them in ordinary life; even the confession-specific differences of their religious mindset influence unmistakably their portrayals of heaven or hell. (Splittgerber 1866, 337–8; trans. mine)

Half a century later, in 1927, the same idea is expressed by Walter Y. Evans-Wentz (2000, 33–4) in his description of the after-death experience in the *Tibetan Book of the Dead*: "Accordingly […], for a Hindu, or a Moslem, or a Christian, the *Bardo* experiences would be appropriately different: the Buddhist's or the Hindu's thought-forms, as in a dream state, would give rise to corresponding visions of the deities of the Buddhist or Hindu pantheon; a Moslem's, to visions of the Moslem Paradise; a Christian's, to visions of the Christian Heaven, or an American Indian's to visions of the Happy Hunting Ground." In conclusion, "this psychology scientifically explains why devout Christians, for example, have had […] visions (in a trance or dream state, or in the after-death state) of God the Father seated on a throne in the New Jerusalem, and of the Son at His side, […], or of Purgatory and Hell" (34).[3] On the *petitio-principii* basis that there *is* an afterlife to be experienced, Evans-Wentz can add in a complacent and patronizing manner that, along these lines, "the materialist will experience after-death visions as negative and as empty and as deityless as any he ever dreamt while in the human body" (34). Moody therefore could build on this tradition in his observation that the identification of a "Being of Light" will vary according to the interviewed person's religious background.

---

[3] This opinion has been variously voiced about Tibetan teachings, e.g. by Alexandra David-Néel. She narrates ([1961] 1978, 85–6) that she got as answer by a Tibetan lama that Christians, too, will certainly enter the bardo, but instead of Buddhist emanations "they will see Issou [Jesus], the angels, the demons, paradise, hell, etc." In the same vein, Sogyal Rinpoche (1992, 284), answers the question if the Tibetan deities may also appear to Western persons as follows: manifestations of the Tibetan "bardo" experience emerge depending on "our conditioning," and they "take on forms we are most familiar with in our lives. For example, for Christian practitioners, the deities might take the form of Christ or the Virgin Mary" (cf. Rawlings 1978, 86; Fox 2003, 94).

That is, all will see the bright light invariably as "the Light"—but Christians as Christ, Jews as an "angel," whereas an individual who "had no religious beliefs or training at all prior to his experience simply identified what he saw as 'a being of light'" (Moody [1975] 1976, 59).

Hence this claim corresponds to the idea of an ontologically real, but, at the same time, subjective nature of the experience of the beyond. However, we assume that if such personalized expectations are formulated, they will guide the respective interpretation by the individual, and, finally, structure their narrative report. In many cases, near-death and fear-of-death situations can be regarded as a trigger—a trigger that I suggest in a later chapter naming "death-x-pulse." This trigger, I will argue, induces the conscious mind to draw from memory a quintessence of all these former reflections, experiences, and expectations. However, not all narratives of experiences near death occur in dependency of a distinct, sudden trigger; we must therefore abstain from overemphasizing the "death-x-pulse," which can highlight only certain aspects of those reports.

Additionally, to these expectations that may unconsciously structure the reported experiences, there is another, now conscious, expectation strategy at work, which we may term the "Pascal's Wager" argument of the assumed truth of near-death accounts. In short, Blaise Pascal argued in his *Pensées* that a person will be better off if he or she assumes that God exists, and acts accordingly. Only then there will be an infinite gain if this turns out to be true in the afterlife. If it turns out to be wrong, nothing is lost; disbelief, however, may lead to an infinite loss. In sum, this is an argument for an "induced faith"—if one does not believe, Pascal (1660 [1910] §§ 231–241), argues, one should simply follow conventional religious practice. A famous ancestor of this idea has been Plato's Socrates—a fact that has, in the context of near-death experiences, been outlined by no less than Raymond Moody himself. In the *Phaedo*, Socrates, aware of his imminent death by poison, presents the "myth" (at that time, a term without any negative association of "phantasy") about the afterlife, encompassing the judgment of the departed souls and their journey to the underworld (cf. 107d–108c). Socrates is not afraid of death, he says, because he knows his soul to be immortal, and expects a punishment of the bad, but a reward of the philosophers in the beyond (cf. 113d–114c). And then he articulates a "noble risk":

No sensible man would insist that these things are as I have described them, but I think it is fitting for a man to risk the belief—for the risk is a noble one—that this, or something like this, is true about our souls and their dwelling places, since the soul is evidently immortal, and a man should repeat this to himself as if it were an incantation, which is why I have been prolonging my tale. That is the reason why a man should be of good cheer about his own soul, if during life he has ignored the pleasures of the body [. . .], but has seriously concerned himself with the pleasures of learning, and adorned his soul not with alien but with its own ornaments, namely, moderation, righteousness [. . .], and truth, and in that state awaits his journey to the underworld. (114d–115a; Grube 2002, 150–1)

In other words, Socrates recommends his followers to "risk the belief," to repeat the story of the assumed postmortem existence of the soul to ourselves as though it were, in Plato's word, an "incantation"—even though literary details of the story, or of the tale, may be otherwise—which means: The afterworld may look different. Doing so will "charm away the fears of death" (cf. 77e),[4] keep the soul on a moral track, as is the case in Pascal's wager. Moody (2012, 83) points to exactly these "charms" of repeating stories of the afterlife, arguing that Plato makes two important points: First, that there "always has to be a narrative element in studying the afterlife because that is how people connect with concepts of living beyond physical death," second, that there is a logic, a conceptual means, for the "truth seeker" to get "beyond just stories and into the stream of objective truth" (84). Moody comments that "talking about the afterlife is a form of incantation or 'magic words,'" because Plato had already advised that "we ought to repeat them to ourselves over and over to arm ourselves against the vicissitudes of life" (84). Actually, I could not express better the workings of general expectations regarding near-death experiences. Because of their convincing storylines, the reports of those experiences are easy to grasp, to memorize and to reproduce, and may internalize, configure, and stabilize one's own "high" expectations. It is important to acknowledge that the content of expectations, however, cannot simply be judged as mistaken and false or as true and real. The relationship of expectations and subsequent experiences is more complex, because expectations *form* experiences (cf., in respect to mystical experiences, Proudfoot 1985, 121–3). As such, they exert a stronger influence than the well-known "confirmation bias," that is, to ignore countervailing information (cf. Fischer and Mitchell-Yellin 2016, 149–56). Any attempt to verify the "reliability" of near-death testimonies from a neutral, external point of view builds on the idea that sources of individual error can be identified. Yet, if expectations, experiences, and the reporting are self-stabilizing processes, such a verification attempt will usually be of no avail. Therefore, in the main part of the book, I focus on the *narratives* of these experiences, and, in the final part, on the experiences *as* narratives.

In addition to more general prefigured expectations that may be triggered in situations near death, we even meet reports that openheartedly admit examples of self-suggestion—especially of one of the most prominent elements of near-death experiences, the out-of-body experience. To quote a characteristic account, reported in the 1930s of a certain Prof. M. B. in Ledeč (Bohemia; communicated by Karel Kuchynka 1931, 171–2): "In the

---

[4] Earlier in *Phaedo* (77e), the interlocutors, being afraid, urge Socrates to change their minds: "perhaps there is a child in us who has these fears; try to persuade him not to fear death like a bogey," and Socrates answers, they should "sing a charm over him every day until you have charmed away his fears" (Grube 2002, 116).

year 1912 I had to study late at night, while in my atelier, material that I needed for my work on ancient oriental art. [. . .] Accidentally [*sic!*], a work on 'Yogism' came into my hands. Included was an instruction on how to get out of one's body. In that respect I am a great skeptic and I never encountered any phenomenon that could not be explained by the natural or physical laws known. Following an adventorious inspiration, and for proving to myself the voidness of such phantastic talk, I practiced very diligently the prescribed exercises. Of course, without success." He therefore put the book aside and resorted to the bedroom, where, reading an "insignificant" book, he fell "presumably" asleep. And Prof. M. B. continues:

> In the next moment, I awoke as if from a bad dream, but my eyes shut. I felt, however, that I was no longer in the same position, that is, on my back, but that I hovered horizontally with my face downwards. [. . .]. As if I had seen it today, I remember the following picture: [. . .] on the bed, my own face with closed eyes, with the features of a corpse and with teeth clenched in death struggle. [. . .] This feeling, that I would not even be able to die, stirred a boundless shudder in me, of a kind that I never experienced ever before or thereafter. The thought came to me, how my body would be found and buried, but I am not yet dead and unable to communicate this to anybody![5]

The following morning, he awoke, still being able to remember his elevated perspective. The description is a perfect example of a longed-for experience, raised and motivated by a literary account—in this case, a "yogic" instruction, probably of Western origin, and most likely dealing with "astral travel." To provide here just one illustrative example of such a lesson on how to develop "psychic powers" and undertake "astral travels,"[6] I may cite Yogi Ramacharaka (William W. Atkinson),[7] whose very successful book *Fourteen Lessons in Yogi Philosophy and Oriental Occultism* (1903; some 60 reprints up to 2017) gives the following instruction for a "trip" of the disembodied soul:

> Are you ready for your trip? Well, here is your guide. You have gone into the silence, and suddenly become aware of having passed out of your body, and to be now occupying only your astral body. You stand beside your physical body, and see it sleeping on the couch, but you realize that you are connected with it by a bright silvery thread, looking something like a large bit of bright spider-web. You

---

[5] Trans. mine. Quoted also in Mattiesen 1931, 321–2.

[6] Ramacharaka (1905, 192) explains that it is possible for a person "to project his astral body" and to travel with it "to any point within the limits of the earth's attraction, and the trained occultist may do so at will, under the proper conditions."

[7] Ramacharaka is a good example of a multiple religious identity, combining Theosophy, occultism, mysticism, Christianity, and Indian Yoga.

are conscious of the presence of your guide, who is to conduct you on your journey. He also has left his physical body, and is in his astral form [. . .] which can move through solid objects at will. Your guide takes your hand in his and says, 'Come,' and in an instant you have left your room and are over the city in which you dwell, floating along as does a summer cloud. (Ramacharaka 1905, 195)[8]

For many researchers of near-death experiences, these Indian yogic ideas do not attest to processes of transcultural reception, but point to the culture-transcending experience. Walker and Serdahely (1990, 107), for example, hold that *within the Indian culture*, yoga has served as an important tradition whereby *we* are aware of the possible separateness of body and consciousness" (italics mine). Nevertheless, Ramacharaka's description is far less than a "Yogic" account—it offers distinct elements of Western esotericism, for example, the astral lifeline cord, or silver thread, that connects the astral body to the physical body. Especially in the theosophical discourse of the early 20th century, the silver cord is a significant element of both—intentional travels of the astral soul and dying. A spiritual "umbilical cord" (H. P. Blavatsky), it reassures, so it seems, practitioners eventually to return to the body. A rupture of the cord, then, would mean for the astral body to be irreversibly set free. Although there are attempts in Theosophy to connect this "silver cord" also to Indian sources, it is a significant Western topos shared by Jewish, Christian, and Spiritualist–Occult writers. Mentioned already in Ecclesiastes 12:6–7,[9] the silver cord shaped Western imagination of the after-death relation of the body and soul over many centuries, especially in mysticism. We return to the Spiritualist–Occult narratives on out-of-body travels in later chapters. Here, it may suffice to note that it was probably this book, or a cognate kind of yogism guide that the Bohemian professor "M. B." had read and followed.[10] Furthermore, his report displays a strategy to downplay the direct relation, and even more, denies that any general interest in out-of-body experiences were already at play. Emphasizing the universality of these experiences, researchers argue, of course, that "spontaneity" and "inadvertent activation" are characteristics of near-death experiences. Shushan (2009, 193), for example, holds, that the "very existence of the cross-cultural similarities indicates that experience preceded conception. To argue the reverse does not explain how a set of thematically similar ideas could be independently invented, or how it could influence/create spontaneous, unsought NDEs." Of course, one can never invalidate the argument of a historical independent emergence of such experiences, if the argument rests on a successfully established "precomparative," universal experience

---

[8] A significant move in Ramacharaka's description (1905, 195–205) of his trip that includes many reminiscences of near-death discourse, is the concept of the "guide"—first, the "guide" is the lesson that follows, and later, it is the disembodied soul's company.

[9] "Or ever the silver cord be loosed [. . .]. Then shall the dust return to the earth as it was: and the spirit shall return unto God who gave it" (KJV).

[10] On Yogi Ramacharaka's significance for the (Eastern) European "orientalist" reception of Yoga cf. Stasulane 2013, 200–1.

that emanates into "similar" historical commonalities. Although I may remain skeptical in respect to such claims, it is equally important to counter the opposite temptation, namely, to deny the possibility entirely that near-death experiences were exactly experienced in the way they are reported. A common trope, however, is to report that the experience had been much "richer;" or that any attempt to convey in words what had been experienced must fail. Some reports, as we will see later, argue that the experience is utterly indescribable, or that communication with a divine presence had taken place without words, and so forth. But still, *this* is communicated, and therefore—in a certain sense—not completely beyond words. In sum, important meanings are conveyed in the way the "indescribable" quality is contextualized. If someone, for example, reports that his or her "beautiful" experience was "indescribable," it means something very different than to report that a "revelatory" experience was "indescribable." Later, I will argue that even the experiencing individual is in principle confronted with the same methodological problem, namely, the lack of intersubjective criteria for the experienced, even though the conviction of certainty usually overrules the need to provide additional criteria. In addition, those experiences, being phenomena of consciousness, cannot be causally related to a fixed set of circumstances, or a set of factors, that will lead without exception to only one effect. This is not tenable, because so far, no experimental setting could be set up that would prove the causal relation between these hypothetical triggers (physiological, psychological, etc.) and the conscious content of these experiences (claimed, again, in first-person narrative accounts). Such arguments suffer from behavioristic and deterministic shortcomings. On the other hand, they suggest a scheme of explanation that does not consider that the postecstatic report of the experiencers necessarily articulates itself through language—a language that encompasses metaphors, images, and so forth. For example, the conveyed experience of a tunnel: As a cognitive metaphor, the "tunnel experience" is not only dependent on the worldly experience of walking or driving through a tunnel. Moreover, it resorts to a large cultural reservoir of images, narratives, and concepts that are at hand—in the case of the tunnel, for example the well-known painting of Hieronymus Bosch (cf. Kellehear 1996, 41). For sure, it is very difficult to ascertain whether individuals were already accustomed to certain afterlife ideas at the time of their experience. But it is highly likely that the reporting individuals, very often raised in religious families, were usually accustomed to at least some narrative topoi of the "life to come." There is a multitude of ways in which these ideas are communicated within cultures: novels, poems, song lyrics; documentaries, movies; paintings; comics and the like; and, most important, personal communications. Moody, it seems, was initially aware of these influences. Yet, taking the various ways of cultural prefiguration into consideration, the problem will not be solved by merely asking "have you ever read the *Tibetan Book of the Dead* prior to your near-death experience?" or "Could Emanuel Swedenborg possibly had been influenced by Tibetan ideas?" (cf. Moody 1976, 126–8).

To summarize, the relationship among (i) situations identified as the trigger of the experience, (ii) the experiences themselves, and (iii) their subsequent verbalization may at best be described in terms of conditional relation, naming a group of factors and circumstances that seem to contribute to conditioned effects, but not in causal dependence. In addition, we may follow Jacques Lacan in his reformulation of Freudian concepts that the discourse of others highly influences a subject's subconsciousness. Narrations of ecstatic experiences, of which most near-death reports are an example, are in principle accessible only by means of postecstatic, first-person reports, are accordingly finalized (if not construed) in the moment of their narration, yet, they are formed in numerous ways by the discourse of others. Finally, reports of experience generate a new, discursive reality—in other words, they will become, if repeated and enriched by reports of others, a social institution.

What is more, we do find self-referential comments within the near-death reports: From early on, the reporting individuals, for example, Montaigne or Admiral Beaufort, suggest how to "read" their testimonies. In more modern collections of reports, we must count with a cognate tendency: Because many reports go back to interview surveys (from Moody up to the present day), it is crucial to consider what the interviewees assumed as motives of the interviewers. They suggested reading them as experiences with death, but also as experiences of a disembodied soul, or of the beyond, and afterlife, and so forth. However, I understand any state of unconsciousness (coma) that is reversible—that is, which is followed by another state of consciousness—not as death, but as a continuation of life. Yet, this does not mean that we are—from an epistemological point of view—able to decide with final certainty that there is no afterlife. According to my premises, however, all human experience is bound to consciousness. Various philosophers, ranging from Immanuel Kant to Peter Strawson, argued that a concept of "unbound" consciousness would disable any kind of individual existence, of sense perception, or personal experience. Reviewing these arguments, I will refrain from any materialist reductionism about near-death experiences. Following Thomas Nagel and others, I will argue that the descriptive frame of "consciousness," the non-objectifiable first-person perspective, does not allow for conscious content to be reduced on a one-to-one basis to brain states. Although these phenomena are bound to human consciousness, I will occasionally point to current research in neuroscience that seems to offer additional evidence as to why certain elements of the reported experiences tend to show up in the "dying brain."

Outline of the Argument and Remarks on Method

⌒⎯⎯⎯⎯⎯⎯⎯⎯⎯⎯⎯⎯⎯⎯⎯⎯⎯⎯⎯⎯⎯⎯⎯⎯⎯⎯⎯⎯⎯⎯⎯⎯⎯⎯⎯⎯⎯⎯

THIS BOOK HAS five parts, each of which prepares the ground for the next part. In Part I of this study, I will outline our main thesis that the discourse of near-death experiences can be read throughout as a discourse on religious experience. As such, it has been advanced as a search for existential meaning of often incommensurable experiences, as a reinforcement of personal survival of the soul, the "astral body," or consciousness, and as an evocative discourse to encourage individual expression of somehow revelatory experiences in critical times of religious individualization. In Part II, I will show how the different strands of religious metacultures in the West, most prominently Christian, Gnostic–Esoteric, and Spiritualist–Occult, initiated and catalyzed the ongoing interest in these experiences. Only occasionally, elements of the reported experiences were treated by protagonists of a naturalist perspective aiming to explain them with neurological, pathological, or psychological paradigms of their time. Part III will investigate more specifically the conditions that led in the 1960s and 1970s to a finalization of the concept of "near-death experiences." Key factors that contributed to this development were, on the one side, the improvement in the survival rate of individuals in life-threatening situations. On the other hand, the increase of reported experiences goes hand in hand with the use of psychotropic substances—in medical contexts such as general anesthesia, but most importantly, "psychedelics" such as LSD. This outcome resonates with a result of the historical genealogy, namely, that important protagonists of near-death discourse in the 19th century had already reported similar experiences resulting from opium and hashish consumption. A so far underrepresented aspect that led to an increase of reported near-death experiences is the heated discussion on the criteria of "brain death." The definition of irreversible coma and brain death, installed in the late 1960s, and the emerging practice of organ transplantation from brain-dead bodies, triggered fears, but also resistance. As I will show, several reports of near-death experiences, often communicated by individuals who underwent operations and intensive medical care, include comments on the "materialism" and "soullessness" of modern medicine. Especially its negligence and suppression of dying and death—in sum, the "inhumane" nature of modern medicine—are criticized by individuals who reported to have been granted mystical and revelatory religious experiences before being reanimated. Finally, the impact of the institutional change of religious practice and belief in Western countries should be acknowledged, namely, the general crisis of the major church-based traditions in the 1960s and 1970s, the importance of the ecumenical movement, the trend toward eclecticism, and the "imperative" of individual experience.

In Parts II and III, I exclude any possible appraisal of epistemic and ontological claims of the "experiencers," and will, as previously said, treat them as reports. Having accomplished the reconstruction of near-death discourse, I will, in Part IV, shift my focus from the reports as narratives to the experiences themselves. Is there any way to find out if certain traits of experiences near death rest exclusively on expectations of what to experience near death, or on retroactive imputations? Or should we grant that some traits should be acknowledged as experiences? Although I remain skeptical toward attempts to causally "explain" near-death experiences with impaired brain states, I will explore whether narratives of mental acceleration and the "panoramic life review" can be more properly understood using "wake-up dreams" as a hermeneutic tool. Surely this model is no "Swiss army knife" for understanding all narrated content of the reports. Moreover, I must admit that the assumption of an existential "wake-up call," which I will term "death-x-pulse," rests on theories of human consciousness that, in this part, guide our interpretation. I will therefore recommend reading it as an excursus.

In the concluding Part V, I will reflect on the historical and systematic findings, pursuing to portray the different functions of near-death experiences in—and for—religious discourse. Beginning with some observations in respect to the reports, I will distinguish among ontological, epistemic, communicative, and ethical functions of these experiences in the religious domain. These functions vary in the respective religious metacultures. Crucial, however, is their instrumental value for restoring the meaning of religious experience in an age of uncertainty. A substrategy for achieving this goal can be seen in their psychological relevance for a reduction of existential distress—dying, we are taught by almost all "experiencers," is not painful, and there is, though declared with different degrees of certainty, an afterlife.

REMARKS ON METHOD

Though the reporting of those experiences is intricately interwoven with individual biographies, I decided not to stick to an explicitly biographical approach. Instead, it will be my aim to show that the reports bear witness to the fact that the individual memoirs are—in the way they were formed and reported—embedded in social communities and collective, communicative memory. In respect to the sources considered here, I will treat the discourse on experiences near death in the Western world as an interconnected field in a global arena. To put it in other words, this study will not search for the needle in the haystack—it will try to picture the haystack itself. Accordingly, I will not indulge in the idiosyncrasies of specific languages (reports published in English, French, German, etc.), or the differences in national cultures—for example, the European–American divide. Specific cultural backgrounds will be discussed only if problems of understanding arise. As a method to find relevant memoirs or narratives, more recent collections of near-death experiences were systematically searched for earlier quotations, which were consulted. In addition, I made use of various searchable digital corpora. Interestingly, a prominent, often reliable term for identifying relevant passages that emerged in the course of the study was the term "body" (and its lexical synonyms in the respective languages dealt with here). This led to the hypothesis that the discourse on near-death experiences is, in an almost dialectical manner, tied to the "soul's other," namely, the "body." However, to repeat, with this method, I may have missed reports that did not make their way, for whatever reason, into the ongoing discourse. On the other hand, being interested in the general picture, I hope to have been able to identify the general strands. Yet my approach builds on sources defined, to a certain extent, on pragmatic terms—for example, in respect to the discourse in other languages than those previously named. However, especially in Esoteric and Spiritualist discourses, decisive for the coming-together of a systematized description of those experiences, I encountered a highly interconnected discursive field. In the 18th century, for example, it was very common to translate the respective works almost at once into other European languages. Devoted actors in the field traveled extensively to share their experiences and insights, and relevant journals reprinted their memoirs and interpretations time and again. Another decision that might meet a critical response is our focus on Western discourse. Non-Western texts, practices, and religions will be dealt with only if they were of influence in the Western discourse—an influence, as will be subsequently seen, that was highly important. However, I will not expand on the question if experiences near death are to be found within, for example, Middle Eastern, Asian, or Native American traditions. Moreover, respective studies, often straightforwardly interested in demonstrating the transcultural quality of the experiences themselves, are often methodologically flawed. Focusing on Western discourse, I should mention explicitly that the discourse genealogy outlined here does not imply any normative concept of Europe or the West. Our *terminus post quem* will be the fully established, systematic concept of near-death experiences that is accomplished in 1975, exemplified in Chapter 1.3 on the decisive contributions by Ritchie, Moody, and Hampe.

As said above, Part II will encompass a historical reconstruction of the Western discourse ranging from 1580 to 1975. In general, the method used here will be a historical discourse analysis, pursuing the question of how texts present these experiences and the situations in which they occurred. Very rarely, the reports are conveyed in their raw form, that is, as arduous struggles to communicate intensive experiences. As such, they present themselves with fractures, sudden turns, or idiosyncratic phrases. In contrast, and considerably more often, reports are comprehensible, concerted narratives that leave the mark of having been told and retold over and over again, and finally of having assumed by means of this evolutionary process a narrative structure that incorporates the intention to evoke the best possible cognitive, emotional, and spiritual reaction by hearers and readers alike. In other cases, reports follow closely literary models of complex visions: heavens and hells, journeys to the otherworld, or blueprints of Utopian societies.[1]

Of crucial importance are the self-reflective comments on the meaning of these experiences. These comments, corollaries to the memoirs, usually introduce a larger framework of interpretation, classifying the status of these experiences—for example, as "dreams," "visions," "memories,"—or making sense of their contents, for example, as "experience of the afterlife," or "travels of a disembodied spirit." I assume that especially in modernity *narrated* experiences contribute to the discursive construction of "death" and the "beyond," being themselves pathways of how death, dying and the beyond had been conceptualized in a certain historical period. More precisely, the hypothesis pursued here builds on the observation that even more important than the religious imagery of the visionary content of a significant portion of reports (paradisiacal landscapes, angels, a being of Light, meeting deceased, etc.) is the experiencer's *reaction* in the aftermath of his experience. These transformational reactions are, however, in many cases unverifiable parts of the narratives themselves, and should be treated as such. I will define the entire narrative—including the description of the life-threatening situation, the memoir of what has been experienced, and what the individual reports as meaning of the experience, or of changes in life orientation—as the "script" of near-death experiences. With current narrative theory, a script functions as a scheme that triggers in the recipient an imagined, typical sequence of events.[2]

There is, indeed, a continuous strand of contributions on near-death experiences—including, of course, Moody's seminal work—that preeminently argues with the effects these experiences have on people's lives. The first to theorize that the validity of religious

---

[1] Kellehear (1996, 97) even reckons that portrayals of "ideal, Utopian societies" are a dominant element of near-death experiences, building on the idea that though "highly personal" in experience, the message is "commonly social rather than religious and critical rather than affirming of present social conditions and attitudes" (cf. 100–15). Although I follow Kellehear in his appraisal of the "social" message, we will subsequently see that in the sources analyzed here, Utopian societies are only occasionally portrayed, and if so, obviously in a religious frame.

[2] For example, being told of attending a Sunday Mass will trigger typical elements such as entering a church for a certain amount of time, to pray and sing in community, a sermon and readings, and further aesthetic and emotional aspects that are included in the typical sequence, or script, of "attending a Sunday Mass."

experience rests upon visible changes in lives—in other words, transformational effects it produces—was the psychologist and pragmatist philosopher William James in his work on religious experience (1902). But can those reactions truly be transformed into a way of validating or verifying the "truth" of experienced content, as James and Moody thought? Remaining faithful to the method chosen, I am inclined to argue that *reported changes* of spiritual reorientation in life form an essential part of many *narrative embeddings* of near-death experiences. By this, too, they become religious narratives. Quite often, reported reactions do not build on the more obvious religious imagery, but on altered cognitive perspectives reported by experiencers: namely, to get out of one's body and to view the "old" body from the outside and to experience a higher awareness, a mental lucidity, or the so-called "panoramic life review."

On a more principal level, we will also have to inquire into the relationship among experience, verbal testimony, and the final report. The close reading of the latter will include a special focus on the narrative structure of the reports and the metaphors used. Metaphors are central for two reasons: First, metaphors allow delineating elements of human life-world experience that are used as a background in near-death reports—for example, if texts make use of artefacts such as a "film projection" or a "tunnel." Second, metaphors are a decisive feature of religious texts in general, since these texts often seek to express experiences that are difficult to visualize otherwise.[3] As such, a genealogical reading of conceptual metaphors may also help to uncover the religious dimensions within—at first glance—"secular" strands of near-death discourse. To illustrate this grasp on metaphors and to further delineate our cognitive interests, we may take as an example the "sheep–goat-effect" outlined by Gertrude Schmeidler. Interested in "extrasensory perception," Schmeidler claims to have found a psychological effect that individuals who stated before an experiment on extrasensory perception (and other psi phenomena) that they do believe in the existence of those phenomena score above random chance at a statistically significant level. Self-confessed disbelievers, in contrast, scored significantly lower. Yet the outcome, presupposing not only verifiable paranormal effects, but also a detectable "underperformance" of skeptics, may raise doubts regarding the execution of the experiment, including the evaluation of its results. For our purpose, it is, however, more interesting to focus on the terms that Schmeidler introduced for classifying the two groups. Tellingly, she called believers in the paranormal "sheep" and nonbelievers "goats" (cf. Schmeidler and McConnell 1958, 24–5). Applying cognitive metaphor theory, I presuppose that metaphors are not used accidentally and may not pass unnoticed. In this case, though Schmeidler does not expand on their origin, "sheep" and "goats" may allude to the metaphorical quality of "sheep" as somehow "naïve," and of "goats" being "strongminded" (though the latter are not particularly famous for being "clever"). In this special constellation, "sheep and goats," will unquestionably rely, if consciously or not,

---

[3] Cf. Slingerland 2004; Blumenberg 2010; Schlieter 2013.

on the Christian imagery of the fate of humans in the afterlife. In the final judgment, the well-known parable in Matthew 25:31–46 insinuates, sheep (following the Lord as "shepherd") will be on His right side, the goats on His left side. The sheep shall "inherit the kingdom prepared," eternal life, whereas the goats are destined for eternal punishment. Transposed on personal attitudes on paranormal phenomena reported of near-death experiences, the conceptual metaphors used by Schmeidler uncover the still religiously impregnated hopes dominating the parapsychological discourse on extrasensory perception. An analysis of metaphors such as the rewarded "sheep-believer" will help to uncover the religious longing engrained in the main strands of reports on near-death experience. In this specific case, the sheep metaphor concurs with an opinion widely shared in near-death discourse, namely, that believers in the supernatural will likely be granted such insights if they happen to get near death, whereas skeptics will, in similar situations, experience nothing.

Analyzing features and currents of a polyphonic discourse, I will, moreover, ask how certain historical transformations within near-death discourse can be explained. These transformations may sometimes emerge from intrinsic, "endogenous" alterations within the discourse; in other cases, it becomes obvious that innovations within society, for example, the invention of general anesthesia and surgery in operation theaters, should be acknowledged as an almost indispensable precondition for the emergence of new discursive elements within near-death reports. Reviewing these preconditions, I will neither argue that they are "only" discourse in the most radical constructivist sense, nor that they are objectively untouched "extradiscursive" elements. The fact that the world is construed and perceived through language simply does not imply that everything is discourse. In any case, I will aim to demonstrate how the strand of late medieval Christian deathbed narratives is constantly enriched by new features—namely, the emergence of the "panoramic life-review" feature, the inclusion of autoscopic perspectives "out-of-body," theosophical narratives on travels of the "spiritual body," or the "tunnel" experience.

PART ONE

Near-Death Experiences as Religious Discourse

First our pleasures die – and then
Our hopes, and then our fears – and when
These are dead, the debt is due.
Dust claims dust – and we die too.
"Death" (stanza III)
PERCY B. SHELLEY (1792–1822)

1.1

Introduction

FOLLOWING MOODY, NEAR-DEATH experiences have been primarily studied as "experiences." In respect to the "wild beast" of experience, the imminent question that will arise is, of course, if these experiences (or: which of these) represent an actual encounter with "postmortem worlds" or if they are simply hallucinations, dream-like memories, and so forth. To speak of experiences will inevitably feed the legitimate need for ontological clarification. Whether experience is defined here as "empirical knowledge" (or "a posteriori knowledge," somehow grounded in sensory experience) or as some kind of "mystical experience" of transcendent insights—in both cases the question of factuality arises, namely, if the experience-*cum*-experienced is real. A usual way to avoid the ontological question in respect to the supernatural content of those experiences (e.g., encounter with deceased, spirits, a being of "Light," or transmortal judgment scenes) is, however, to argue that the validity or authenticity of "first-hand experience" can be shown by the individual's sincere reaction, namely, the change it has brought about for the respective individual. According to this criterion of religious or spiritual experience, one would correlate experience only as a certain exposure to situations with (more or less observable) changes, which the individual himself connects causally with this experience. This will, however, not free us from the dilemma to answer the question if what has been "experienced" can be determined as "real."

1.1.1 NEAR-DEATH EXPERIENCES AS MEMOIRS AND REPORTS

To take a new point of departure, instead of near-death experiences, I speak of "near-death reports" (in the case of reported memoirs), and of the "script of near-death experience," if the memoir is framed by descriptions of significant changes in life: orientation, conversion, increased religious or spiritual belief, and so forth. The "near-death memoir" is, in other words, the memorized experience of a sequence of events, represented in form of a causal chain initiated by a near-death situation that finds its closure by the individual regaining full conscious awareness. The script encompasses the memoir and its narrative framing, including added autobiographical information, third-person testimonies by relatives, friends, or doctors. Methodologically, I treat experiences near death as significant from, and for, the effective date at which they were reported—either in oral, written, or other media communication. Only occasionally, it has been suggested not to put undue trust into reports of near-death experiences, but to conduct primarily research on the reports as self-narratives (see Kastenbaum 1996, 254–8). Kastenbaum, however, turns his attention as a psychologist to the "functional value" (cf. 261–3) of the experiences, without being further interested in the cultural transmission of the topoi reported in the near-death memoirs. This implies that we will have to confine ourselves to what we have: reports of experiences, embedded in autobiographical narratives. In many, especially premodern cases, we rely on third-person accounts—again, of those reports, and sometimes enriched by descriptions of the near-death situation from which those experiences are said to have emerged. Given this situation, it is a methodological necessity to analyze experiences near death primarily as near-death reports—as documents that represent the state of affairs at the date of their final revision and publication. To focus on reports is not be understood as a hypercritical attitude relativizing the meaning and impact of the near-death episode. Instead, I want to lay emphasis on the fact that what we usually deal with are the reports—and by and large *only* the reports. Of course, according to several near-death reports, external observers were present and could witness first-hand the life-world situations to which the reporting individuals attribute their experiences. Nevertheless, even these observers can, strictly speaking, attest to only external circumstances. In some classical cases, however, these external observers did not only report what they had heard from the experiencers—they also corroborated "eyewitness" evidence, for example, for the claim of a comatose patient to have been able to identify medical instruments unknown to him or to have been able to follow conversation in the operating theater, and so forth. The problem of all those reports (and equally of the latest experiments of Sam Parnia and others) is the fact that these reporting parties often share the paranormal beliefs of the experiencers. Hence these third-person verifications are often simply taken for granted. For example, the philosophical reflection on "empirical arguments" for postmortem survival, recently undertaken by Michael Sudduth (2016), neglects to even question the problematic status of psychical researchers' classical reports on near-death and disembodied experience, that is, the general desirability of veridical accounts of paranormal experience, shared by experiencers, reporters, and collectors of these reports. Actually, Sudduth (cf. 47–8; 306) defines reports of near-death experiences as "empirical data," arguing that experiences were documented in which the respective individuals were able to observe occurrences in the external world while, for example, in a comatose state (cf. 54–5; 59–65). Sudduth takes these reports straightforwardly as veridical experience but confines himself somehow paradoxically to show that the classical "empirically based" arguments for postmortem survival fail to accomplish what they intended to argue for (cf. 307). Although he disapproves of philosophical arguments for survival, the individual experiential cases are still in place. Sudduth, for that matter, takes leave of the reader by quoting an indeed unchallengeable dictum of philosopher Charlie D. Broad (1962, 430): "one can only wait and see, or alternatively (which is no less likely) wait and not see," which is in a way an unconditional surrender to the "truth" of individual experience.

Taking our departure by analyzing the reports and their corollaries will allow us to look at the processes of literary articulation that may locate the individual's actual attempt to verbalize an experience in the broader field of literary prototypes and culturally transmitted expectations of what is to be experienced near death. This neither means that we doubt that such experiences occur, nor that authentic accounts are in principle impossible. However, a focus on the reports may allow deciphering different processes that influence the communicated content—a so-far-neglected task. Actually, it can be observed that in recent scientific research on near-death experiences, remarks on the literary and narrative forms have been astonishingly commonplace. In contrast, research adopts almost exclusively, as does Kellehear (1996, 43), the perspective to "examine the experience from the point of view of the experiencer." The generic concept of a "near-death experiencer," adapted in near-death discourse in the late 1970s, reified the "experiencer" as a category of persons who went through this life-transforming experience.[1] Interestingly, the technical term "experiencer" had been used in the 18th century mostly for a subject that makes scientific trials and experiments, whereas in the 19th century, it became most popular as a term for translating certain classical passages of Indian philosophy, especially the Yoga Sūtra of Patañjali, which defines the relationship among the "experiencer," the "experience," and the "experienced" (cf. Ballantyne 1852, 9; 26; Mitra 1883, 1; 82–5). In the first half of the 20th century, the concept of an experiencer, although still used in Indian philosophical context, had been adapted in parapsychology, mysticism, and esotericism, which prepared the ground for the near-death experiencer.

Psychologically, near-death reports should be located in a complex network of expectation, anticipation, and confirmation of the anticipated. Nevertheless, for many

---

[1] Kinsella notes (2016, 10) that in a more recent IANDS convention in Virginia (2013), experiencers wore special ribbons attached to their name tags and were sought after and venerated by the more "ordinary mortals" attending the event. Already Moody (cf. 1977a, 140–1) mentions that he had brought experiencers together in groups to discuss and share their experiences.

near-death researchers, the concept of experience is, for systematic reasons, an almost indubitable category, which hinders even thinking of the creative dimension within the reports. A typical example can be found in Hampe's attempt to draw a distinction between "spiritualist" accounts of mediums claiming to be able to communicate even with long-deceased persons and, on the other side, near-death testimonies more properly. Hampe ([1975] 1979, 115) argues: "The experiences of the dying we have been considering in this book derive from people who have gone through these experiences. However we judge them, they remain the authentic testimonies of these men and women. They have experienced dying in their own minds or souls." We may add that the problem of authenticity, largely overlooked in scientific near-death literature, becomes apparent in research on the phenomenon of "cryptomnesia," namely, if an individual believes a certain element (e.g., an experience, an image) to be absolutely new. The individual, however, is merely unaware of its original source that may be a revived memory or even a report of someone else. Cryptomnesia therefore can be categorized as unintentional plagiarism (cf. Marsh and Bower 1993).

1.1.2 FICTIONAL NEAR-DEATH REPORTS AND AUTOBIOGRAPHICAL NARRATIVES

For pragmatic and methodological reasons, I exclude fictional descriptions of near-death experiences. Surely, there are numerous instances of fictional experiences near death depicted in literature or in movies. The latter comprise, for example, the film "Outward Bound" (1930), the musical fantasy film classic "The Wizard of Oz" (1939), or the movie "A Matter of Life and Death" (1946).[2] I also abstain from considering paintings, although the tunnel vision—if it *is* truly a tunnel—depicted in "The Ascent Into the Empyrean or Highest Heaven" by Hieronymus Bosch (ca. 1490) may be the most famous, almost emblematic, illustration of near-death visions. Without question, fictional accounts of experiences near death will certainly have had a considerable influence on expectations of what to experience near death, on the experience itself, and the final reporting. The pragmatic reason to exclude them here is the sheer abundance of material one would have to incorporate. Among influential literary accounts are already premodern instances such as the "Pearl," an English poem of the 14th century, which narrates an experience of traumatic loss that seemingly includes almost two-thirds of Moody's 15 elements (cf. Gunn 1995, 135). Famous descriptions are to be found in Edgar Allan Poe, for example, in "A Tale of the Ragged Mountains" (1844),[3] Ambrose Bierce's "An Occurrence at Owl Creek

---

[2] "The Wizard of Oz," directed by Victor Fleming (MGM); "Outward Bound," directed by Robert Milton (Warner); "A Matter of Life and Death" ("Stairway to Heaven" [US]), directed by Michael Powell and Emeric Pressburger (Eagle-Lion Films, UK; Universal Studios, US).

[3] Cf. Dieguez 2013, 104–7.

Bridge" (1891), or Karl May's *At the Beyond* (*Am Jenseits*, 1899).[4] I am convinced that a closer look at fictional near-death narrations and their embellishments will reveal that in many instances the authors had an intimate knowledge and personal interest in matters spiritist and occult. For example, Poe—though no Spiritist—was fascinated by Andrew J. Davis's mesmerism lectures.[5] Karl May, a declared Spiritist, visited séances and had worked through a large number of Spiritualist–Occult books.[6]

In contrast, I rest my analysis on those reports that claim to be actual, autobiographical experiences, that is, on reports that presuppose a first-person perspective—defined as the capacity to think of *oneself* as the actual *subject of experience*. In principle, accounts must claim to be authentic reports of a certain individual's biographical memoir of what had happened to her or him. It should be mentioned here that the historical formation of autobiographical writing (cf. Mascuch 1997) was, I subsequently argue, a prominent, if not causative, condition for the coming-together of reported experiences near death, particularly the "life review."

Fictional and religious narratives, however, can be distinguished on the basis of the author's "reference ambition," as has been convincingly argued by Markus Davidsen (cf. 2016, 528–9). Authors of fictional narratives usually lack this ambition, whereas authors of factual narratives aim to refer to a text-external world. Fictional accounts certainly provide important story worlds of experiences near death, including new metaphors and topoi, innovative storylines, or plots, but also cognitive maps of the "beyond." The latter may offer detailed spatial and temporal frames as outlined in more recent cognitive theory of narratives. In addition, fictional accounts probably also configure schemes for how the biographical setting of these experiences may be depicted—including, most prominently, the life-threatening situation. Nevertheless, the reference ambition of experiencers to report of authentic experiences (autobiographical memoirs, either directly disclosed to a broader audience by the experiencers themselves or reported of them by others)[7] is an essential precondition for their religious significance and is a requirement for including them here.[8]

---

[4] On near-death experiences in literature, see Audette 1982; Dieguez 2010, 2013.

[5] Cf. E.A. Poe's "The Facts in the Case of M. Valdemar" (1845); for Poe's relationship to Spiritualism cf. Manson 2013.

[6] Cf. on May's relationship to Spiritualism and Occultism Sawicki 2002, 324–30.

[7] In his extensive study on "Claiming Knowledge" in Esoteric traditions, Olav Hammer (2004, 504–5) divides narratives of experiences in first-, second-, and third-person accounts. First-person narratives may claim "privileged experience," whereas second- and third-person narratives offer somehow more "democratic" instructions. Experiences near death, though communicated as first-person narratives, are, however, often not privileged experience and rather contested in their claims.

[8] This statement does not exclude that fiction-based religions (e.g., "Jediism") are possible. Yet, it seems unlikely that *fictional* accounts of unique but contingent experiences near death are especially suitable for being endowed with religious meaning.

A certain intermediate position between fictional and autobiographical narratives occupies those visionary accounts that still claim to be reports. For example, an anonymous American Christian writer, claiming to have access to the secret thoughts of other Christians, published a *Book of Visions* in 1847. It included the following, rather spectacular case: being at the bedside of a Christian friend dying, the author is able to see and mind read the near- and after-death thoughts of his friend: "As I gazed steadfastly upon his cold, pale features, once more my vision was obscured for an instant, and when sight was restored to me, I beheld the spirit of my deceased friend, standing by my side, and an angel holding him by the hand. We were in the world of departed spirits: the corpse still lay before us, and the mourners were there; but there was between us and them a transparent wall of separation" (Anonymous 1847, 127). A few feet above the heads of the "breathing mortals," he can, finally, accompany his friend—whose appearance miraculously assumes an ethereal beauty—into a paradisiacal congregation of departed spirits. Actually, some of these "telepathic" examples present narratives that will become influential in the emerging near-death discourse. Wellesley Tudor Pole, a "medium" with inclinations toward psychical research and theosophy, presents himself as capable to receive a message of a deceased per automatic writing in 1917, namely, the near-death experience of a certain Private Dowding. For the latter, however, the experience near death ended in death proper, so that it is Pole more properly who claims to voice the former's experience. I do not include such visionary accounts in the genre of near-death reports if they miss a connection to a person's claim to render autobiographical information (of himself or herself, or of someone else). However, it is necessary, as became obvious in the previously mentioned case of Professor M. B., to incorporate some reports on disembodied journeys to the "afterlife," for example, on "astral travel" of the disembodied soul, which, though not in the context of dying, are presented as true out-of-body experiences.

Surely, examples in literature, painting, and film entertain close intertextual and intermedial relations with personal, autobiographical reports, and may on their part be grounded in personal experiences. Nevertheless, as outlined, I confine my study to depictions that are avowedly declared to be real experiences.

I. P. Couliano (1991, 7) rightly pointed out that "otherworldly journeys" can undeniably be "envisioned as a literary genre," to be characterized by "intertextuality" that points to "our mental tendency to cast every new experience in old expressive molds."[9] Furthermore, "every individual thinks part of a tradition and therefore is thought by it; and in the process the individual obtains the cognitive self-assuredness that what is thought is experienced, and whatever is experienced also has an effect on what is thought" (11). He goes on to contrast dream interpretation and reports of visions: "The visions are

---

[9] Fox (2003, 79), confronting Couliano with the traditional judgment of a theologian that he leaves aside "whether any kind of common experiential core may underlie the varieties of reported experience," oversees that Couliano actually affirms mystical dimensions of religious experience.

more complex, in that their recipient is usually acquainted with literary precedents, and if not soon becomes so with the help of others. Here, intertextuality can, most unconsciously, interfere with the original version to the point that the visionary is convinced that his or her experience falls into an ancient and venerable pattern illustrated by many other visionaries" (7). Intertextuality, Fox (2003, 79) comments, visualizes an influence of one text or narrative on another "in such a way that certain details of plot or characterization in one may be accounted for by the influence of the plot and characterization of another." However, despite his own insights into the intertextuality at play in otherworldly journey reports, Couliano does not read the latter as documents in their own right. Instead, he assumes that "out-of-body" experiences, for example, were "altered states of consciousness" and more or less within the reach of ordinary human cognitive capabilities. In effect, near-death experiences become an ahistorical quality of the human mind. Couliano, however, conceptualizes the intertextuality of near-death narratives as a process of homogenization. New experiences will be adjusted to cultural expectations that, in visionary literature, consist of a basic "mystical theme"—accordingly, they will be fused and harmonized with an "ancient and venerable pattern illustrated by many other visionaries" (Couliano 1991, 7), which guarantees their relative consistency and contributes to the impression of an apparent universality.

Focusing on reports of experience, however, an objection might be raised. In cases of interviews, conducted with the interviewee immediately after the near-death event, so it could be argued, the reporting should be more reliable and trustworthy. Kellehear (1996, 187) argues that it was "Moody's, Ring's and Sabom's in-depth interviews that gave us the first full phenomenological accounts of the experience," and that for "consistently sharp details of the NDE as a personal experience, the interview has been an excellent revelatory tool." Although in comparison with memoirs narrated for—or after—decades, this assessment may be correct, we must nevertheless emphasize that, even in this case, the contents of the experience cannot simply be construed as a "phenomenological account," insinuating that we are informed of what an experiencer saw, felt, or heard. We must take into consideration that the individual's expectations, readings, and so forth, are intricately present in the experience and, likewise, in the reporting.

In terms of genre, the final constitution of near-death experiences presents itself as the process of collecting, corroborating, and systematizing the reports. This becomes obvious in the work of Moody, though his collection was by far not the first. For these sources, I introduce the term "near-death report collections." Arguably starting in the 17th century as collections of supernatural visions and experiences, near-death report collections slowly developed into a genre on their own (cf. Audette 1982, 31). The case collection of Albert Heim, published in 1892 as a description and interpretation of experiences reported from nearly fatal falls in the Alps, is usually seen as the first specimen of this genre. These collections—of which the Christian "compilations of visions" are important late medieval forerunners (cf. Gebauer 2013)—did (and still do) not only structure the material. Usually, they follow cognitive interests within their metaculture—be they

Spiritualist, Christian, or, although quite rarely, Psychological–Naturalist. Last but not least, collections follow criteria of inclusion and exclusion and therefore canonize the narratives into "core experiences." Strictly speaking, this final phase does not belong to the configuration of near-death reports; yet the emergence of those collections encouraged further reporting—in consequence, we add the "collection" as the concluding phase.

1.2

Experiences of Dying and Death

⌒————————————————————————————————

HOW DO REPORTS that usually entail both an intersubjective objectifiable part (namely, the situation being close to death or being declared "dead," the medical records, external third-party observations, etc.) and a solely subjective, first-person report on experience, relate to an experienced reality? How should we respond to truth claims of these reports? As a literary genre, near-death reports often use a unifying strategy to interweave both perspectives in *one* report—for example, the parallelization of inner experiences ("then I saw the doctor who declared me dead") and external, intersubjective events (the localizable speech act of a doctor who informs other persons that the patient must be declared "dead"). Applying recent narrative theory here, I may call this with Markus Davidsen (see 2016, 524) an "anchoring mechanism," which aims to link the story world of inner experience with the actual world. In fact, doctors will usually inform patients later on that they *were* declared dead at a certain time.

Although I may not provide an extended discussion of the general relationship between subjective report and experienced reality here, it seems necessary to discuss some specific claims of near-death reports. In a large group of reports, this claim—that is, the script—is conveyed in the following manner: "At the time I had my near-death experience, I *was dead* (because I *was declared* dead). In my experience, I crossed the borderline of life and death, had significant experiences in the beyond, but returned to life." The claim is, in principle, twofold: first, the insights or revelations gained; second, the fact of postmortem survival itself, seen as evidence for a noncorporeal consciousness, or, for that matter, the soul's immortality. The more specific claims differ in regard to the metacultures in which they are usually grounded—most prominently, Christian, Esoteric, or Spiritualist metacultures (as subsequently defined). Philosophers, anthropologists, and theologians will usually argue that truth claims of first-person reports should be evaluated on two levels: in regard to their subjective and their intersubjective realities. If a person claims in her first-person account that what she experienced in a near-death situation has an intersubjective quality—for example, that a postmortem, "otherworldly" state has been revealed—one will of course ask for criteria that allow these claims to be validated. In contrast, if these experiences are conveyed as a dream-like or hallucinatory quality, it will be easy to locate them within a framework of subjective mental states that do not fulfill the criteria of "experiences." Yet, given that "states of affairs" in experiences near death are solely accessible through later reports by the affected individuals, we are in the same situation—we lack criteria to evaluate claims in regard to the "experienced" postmortem reality. Unless we claim the possibility of "pure experience" as an experience without intentional relations to an experienced reality, or some kind of "self-luminosity," or, as Zaleski holds, a "bottom layer of actual experience" (1987, 86),[1] it remains doubtful if we can conceptualize the respective states of consciousness as experiences.

However, a position articulated in various Gnostic–Esoteric or Spiritualist–Occult sources holds that there *is* intersubjective validity. There are known instances, it is argued, in which two reporting individuals, while out of their bodies, met in their respective near-death experiences. This claim is, of course, a well-known argument of those traditions that do not wait for a rather unlikely situation of parallel near-death experiences to happen, but initiate intentional travels in the after-death realm on a regular basis. Alfred P. Sinnett,[2] an influential theosophist and important precursor for the later formulation of "out-of-body experiences," argued, for example, that the concurrent testimony of disembodied souls, experiencing not only the same "astral plane" of existence but also experiencing each other while "being there," will weigh more than double. Such an abiding familiarity, Sinnett (cf. 1918 [1896], 12–13) holds, can be observed in Indian and Western theosophists.

For psychologists such as Susan Blackmore, arguing that people in near-death situations are in some kind of impaired or even "pathological" mental states, the question of inter-subjective, and even of subjective, truth claims can easily be dismissed. The affected individual may neither be consciously aware nor be able to remember that she or he had been in an abnormal mental state, because, as Michael N. Marsh (2010, 242) explains, "hallucinatory hypnagogic and hypnopompic dream imagery is intensely vivid and memorable."

---

[1] Even when a vision did occur, Zaleski holds (1987, 86), it has likely "been reworked many times before being recorded." The vision, she argues convincingly, is "a collaborative effort," produced in interaction with "neighbors, counselors, the narrator," and others. Actual experience may be present, but their contours, she holds, "are nearly indistinguishable from those of the superimposed images through which we discern it." Although being aware of the literary processes, Zaleski sticks to a pure, basic visionary experience that cannot be construed without its "literary wrapper," or touched upon as an "unembellished event" (86; cf. the discussion in Fox 2003, 87).

[2] For biographical information on Spiritualists and Occultists, I have drawn from Melton (ed., 2001) and Hanegraaff (ed., 2006).

If the neurophysiological basis of impaired mental states is the underlying explanatory model, the incredibility of near-death reports is only a natural consequence:

> Also, we note the banality and bizarreness of many published narratives, the absurd content of some of the reported conversations with either divine or deceased persons, their ephemeral nature, and the abruptness with which many experiences terminate. The phenomenology, viewed critically, is more akin to subconscious oneiric experience than to robust, credible accounts of an authentic, veridical glimpsing of the hereafter. (261)

The concept of "hallucination," however, is far too simple. Judged from the reports, it can in principle not be excluded that the reported experiences are pointing to something real. In our view, answers given on "What is it like to be dead?" affirm a disembodied observer and therefore an afterlife. In consequence, they have—whatever the answer will be—an inherent religious significance: The belief in postmortem survival, even if envisioned as purgatory or hell, seems as such to serve as basis for hope and consolation. In contrast, down-to-earth answers on "What is it like to be dying?" usually attract much less curiosity. We may therefore detect in many systematic accounts of near-death experiences not only strategies to blur the distinction between death and dying, but even strategies to dissimulate awareness of the difference between the two questions.

This may be illustrated with an example from the spiritual autobiography of John Godolphin Bennett (1897–1974), a British mathematician, author, spiritual teacher, and follower of George Gurdjieff, Bapak Mohammad Subudh, and others. In his autobiographical work *Witness. The Story of a Search*, he bears "witness to the truth revealed to him" (Bennett 1962, v), starting in the first chapter, "Near-Death and Marriage," with an homage to his experiences near death: "There is a world of difference between seeing death nearby, but outside, and seeing death from the inside. Several times in my life, under very different conditions, I have known what it is like to be dead" (11). The first experience dates back to March 21, 1918, in the final phase of World War I in France. Bennett, at that time an officer in the British Army, came under attack from German artillery while riding his motorcycle. He fainted and woke up in a hospital. There, he claims to have left his body, surveying the wounded placed on stretchers around him. "At that moment, it was perfectly clear to me that being dead is quite unlike being very ill," and he adds, "So far as I am concerned, there was no fear at all" (13). After undergoing an operation, he was in a coma for six days. But most important, what did not leave him after the experience of near death "is the awareness that I entered some realm of experience where all perceptions are changed and our physical bodies are not required" (14; cf. 291). For Bennett, however, it was clear that he had in reality experienced "death." Accordingly, the return to life was also a birth or rebirth. Although the dominant content of the experience was the *dédoublement* [splitting into two] itself, on which he could shortly thereafter converse with Henri Bergson (cf. 16), it becomes obvious that for Bennett, this disembodied

experience proved to him the existence of a "world without bodies" (15), for which his entire life to come—filled with spiritual exercises and mystic experiences of various Eastern
origins—indeed bears witness. In other words, Bennett, by starting his autobiography
with the personal experience of "what it is like to be dead," transforms his experience into
a revelatory initiation. How this experience serves this function is reinforced in his description of a cognate experience of his second wife, Winifred. Attempting suicide with
an overdose of sleeping medicine in 1937, her experience "out of the body" included the
joyful experience of heavenly music, of peace, and an encounter with "Him," the presence
of Jesus. However, she felt the "call" of her husband to return, and "to live" her "life out"
(183). Bennett comments: "After her experience of death my wife was greatly changed.
She acquired a degree of non-attachment that I had never seen in her before," a positive
and happy detachment, as Bennett quickly adds. And, he continues, his "deep conviction that the unseen world is more truly real than the visible world, had been reinforced
by my wife's experience" (184).[3] Even in his wife's case, the experience near death serves
the function of a revelatory experience that, in her case, gets formally acknowledged as
such by the spiritual teacher Pyotr D. Ouspensky, with whom both Bennett and his wife
had an intimate pupil–teacher relationship.[4] In conclusion, experiences near death are
of exceptional religious meaning throughout Bennett's book, which is further attested
by various instances in which the author reports to have intentionally or unintentionally
left the body.

How to deal now with the common belief of experiencers that they can provide verbal
testimony of what it has been for them to be dead? As we can see in Bennett's portrayal,
their description rests heavily on how "death" gets defined, usually blurring the distinction of death versus deprived states close to death. Bennett himself speaks ambiguously
of being "near death" *and* "being dead"—in the sense of having left the body. Defining,
in contrast, death in its ontological irreversibility, we need to take a quick look at what
will be irreversibly lost in death. For that purpose, I apply the traditional concept of consciousness. If consciousness and death are conceptualized as mutually exclusive states, any
individual's near-death report, grounded in conscious experience, will report events of a
"dying" person, not of "death" (cf. Marsh 2010, 262). That death cannot be consciously
perceived is, however, exactly a position targeted by many protagonists of (near-) death
experience. The psychical researcher James Hyslop (1898, 250), for example, expands in
his article "The Consciousness of Dying" on how he had been able to accompany a dying
individual who in the moment of death *did* communicate (the arrival of) death. And
he continues to argue that, if materialism is true, it is impossible to be ever conscious of

---

[3] Compare, moreover, Bennett's mystical experience of Jesus as God's love, and his wife's approval that this had
been the essence of her experience when "she had been dead" (192, 206).

[4] Significantly, Winifred had also received, Bennett reports, in addition to the communicated content of her experience, knowledge that concerned Bennett's own future—a knowledge that is of a strategic quality, and, as we
subsequently see, often claimed in occultist and spiritualist accounts.

dying, "that is, conscious that consciousness is being extinguished."[5] Hyslop, however, takes an unexpected turn in his argument. Applying as an "inductive" thought, that death might not be extinction, as "long religious teaching has made general," and, building on his equally inductive, idiosyncratic experience while escorting a dying person, he concludes: If, indeed, it is not possible to be conscious of one's own extinction, then it follows that it is not extinction that is experienced, because there is none, but merely the departure of consciousness, that is, the "*severance* of consciousness from the body" (254). That individual consciousness will not be extinguished but merely withdrawn is, as we will see, a crucial aspect of the so-called "filter theory" or "transmission theory," advanced by philosophers and psychologists such as Ferdinand Schiller, William James, Henri Bergson, or Frederic W. Myers. All of them shared a special interest in experiences near death and saw the filter theory as a plausible explanation—in particular, of the "life-review" phenomenon. According to this theory, the human brain is a transmission device only, a device that usually serves as a filter that constrains what may appear in the individual consciousness. Once consciousness is disconnected from its bodily constraints, adherents of this theory generally hold, it may potentially perceive without eliminative boundaries. Such a theory, which is, not so surprisingly, an important corollary of modern-near death discourse from Moody to Pim van Lommel, can be easily advanced into a theory of a transpersonal superconsciousness, which happened, for example, in the 1960s.

---

[5] Cf. Muldoon and Carrington 1929, 228.

1.3

The Formation of Near-Death Experiences

MOODY, RITCHIE, AND HAMPE

IN 1975, RAYMOND A. MOODY (born 1944) introduced the designation "near-death experience" for a standard model of about 15 distinct elements that kept recurring in the reports he had collected.[1] This most influential construct of an "ideal" typology has been understood as—if all elements are reported—describing a "deep," or "full" near-death experience. Without doubt, Moody's ingenious idea was to order these 15 elements in the form of a short narrative, which encompassed all elements comprising a "core experience" near death, which is subsequently quoted and discussed. Moody's book *Life After Life* (1975) was an immediate bestseller.[2] In contrast to his self-presentation and in contrast to the initial public perception, Moody built his insights on various literary sources on near-death reports within the three affirmative metacultures already outlined, which, finally, were of eminent use to him for defending a certain religious position, namely, the death-surviving soul. For my purpose, it is central to highlight these influences and also the specific intentions that led Moody to publish his work. Other influences, "triggers," as I proposed to call them, include the social circumstances of modern medicine, institutionalized dying, the use of anesthesia and hallucinogenic drugs, and the "brain-death" debate. But how can we assess the impact of these elements for Moody's project? In that respect, a similar study by German Lutheran minister Johann Christoph Hampe

---

[1] The genre and the specific style of Moody's book have been analyzed in Fox 2003, 15–23; for the ongoing discussion regarding Moody's claims, cf. Marsh 2010, 33–5.

[2] Unfortunately, the first edition has been unavailable to me. Instead, I quote from the unaltered text of the 1976 paperback edition.

(1913–1990) will be a very valuable means of comparison. It appeared, independently of Moody's work, in exactly the same year, 1975, under the title *Sterben ist doch ganz anders. Erfahrungen mit dem eigenen Tod* [*Dying Is Yet Completely Different. Experiences With One's Own Death*]. Although the German edition saw several reprints, the English translation of Hampe's work, which appeared under the title *To Die is To Gain* in 1979 in Great Britain and the United States, attracted considerably less attention, which might be an outcome of its strong theological interests. Far less than nondenominational, Hampe's study seems to represent the very first attempt to investigate those experiences near death "from within the context of theology" (Fox 2003, 55). Methodologically, both men took the reports at face value. They "remain authentic testimonies," as Hampe and Moody repeatedly reassure their readers (Hampe 1979, 115, cf. 111; cf. Moody [1975] 1976, 138–40). I return to Hampe's work in Section 1.3.3.

1.3.1 GEORGE G. RITCHIE AND RAYMOND A. MOODY

Biographically speaking, Moody was introduced to the phenomenon as a philosophy undergraduate at the University of Virginia in 1965, where he was able to hear the report of George G. Ritchie (1923–2007), teaching psychiatry at the school of medicine (Moody in Ritchie [1978], 9). The fact that Ritchie's account and interpretation had a central impact on Moody becomes clear by the latter's dedication in *Life after Life*: "To George Ritchie, M.D. and, through him, to the One whom he suggested." Ritchie, informed that the book would be dedicated to him, had suggested to Moody that the work should be dedicated to Jesus Christ, to whom he would owe the experience. Moody, reluctant to see his book solely "aimed at a Christian audience" (Moody 2012, 94), declared that the actual wording of the dedication satisfied both interests.

In the late 1960s, Ritchie spread freely his account of a near-death experience that had happened to him as an Army private in December 1943. Obviously, these "epiphanic" experiences in a very critical health condition made for Ritchie a major change in his life, in short, a conversion, which, from that time, never lost momentum (cf. Ritchie 1991). Central elements in the first published report of 1964, and the subsequent, narrativized account of 1978 that had been coauthored by a Christian writer,[3] proved to be important

---

[3] The author of evangelical Christian bestsellers, Elizabeth Sherrill interviewed Ritchie (June 1964) in the series "Life After Death" in the faith-based magazine *Guideposts* (1963–1964). Later, she published another interview (1977) and coauthored with him a book, *Return From Tomorrow* (1978), that presents a more elaborate version of the account. This work that Zaleski depicts as a "tale" (1987, 101) is, again, a complex product of various influences. Sherrill's Christian stance, however, becomes clear in her description of Ritchie's report: "Light, so central to George's story, was a common report, though unlike his, the light usually appeared far off at the end of a tunnel [. . .]. Present in his, though, and missing from most others, were two elements: a vision of hell as well as heaven, and the absolute centrality of Christ. [. . .] [T]he title of this book might well be 'An Encounter with Jesus'" (on her homepage: http://www.elizabethsherrill.com/return-from-tomorrow-book-desc.html; 10.06.2016).

impulses for Moody. To understand these impulses, it will be of help to give a short summary of Ritchie's report here. Because of lobar pneumonia, he seemed to have suffered from a cardiac arrest and was pronounced dead. During nine minutes "beyond life," he had experiences that, according to the published account of 1978, show substantial elements of Moody's near-death experiences. In line with Christian metaculture, Ritchie later said that his experience, in which he met Jesus Christ and saw the "Light," changed his life orientation.[4] Ritchie is brought back to life by an almost desperate measure, that is, a shot of adrenaline into the heart muscle. This was, Ritchie comments, "medically ridiculous." Adrenaline injected into the heart was, he says, "occasionally attempted in cases of heart arrest. But this was only done when the heart had stopped because of some trauma in a basically healthy patient [. . .]. But when the entire system has deteriorated from an illness like pneumonia, simply getting the heart muscle to contract a few more times achieves nothing" (Moody in Richie 1978, 79–80).

Finally, Ritchie became aware that he was "out-of-the-body" (in this older diction), realizing that he, lying in a small room after an x-ray had been done, could see himself from the outside. He "identifies" himself by a fraternity ring he is wearing. Walking through the hospital, he realizes that he is not heard or perceived by others, and, most drastic an experience, that he can pass right through the bodies of others. Interestingly, he can still hold on to the wish to travel to Richmond for spending Christmas at home, and "runs" or "flies" as a disembodied spirit in that direction. However, at a certain town he realizes that he has to go back in order to reunite with his body. Having finally found his body and suddenly realizing that he was indeed "dead": "And there, standing before this problem, I thought suddenly: 'This is death. This is what we human beings call 'death,' this splitting up of one's self.' It was the first time I had connected death with what had happened to me" (Ritchie [1964] in Weiss 1972, 65). But then the room began to fill with a brilliant light of ineffable quality.[5] "The light which entered that room was Christ: I knew because a thought was put deep within me, 'You are in the presence of the Son of God.' I have called him 'light,' but I could also have said 'love,' for that room was flooded, pierced, illuminated, by the most total compassion I have ever felt. It was a presence so comforting, so joyous and all-satisfying, that I wanted to lose myself forever in the wonder of it" (65). Simultaneously with the appearance of Christ, "every single episode" of his entire life appeared, as a "series of pictures," all of them asking for a moral judgment: "'What did you do with your time on earth?'" (65). He even "hears" Christ saying, "'Did you tell anyone about me?'" which has been obviously understood (and therefore related) by Ritchie as to make him aware of a major negligence and a kind of twofold "great commission": to become a physician, and to serve God (65). There is an

---

[4] "The cry in my heart that moment has been the cry of my life ever since: Christ, show me Yourself again" (Ritchie in Weiss 1972, 67).

[5] According to van Uytfanghe (see 1991, 458–9, 461–2), the topos of an ineffable quality of experience has a long-standing history in depictions of heaven and afterlife and, occasionally, of hellish experiences.

overwhelming moral quality in Ritchie's report, which is equally present in the next episode. Ritchie follows Christ into different worlds, the first one being a realm of everyday
human suffering (identified as "hell," namely, as a state in which a hopeless occupation
with earthly things is endlessly prolonged in the afterlife).[6] The second "world" is made
out of the human endeavor of searching truth, the third is a city made of light. The last
vision is commented on by Ritchie: "At that time I had not read the Book of Revelation,
nor incidentally, anything on the subject of life after death. But here was a city in which
the walls, houses, streets, seemed to give off light, while moving among them were beings
as blindingly bright as the one who stood beside me" (66–7). I may note in passing that
the statement "at that time I had not read" is an important element of the script of several near-death reports. Furthermore, Ritchie alludes, surely, to the City of Light ("New
Jerusalem," Revelation 21:23).[7] The rhetorical figure aims not only at increasing plausibility to his own account, but indirectly lends also new credibility to the biblical text of
the Revelation. Ritchie could actually see the City in his vision without even knowing of
the biblical text, as he says. With this vision, his after-death journey comes to an end, and
in the next moment he returns into the little room and his body, and falls asleep.

Now, in terms of a plausible narrative, we need further evidence that Ritchie had been
dead. Ritchie adduces evidence for this by quoting from his chart "Pvt. George Ritchie,
died December 20, 1943, double lobar pneumonia," which, he adds, had been reaffirmed
in a personal conversation with the doctor who had signed the report. Moody (cf. 2013,
58–61), obviously deeply impressed by Ritchie and his narrative, informs us that he had
attended a lecture of Ritchie's in which the "death certificate" had been passed through
the audience, thereby "proving,"[8] at least to Moody, Ritchie's reversible death and out-of-
body travel. The two men became friends and discussed those experiences extensively.
Whereas Ritchie was deeply convinced of their Christian meaning, Moody relates in his
autobiography (see 62–3) several instances of evidencing Ritchie's "paranormal" abilities,
which we can take as an indication that Moody, while becoming interested in near-death
reports, was already open to their parapsychological dimensions. This openness is present
in Moody's original 1975 work. Accordingly, they are also included in his well-known
narrative condensation of near-death experiences which still is the decisive turning point
in near-death discourse. I therefore think quoting the passage in full is appropriate here:

*A man is dying and, as he reaches the point of greatest physical distress, he hears him-
self pronounced dead by his doctor. He begins to hear an uncomfortable noise, a loud*

---

[6] Interestingly, in the 1978 version, these worlds are much closer to common descriptions of hells, e.g., the hell of
people who ended their lives in a suicidal manner. Moreover, he can "mind-read" the suffering of others, while
in the earlier account he just observes unhappy faces, etc.

[7] See on the Utopian visions of cities and ideal societies Kellehear 1996, 100–15; on Ritchie, in this context, 184.

[8] Cf., in contrast, his statement: "I declared openly—in both the book and my lectures—that these experiences
were *not* proof of an afterlife" (Moody 2012, 101).

ringing or buzzing, and at the same time feels himself moving very rapidly through a long dark tunnel. After this, he suddenly finds himself outside of his own physical body, but still in the immediate physical environment, and he sees his own body from a distance, as though he is a spectator. He watches the resuscitation attempt from this unusual vantage point and is in a state of emotional upheaval. After a while, he collects himself and becomes more accustomed to his odd condition. He notices that he still has a "body," but one of a very different nature and with very different powers from the physical body he has left behind. Soon other things begin to happen. Others come to meet and to help him. He glimpses the spirits of relatives and friends who have already died, and a loving, warm spirit o f a kind he has never encountered before—a being of light—appears before him. This being asks him a question, nonverbally, to make him evaluate his life and helps him along by showing him a panoramic, instantaneous play-back of the major events of his life. At some point he finds himself approaching some sort of barrier or border, apparently representing the limit between earthly life and the next life. Yet, he finds that he must go, back to the earth, that the time for his death has not yet come. At this point he resists, for by now he is taken up with his experiences in the afterlife and does not want to return. He is overwhelmed by intense feelings of joy, love, and peace. Despite his attitude, though, he somehow reunites with his physical body and lives. (Moody [1975] 1976, 21–3; italics in orig.)

Indeed, this portrait unfolds an almost perfect literary narrative.[9] It begins with a clear exposition, a life-threatening situation. It is crucial for the continuation of the narrative that the person has these experiences in a state that counts no longer as "life" but as death. Moody (in technical terms, the omniscient narrator) settles this problem by naming an element that may indeed be encountered in many reports: The affected persons report that they were actually able to hear doctors or other personnel who declare them to be "clinically" dead—most often in the emergency room. The diagnosis of being dead is therefore constitutive for the evaluation of that state in which these experiences are located.

After the topos of being "declared dead" by a medical doctor, the narrative combines the internal visions of an experiencing mind with external data. The internal visions provide a new, supra-empirical environment—after the "tunnel" is passed, the person may, in a somehow "new," spiritual body, watch scenes within the world, but may move on to otherworldly scenes. Being slowly accustomed to this new environment, the "dead" encounters other characters (i.e., other deceased), before finally meeting the major character. Here, we get to the climax of the plot: This major character, a being of light, nonverbally asks the protagonist to evaluate the life lived, resulting in the life review

---

[9] This narrative is so compelling that even a sociologist such as Kellehear (cf. 1996, 163–4) felt an appeal to summarize his interpretation (i.e., such experiences emerge from social experiences of "crisis") adapting Moody's narrative form.

"projected" by the being of light. After this plot, the narrative turning point unfolds: The protagonist's feelings of peace and joy substantiate the longing of going into the irreversible "beyond." However, a conflict emerges—the protagonist reaches a barrier, or he is sent home. Therefore, the resolution, or *dénouement*, of the story is reached: The protagonist returns into his body. Now, enriched by the transformational experience, he is somehow "awake" and may never return to his former careless life.

Interestingly, Moody himself (2013, 239) describes in his autobiography his method of studying near-death and other experiences by "dissecting them into their elements"; for us, much more important is his opposing move to formulate this narrative synthesis, claiming to describe a homogenous realm of near-death experiences. Moody uses the term "near death," although by his interpretation it becomes clear that he is looking at the reports as glimpses into an "afterlife" (cf. the title of the book). Nevertheless, Moody hesitates to claim that these reports offer any kind of "proof" for an afterlife—a statement that serves, above all, a rhetorical function, demonstrating an awareness of the problems of "scientific proof" (cf., for example, the well-known theory of Karl Popper's "fallibilism"). In regard to the question of where to locate these experiences, it is crucial to become aware of the fact that the official biomedical definition of "death" did change in the late 1960s. "Clinical death," the medical term for the cessation of blood circulation and breathing and a designation championed in many near-death accounts, is rather imprecise, because it leaves open whether a person is irreversibly "brain dead," or suffers—reversibly, as it may happen to be—a "cardiac death." Yet, in the late 1960s, the concept of brain death and the respective diagnostic methods officially replaced the concept of "cardiac death." Obviously, Moody and several other medical professionals, who, following him, dealt with near-death experiences, use deliberately the word "clinical death," the motives of which are subsequently discussed.

In combination with the reports of the affected persons (or the patients, to be more faithful in regard to the situation they were in), a second element is of importance. According to Moody, they were able to observe from an out-of-body perspective how they were reanimated. For example, Moody ([1975] 1976, 44) provides us with the following report: "The doctors and nurses were pounding on my body to try to get IV's started and to get me back, and I kept trying to tell them, 'Leave me alone. All I want is to be left alone. Quit pounding on me.' But they didn't hear me. So I tried to move their hands to keep them from beating on my body, but nothing would happen. I couldn't get anywhere. It was like—I don't really know what happened, but I couldn't move their hands. It looked like I was touching their hands and I tried to move them—yet when I would give it the stroke, their hands were still there." Moody emphasizes that the affected individuals told him how they suffered from the experience to be alone and their inability to communicate: "Communication with other human beings is effectively cut off, even through the sense of touch, since his spiritual body lacks solidity. Thus, it is not surprising that after a time in this state profound feelings of isolation and loneliness set in. As one man put it, he could see everything around him in the hospital—all the doctors, nurses, and other personnel going about their tasks. Yet, he could not communicate with them in any way, so 'I was desperately alone' " (53).

Not being able to communicate while watching the scene from an "out of body"-perspective is a well-known feature from the *Tibetan Book of the Dead*—a work that Moody quoted fairly often in order to substantiate the plausibility of these experiences. Nevertheless, although in Moody's typified report the "spiritual body" looks down at his own physical body in the setting of the modern hospital, namely the emergency ward, there is an important difference in regard to the respective Tibetan Buddhist account of the 14th century. There, the "consciousness principle" of the deceased is not interested in his "corpse" but is highly uncomfortable in seeing his relatives weeping and crying. We again subsequently return to a more thorough discussion of this significant difference.

It is by no means a great surprise that Moody's informants were visioning and envisioning their own reanimation in the modern hospital, being in most cases hospitalized patients.[10] Nevertheless, the setting of the visionary scene seems not only to react to certain expectations of patients who were to a significant number still conscious while being wheeled into the emergency room. Likewise, it is an important element of the definition of the state they are in. A patient will—after a cardiac arrest (*nota bene*: the by then, in the 1970s, largely abolished criterion of death)—be "brought back" into life by cardiopulmonary resuscitation: defibrillation, heart massage, artificial respiration, or, as in Ritchie's case, further measures such as the nowadays rarely used intracardiac epinephrine (adrenaline) injection. That he or she is—at that time—dead is secured by the statement of the doctors declaring him or her "dead," which is, in turn, heard and "witnessed" by the experiencer. The narrative of this scene serves obviously the following functions: First and foremost, cardiac death is accepted as complete death that is then survived by the noncorporeal soul, consciousness, or "spiritual body" (Moody). Implicitly and tacitly, this narrative despises the criteria of brain death. In particular, out-of-body experiences serve a function here. In this key scene, the "soul" witnesses its own, and necessarily successful, resuscitation. At the same time, the whole process of resuscitation is relativized "from above": What came back to life is only the body, whereas the spirit could never be affected—it did not die here. The hope is raised and nurtured that the spirit would not have died, even if the resuscitation attempt had not been successful. Nevertheless, if a person in that specific situation is most terrified, helpless, and largely not able to communicate (especially if artificial respiration measures were taken), it seems a possible, if not plausible, reaction that consciousness imagines itself as going "outside," leaving this depressive scene.[11]

---

[10] The usual setting of the hospital environment has, as Kellehear (see 1996, 10, 119–21) points out, also paved the way for medical explanations of these experiences.

[11] Cf. Lilly's experiments on sensory deprivation subsequently discussed.

Second, in the narrative order of the first-person report, this element allows a "synchronization" with the life-world situation. More precisely, it permits arguing that all content that a person reports as near-death experience has happened *after* this decisive moment of being "declared dead." The most prominent are those accounts that parallel certain elements of the (first-person) near-death experiences with events that happened in the external world, witnessed (or, to be more cautious here, observable) by third parties present (doctors, medical personnel, relatives, etc.). The affected persons and—perhaps even more important—near-death researchers themselves will be thus able to argue that the most significant experiences happened exactly at the point at which they were in deepest coma. In contrast, Marsh and others have argued that it seems much more plausible to assume that certain elements of those experiences, if not the experiences as a whole, take place in the initial phase right before slipping into coma or in the final phase of regaining consciousness (cf. Marsh 2010, 86–9; Fischer and Mitchell-Yellin 2016, 17–24).

Consider, for example, the following report of one of Moody's informants. Being scheduled for an operation and obviously in a deteriorating condition, this patient experienced—after details of the projected operation had been disclosed—an out-of-body experience in which a "being of light" showed up: "I could see a hand reach down for me from the light, and the light said, 'Come with me. I want to show you something'" (Moody [1975] 1976, 102). And the being guides him to the recovery room: "That's where you're going to be. When they bring you off the operating table they're going to put you in that bed, but you will never awaken from that position. You'll know nothing after you go to the operating room until I come back to get you sometime after this" (103). By the report it becomes clear that the patient is still conscious, but fully absorbed in visions that deal with the expected operation. The "being of light," seemingly well versed in operational sequences of modern medicine and accustomed to the procedures in this specific operation unit, announces how he will later on offer his guidance.[12]

1.3.2 MOODY'S READING OF "PARALLELS": THE EXAMPLE OF THE *TIBETAN BOOK OF THE DEAD*

After the initial "archetypal" narrative, Moody proceeds to portray its approximately 15 elements, usually providing several rephrased excerpts from testimonies that, Moody declares, were personally reported to him (chapter 2). In the subsequent chapter with the title "Parallels," Moody points to four sources that he identifies as parallel testimonies for (certain elements of) these experiences: The Bible, Plato, *The Tibetan Book of the Dead*, and the theosophical–mystical teachings of Emanuel Swedenborg (1688–1772). The "similarities and parallels" between these and "the reports of modern Americans"

---

[12] The informant declared that he knew the "being" wanted to take his fear away, but might not be there in time (see Moody 1976, 103–4).

surviving death, Moody says, is "a striking, and, so far, not definitively explicable fact. How is it, we might well ask ourselves, that the wisdom of Tibetan sages, the theology and visions of Paul, the strange insights and myths of Plato, and the spiritual revelations of Swedenborg all agree so well, both among themselves and with the narratives of contemporary individuals who have come as close as anyone alive to the state of death?" (Moody [1975] 1976, 128).

Moody, by asking this question rhetorically, assumes a universality of the respective experiences. However, his description—and also some of the testimonies he could assemble—make it highly probable that he was well versed in these "parallels" while composing the elements of his "standard model."[13] Therefore, it seems safe to conclude that the ideas expressed in the Tibetan work (or group of works on "bardo" teachings) that became popular through the translation of Lama Kazi Dawa Samdup and Evans-Wentz (1927) may not come simply as parallels, detected *after* the standard model had been formed, but served Moody, and a large number of his followers, as a kind of "hermeneutic" for his model of near-death experiences. The fact that Moody identifies these parallels is by no means a coincidental discovery—it follows established currents that are subsequently discussed. Moody had read the *Tibetan Book of the Dead* in Evans-Wentz and Samdup's translation, which I in the following quote and further discussion refer to as the *Book*. The latter's general success, attested by more than half a million copies sold up to today—not counting the various other translations that have been prepared in the meantime—had a crucial impact on the Western imagination of dying, death, and the afterlife. Donald Lopez (2011, 8), who published a "biography" of the *Book*, observed that "beyond the historical exigencies of its publication, The Tibetan Book of the Dead has proved remarkably resilient [. . . . . .], gaining far more readers in its English version (with subsequent translations into other European languages) than the Tibetan text," he says, "ever had in Tibet." For example, resulting from the popularity of the Book, the Tibetan term for after-death states, *bardo*, was included in *Webster's Dictionary* (cf. 7).

According to Moody ([1975] 1976, 120), "the book contains lengthy descriptions of the various stages through which the soul goes after physical death. The correspondence between the early stages of death which it relates and those which have been recounted to me by those who have come near to death is nothing short of fantastic." And he proceeds by introducing the out-of-body experience witnessed by Tibetan Buddhists, in which "the mind or soul of the dying person departs from the body," enters a "swoon," and "finds himself in a void—not a physical void, but one which is, in effect, subject to its own kind of limits, and one in which his consciousness still exists." Being now out of the body, Moody mentions how the *Book* depicts the disturbing noises, and how the consciousness

---

[13] Cf. further examples in Moody's second book (1977a, 65–77), which lists in its bibliography several books that are important milestones treated in the further discussion, e.g., Barrett (1926), Delacour (1973), Jung (1963), Osis (1961), Uxkull [1934]—books that document Moody's familiarity with near-death discourse in religious metacultures in 1977 (at the latest).

"sees and hears his relatives and friends mourning over his body and preparing it for the funeral and yet when he tries to respond to them they neither hear nor see him. He does not yet realize that he is dead, and he is confused. He asks himself whether he is dead or not, and, when he finally realizes that he is, wonders where he should go or what he should do" (121). In following paragraphs, Moody lists further parallels—for example, the "regret" of the (nearly) deceased, his noncorporeal body, the "lucid" mind, feelings of peace, a "mirror" in which the entire life is reflected and open for ethical judgment—in conclusion, "it is quite obvious that there is a striking similarity between the account in this ancient manuscript and the events which have been related to me by twentieth-century Americans" (122).

Indeed, some of the similarities are remarkable (cf. Shushan 2009); nevertheless, there are also significant differences (cf. Nahm 2011)—most centrally, that the *Book* does not relate these "experiences" (a problematic term in this context) to a *near*-death but to an *after*-death state. Some of these experiences may happen weeks after "death" (defined, from an external point of view, e.g., as the cremation of the body). So if Moody and others argue for strong similarities, it can make sense only if it is taken for granted that Tibetan views on what happens in the after-death state are, on their part, based on near-death experiences of its Tibetan authors or their informants. This opinion, however, either transforms the Tibetan dogmatic teachings of after-death experiences into near-death experiences most properly or it has to explain the Tibetan teachings as reflecting those experiences that are then declared to be a deeper anthropological or ontological expression (beyond the life–death divide).

Moody ([1975] 1976, 127) reassures us that among the informants who had reported their experiences to him, "none were aware of the existence of such esoterica as the works of Swedenborg or The Tibetan Book of the Dead." Even though we may not be able to offer any kind of proof that Moody is dishonest here, we may nevertheless presume that some of his informants had some knowledge of these teachings—given the enormous popularity of the *Book* especially from the 1950s onward. Moreover, as Moody did not offer transcriptions of his interviews, it is also possible that his own rephrasing altered some narratives in order to fit with the Tibetan account. This possibility seems rather likely, as we can observe this hermeneutic process in Moody's portrayal of the ideas expressed in the *Book*. Moody, for example, explains: "The book also describes the feelings of immense peace and contentment which the dying one experiences, and also a kind of 'mirror' in which his entire life, all deeds both good and bad, are reflected for both him and the beings judging him to see vividly" (122). Actually, the *Book no-where* describes feelings of peace or contentment on the side of the dying. As is stated repeatedly, dying and death are both, in contrast, for "ordinary humans" and their karmic burden a terrifying, disturbing and fearful experience. So how could Moody hold that "feelings of immense peace and contentment" are described? The answer seems rather simple: At various places in the *Book*, "Peaceful Deities" are mentioned—beginning with the full title that reads: "Herein Lieth The Setting-Face-to-Face to the Reality in the

Intermediate State: The Great Deliverance by Hearing While on the After-Death Plane, From 'The Profound Doctrine of the Emancipating of the Consciousness by Meditation Upon the Peaceful and Wrathful Deities" (Evans-Wentz [1927] 2000, 83). The *Book*, however, explains that these deities should be recognized as apparitions of one's own mind. They are not simply peaceful experiences of the dying. On the contrary, the *Book* reminds its readers (and, originally, its hearers): "May I not fear the bands of Peaceful and Wrathful [Deities], mine own thought-forms" (103). And finally, Evans-Wentz argues in a footnote for the necessity of unpleasant experiences in the bardo states: "Had the deceased been developed spiritually, his Bardo existence would have been peaceful and happy from the first, and he would not have wandered down so far as this" (164, note 2). So we must conclude that Moody took the nature of "Peaceful Deities" for "peaceful experiences" of the dying, thus overwriting more counterintuitive elements in the *Book* with Western preconceptions.

1.3.3 JOHANN C. HAMPE AND THE CONTINENTAL DISCOURSE ON EXPERIENCES OF THE DYING

Parallel to Moody, Johann C. Hampe followed the same central idea to describe the *Experience of One's Own Death*, as the subtitle has it.[14] As Mark Fox (2003, 55) observes, Hampe's work is, in contrast to Moody's, "largely based around experiences that had already been published [. . .], many of them in psychic and paranormal publications and including experiences of victims of mountain-climbing accidents and the proceedings of the *Society for Psychical Research*." Hampe (1979, 31; cf. 124) builds on oral testimonies presented to him, following in his emphatic attempt to "let the dying speak for themselves," the newly introduced approach of Elisabeth Kübler-Ross. At the same time, Hampe adduces an extensive number of "spiritual" and "paranormal" reports, including the systematic collections by Splittgerber, Mattiesen, Barbarin, and Martensen-Larsen (cf. 140–5). In contrast to Moody, he abstains from any attempt to downplay these precursing informants. Their guiding influence becomes apparent in Hampe's terminology while systematizing the reports. Three elements of the unfolding experience of dying occur time and again, Hampe argues, namely, the "escape, or exit, of the self; the account rendered by the self, or the 'life panorama'; and the expansion of the self"[15] (32; cf. Fox 2003, 55). The "exit of the self" ("*Austritt des Ich*," akin to Moody's out-of-the-body experience) follows clearly Emil Mattiesen, a Baltic German parapsychologist who had published in the 1930s an extensive, three-volume work on the *Personal Survival of Death: The Empirical Evidence*. As subsequently shown, Mattiesen had collected

---

[14] Hampe himself was inspired by Eckart Wiesenhütter who had published in 1974 a work dealing with experiences near death from the perspective of psychotherapy and psychoanalysis.

[15] "Austritt des Ich, Rechenschaft des Ich, oder 'Lebenspanorama' und Weitung des Ich" (Hampe 1975, 45).

evidence of "personal survival" from the "anticipation of dying," starting with reports of an "Exit of the Self [*Austritt des Ich*] With Perception of One's Own Body." Mattiesen (1936, I, 297) argued that the "unmediated evidence" of this "proof" rests on the fact "that it is **immediate experience [*Erfahren*]** of that to be verified; an experience that we must perceive **as anticipatory experience [*Erleben*] of the dead's status**—a status which proves to be **a conscious, yes, self-conscious life of the Self**, which is actually the original content of the 'spiritist assumption'" (my trans., emphasis in orig.). Obviously, Hampe adopted Mattiesen's technical term, "exit of the self." The second element, the "life panorama" [*Lebenspanorama*], was a common concept of the discourse on dying in the 1970s—an established idiomatic expression in nearly all European languages. Similar to Moody, Hampe (1979, 50–1) points to the possible "self-judgment" as an aspect of the life panorama. The third element, "the expansion of the self" [*Ich-Ausweitung*], encompasses mental lucidity and a broadening of consciousness, unusual visions of light, heavenly music, and feelings of boundless peace. The idea of such an expansion of the self is, again, already to be found in the Western reception of Indian yoga philosophy (cf. Ramacharaka 1906, 47–70).[16] The technical concept of "self-expansion" with the meaning of personal growth, however, had been introduced by psychoanalyst Sándor Ferenczi (1912, 200) in the early 20th century; in the 1970s, it was still a common concept in psychoanalytic discourse, for example, in the popular book of Ernest Becker, *The Denial of Death* (1973), merging, however, slowly with the concept of "self-actualization."

In contrast to Moody's construction of the around 15 elements of near-death experience—arranged, as previously shown, in a narratively convincing story—Hampe (1979, 75) confines himself to subsuming the whole variety of reported experiences, as said at the beginning of this chapter, under three central headings: exit of self (out of body); life panorama and judgment; and self-expansion or weightless floating—which may usually be experienced in this succession. The final stage, however, is "frequently described as the ultimate and uttermost happiness [...]. It is not only that the world has changed; the dying person has been transformed and strives towards new being" (75). Moody (cf. [1975] 1976, 28–9), on the other hand, emphasizes that feelings of peace and love prevail in the reports, whereas the element of happiness is more in the background (his reports and his systematization speak of "joy" and "pleasant feelings"). In regard to the conclusion that, in its final stage, dying is a happy experience, Hampe's interpretation of near-death reports seems to share certain elements of Albert Heim's seminal interpretation (whom he quotes). Heim, and also especially Oskar Pfister and Viktor Frankl, saw in these experiences an "escape from reality" at work—a happiness resulting from active suppression of life-threatening danger in the Freudian sense (cf. Pfister 1931, 24).

---

[16] The lesson "Expansion of the Self" aims to direct the attention to "the relationship of the 'I' to the Universal 'I,' and will endeavor to give him an idea of a greater, grander Self, transcending personality and the little self that we are so apt to regard as the 'I'" (Ramacharaka 1906, 47).

Yet, Hampe (see 1978, 94–119), firmly based in Protestant beliefs, acknowledges in this happiness the "freedom in dying"—the "exit from all struggle and pain, the receiving of pure creatureliness, the creatureliness of Adam" (100), the "new heaven and new earth" of the Bible. "Dying," in consequence, is to "gain," but not only as a disembodied soul's existence, but as body and soul (102). Rejecting every kind of "spiritualist" belief in a pure soul and repudiating any Platonic dualism, Hampe adheres to the belief that "death is absolute remoteness from God" (109), and dying, therefore, a passage toward life again.

Although Hampe shares with Moody a certain number of beliefs and obervations, there is an interesting crosswise relationship: In contrast to Moody, Hampe openly pays tribute to various systematic collections of near-death reports, many of them from para psychological and spiritualist–occultist authors, but, being a self-confident and professed theologian, disavows their "occultist" or "spiritualist" interpretations. Moody, on the other hand, sympathizes with supernatural and mystical readings of near-death experiences, but, stressing repeatedly his medical professionality and conventional Christianity, disavows his systematic interest in the paranormal. Clearly Moody believes that the experiences are actually experiences of the "beyond," whereas Hampe is much more cautious—for him, the experiencers are on "this side" of the threshold. If one takes them as "witnesses as to what comes afterwards," "the door to occultism is wide open" (Hampe 1979, 114). Nevertheless, he expresses certainty that, in contrast to psychedelic drug experiences, "among the dying and visionaries, the consciousness reaches beyond itself into what we have called super-consciousness [*Überbewusstsein*]" (117).

Although both point to C. G. Jung's analytic psychology, Hampe shows, moreover, a pronounced interest in other strands of psychology—carefully avoiding, however, any naturalist stance in regard to the religious significance of the reports. As for Moody, one of the important testimonies for the universality of the experiences described is the *Tibetan Book of the Dead,* quoted extensively by Hampe (63–4, 79). In addition, one of the personal accounts quoted by Hampe reveals an intimate familiarity with Buddhist philosophy (cf. 106–7, 81–2).

Another astonishing similarity to Moody's book can be seen in the almost identical critique of modern biomedicine, the naturalist paradigm, and "positivist philosophy." The "modern viewpoint, which I believe to be wrong" (3; 23),[17] Hampe holds, resolved into fear of death and medical life prolongation at all costs. Again, in the reports quoted by Hampe, we encounter explicit statements of reanimation attempts by doctors, witnessed by the disembodied, autoscopic observer. In a personal report of a car accident, we read, for example, "He said that he was the doctor who had given me the life-saving cardiac injection—I myself would say the 'devilish' injection, because it was with the injection that my suffering began," that is, the interruption of the "divine harmony" (47; cf. 84). In

---

[17] "Almost every death proceeds from the mind," even "what we call the 'natural causes' of death—the wear and tear on our organs," as Hampe reflects (1979, 20).

the same vein, Hampe refers to the case of the famous Russian physicist and Nobel Prize winner Lev D. Landau, who, after a fatal car accident, was repeatedly reanimated and underwent extensive brain surgery—a "triumph for the whole of medicine," Hampe adds seemingly ironical, referring to reports that Landau never regained his former presence and creativity. Landau's life was, most significantly, retold in a biography with the title *The Man They Wouldn't Let Die* (87). Accordingly, Hampe asks in his last chapter for "consequences" the experiences of dying should bear for doctors and the hospital, where most people nowadays die. The "doctor-as-mechanic" (120) must give up "enmity towards dying"—the patient is "not an object; he is a person before God" (123). Hampe's final conclusion pertains to pastoral counseling in intensive care units, championing the Protestant bioethical discourse of "natural dying" against the helplessness and vacuum of a life artificially prolonged at any cost (cf. 23–6, 130–1). In that respect, in this explicitly religious sense, dying is a "gain": "Life is God's gift to me. But I am not identical with that life. So I can even leave it behind me when I am called" (130).[18]

Apart from several commonalities in Moody's and Hampe's reports and their parallel attempts to offer a systematic interpretation,[19] it should have become apparent how both discuss near-death experiences with a spiritual, religious, and, in Hampe's case, theological interest. Both of them strongly believed that the reported experiences highlight how modern medicine's biological definition of life and treatment of the dying are entirely wrong. One of Moody's most important contributions was to declare autoscopic out-of-body experiences (mostly in the hospital setting) as essential parts of near-death experiences, therewith abstracting from other contexts and sources in which these experiences were reported—most prominently, drug intoxication, voluntary exercises (yoga, astral projection, etc.), religious or "mystical" experiences, or "fear of death" situations.

1.3.4 RELIGIOUS, SPIRITUAL, OR PSYCHOLOGICAL SIGNIFICANCE? THE SECOND GENERATION OF SCHOLARS OF NEAR-DEATH EXPERIENCES

Three years before Moody suggested the technical term "near-death experience" in 1975, it emerged, as subsequently shown, in a work by John C. Lilly. In April 1975, the psychiatrist David H. Rosen used it for the first time as a generic term (Moody's book appeared in November of that year). Only two years later, in 1977, the term was a coin of fixed value. In this year, Moody published, next to his *Reflections on Life After Life*, an article that already in its title spoke of near-death experience (Moody 1977b), while

---

[18] For Hampe's theological position see Fox 2003, 60–1.

[19] Fox (2003, 60–1) concludes that Hampe did "*not* detect certain features of the model NDEs produced by his American counterparts: there are no reports of Moody's buzzing, ringing noise, for example, and few of Hampe's respondents appear to encounter deceased relatives. Nonetheless, many if not most of the characteristics of the American researchers' early models *are* present."

other scholars of near-death reports adapted and established the term—among many others, Elisabeth Kübler-Ross (e.g., in Grof and Halifax 1977, iv), Stanislav Grof and Joan Halifax (1977, 136), Michael Sabom (1977; 1978), Ian Stevenson and Bruce Greyson (1979, Russell Noyes (1979), and Kenneth Ring (1980). Although the new term itself was hardly disputed, some scholars such as Karlis Osis and Erlendur Haraldsson (*At the Hour of Death*, 1977) used it only occasionally, keeping instead to the classic term "deathbed visions." Yet it is safe to assume that the establishment of near-death experiences as a new concept of scientific value proved to be successful within no more than four to five years after its introduction.[20] Its final acceptance in the scientific discourse of various disciplines was made apparent with the publication of handbooks (1979–1984) on near-death experiences, for example, by Kastenbaum, Lundahl, or Greyson and Flynn.

However, the religious dimensions present in a large number of reports and the subsequent existential changes of lifestyle and orientation reported by affected individuals were already in this generation of the founding fathers of the concept of near-death experience a matter of dispute. Diverging views of two of these—Sabom and Ring—culminated almost three decades later in an intensive battle on the religious and spiritual meanings of those experiences. Sabom had published in 1998 a new book (*Light and Death*), in which he reevaluated his own contribution in the light of his new religious orientation. In 1993, Sabom had joined the Presbyterian Church of America, which had led him to criticize not only the neglect of religious and spiritual dimensions in his own earlier contributions (see Sabom 1998, 107–8, 140–1), but also to point to an apparent fable for "New-Age" conceptions in his earlier companion Kenneth Ring. Now Sabom holds that Ring had fallaciously thought that near-death experiences would contribute to a shift from institutionalized religion to individual spiritual practice. In his response on "religious wars" in the Near-Death Movement, Ring, in contrast, quickly distanced himself from his former New Age predilections while, at the same time, criticizing Sabom's biblicist reading of the respective experiences. Ring argued (cf. 2000, 223) that near-death experiencers are not inclined to trigger specific beliefs or creeds, but will usually reinforce one's preexisting faith.[21]

As previously seen, Moody argued that neither were the experiences essentially part of a religious discourse, nor was he himself particularly interested in religion. The latter disclosure, being a form of a *captatio benevolentiae* ("I do not understand anything of religion, but . . . ") will not hinder us from delineating in Part II of this study how religious narratives were transmitted in an uninterrupted manner, being a large stream with various currents of near-death narratives.

---

[20] As a discursive consequence of its establishment, Ring (see 1980, 102–3) did not only present a new list of core features or elements, but also a quantitative scale for measuring the "relative depth" of near-death experiences (cf. 32–3). In this scientific mood, several attempts for quantifying and weighting core elements followed, as the one by Greyson discussed earlier.

[21] Cf., on this debate, Fox 2003, Greyson 2006.

1.4

Near-Death Experiences and the Religious Metacultures
of Western Modernity

IN INVERSE PROPORTION to the decrease of institutionalized religion and its orthodox visions of what to expect in the beyond, near-death reports became an important foothold for the individual's claim to authentic religious experience. Near-death reports, for that matter, follow a religious imperative that becomes increasingly influential in the 1960s and 1970s, claiming that a subject may prove his or her experiences as distinctively individual experiences—instead of being mere repetitions of collective narratives (myths and dogmas, hagiographical narratives, or religious "blueprints," etc.). Peter L. Berger (1979) has termed one effect of this imperative as "heretical," namely, that, in the crisis of religious affirmation in modernity, there is a necessity to choose. The need to be heretical as an outcome of "choosing (one's) religion" focuses on a special aspect—the deviation from institutionalized "orthodoxy." Charles Taylor, in contrast, emphasized the aspect of "authenticity." Originating, Taylor (cf. 2007, 437–78) holds, in the Romantic period, but probably even earlier (cf. Mascuch 1997), and getting traction in the 1960s, the "age of authenticity" unfolds as an expressive individualism. It does not only imply "bare choice" as a prime value, but to find one's own way and to express how one has achieved individual autonomy, escaped conformity, and so forth. I speak of this imperative more broadly as the (not only modern) need to express individual "existential" experience in order to become a subject in its emphatic sense. As I understand it, this need has its roots within Christian, and especially, Protestant metaculture. This includes the fact that persons may self-affirm their individuality exactly *through* individual biographical narratives. Therefore, in the context of life writing, the near-death memoir must include references to distinctively individual elements, for example, the meeting of deceased family members or friends, which as an element was absent in premodern reports of dying. The latter, however, include to a much greater extent meetings with Jesus Christ, angels, but also with Satan or demons (cf. van Uytfanghe 1991, 473–5)[1]—all of them being nonindividual, nonhuman (in the case of Jesus, "more-than-human") actors. Accordingly, to such figures one may not entertain individual personal relations in the usual understanding.

In fact, both elements are indispensable for a near-death report to become significant. As an element of modern religious discourse, they must include individual experiences (a "must" for lending credibility to the report). Equally, the inclusion of nonhuman beings or supernatural elements is paramount. By including the latter, namely, "human interaction with supernatural agents," they will become more decisively *religious* narratives (cf. Davidsen 2016, 528). The absence of these elements would make it difficult for others to relate to them as harboring intersubjective meaning. A richness of meaning that allows inferences on how the reported experience may be relevant for the recipient's concept of postmortal existence will, in other words, usually include supernatural elements (a "Being of Light," angels, and other supernatural actors, final judgment, mystical unity, or a world-transcending bliss). The common definition of religion as including interaction with supernatural agents (cf. Boyer 2001, 7, 138), however, is too narrow to be of use here. Experiences near death may harbor religious meaning without any soul's encounter with supernatural agents. Even in the absence of such agents, experiences can include and reveal deep convictions of the soul's survival, all-encompassing gratitude, and unconditional love, or insights into the "real"—especially in occult and esoteric reports.

Despite the imperatives of religious individualization and authenticity, we must equally acknowledge that more recent near-death reports harbor important elements of premodern European religious traditions. In their attempt to show the transcultural occurrence of near-death experiences, some modern researchers, however, were quick in amalgamating an overall scheme of "spirituality" built by the narratives and visions of various religious traditions. For example, Bruce Greyson's "near-death experience scale" (1983) distinguishes between the "paranormal" and the "transcendental cluster," which, at first glance, might be a sufficient instrument for distinguishing between esoteric elements of the paranormal (i.e., precognition) and classical elements of religious discourse on transcendence (i.e., to envision a mystical realm or to encounter spiritual beings). In contrast to extensive "otherworldly journeys" of premodern deathbed visions, many modern near-death accounts combine personal "life-world" experiences—reported, however, from the "beyond"—with only some supernatural elements. This can be illustrated with the more recent account of Eben Alexander that garnered much attention. As previously mentioned, he reported in his *Proof of Heaven* (2012) a near-death experience with two outstanding supernatural elements—the message of "being loved," communicated

---

[1] In the words of Dinzelbacher (1989, 29), "transfigured persons of the religious sphere" (cf. Zaleski 1987, 127–8).

through a butterfly-riding woman, and the encounter with a (invisible) God.[2] One might argue here with the necessity to present a "cognitive optimum" in the way it has been theorized in the *Cognitive Science of Religion*. The audience's attention will be raised and personal memory will be enhanced if there are only a limited number of "counterintuitive elements" such as violations of cognitive life-world expectations (e.g., "a tree does not speak"). A cognitive optimum is reached by "a combination of *one* violation with preserved expectations" (Boyer 2001, 86; cf. Barrett, Burdett, and Porter 2009). In that respect, modern reports usually contain only a limited number of supernatural elements.

For my purpose here, which is to outline the religious origins and functions of near-death narratives, it seems necessary to provide some preliminary basic categories for naming the different religious topoi and strands visible in modern near-death experiences. A recent paradigmatic shift, moving from the segregated study of "religions" to a more encompassing study of entangled traditions, allows us to speak of Western history of religion as a field of continuous exchange and close interaction of religious actors, discourses, and institutions. Nevertheless, in regard to specific near-death narratives reported, I may still—in an ideal-typical fashion—designate these narratives according to their function in and for religious discourse.

1.4.1 NEAR-DEATH EXPERIENCES AND THEIR RELEVANCE FOR RELIGIOUS BELIEFS

The most prominent position regarding the religious significance of near-death experiences pertains to the relationship of the "body" and the "soul." I locate all those reports (and collections of reports) assuming a survival of the soul within the religious domain, whereas positions holding that these experiences yield no insight regarding an afterlife or the beyond are pooled as "naturalist" positions. Within the domain of the soul's survival, I distinguish different strands in respect to its (a) ontological, (b) epistemic, (c) intersubjective or communicative, and (d) moral significance.

In respect to the *ontology of the soul or of consciousness* (a), we meet positions that build on the belief that the soul, spirit, or consciousness does not die—that is, it is indestructible and immortal. Thus, to "die" will be meaningful only as a separation of body and soul. According to one strand of this belief, there is "conscious life" in "death," and the disembodied soul will still be able to experience its new environment. A stronger ontological claim expresses itself in the words that there is ultimately no death but only life, or, the soul is the only true matter of human existence. In other words, the ontology of the soul is closely intertwined in respect to the ontological status of the body—the

---

[2] We should, however, mention that Alexander's account encompasses also additional counterintuitive elements, for example, that he later identified the woman on the butterfly wing as the "heavenly self" of his deceased biological sister Betsy whom he had never met or seen (see Alexander 2012, 165–9).

latter being an ephemeral habitat that will not survive separation; or even, as long as the worldly presence of the soul lasts, its "prison." However, certain ontological views may also rest on the premise that the immortal soul may only exist embodied and will therefore either assume a new body in the postmortal realm or be reborn in another body. Of ontological quality are, moreover, reports that include the soul's capability to separate from the body and to "travel" in this or another world.

Epistemic aspects (b) comprise the ability of the soul (or of consciousness) to develop at the moment of death or thereafter higher spiritual faculties. These may allow it to become aware of the true nature of the (immortal) soul, ascertain a "true Self," or to develop (into) a "superconsciousness" (cf. Hanegraaff 1996, 266).[3] Epistemic claims also comprise the belief that dying persons may develop clairvoyance or other telepathic powers (either as cognizing distant places in the life world or being able to communicate with the "beyond"). Within this field, we may also encounter the belief that highly developed minds, or specially gifted persons, may be able to "see" deceased souls, or the soul's "aura" around the body, and so forth. Finally, epistemic claims are voiced if it is reported that in the aftermath of an experience near death, the individual could retain all or some of the mental abilities achieved.

In regard to *intersubjectivity* (c), we will notice narratives and beliefs that dying or dead persons may come into contact with other minds (deceased, "guides," etc.), or with God, Jesus, Satan, angels, and so forth. A variant with intersubjective significance reports that two persons, while both in near-death states, were able to meet in the beyond. An intersubjective and communicative quality can additionally be found in those reports that deceased or—to be more precise—departed souls may be able to communicate with the living or depart and return into the realm of the deceased at will.

Finally, the *moral significance* (d): It includes beliefs that within the near-death experience the soul encountered a judgment scene, became aware of the ultimate moral significance of the life lived or of highest values such as love and empathy. Here, consciousness or the soul may recognize the moral law of sin and retribution, the law of karma, or the true existence of heaven or hell. Other reports of moral quality are the soul's new awareness of the insignificance, or lower worth, of the body. Moreover, this may imply the return with a higher, religious mission.

Surveying these different strands of reasoning on death, the soul, and the afterlife, I may add the observation that quite often discourse on death and the afterlife has an immediate impact on understanding body, soul, and consciousness "in this life." Assuming the after-death existence of a disembodied soul will, in other words, counter materialist and reductionist views of the individual's "conscious existence" in its this worldly,

---

[3] The mainstream New Age vision, for example, holds, in Hanegraaff's terms (1996, 266), that at death "one regains awareness of one's larger identity or 'Higher Self'; the limited 'ego' personality is in most cases believed to perish together with the physical body"—a belief that I address as Gnostic–Esoteric, as subsequently described.

embodied form. It must, however, be admitted that it is fairly complicated and a rather theoretical undertaking to distinguish between these interrelated aspects of the belief in a soul or superempirical consciousness.

I.4.2 FOUR METACULTURES OF MODERNITY

Being aware of its necessary shortcomings, I will nevertheless introduce for our purpose four different "metacultures" as analytical categories. Three of these metacultures articulate religious aims, namely, the *Christian* (and especially the Christian Protestant), the *Gnostic–Esoteric*, and the *Spiritualist–Occult*; the fourth, however, the *Naturalist metaculture*, is nonreligious in outlook. This group of Naturalist positions will embrace all those positions that argue that experiences near death are significant only as elements of "natural" human life.

According to a view held by a considerable number of scholars in the academic study of religion, it is impossible to operate with esotericism, the occult, or even Christianity as concepts. Some proponents of discourse analysis argue that it is equally impossible to provide precise definitions, for example, of "esotericism," as it is impossible to identify a delimitable object of study designated with this word. In the following discussion I outline how to define these metacultures for my analytic purposes. In general, metaculture, though sometimes understood as a way in which a culture speaks of itself, will designate here a set of narratives, ideas, practices, and salvific goals as they become visible in a text. A discourse analysis in the tradition of Michel Foucault, or, equally, an analysis of class and "habitus" (Pierre Bourdieu), will not contribute much to satisfy our cognitive interests. Even if questions of discursive power, competition, censorship, processes of "othering," and the like, would be sufficiently answered, central aspects of near-death experiences as a religious discourse would be left untouched. Power relations or identity formation, though they are relevant, inhabit only the periphery of the questions pursued here. Narratives of existential, first-person experiences in religious terms is the heart that pulsates in its center. Even if the "boundary-maintaining work" of reporting individuals will undeniably encompass their religious belonging and their "othering" of competing religious claims, practices, or communities, it is, for me, less relevant. Central, however, is the question whether reports are enacted in principal elements of religious metaculture or if they stick to a naturalist framework of interpretation.

To get back to the fourfold classification of metacultures, I may take up a thread on religious metacultures presented by American sociologist Edward Tiryakian. Tiryakian (1996, 103) conceptualized modern Western culture from the broadest possible angle and hypothesized that there are essentially three "metacultures of modernity," namely, the Christian, the Gnostic, and the Chthonic metacultures.[4] As the Christian metaculture, he defines the "core symbolism" as "emphasis on the salvation of each and all through

---

[4] The Chthonic metaculture, which is the fuzziest of Tiryakian's metacultures, pools together all those orientations that follow the lead of an inner-worldly cultivation of life forces and an ontological affirmation of

the redemptive sacrifice of Jesus Christ, the divine savior who is both 'Son of God' and 'Son of Man.'" In fact, within Christian metaculture "the constraints of 'conscience' and 'sin'" served to "enhance the process of individualization by expanding the sphere of autonomy while making persons accountable, not so much to the immediate social group but the Godhead internalized in the self" (103). Most important, the individual's "set of activity has to be evaluated in short term against or in the light of 'conscience,' and long term (i.e., on death's bed) on the adequacy of the life course for gaining 'eternal salvation' in Heaven, as judged by God himself" (104). The latter, the hope to be saved from everlasting death, is, of course, central for the Christian depiction of the afterlife. Certainly, the internal differentiation of Christian traditions in the West has led to very different accounts of the meaning of this life and the beyond. Nevertheless, taken in this generality, Christian metaculture can be grasped in various (pre)modern near-death reports in which, such as in Ritchie's *Return from Tomorrow*, a predominantly ethical message of the postmortal encounter with Jesus Christ is conveyed. I exemplify elements of this view more closely in an early modern near-death report by Johann Schwerdtfeger in 1733 (see Kern 1734a; 1734b) in the following discussion.

For Tiryakian (1996, 104), the "Gnostic metaculture" is, in contrast, "seeking salvation through 'divine knowledge' of the hidden truths of the universe. The Gnostics feel thus uncomfortable, or alien, in the world which there is." A basic Gnostic topos is the contrasting juxtaposition of "darkness" and "light" and the contaminated nature of our world of darkness, revealed through the superior knowledge of the "initiated." Although Tiryakian admits that it is difficult to delineate this opaque, sometimes secret, and often suppressed and marginalized "metaculture" of the West, I use Tiryakian's characterization as a point of departure, reframing it, however, as "Gnostic–Esoteric." By putting Gnostic and Esoteric together, I may follow the introduction of the substantive "esotericism" [*l'ésotérisme*] in the study on Gnosticism by Jacques Matter in his *Histoire critique du gnosticisme et de son influence* (1828, quoted in Zander 2007, 46).[5] It combines "the teachings of Christ on the one hand, and Oriental, Jewish and Greek religio-philosophical traditions on the other" (Hanegraaff 2006, 337). Although the internal diversity and interwovenness of "esotericism" has been continuously stressed,[6] it seems helpful for my purpose to define some traits that will be understood as elements

---

the earth. As such, it is not salvation oriented. Adapted to near-death discourse, we will replace the concept of a Chthonic metaculture by the category of Naturalist metaculture.

[5] Hanegraaff comments (1996, 394) that the popularization of the term "esotericism" came along with the work of Éliphas Lévi since 1856; in the English language, however, as late as with the work of the theosophist A. D. Sinnett in 1883.

[6] According to Kocku von Stuckrad (2014, 223), most scholars share the opinion that esotericism encompasses "Gnosticism, ancient Hermetism, the so-called 'occult sciences,'" but also "Christian mysticism, Renaissance Hermeticism, Jewish and Christian Kabbalah, Paracelsianism, Rosicrucianism, Christian theosophy, illuminism," and related currents up to "'New Age' spiritualities." On the historic emergence of esotericism as an analytic category, see Neugebauer-Wölk 2013.

of a Gnostic–Esoteric metaculture here. Most centrally, it may include the idea of a hidden or secret knowledge that, if developed methodically, may help the individual to master a process of spiritual transformation, a "gnosis" that may raise awareness of the divine, catalyze personal spiritual regeneration or enlightenment, and may lead, finally, to liberation. If near-death experiences are held to initiate or contribute to such a kind of knowledge, I will designate them accordingly as comprising topics and claims of the Gnostic–Esoteric metaculture.[7] Additionally, it is predominantly in this metaculture that the belief is expressed that there is a large concordance among almost all spiritual traditions (cf. Hanegraaff 2006, 340). This belief is found in many more modern systematic treatises, and shared, for example, by Moody. Esotericism has been marked as "rejected knowledge" (cf. Hanegraaff 2012)—rejected especially by proponents of demystifying enlightenment discourse. Indeed, we may find such rejection regarding the experiences in question in what I call "Naturalist metaculture." However, I may add that reported experiences near death are exactly cases in which knowledge classified as "other"—paranormal, esoteric—is often not outright rejected. For example, there is a shared interest in certain elements of "deathbed visions" in Gnostic–Esoteric, Spiritualist–Occult, and Christian metacultures. From the quality of being reports of personal experience, we may observe that certain currents in the Protestant substrand of Christian metaculture in the 17th century were already receptive to Gnostic–Esoteric claims based on these reports. This observation fits perfectly well with what Neugebauer-Wölk (2013) could show, namely, that Esoteric and Christian practices and discourses are, in pre-1800 Europe, sometimes hardly distinguishable. Elements of the Spiritualist–Occult metaculture will comprise, in contrast to the Gnostic–Esoteric, those beliefs that are especially tied to "intersubjective" narratives: that the soul (the spirit) may leave the body temporarily through certain occult practices, or that individual souls who left the body permanently ("died") are able to communicate with the living through suitable channels in special séances. Occultism, sometimes used in the general sense of denoting "esoteric" practices in their entirety, was probably introduced into the English-speaking world by Helena P. Blavatsky (Yelena Petrovna Blavatskaya, 1831–1891) in 1875 (cf. Baier 2009, I, 254). Spiritualism is usually described as emerging in the United States of the 1840s, influenced by Christian Protestant metaculture, with the central belief that one may attain a direct knowledge of an afterlife, for example, by making use of a guide or a "medium," hypnotic séances, and so forth. Spiritualism, from around 1840 to the 1920s largely followed in the West, was influenced by the thoughts of Emanuel Swedenborg (1688–1772) and the teachings of Franz Mesmer (1734–1815). For our purposes, the most

---

[7] Some protagonists of the Esoteric–Gnostic metaculture entertain an intimate connection to Spiritualist–Occult practices. Hammer's description of Gnostic conceptions of the higher Self in Esotericism, however, underscores the relation to exercises, but also to superhuman agency: "We are often unaware of this higher Self, and need an awakening call or spiritual exercises to get in touch with what is perceived as the 'true' essence of our persons" (Hammer 2004, 55).

prominent protagonists are the various strands of Theosophy. Regarding the intimate relationship between Gnostic–Esoteric and Spiritualist–Occult metacultures, we may follow to a certain extent Tiryakian's line of thought (cf. 1974, 265), who defined esotericism as the religio-philosophical belief system that forms the background of specific occult practices and procedures.[8] Being certainly closely related, I nevertheless argue that it is helpful to distinguish between those two metacultures. For example, if it is narrated or held that near-death experiences are suitable to come *intentionally* into contact with deceased persons, or, more dramatically, that those experiences, because of their quality of enabling interaction with spirits, may intentionally be sought after, we meet elements of a specific Spiritualist–Occult metaculture. Moreover, Spiritualist–Occult elements may be found in the parapsychological interest in these experiences (e.g., the willingness to interpret anomalous perceptions as merely indicating a paranormal reality), while at the same time elements of the Gnostic–Esoteric metaculture may be absent.

To summarize, the Spiritualist–Occult metaculture builds on ideas and practices of mediumistic interaction with a supersensory world in which, most prominently, "spirits" may speak to the living. This may happen in various suitable situations—one of them being experiences near death.

The Spiritualist–Occult metaculture is, I aim to show, of utmost importance for the systematization of near-death experiences, as it paved the way for bringing "out-of-body experiences" to the attention of a broad audience. It is, furthermore, the background of Evans-Wentz, the initiator for the first translation of the *Tibetan Book of the Dead*, and therefore a link paramount for the reception of the Tibetan "near-death" teachings in the West.

1.4.3 NATURALIST METACULTURE AND SCIENTIFIC EXPLANATIONS
OF NEAR-DEATH EXPERIENCES

Finally, I assemble under the umbrella of the Naturalist metaculture all those positions taken in medicine, psychology, psychoanalysis, (neuro)biology, or philosophy that do not assign a deeper meaning to near-death reports, especially denying that something "otherworldly" or hidden has been revealed in these experiences. As outlined, the study will focus on the historical continuation and innovation within near-death discourse. If taken as experiences and combined with truth claims about the reality of the experienced state beyond death, it is surely not astonishing that, from the beginnings of a Naturalist metaculture, near-death experiences have been explained with medical, neurobiological, and neuropsychological theories. Here, these experiences are addressed as "dreams," "vivid memories," "altered states of consciousness," "fantasies" or even "hallucinations."

---

[8] As Hammer (2004, 6) argues, a clear-cut distinction between esoteric beliefs and occult practices would be quite artificial.

Regarding their psychological functions, they may yet be coping strategies for life-threatening danger. In that respect, these experiences bear witness of the individual's conscious will to live or to survive.[9]

For the broad variety of the reported experiences several models have been offered as "scientific" explanations, which means, in this context, a reduction to psychophysiological dysfunction or impaired brain structures. Neurological models of explaining these experiences include epilepsy, temporal lobe disorders, and other more severe impairments of the brain. Neurobiological models suggested altered blood gas levels, anoxia, and hypoxia (deprivation of oxygen), or hypercapnia (increased CO_2 level in the blood), or the like. Finally, there are neuropharmacological theories that aim to explain certain near-death experiences as caused by ketamine, steroids, opioids, or hallucinogenic drugs (see Engmann 2014, 81–96). From as early as the 17th century, medical as well as psychological theories present a "pathology" of these experiences: brain malfunction, acute depersonalization, dissociation, or, more recently, of (multiple) personality disorders, trauma, or "false memories." I will not deny that all these factors and descriptive models are important for understanding certain "experiences." Yet, these descriptions and explanations are part of a certain metaculture that describes itself to be the dominant paradigm for understanding more truly the unconditional and irrefutable basis of these experiences. Dealing with reported experiences, influenced by the cultural transmission of cognate reports, the focus on pharmacological, neurological, or psychological explanations of experiences is much too narrow. On the contrary, Naturalist metaculture is but one current that influenced the discourse of religious metacultures, for example, by putting a constant pressure on how to justify the meaningfulness of experiences near death. On a more general level, naturalist explanations of ecstatic or religious experiences were, in contrast, an important framework for near-death discourse, because these explanations of the "pathology" of religious beliefs contributed to the view of near-death experience adherents that naturalist explanations (hallucination, dream, etc.) are of no importance if these mental states "reveal the truth." A telling example of this attitude can be found in Fyodor Dostoevsky's short story "Dream of a Ridiculous Man" (1877), in which the protagonist asks: "But does it make any difference whether it was a dream or not, if this dream proclaimed the Truth to me?" (Dostoevsky 2011, 326).[10]

Taken together, I will use the three-plus-one metacultures as a heuristic device. Although there are significant differences among, say, the discourse of American, British,

---

[9] This naturalist perspective on "survival" would fit to Tiryakian's example of Nietzsche's enactment of "early Greek chthonic metaculture" (1996, 107).

[10] Even if I will not rule out that physicalist explanations must not oppose respective experiences to be deeply meaningful, and "capable of inspiring awe, wonder, and hope" (Fischer and Mitchell-Yellin 2016, 157), I am not fully convinced that brain-based explanations of the "experiential event," or "event cognition" (cf. Taves 2009, Asprem and Taves 2017)—leaving aside the specific biography and religious socialization of the respective individual—will be much of help (cf. Part V).

French, or German protagonists, it is nevertheless my aim to show how the discourse on "what it is like to be dead" could merge into one—a process that found its completion by the successful global acceptance of the generic term "near-death experiences." As a preparation stage to this acceptance, near-death discourse proved itself as an increasingly transnational phenomenon. An amazing fact of Esoteric and Spiritualist metacultures in the 19th century is the impressive number and speed in which translations were produced. For example, French books by spiritualists, occultists, and scholars of "abnormal" psychology alike saw almost immediately translations into English and German, and vice versa. Moreover, we can witness a close interaction, and sometimes even a personal union, of scholars studying Spiritualism on practical terms, and those interested in Spiritualism as a legitimate part of general psychology. As will become clear, Spiritualists were quite often on equal terms with physiologists and psychologists in advancing latest models of how to explain experiences near death.

PART TWO

The Different Strands of Death

WESTERN DISCOURSE ON EXPERIENCES NEAR DEATH
(1580–1975)

2.1

Introduction

CERTAIN HISTORICAL FACTORS, reports, and discourses, culminating in the two preceding decades of the 1970s, allowed Moody to construct near-death experiences as systematic phenomena. If this holds true, it should be possible to show a *terminus ante quem* at which elements of near-death reports had either not emerged or were part of other discourses unrelated to each other. I subsequently show that the earliest systematic report collections of experiences near death, emerging in the second half of the 19th century, already entailed the elements of blissful feelings, or the "panoramic life-review" feature. Accounts of "out-of-body" experiences, or visions of a "Bright Light," encountering deceased, precognition, or entering a tunnel, were at that time still elements handed down as specific, unconnected features in Christian, Spiritualist–Occult, or parapsychological discourses.

Interestingly, historical studies of experiences near death—especially by the religious scholar Carol Zaleski and somewhat less by the medievalists Peter Dinzelbacher and Marc van Uytfanghe—largely followed the pattern of taking modern near-death experiences as a homogeneous group of phenomena that can be directly compared with medieval visions of the otherworld. Thus they invoke the picture that medieval and modern experiences—the latter's direct dependency on the former to be ruled out—share "perennial insights" of life beyond death. In other words, it was not only an accidental negligence of former studies to skip over centuries—it was essential to their argument. Zaleski (1987, 6) defines in her prominent study *Otherworld Journeys* the purpose of her study as an examination of the return-from-death story in two widely separated settings: medieval Christendom and modern "secular" and pluralistic society. Comparative study will highlight features that are not otherwise obvious, putting into sharper relief the elements that are culturally specific and at the same time drawing attention to perennial aspects of otherworld journey narration.

Zaleski refrained from writing a continuous history of "return-from-death narratives"—instead, she presented "two periods of peak interest in this subject" (7) that crystalized in reports that seem to her to be more "authentic." As to the Middle Ages, her study covers stories from the sixth to the early 13th centuries, focusing on return-from-death stories that, on their part, are rooted in the apocalyptic traditions of late antiquity.

In the centuries that follow medieval times, visionary stories from the otherworld tend to become "a deliberate literary construction, self-conscious and systematic in its allegorical themes and classical allusions, and without the connection it formerly had to experience-based reports" (6). During the Reformation, she holds, stories of experiences near death declined but "reappeared in connection with some of the evangelical, separatist, and spiritualist movements of the nineteenth century" (5).

This notwithstanding, Zaleski limits her study to only a few comments alluding to accounts of near-death reports that predate Moody's collection. "Although," she argues, "*Life After Life* and its progeny break with the past in some ways, they cannot help but inherit the traits of older generations of explorers. A little digging at the roots of this family tree reveals, for example, that the mid-1800s witnessed a spate of books combining visionary testimony of the hereafter with edifying descriptions of death" (98). Astonishingly, there remains in Zaleski's account, and not only hers, a gap between 1300 and 1975 that is sparsely covered, a neglect presumably motivated by (a) an assumed lack of "authentic" experiences or sources (or both), and (b) an underlying premise to highlight the transcultural core of those experiences.

In the same vein, Peter Dinzelbacher argues that after the Middle Ages came to an end, the interest in visions of the beyond ceased, too. On the one hand, Dinzelbacher (1989, 10–11) argues, reformed theologians declared medieval accounts of holy visionaries as legendary, whereas, on the other hand, in the context of the Fifth Lateran Council (1516), Catholic theologians relativized deathbed visions as "private apparitions and revelations." However, he, too, is convinced of the authenticity of medieval reports as "reported experiences" (cf. 84). To him, all reports express cross-culturally "similar experiences which get immediately interpreted in diverging ways in different cultures, and are expressed differently" (12; my transl.). On these grounds, Dinzelbacher argues against scholars who take medieval visions as literary topoi. If modern thanatologists could record "completely analogous experiences of dying," and, moreover, a dependency of a "literary tradition" bridging from modernity to the Middle Ages is "fully out of question, because neither these thanatologists nor the reporting patients are philologists"

(85), then we are forced to conclude that converging experiences will lead to converging reports independent of each other.

There are several shortcomings in this reasoning. First, it is shown here that there are in fact various elements that modern near-death reports owe to ancient and medieval literature. Second, and more basic, the phenomenological perspective that takes reports for experiences suffers from a more general failure, namely, to project the radical individuation of dying (of an autonomous individual), which is, existentially speaking, certainly the case, into the "authenticity" of the reports. As I aim to show, the reports are, in contrast to their individual emergence, part of a communal discourse—be it in ancient, medieval, early modern, or contemporary culture. Dinzelbacher, however, correctly assumes the role of an individual "horizon of expectation" (77) that will not just influence the literary form of the report, but will be already effective at a much earlier phase, namely, when the individual undergoes the experience.

Finally, and equally important, it should be acknowledged that every historical account of experiences near death presupposes the perspective of modern near-death studies, which led to an extraction of near-death experiences in the respective ancient or medieval literature. In other words, the testimony of real and authentic modern reports— evaluated by its supposedly individual, autobiographical expression of correctly rendered "experience"—is used as the blueprint to single out exactly those elements of afterlife narratives that converge with modern reports.[1] Thus both perspectives are interrelated and interdependent. In its final consequence, such an approach may not be even able to address the questions of psychological expectations and literary dependency raised here, because it is clear from the outset that universal experiences are translated into reports, which makes the reverse process, the translation of reports into experience, superfluous.

In his comparative study of afterlife conceptions in early civilizations, Gregory Shushan (2009, 155) argues, "Obviously, the structure 'afterlife conception' is consistent crossculturally, or there could be no present book. We have also seen that the mythemes are consistent cross-culturally, while the symbols utilized in the expression of the mythemes are largely culture-specific."[2] In other words, every "journey to an afterlife realm" expresses through its "symbols" certain "mythemes" of intrinsic meaning beyond any cultural specificity, for example, ascent, judgment, or annihilation (cf. 154). Far from being precise, Shushan invokes several other categories to circumscribe the status of these universal mythemes, which, for him, are in essence the same in myths and modern near-death experiences: "symbols express mythemes, and mythemes are combined to form the

---

[1] Unfortunately, even the brilliant study of Jan Bremmer, *The Rise and Fall of the Afterlife*, occasionally uses (see 2002, 94; 100–2) the legacy of modern "authentic reports" in order to qualify certain reports of ancient and medieval times as mere "literary compositions."

[2] "It is not surprising that these details/symbols would be culture-specific, as they are plainly influenced by environment, history, social organization, and so on. Conceptions of afterlife hierarchies, for example, reflect earthly social hierarchies; and earthly societies are not identical to each other" (Shushan 2009, 155).

overall narrative structure (myth or NDE report), like a collection of metaphors organized to form an allegory. [. . .] The similarities are largely on the mythemic, (quasi-) universal level" (156). If the relationship of "symbols," "metaphors," and "narratives" on the one side, and mythemes on the other will not be more thoroughly defined, comparative analysis is threatened by the danger of not being an analysis at all, merging all accounts into a prestabilized harmony of supra-empirical experience. In this vein, Shushan argues that these experiences are not dependent on belief—exactly the opposite. They already influenced the conceptions of afterlife experience in major ancient civilizations. To argue that "the experience is dependent upon belief, would not address the cross-cultural, cross-temporal, and cross-contextual similarities outlined above" (165). Applying William James,[3] he concludes: "Regardless of its veridicality or otherwise, the NDE is indeed 'scientific fact' " (165).

I. P. Couliano, resonating with paradigms of the "esoteric metaculture" and a phenomenological description of the history of religions, could contextualize out-of-body experiences as cognitive capacity visible in almost all religious traditions, ranging from "shamanism" to modern esotericism. Taking them as experiences expressed in texts, Couliano treats them as human traits with Paleolithic roots (cf. 1991, 233). Voicing furthermore the opinion that in the meantime "no ancient otherworldly beliefs have been completely abandoned" (235), Couliano relativizes again the need to study the literary testimonies more closely—a task we carry out here.

According to Couliano's point of view, otherworldly journeys of a "separated soul" seem to have lost their moral features of punishment or hell quite recently. Equally, the conviction of a "separable soul" seems to have lost ground. Nevertheless, Couliano himself evidences the possibility of experiences out of the body with the multidimensional universe conceptualized in modern physics (see 32; 234). Interestingly, he concludes that his treatise "arrives at no particular conclusions" (232). Still, Shushan and Couliano transgress the boundaries of a historical survey, expressing a general conviction that there is a space of our disembodied mind in its own right. The final study that we may mention here is the work by the historian of ancient religion, Jan N. Bremmer, aiming to show how afterlife beliefs emerged in ancient Europe, were popularized in Christianity, and changed dramatically with the lost belief in the "soul." In this context, Bremmer (2002, 94; cf. 102) argues that modern near-death experiences, while often resulting in "a kind of conversion," depart in several respects from their medieval cognates. Nowadays, he holds—erroneously, as we subsequently see—that "hell, frightening demons or a kind of Last Judgment are generally absent from the NDEs," and therewith no longer convey the idea of a religious conversion but display a modern, personal religiosity beyond God and

---

[3] In Shushan's words (2009, 165), the belief that universal "primary experiences" "contribute to the formation of religious beliefs, thus accounting for the cross-cultural similarities of such beliefs."

a belief in a soul. Rather simply, "the NDE makes people a better person" (102). Heaven and salvation is "within us," and no longer a "final destination." Counterintuitive as it may be, Bremmer concludes that such modern experiences merely illustrate the continuing decline of the afterlife, attesting to an "empty" heaven in which "God is no longer there" (102). Although some reports in Moody's book may reinforce Bremmer's view of "modern secularization" (102), there is broad evidence that Christian metaculture is still an important background in a considerable number of modern reports.

Let us summarize the premodern elements of near-death reports identified by the respective historical research that has so far been undertaken. In general, scholars agree on the dominant literary form of the visions communicated in medieval Christian (and even ancient) sources: Near-death experiences are, as stated in the title of Zaleski's study, composed and reported as "journeys" of the (temporarily departed) soul. Shushan (2009, 148), following the archetypical model of experience, admonishes the reader to keep in mind "that NDErs primarily describe the afterlife journey." For him, the depiction of a "journey"—as opposed to a static "destination"—"reflects the main function of the texts: to instruct and assist the deceased on the afterlife journey" (160). More specifically, the most central episode narrated of these journeys is the "judicial assessment of deeds" (Zaleski 1987, 27; cf. Dinzelbacher 1989, 64). These episodes provide a hermeneutic key both for reading the journeys as "essentially an encounter with oneself" and for understanding the "imaginative laws"—essentially moral laws—"at work in visions of the other world" (Zaleski 1987, 27). According to Zaleski, the "encounter with one's deeds"[4] that reaches back to biblical sources highlights also the "imaginative quality" of these visions of an afterlife:

> In the encounter with deeds, the protagonist is, in effect, turned inside out; his inner state, the acts and impulses that were hidden even to himself, are projected outward onto the stage of the other world. The encounter with deeds is in this respect perhaps the most significant moment, even the epitome, of the otherworld journey; never is it more clear that the other world is the domain of the imagination." (73)

A second element is the separation of body and soul, and the "ascent" of the latter, which must "rise up out of the body" (58). However, repeatedly referring to the ambivalent description in St. Paul's account, "whether in the body or out of the body I know not, God knows" (93),[5] Zaleski seems hesitant to declare journey narratives of medieval

---

[4] Zaleski (1987, 75) provides an observation of Caesarius of Heisterbach that uncovers the by-then predominantly moral framework of afterlife narrations: "Read the visions of Wetti, Gottschalk, and others to whom it was granted to see the pains of the wicked and the glory of the elect: the vision of punishment always comes first."

[5] Cf. 2 Cor. 12: 1–5, 7; for a discussion see Zaleski 1987, 26–7.

texts straightforwardly as examples of out-of-body" experiences, being aware of the modern "paranormal" use of the term. In consequence, she avoids taking a position regarding the reality of out-of-body experiences. In contrast, for Dinzelbacher the case is obvious. From the sources, he argues, "something is evidently proven, namely, that the soul, whatever it may be, has the capability to leave for a certain amount of time the body and to return into him. This fact is adamant in the numerous testimonies of an 'astral body,' too, which may in some bodily unconscious individuals dissolve from the material body" (Dinzelbacher 1989, 93). Interestingly, the author resorts here to a concept of the esoteric metaculture, "astral body," applying it to premodern reports. Likewise, Shushan argues (2009, 112, with Sheils 1978) for the centrality of out-of-body experiences. Appealing to Shamanic flights of the soul (as did already Ehrenwald 1974, or, extensively, Duerr 2015), Shushan takes them as real experiences of an afterlife realm too: "Thus, while there are diverse methods of ascent (on cremation smoke, ladders, dragons, chariots, celestial bodies, spiritual bodies, etc.) and various modes of evaluation of one's earthly conduct, all the traditions and the NDE contain the *concepts* or themes these *symbols* express: ascent/OBE and judgment" (155; cf. 167). Further topics narrated in ancient and medieval otherworld itineraries are categorized by Zaleski (1987, 45–94) as pertaining to the "exit" and the "journey" itself, to "guides" of various kinds escorting the souls through heavenly or hellish realms, to "obstacles" encountered (e.g., fire or the "test-bridge"), to the "reentry," and finally, to the postecstatic transformation of the visionary, for example, by taking up the new role of a messenger. In his broader treatment of early civilizations, Shushan arrives at "a more or less *fixed set* of nine elements"[6] or "similarities." Supported by selected textual references, Shushan's set (2009, 157–60) of nine categories comprises the following: (1) OBE/Ascent; (2) Corpse Encounter; (3) Darkness/Tunnel; (4) Deceased Relatives/Ancestors; (5) Divine Presence or Being of Light; (6) Conduct Evaluation/Life Review; (7) Barriers/Obstacles; (8) Divinization/Oneness/Enlightenment; (9) Other Realm/Origin Point. In comparison with Zaleski's (cf. 1987, 134–5) or Dinzelbacher's (1989, 48) treatment of medieval Christian texts, this set includes many more categories of modern near-death discourse. For example, the vision or meeting of deceased relatives or ancestors (4) is, as topos, largely absent in Christian medieval literature.

To summarize the topoi of journeys to the otherworld in medieval Christian literature: Structurally, the returned visionary gives testimony of a vision that is thought to be a significant warning: to refrain from sins; to believe in retributive justice; to trust in Jesus. In that respect, we may speak of conversion narratives following, as Zaleski (1987, 81) puts it, "an intricate set of literary conventions" (cf. Benz 2013).

---

[6] "It is as if these nine key elements of the NDE were imported whole as a set into the afterlife conceptions of each of the civilizations" (Shushan 2009, 157). We may ask here, imported from where?

The question remains if, and how, a historical chronology of near-death reports is possible.

The first to present such a periodization—though more broadly of contributions on experiences related to human survival of physical death—had been Ian Stevenson, whose "reincarnation research" is subsequently treated. In what he conceptualized as the first period, ranging from the 1880s to the 1930s, investigators were "mainly engaged in collecting, classifying, and analyzing spontaneous experiences of persons who saw apparitions of deceased persons or had other experiences that suggested to them some communication from a discarnate personality" (Stevenson 1977, 152)—in other words, a period in which, mediated by Theosophy, the Spiritualist–Occult metaculture, including parapsychological research, became dominant. In the second period, extending from the 1930s to the 1960s, "most parapsychologists neglected the question of the possibility of man's survival after physical death"—as it seems, in reaction to an obvious rise of the Naturalist metaculture. Finally, in the third period, lasting from around 1960 to the by-then present, the mid-1970s, a new parapsychological interest began to focus again on out-of-body phenomena, on evidence of communication from deceased and reincarnation as survival of death—while, at the same time, being under continuous attack from the now-dominant paradigm of scientific naturalism.

Although this periodization—more properly a model of successive phases of parapsychology—has been followed by some scholars such as Barbara Walker and William Serdahely (1990), it has certain shortcomings. Stevenson's decision (1977, 153) to assign the beginning of "scientific research" on whether humans may survive physical death to the 1880s, substantiated by the foundation of the "Society for Psychical Research" in 1882, allots all precursory studies or observations to a "prescientific" realm. Moreover, Stevenson does not present a periodization of the entire near-death discourse, but, because of his predilection for the "scientific" discipline of parapsychology, leaves especially the respective discourse in Christian, Gnostic–Esoteric, and Naturalist metacultures out of the picture. Walker and Serdahely (1990, 109), for their part, use these three periods for an overview of near-death research more properly, sharing, however, the opinion that "contemporary near-death research is a derivative of early paranormal experimentation and observation." And again, there is a preference for the Spiritualist-Occult discourse; moreover, French and German studies are largely absent.

In conclusion, I neither stick to the three periods proposed nor present a new periodization here. In contrast, I aim to show that there is, and has been, a continuous process of broad reception of single reports and collation of these reports, and respective research. So far, only a few scholars have emphasized the continuity of those reports, speaking, however, usually of "experiences," or near-death episodes. Near-death researcher John R. Audette (1982, 39) concludes his paper on historical perspectives by saying that there is "a historical continuity and a compatible relation between past and present accounts of near-death episodes and experiences" that "span centuries of recorded human history." Of course, we can determine waves of popularity or the emergence of new conceptualizations and theories, which present themselves often as "discoveries," but much more obvious is the uninterrupted continuity of these narratives. Being aware of the arbitrariness of this decision, we next raise the curtain in 1580, the year that saw the first early modern autobiographical description of an experience near death, communicated by the French philosopher Michel de Montaigne. Because of its specific importance, the integration of out-of-body experiences, which became visible in the last two decades of the 19th century, is treated in a separate chapter.

"The past is never dead. It's not even past."

WILLIAM FAULKNER, *Requiem for a Nun* (1951)

2.2

Currents of Early Modern Near-Death Discourse

STUDIES OF NEAR-DEATH experiences have focused so far, as said, on ancient, medieval, or very recent cases. The early modern phase, up to the 1850s, has been largely neglected. In the following, I set out to show that there has been, in the respective centuries, a continuous flow of what people have reported as experiences near death. There is evidence that within the period of 1580–1970 three affirmative religious metacultures expressed themselves in—and by means of—these experiences, which finally enabled systematic accounts of near-death reports. The respective experiences were discussed and narrated in social communities, handed down initially in autobiographical first-person descriptions, and were finally enclosed in case collections from a third-person perspective. Thus Moody did not "discover" these experiences in the 1970s, but bundled these well-established strands of near-death discourse into one homogeneous whole. It must certainly be admitted that there are always some contingent decisions at play in the definition of the beginning of a certain discourse. I start the historical probe, however short and inconclusive, with early modern discourse, because it is here that we are able to cut through hagiographic patterns of exemplary subjects and meet ordinary individuals trying to express experiences that they had in the context of critical accidents. Literary historian Stephen Greenblatt argued that it is exactly the 16th century in which an increased self-consciousness or "self-fashioning" emerged—a discovery of individuality that finally resulted in the new genre of autobiography, even though the word "autobiography" emerged in the late 18th century (see Davis 2006, 19). Mascuch (1997, 19) shows convincingly that the origins of the "individualist self lie in the advent of modern autobiographical practice"—an important observation that becomes relevant in the subsequent discussion.

2.2.1 MICHEL DE MONTAIGNE AND THE BIRTH OF AUTOBIOGRAPHIC REPORTS OF EXPERIENCES NEAR DEATH

The first account in this mood, which is seen by many as the earliest near-death experience, is a personal report and philosophical reflection on a nearly fatal horseback riding accident by the famous philosopher Michel de Montaigne (1533–ca. 1593). It is unanimously regarded as the first early modern report of such an experience within an autobiographical context. In his *Essais* (1572–1592), establishing thereby the new literary genre of "essayistic literature," Montaigne described his almost catastrophic accident in a chapter with the title "De l'exercitation" (["On Exercise," or "Use Makes Perfect"]; book II, ch. 6 [1580]), which I quote in Charles Cotton's classical translation. We should, Montaigne (1849, 169) sets out to argue, "exercise and form the soul by experience to the course for which we design it; it will, otherwise, doubtless find itself at a loss when it comes to the pinch of the business." "But in dying," he proceeds, "which is the greatest work we have to do, practice can give us no assistance," because death can only be experienced "but once" (169).

The accident, which is, however, only incidentally described as a kind of background information for the philosophical reflection (and the subsequent changes in Montaigne's life) it initiated, seems to have happened when Montaigne was 37 years old. A reckless rider, galloping full speed, had bumped into him so that he and his horse came to fall, turning, as he reports, over and over again. Fully unconscious for quite a time, Montaigne was thought to be dead. While being carried to his house, he began to move again and showed signs of a serious traumatic brain injury—choking blood, vomiting, and so forth. It is in this context that Montaigne describes his experiences. Even hours after the accident, he discloses, he was fully disoriented:

> I knew not any more whence I came or whither I was going, neither was I capable to weigh and consider what was said to me: these were light effects that the senses produced of themselves, as of custom; what the soul contributed was in a dream, and lightly touched, as it were, merely licked and bedewed by the soft impression of the senses. Meantime my condition was, in truth, very easy and quiet; I had no affliction upon me, either for others or myself [...]. And, in earnest, it had been a very happy death; for the weakness of my understanding deprived me of the faculty of discerning, and that of my body of the sense of feeling [...]. When I came again to myself and to re-assume my faculties [...] I felt myself on a sudden involved in terrible pain [...], that I thought I was once more dying again, but a more painful death [...]. [T]he very next day when my memory began to return and to represent to me the state wherein I was at the

instant that I perceived this horse coming full drive upon me [. . .], it seemed to me like a flash of lightning that had pierced through my soul, and that [I] [1] was coming from the other world. This long story of so light a matter would appear vain enough, were it not for the knowledge I have gained by it for my own use; for I really find that, to get acquainted with death, you have but nearly to approach it. (171–2)

Several elements of this description deserve special mention. First, and in sharp contrast to medieval Christian visionaries, Montaigne no longer expresses his experiences in terms of an overly religious otherworldly journey into a "beyond." Instead, he recounts from a biographical and worldly perspective. After the full recovery of his memory, he is able to revive the accident and its circumstances. There is no allusion to an after-death state, although one might interpret the last remark of his description—that is, that it seemed to him that he had come "from the other world"– as pointing to a beyond. However, to me, a more plausible interpretation, in line with Montaigne's point of departure that death can only be experienced but once, will take the "other world" as a more general metaphor for the memorized experiences of a "shock" state disconnected from the usual life world. Such a reading would be, moreover, in line with Montaigne's skeptical approach. Most prominently, Montaigne's account documents the new importance given to individual, first-person experience. In this mood, he characterizes his own experience close to death as a perplexingly blissful and peaceful state of mind characterized by the absence of pain. This, the narrative of a calm, peaceful, and happy death, is still in line with medieval accounts (cf. van Uytfanghe 1991, 460–1). However, Montaigne does not report any experiences out of his own body or the topos of the panoramic life review, nor does he speak of any supernatural or paranormal encounters of deceased persons, Jesus, or a bright light.

Shall we, then, call Montaigne's account a near-death experience? Certainly it articulates an experience of approaching death. From a modern point of view, the description given points in diagnostic terms to a traumatic brain injury followed by a posttraumatic stress disorder (cf. Sperber 2012). Yet, to argue that Montaigne describes a near-death experience in the modern, post-Moody use would overstretch the evidence. On the one hand, Montaigne does not straightforwardly speak of a postdeath experience. On the other hand, we do find only allusions to mental states, which are, he assures us, somehow indirect memories of those states he had experienced. Nevertheless, he saw in his experience a fundamental turning point in his life, which at least structurally accords with an important element of later near-death discourse. Montaigne's report can indeed be seen as a precursor for modern near-death experiences, because the experience

---

[1] Later editions of Cotton's translation read correctly, "and that I came from the other world" ["et que ie revenois de l'aultre monde"] (Montaigne 1827, 344).

is reported of a clearly life-threatening situation. Yet, only few of Moody's topoi are part of the narrative.

2.2.2 EARLY CHRISTIAN ACCOUNTS OF NATIVE AMERICAN AFTERLIFE EXPERIENCES: THOMAS HARRIOT

As has been aptly argued by Mascuch, the *ars moriendi* [art of dying] literature of the early 16th century already prefigured the idea that, to have a holy and blessed death, one should practice diligently a self-examination that prefigures later autobiographical practice and, therewith, first-person biographical accounts of experiences near death. In Jeremy Taylor's "Holy Dying" (1651, II, 55), we read, "we are here to follow S. Paul's advice; *Judge your selves and you shall not be judged by the Lord*" (quoted in Mascuch 1997, 62), to which I return when discussing the "life review."

The remarkable traits of Montaigne's account become more apparent if compared with reports of deathbed visions in Christian metaculture. Two stories of two persons who recently had been dead and revived again are included in *A Briefe and True Report of the New Found Land Of Virginia* (1588), in which the British polymath Thomas Harriot (1560-1621) documented his travel to present-day North Carolina. In a section on customs and beliefs of the American Indians, he explains that the Indians believe in "the immortalitie of the soule," that at death the soul departs, according to the "workes it hath done," either to heaven as a place of perpetual happiness, "or els to a great pitte or hole, which they thinke to bee in the furthest partes of their part of the worlde towarde the sunne set, there to burne continually: the place they call *Popogusso*" (Har[r]iot 1588, 37). For confirmation, his native informants told him the following cases:

> [T]he one happened but few yeres before our comming in the countrey of a wicked man which hauing beene dead and buried, the next day the earth of the graue beeing seene to moue, was taken vp againe; Who made declaration where his soule had beene, that is to saie very neere entring into *Popogusso*, had not one of the gods saued him & gaue him leaue to returne againe, and teach his friends what they should doe to auoid that terrible place of torment. (37)

This second narration pertains once more to

> one being dead, buried and taken vp againe as the first, shewed that although his soule was aliue, and had trauailed farre in a long broade waie, on both sides whereof grewe most delicate and pleasaunt trees, bearing more rare and excellent fruites then euer hee had seene before or was able to expresse, and at length came to [...] houses, neere which hee met his father, that had beene dead before, who gaue him great charge to goe backe againe and shew his friendes what good they were to doe

to enioy the pleasures of that place, which when he had done he should after come againe." (38)

Reading these two reports, we should be aware of the hermeneutics that govern Harriot's perspective. As he says, "Some religion they haue alreadie, which although it be farre from the truth, yet beyng as it is, there is hope it may bee the easier and sooner reformed" (35). Therefore it may not astonish us to read in both accounts of almost Christian visions of hell and heaven. Both accounts end with the same, essential moral message, namely, the relevance of deeds done in this world. Interestingly, in the first account, it is one of the "gods" that sends the individual back to the world, whereas the second narrative depicts the deceased father sending him back. In that respect, the two narratives harmonize well with late medieval Christian deathbed narratives. Nevertheless, it should be worth mentioning that these reports of Native Americans fulfill for Harriot a special function—to demonstrate the universal prevalence of religion, the belief in the soul's immortality, and moral retribution in the afterlife existence. In the same way, Harriot's secondhand report, rephrasing third-person stories told by Native Americans, is drawn as evidence for the cross-cultural salience of near-death experiences. Shushan (2016, 72), for example, writes that Harriot "related the experience of an Algonquin man he met. The man reported that he had died and left his body during his own funeral, seeing his corpse below him." This is a perfect example of how post-Moodian beliefs are read into a historical document. In fact, there is no mention of any autoscopic interest into the body.[2] Without being able to discuss here how Harriot may have "heard" Indian narratives[3] as evidence of his own convictions, it should be obvious that such documents cannot be taken as immediate evidence for transcultural, ubiquitous experiences.

2.2.3 ANNA ATHERTON'S "MIRACULOUS PROOF OF THE RESURRECTION" (1680)

I now turn to what seems to be the oldest early modern report that encompasses main elements of near-death experiences. It has been disclosed by Henry Atherton, a physician in Wales, published probably in 1680.[4] Without doubt, already the programmatic

---

[2] Moreover, Shushan (see 2016, 72) deals with both reports as a single narrative and says that the "experiencer" had reported this story to Harriot, though it is conveyed by further informants.

[3] In the *Historia Antigua de México* (1780), Jesuit preacher and historian Francesco Clavigero (English translation 1787, I, 230) reports another "Indian" case, this time of a "Mexican princess," describing her experience (1505): "'After I was dead, or if you will not believe that I have been dead, after I remained bereft of motion and of sense, I found myself suddenly placed upon an extensive plain [...]. In the middle of it I observed a road [...], and on one side ran a great river whose waters made a frightful noise. As I was going to throw myself into the river to swim to the opposite bank, I saw before me a beautiful youth [...], clothed in a long habit, white as snow, and dazzling like the sun; he had wings of beautiful feathers [...], and laying hold of my hand, said to me, *Stop, for it is not yet time to pass this river*.'"

[4] Cf. Shaw 2006, 59–60; Morse 2008a, 2008b.

title[5]—as a metacommentary in regard to the hoped-for effects of disclosing this example—makes it perfectly clear that the report and its supernatural circumstances are thought to be a powerful device against the impending scandal of "Atheism" in contemporary society. The anonymous report builds on Henry Atherton's narration of his 14-year-old sister Anna (ca. 1655–1672). She fell sick with symptoms of ague in November 1669. In slowly deteriorating health, she lost weight and, on one day in February 1670, she seemed to be dead. Neither a looking glass under her nose nor hot coals applied to her feet made her display signs of life. However, her burial was delayed, and after seven days she "recovered all her senses," desired to see her mother and reported her experience:

> "8. O Mother! Since I was absent from you, I have been in Heaven, an Angel went before me to conduct me thither; I passed through three several Gates, and at length I came to Heaven Gate, where I saw things very glorious and unutterable, as Saints, Angels, and the like, in glorious Apparel; and heard Unparalleld Musick, Divine Anthems and Hallelu-jahs. 9. I would fain have entred that glorious place, but the Angel, that went before me [...] told me, I could not be admitted now, but I must go back, and take leave of my Friends, and after some short time, I should be admitted. 10. So he brought me hither again, and is now standing at the Beds-feet; Mother! You must see him, he is all in white. Her Mother told her, It was but a Dream or Fancy [...]. 11. But for the greater Confirmation, she told them of Three or Four Persons that were dead, since she was deprived of her Senses, and named each Person; (one of them was dead, and they knew not of it before they sent to en-quire:) she said, she saw them passing by her while she stood at the Gate.
>
> 12. One whom she named was reputed a Vicious Person, came as far as the Gate, but was sent back again another way. All the Persons named, dyed in the time she lay in this Trance" (Atherton [1680], n.p.). Finally, the report concludes, that she lived in "perfect health" for another two years, and "then dyed in great Assurance of her Salvation."

I do not discuss at length the well-known elements of Christian metaculture in this report, which proves an unbroken continuity of medieval near-death discourse. Among the elements being in line with the script of otherworldly journeys are heavenly gates, an angel in white, music, being sent back, or the reinforcement of the world's moral order by alluding to the transmortal judgment that awaits the "Vicious Person." Of significance

---

[5] The title of this pamphlet, most probably drafted by Henry Atherton (cf. Shaw 2006, 60), runs: "A Miraculous Proof of the Resurrection, or, The Life to come Demonstrated. Being a Strange but True Relation of what hapned to M[ris] *Anna Atherton*: Who lay in a trance 7 days, and had burning Coals applied to her feet, but no life appeared: and liv'd comfortably 2 years after [...], *An Invitation to an Holy Life* [...] *in this Adulterous and Atheistical generation, wherein neither God, Christ, Soul, Heaven nor Hell are minded; but drinking, whoring, swaring, lying, &c.*"

is, furthermore, the overtly geomorphic and anthropomorphic accessibility of the heavenly realm presented. Anna describes a spatio-temporal location through which one may be guided, encounter artefacts such as gates, and in which the sequential order of action is identical, or at least parallel, to the sequential order in our life world. In other words, this report speaks neither of some kind of omnipresence, nor of a heightened awareness, nor of an altered sense of time, which will become prominent features of 19th- and 20th-century esoteric accounts.

Furthermore, the report does not mention an out-of-body experience nor the life-review feature. As said, a structurally significant element of the narration is its attempt to classify the experience as real. In other words, otherworldly reports were already subject to criticism. Dramaturgically skillful, the mother is depicted as suggesting that it might be nothing but a dream. To counter this suggestion, Anna not only reaffirms her claim, but additionally names deceased persons she saw arriving at the gate of heaven. Not enough—one of these persons had not been known to be dead. It was, the report says, confirmed later that he had died exactly within the period of Anna's "trance." This, of course, serves as an "veracity mechanism" (Davidsen), lending credibility to her account, and connecting the peer's life world with justice restored in the beyond. Interestingly, this sort of a paranormal element—structurally similar to clairvoyance—is a characteristic feature of the early modern Protestant strand of Christian metaculture, as Jane Shaw could aptly demonstrate in her study on miracles in Enlightenment England (cf. Shaw 2006). English Protestants in particular reported numerous miraculous events. In the context of the report, it obviously serves to introduce an empirically testable confirmation, suitable to scientific minds of the "Atheistical Generation." The same purpose—actually, to draw a "scientific" conclusion from Anna's case—is laid down in the last sentence of the report: *"I[t] is then necessary all Persons be kept 48 hours before burial, lest they should be buried alive"* (Atherton [1680], n.p.), which finishes with a decidedly neutral, medical interest in the case. In these days, fears of premature burial emerged, though it will be in the 18th and 19th centuries much more prominent (see Bondeson 2001, 22–8; 278–80). But, of course, the major purpose of this account is to offer a proof for the doctrine of resurrection.[6]

2.2.4 JOHANN SCHWERDTFEGER'S "VITAL EXPERIENCE" OF DEATH (1734)

Whereas the reports of Montaigne and others are regularly invoked in modern near-death studies, the narrative of Anna Atherton has only recently attracted the interest of the research community (cf. Morse 2008b; Greyson 2010; Duerr 2015). But there are still other testimonies that deserve our attention. A case reported and discussed, as

---

[6] Anna's report was reprinted by William Turner in his *Compleat History of the Most Remarkable Providences* (1697), as a proof of resurrection (cf. Shaw 2006, 60).

it seems, exclusively in German texts of the 18th and 19th centuries, is the following of Johann Schwerdtfeger, who died in 1733 in a small town near Magdeburg, Germany. It allows us to show how a certain narrative, combining hagiographical and dogmatic topoi with personal biographical accounts, developed. The original report by Prussian pastor Gottfried Kern appeared in 1734 in the journal *Geistliche Fama* (*Spiritual Fame*), edited and authored by radical Pietists from 1730 to 1740. The overall aim of the journal, which was distributed not only in Europe but was also read in American Pietist circles, for example, in Pennsylvania, was to provide a communication platform for the community of "Reborn" Christians of the "Philadelphia Movement,"[7] to inform of "Godly Awakenings," to provide spiritual guidance, and so forth. The second volume, edited by Pietist physician Johann Samuel Carl,[8] includes an enclosure[9] in which Pastor Kern reports the "veritable case" of the deceased, whom he visited several times. An acute and severe fever took hold of Johann Schwerdtfeger, which developed into pneumonia. Moreover, he took a medicine that made his condition even worse. After some days of growing weakness and repeated visits by the pastor, from whom he already had received "the Lord's supper," he called, after being unconscious for some hours, for the pastor again, and delivered the following report. He had been on a small path, difficult to travel because of stones and thorns, but, because he remembered God's words that the way to Heaven has to be like this,[10] he went on. But then he heard a loud voice proclaiming that it is not yet time for him to die and that he should return in order to investigate his life; this being done, he may reappear in front of the judgment seat. Two days after this first report, he fainted again and was unconscious for four hours. Regaining consciousness, he "revealed" [*offenbaren*] what he had experienced this time. Strong as if nearly recovered, Pastor Kern (1734a, 107) narrates, Schwerdtfeger told him the following: He had truly been before the judgment seat, where a black register had been opened and "my sins had been read from it—among them some which in my life I would certainly not have been able to remember, but for all that, they appeared to me as if I had committed them at the same moment." Being accused by a horrendous "Satan," Schwerdtfeger, in full fear and terror, looked around and called for Jesus, praying that he might help him to escape

---

[7] See Grutschnig-Kieser 2006, 266.

[8] Besides editing the journal *Geistliche Fama* (between 1730 and 1740, the main organ of the Philadelphia Movement) in Sardis (Berleburg), Carl authored some pietist scriptures. For the context of the movement, see Shantz 2008.

[9] *II. Beylage / In einem wahrhafften und umständlichen Bericht von dem verstorbenen Mann in Hornhausen, namens Johann Schwerdtfeger* [. . .] (= Kern 1734a). A second, revised, and enlarged reprint appeared as an independent publication in the same year (Kern 1734b).

[10] According to Zaleski, the thorny way to heaven has been a recurrent Christian motive from early on. She mentions (1987, 56) the vision of Saint Ansgar, an archbishop of the ninth century, explaining that paths toward the other world usually come "in two main varieties: the delightful way [*via amoena*] and the dark or thorny path." Ansgar, for example, is stuck in mud and cannot travel farther but must return and "disavow his childish frivolities," before he may proceed on the "delightful way."

from the might of the devil. Then he noticed a shadowy man standing at the side of the table with the opened register. After some while, he recognized him to be "the mediator between God and men," and he "jumped towards him, and hugged him with tearful eyes; and he looked at me most friendly, and, even apart from that, he appeared to me as if being pure Sun and brilliance. He closed the book and [. . .] announced to me the remission of my sins [. . .] and accepted me as a heavenly member of the Chosen" (108). Thereupon he was led by the mediator to a group of angels, and, in the moment of being included in their circle,

> "cries of joy filled the whole heaven, and it appeared to me as if I heard loud drum rolls, and a powerful sound of many trumpets, and a tuned-in music, of a kind that I had never heard before. Then heaven opened so that I could look inside, and [. . .] my eyes were fully dazzled, and I was aghast by the beauty that I saw. At that moment, I commemorated the words of Paul, 1 Cor. 2:9, 'Eye hath not seen, nor ear heard', etc., and therefore I have to confess that it is impossible to me to speak out what I have seen and experienced, even if I could speak in the tongues of angels. (108)

And Schwerdtfeger concludes his report, that he was brought back to our "vale of tears," but filled with such happiness that "everything [here] stinks. Yes, if the King of Prussia would present the whole principality of Halberstadt as a gift to me, to do with it whatever I want: I would luckily refuse, because in my eyes it is nothing but excrement and dirt. I will not mix the taste of heaven with worldly food and drink; in the meantime, I will wait as long as I will enter my ease again" (109). According to Pastor Kern, he then announced that he will live for two more days, and invited all to visit him to hear of his credentials. As proclaimed, he disclosed after two days that the time had come to die. However, his mourning wife, Kern reports, shouted in his ears and did not let him lay down. She shook his body, so that, in consequence, he awoke again, "and said: You godless people, why do you refuse to grant me ease, which has been granted by God? Now I do have to live for another day" (110), which so happened. And then, finally, he died.

In his second report of the event, Kern (1734b, 2) wants to "give knowledge of other thoughtful circumstances, which may have happened in this incident." Kern's ambiguity in respect to trustworthiness becomes clearer in the next passage. Although such reports of "strange events" are usually suppressed and disavowed, he holds that they nevertheless prove God's capability to make himself, his love, and his justice known. According to Kern's Lutheran pietist belief, God may even beyond the "official ministry [*ministerio*] awake now and then people, to appoint them [. . .], and to grant special abilities to them, who, on their part, testify to others the truth out of vital experience [*lebendiger Erfahrung*] and inner conviction" (2). Interestingly, Kern alters some sentences in his second report , and adds a second biblical reference (the "dirt" of the world: Philippians 3:8). Most important, he reinforces the supernatural circumstances of the incident, namely,

Schwerdtfeger's prophesy concerning his time of death, the miraculous return of his life force, and, finally, his death—now "fully relaxed, without distortion of his face or body" (cf. 8).

Kern's reports, to my knowledge unknown to recent near-death research, combine crucial elements of the Christian metaculture with a personal biographical account. On the threshold of modernity, it pays only occasional tribute to hagiographical standard models, being probably the oldest report of an experience near death in a more focused sense.

2.2.5 KERN'S REPORTS AND THE OLDEST MEDICAL DESCRIPTION OF AN EXPERIENCE NEAR DEATH BY DU MONCHAUX (1766)

The aspects last mentioned become clearer with a report given in Pierre-Jean Du Monchaux's *Anecdotes of Medicine*, published in 1766. It has recently been unearthed and discussed as the oldest medical description of a near-death experience. Here, we read,

> "Sir L. C., one of the most famous apothecaries of Paris had in Italy, 25 years ago, a malign fever, and was treated by French physicians [. . .], and sustained many blood-letters. After the last phlebotomy [. . .] he had a syncope and was unconscious for such a long time that the assistants were particularly worried. He reported that after having lost all external sensations, he saw such a pure and extreme light that he thought he was in Heaven (literally: in the Kingdom of the Blessed). He remembered this sensation very well, and affirmed that never of all his life had he had a nicer moment [. . .]. These observations seem to be comparable to those of a 12th c. theologian, who said that at the moment approaching our body and soul dissolution, the latter is lit by a primary light ray (*luminositas lucis primae*)." (Du Monchaux 1766, 44; trans. and quoted in Charlier 2014, e155).

Most significantly, Du Monchaux alludes to Christian theology but proposes, at the same time, a purely physico-pathological explanation.[11] It represents probably the first documented instance of an interpretation from the perspective of a Naturalist metaculture, foreshadowing the appearance of a new understanding of disease that was an innovation of French physicians in the early 19th century. Now, pathological deviations of human tissue and physiology will inform the explanation of disease—and not lifestyle, character, or the like.

Applying the "Greyson scale" for assessing the depth of the experience in this account, Charlier arrives at a total score of 12 (out of 32), which permits speaking of a moderate

---

[11] Du Monchaux (1766, 45; quoted in Charlier 2014, e155) holds that "the cause of the pleasant sensation" is everywhere the same: It is a kind of blood effusion in the brain vessels that "excites all these vivid and strong sensations."

near-death experience (a total score of more than 7; cf. Greyson 1983, 373). Compared with that, Schwerdtfeger's report includes considerably more elements (cognitive (c), affective (a), paranormal (p), and transcendental (t) components; patient score/maximum score achievable):

1. Altered sense of time (c) 1/2 ("deeds appeared as committed at the same moment")
2. Accelerated thought processes (c) 0/2
3. Past flashed before me (c) 2/2
4. Sense of sudden understanding (c) 2/2
5. Affective feeling of peace (a) 2/2
6. Feeling of joy (a) 2/2
7. Feeling of cosmic unity (a) 0/2 (at least not in modern terms)
8. Seeing or feeling surrounded by light (a) 2/2
9. Senses more vivid than usual (p) 0/2
10. Extrasensory perception (p) 0/2
11. Precognitive vision of personal future (p) 1/2
12. Sense of being out of physical body (p) 0/2
13. Transcendental sense of an unearthly realm (t) 2/2
14. Sense of a mystical being (t) 2/2
15. Sense of deceased or religious spirits (t) 2/2
16. Sense of a border, sent back to life involuntarily (t) 2/2
     Total score 20/32

Schwerdtfeger's report scores rather high on a modern near-death experience scale. However, according to my premises, I refrain from judging the "depth" or intensity of any kind of experience. Instead, the scale allows us to compare the report with modern expectations in respect to the elements that should be part of a near-death experience. Most notably, Schwerdtfeger's report does not include an out-of-body experience.

Kern's report of Schwerdtfeger's deathbed vision immediately triggered some discussion among theologians.[12] Interestingly, the questions raised were similar to those inhabiting the arena of contemporary claims of such experiences. Still in 1734, Johann Christoph Colerus (1734, 30–47), a preacher in Weimar, Germany, discussed the story, reprinting the report of Kern, followed by two comments. Colerus argues that the report is trustworthy simply because it had been noted down by a trustworthy preacher. On the status of Schwerdtfeger's narration, he points out that it is "neither a mere dream, nor mere syncope, but a rapture"—that is, the soul "had not yet left him, nor was he dead" (40). Furthermore, Colerus warns the reader of searching for similar experiences that

---

[12] Cf. the "Gleanings" ["*Nachlese*"], in *Acta Historico-Ecclesiastica*, 1734, I, 150–64.

to him are possible, though not "necessary." Nevertheless, the experience had happened through God's "holy reasons." It should be taken by others as a call to "wake up," which is the right attitude to deal with such a report. "Taunting atheistic speeches" ("*spöttische, atheistische Reden*," 41), that only simple-minded but not sharp-minded individuals will have such experiences, are, in contrast, sinful. In his "prophetic examination," Colerus discusses if Schwerdtfeger's account may be regarded as a "revelation" through which one may gain more universal insights. He discloses that one may speak of a revelation only if supernatural causes are present. The discussed case, however, seems not to be caused by godly "mercy" but by "forces of nature"—a fact that, he surmises, could be uncovered in a joint effort of an experienced physician and a theologian (44). But still, he holds that in the case at hand, "God, and his spirit were very busy in the soul of the patient" (45). Yet Colerus reminds the reader that Schwerdtfeger had been ill, and "all illnesses disturb the soul's faculties." Schwerdtfeger, occupied with his testament, Colerus comments, was already focusing his death, oscillating between existential fears and hopes: "The preacher speaks to his conscience, and reminds him of the impending godly court, and points to Christ, the advocate. These ideas [*Vorstellungen*] reappeared to the patient while being unconscious" (45). So, he argues, his vision did not appear supernaturally. Most significantly, already Colerus, in the 18th century, wonders if patients' obviously religious ideas might have been induced by the counseling pastor. Taken together, all this leads him to believe that it is, even though indirectly induced by God, still the "phantasy of a devout Christian" (46). And he concludes his examination by pointing to—equally natural— occurrences of apparent death and, subsequently, to reports in "other religions," quoting, however, only Erasmus's interpretation of Plato's Myth of Er (*Republic*, 10.614–21).

2.2.6 EMMANUEL SWEDENBORG'S SPIRITUAL RESUSCITATION AND EXPERIENCES OF THE AFTERLIFE

Moving onward to the influential afterlife experiences reported by Emanuel Swedenborg (1688–1772), an eminent Swedish scholar, visionary, and Theosophist, it should be mentioned that he did not report an experience triggered in a confined situation near death (cf. Rhodes 1982). Yet he communicated in his extensive writings his ability to travel freely between the spiritual and the earthly world (cf. Rhodes 1996). His influence on near-death discourse, however, has been tremendous. Goodrick-Clarke (2008, 169) argued that the common theme of the reception of Swedenborg's ideas "relates to the interplay among spirit and matter and after-death states," being "his principal legacy to modern esotericism." Walker argued that it was the experience of out-of-body travels most properly that initiated Swedenborg's spiritual turn.[13] We may leave it to his most

---

[13] Swedenborg had experienced enlightening out-of-body travels for several years, in which "spiritual ideas and deceased people were supposedly revealed to him." In consequence, he turned away from science and

famous early critic, Immanuel Kant, to describe these experiences. Kant ([1766] 1899, 103–4) recapitulates that Swedenborg reported to have been "liberated from the body, in a state mediate between sleeping and waking, in which he has seen, heard, even felt spirits." According to a second kind of experience, he "is being led away by the spirit, when he may be out walking on the street without losing himself, while at the same time his spirit is in entirely different regions and sees clearly elsewhere houses, men, forests, &c., and this perhaps for several hours." The third, and more usual kind of visions, are those "which he has daily while wide awake; and from these visions his stories are taken." Swedenborg has been quoted time and again in near-death literature, markedly by Moody who included him in his section on "Parallels" in his 1975 book (cf. 1976, 122–6). For him, Swedenborg presented "vivid descriptions of what life after death is like" (123), namely out-of-body experiences, meeting angels, the Lord, and spirits of the deceased, direct communication, the lack of the dead's awareness to be dead, bright light, perfect memory of the past life, and the ineffability of higher experience. Indeed, in a central passage in *Of Heaven and Hell* (*De coelo et inferno*, 1758) Swedenborg describes in detail his spiritual resuscitation and experience of the afterlife.[14] However, looking more closely at Swedenborg's text, significant differences come to the fore. To start with a decisive feature, the out-of-body experience: Looking at the process of how Swedenborg describes the coming-together of his experience, it is perfectly clear that although he narrates an identifiable, specific situation in which God made him experience what "death" and "resurrection" will be like, it is framed by speculative and visionary descriptions of the general nature of the afterlife. It will be experienced by all dead passing to the beyond. Additionally, Swedenborg (cf. 1758, 114) refers to a supernatural agency, the "Lord," who actually grants and initiates the experience:

> The spirit of man, after the separation, remains a little while in the body, but not longer than till the total cessation of the heart's action, which takes place with variety according to the state of the disease of which man dies; for the motion of the heart with some continues a long while, and with some not long: as soon as this motion ceases, the man is resuscitated; but this is done by the Lord alone. By resuscitation is meant the drawing forth of the spirit of man from the body [*eductio spiritus hominis a corpore*], and its introduction into the spiritual world, which is commonly called resurrection. (1854, 160; cf. 1778, 291)[15]

---

government to pursue "spiritual truths." The motive of sharing his experiences resides in his hope "of helping others to understand this domain better," claiming a "constant interplay between the spiritual world and the earthly world, serving as the source of our emotions and ideas" (Walker 1990, 107).

[14] The section "De hominis Resuscitatione a mortuis, ac Introitu in vitam æternam" (Swedenborg 1758, 187–90 [nn. 445–52]).

[15] Latin: Swedenborg 1758, 188 [n. 447].

Swedenborg continues that he was granted a demonstration of resuscitation, provided by the Lord: "How resuscitation is effected, has not only been told me, but also shown by living experience. The experiment itself was made with me, in order that I might fully know how it is done. I was brought into a state of insensibility as to the bodily senses, thus almost into the state of the dying; yet the interior life with thought remaining entire, so that I perceived and retained in memory the things which occurred" (291).[16] It is interesting to note that the English rendering of Swedenborg that Moody had at hand, too, translates Latin *experientia* occasionally as experiment, thereby strengthening its meaning as denoting "trial"—and knowledge gained by repetition of experiments—in the emerging culture of scientific experimentation.[17] Probably the allusion to scientific methods was intended by Swedenborg; yet, he still attributed the final agency to God Almighty. However, this passage is, in this aspect, crucial for the shift toward the modern meaning of experience—to be personally involved in a significant, often life-changing event that results through the unforeseeable outcome of situation itself, in new knowledge or skills.

However, Swedenborg's description of the surmised out-of-body experience is emerging from Christian metaculture (cf. his résumé, n. 452).[18] He still holds that it is the gross, earthly human body that hinders the spirit's access to spiritual realms. Therefore his out-of-body experience should more accurately be described as a kind of incomplete and reversible resurrection: "Especially it was given to perceive, and also to feel, that there was a drawing, and as it were a pulling out of the interiors of my mind, thus of my spirit, from the body; and it was said that this was from the Lord, and that thence is resurrection" (Swedenborg 1854, 160).[19] Moody, quoting from the passage mentioned (n. 449), comments that Swedenborg "claims that he himself has been through the early events of death, and has had experiences out of his body" (1976, 123), which seems, judged from the preceding passage, true to the limited extent of Swedenborg describing visionary, ecstatic experiences. Yet he neither mentions autoscopic visions nor describes how his experience ended. In other words, the return into his body is missing in the account.

Swedenborg, to summarize, is a perfect example of how an individual in the early Enlightenment period could treat the experience of an afterlife. On the one hand, he remains in various respects within the currents of Christian metaculture, although with quite unique interpretations of the spirit(s), heaven and hell, angels, and God. On the

---

[16] "Quomodo Resuscitatio fit, non modo mihi dictum est, sed etiam per vivam experientiam ostensum, ipsa experientia mecum facta est, ob causam ut plene scirem, quomodo fit" (Swedenborg 1758, 188 [n. 449]).

[17] We find elsewhere explicit references to such knowledge, too: "It has been granted me to have an *experimental knowledge* of such communication in the heavens from being present with some spirits" (Swedenborg 1778, 169 [n. 268], italics mine). On the history of the concepts *experimentum* and *experientia* see Harrison 2011.

[18] Swedenborg 1778, 294–5. For example, he points to the vision of a transfigured Jesus in Matthew (17:2): "Such was his appearance to his disciples, when they were out of the body, and in the light of heaven" (Swedenborg 1758, 72; cf. 199 [n. 313]).

[19] Latin: Swedenborg 1758, 189 [n. 449]).

other hand, he transgresses the traditional boundaries of Christian discourse on death and dying by introducing visionary accounts, if not practices, of the Gnostic–Esoteric and Spiritualist–Occult metacultures (cf. Hanegraaff 1996, 425–9, 460). Finally, he at least tries to harmonize his visionary insights with the agenda of the Enlightenment and its devotion to scientific explanation and rationality (cf. Stengel 2011).

2.2.7 PIETIST LEGACIES OF REPORTS NEAR DEATH: GEORGE DE BENNEVILLE (1791)

As it seems, German Pietism was a fertile ground for reporting experiences near death, as can be seen in the example of George de Benneville (1703–1793). Descendent of a refugee family of Huguenot French nobility, he was born in London, but lived, at the time of his experience, in Germany, serving as a lay minister and physician. In 1741, he immigrated to America, settling in Germantown, Pennsylvania. The description of his experience near death is to be found in the author's French manuscript that had been translated and published in 1791 by Rev. Elhanan Winchester under the title "A True and Most Remarkable Account of Some Passages in the Life of Mr. George de Benneville."[20] In this autobiographical narrative, de Benneville reports that he had been a Calvinist, adhering to the view that salvation is only for a selected few. In the aftermath of his visionary experience (at the age of 36), he was cast out of the Calvinist Church and "converted," as he says, to Christian Universalism and its doctrine that, "after purification in Hell, *all* will be saved" (Vincent and Morgan 2006, 44; cf. de Benneville [1791] 1890, 16).

After being ill for quite a while with a "consumptive fever," he was merely a "skeleton," but "favored through grace with many visions" (26). At a point, he reports, "I felt myself die by degrees. Exactly at midnight my soul was separated from my body, and I saw the people occupied in washing it, according to the custom of the country. I had a strong desire to be freed from the sight of my body, and immediately I was drawn upward as in a cloud, and beheld great wonders beyond my power to describe" (27). He arrives at a wonderful place with delightful fruit trees, dispersing fragrant odors. He becomes aware of two winged, shining white guardians, "one at my right hand, and the other at my left, beautiful beyond expression, whose boundless love and tenderness profoundly affected me" (28). Then, the guardian to his right says to him "the most Holy Trinity hath favored you to be comforted with an everlasting and universal consolation, by discovering to you in what manner he will restore all his creatures, without exception, to the praise of his glory and their eternal salvation; and you shall be witness of this" (28)—obviously reassuring his new, Universalist faith. Next, the guardian to his left indicates that he will now have to visit "the seven habitations of the damned." Lifted through the air, they pass through dreadful places where he observes how the sinners are confronted each with

---

[20] A German translation appeared in 1798.

"his own sins and iniquities" (29–30). Suffering from compassion toward the tormented, he is lifted again and brought to a secure place. Here, a "messenger" arrives, and he is equipped with the mission that he shall return to his "earthly tabernacle, to proclaim and publish to the people of the world an universal Gospel" (31). A short while later, he sees a figure of utmost brightness, the "Son of the living God," approaching with an innumerable multitude. He hears the masses praise everlasting deliverance, and sees how "they passed through the seven habitations of the damned, and numbers were delivered from each, and being clothed in white robes, they followed the heavenly host" (33). Finally, his guardians conduct him to the "five celestial habitations." Here, he sees, of course, glory and joy, "impossible to describe." "They have no need of any speech there. The language of eternal and universal love is expressed in all their actions" (35). He sees thrones, Adam and Eve, Mount Zion, released spirits, and many other miracles and mysteries, Hallelujah, Amen (cf. 40). Then his guardians reconduct him to his house: "I beheld the people assembled, and saw my body in the coffin, with which I was reunited, and lodged within my earthly tabernacle. Upon gaining consciousness I recognized my dear brother Marsey, and many others, who told me that I was twenty-five hours in the coffin, and seventeen hours out of it [. . .]; but to me they seemed as many years" (40–1).

Several elements in this narrative are highly significant as mediating Christian visionary imagery of deathbed narratives into the 18th century. Certainly, the predominant intention of the narrative is the justification of his newly adopted, Universalist faith. Moreover, the sight of his body that he observes as already being prepared for the funeral is, by the disembodied soul, met with repulsion—an important difference to later, overtly curious autoscopic interests of the soul. There are narratives of wordless understanding, unconditional love, guardians, and hellish punishment; yet the author is not subject to a heavenly judgment, nor is a life review reported.

2.2.8 A NEAR-DEATH REPORT BY AN AMERICAN QUAKER: THE EXAMPLE OF THOMAS SAY

Of several other contemporary visionary experiences of leaving the body while being ill and in critical condition,[21] the report of Thomas Say (1709–1796), an American Quaker minister, is quoted. In 1796, his son published his biography. Say, "a great enemy to atheism and deism" ([1796] 1805, 21), had not only felt in his "trance" an extraordinary bliss, but also witnessed the fate of two others who had died recently. On the ninth day, "I fell into a trance [. . .]. After my departure from the body (for I left the body)"—the formal allusion to Paul's rapture (2 Corinthians 12) is noteworthy here—the attending

---

[21] For example, the narrative of Rev. William Tennent (1705–1777) of the Presbyterian Church, cf. Boudinot 1828, 10–21.

family felt no pulse and thought he was close to death, as was the opinion of the doctor called. At the same time, Thomas Say heard, after leaving the body,

> the voices of men, women and children, singing songs of praises unto the Lord God and the Lamb, without intermission, which ravished my soul [...], also delighted with most beautiful greens which appeared to me on every side, and such as never were seen in this world; through these I passed, being all clothed in white, and in my full shape [...]. As I passed along towards a higher state of bliss, I cast my eyes upon the earth, which I saw plainly, and beheld three men (whom I knew) die. [...] Two of them were white men, one of whom entered into rest, and the other was cast off. There appeared a beautiful transparent gate opened; and as I and the one that entered into rest came up to it, he stepped in; but as I was stepping in, I stepped into the body. When I recovered from my trance, I mentioned both their names, [...] and which of them entered into rest, and which did not. I said to my mother, O that I had made one step further; then I should not have come back again. (87–9)

According to his son, this had happened in 1726. Yet, it had not been a singular experience—some years later, he could, while in bed with "yellow fever," see "the Father, Son and Spirit," all in Light and Glory (cf. 103–6),[22] and could detail not only their vision, but also realized essential Christian teachings. As it seems, his first experience of leaving the body had opened an ability to cross the threshold into the beyond.[23] Say reports to have identified recently deceased persons—a topos that we met in Atherton's report—but this time enriched with additional knowledge: Say is a chief witness to their postmortal fate, being able to tell which of them was chosen to enter into rest. Surely such reported insights will have contributed to Say's authority as minister.

2.2.9 THE EMERGENCE OF NEAR-DEATH REPORTS IN GERMAN SPIRITUALISM: JOHANN CARL PASSAVANT

Moving onward, the next important stage is initiated by protagonists of Western Spiritualist–Occult metaculture. As is well known, the Viennese physician Franz A. Mesmer (1734–1815) popularized the concept of "animal magnetism," a vital force in all organic beings. In this paradigm, widely influential up to the late 19th century, it

---

[22] The vision of a "light" resonates with the Quaker's assumption that the light of God is in every person and that the individual shall let that life be the guide of his or her life.

[23] Although Say's report enacts Christian metaculture in the strand of medieval and early modern deathbed visions, it served alongside with other reports in a work of the 20th century, Graham's *Psychical Experiences of Quaker Ministers* (1933, 22–4), as example in a by-then-modern context of "psychical experiences," i.e., modern Spiritualism and parapsychology.

was the task of the physician to influence positively the vital magnetic fluid for restoring health. In the context of somnambulism—referring to the half-waking trance practiced in animal magnetism—the interest in experiences near death found a broad continuation. Johann Heinrich Jung-Stilling (1740–1817), a German ophthalmologist, edifying Pietist writer, and friend of Johann Wolfgang von Goethe, discussed in his *Theorie der Geisterkunde* (1808, translated as *Theory of Pneumatology*, 1834) the case of Swedenborg. He grants him a certain credibility, but disagrees with him about the source of his vision. The latter is not God or "intercourse with the world of spirits," Jung-Stilling says ([1808] 1832, 95), but comes about "by means of magnetism, by certain diseases, and by other instrumentality," which may include experiences near death, though he does not say this explicitly. However, in the same manner as Swedenborg, he hypothesized that the soul, if irreversibly separated from its body, will gain a complete recollection of its own life in the world. This will, he says, in its initial phase already happen to individuals in somnambulist states: "It is now in the state of a clear-seeing magnetic sleeper, but being entirely separated from the body, its state is much more perfect: it has a complete recollection of its earthly existence from beginning to end; it remembers those it has left behind, and can form to itself a very clear idea of the visible world, of which it is now no longer susceptible, whilst on the contrary, it is conscious of the invisible world and its objects" (62; cf. Alvarado 2011, 67).[24] I am not able to trace the roots of the topos of a "full recollection" of the earthly existence in the disembodied soul here, but it surely relates to Platonic ideas of a full "recollection" [*anamnesis*] in the after-death existence of the soul, if not "truth" as "absence of oblivion" [*aletheia*]—ideas preserved and transmitted in Christian philosophy. For example, Plotinus, who inspired Christian metaphysics, holds that in the soul's career after death, the first phase will be to achieve a complete memory of deeds and experiences of the last existence (*Ennead* IV 3, 27; cf. du Prel 1885, 320).

　　Some 10 years after Jung-Stilling's work, narratives of experiences near death surface, this time explicitly, in the mesmerist tradition. In the work *Untersuchungen über den Lebensmagnetismus und das Hellsehen* ("Examinations of Life-Magnetism and Clairvoyance") by German physician Johann Carl Passavant (1790–1857), which appeared in 1821, Schwerdtfeger's report attracted new attention. Actually, Passavant (see 1821, 253–69) seems to be among the first to devote a full chapter to the topic of "clairvoyance near death." Arguing that the "peripheric powers of the soul" must decrease for the "central life of the soul" to appear, he points to cases near death, in which the "half-liberated souls" are aware of their past and future, free from the bondage of time and death, which also helps "to explain the undisputable facts that dying persons appear to

---

[24] If the human soul, while not entirely detached from its material body, is "capable of such wonderful things," Jung-Stilling (1832, 62) exclaims, "what will its capability be when totally separated from it by death!" Here, the person "falls into a perfect trance or profound sleep. As long as the mass of blood is still warm and not congealed [. . .], the soul remains in it; but as soon as the brain and the nerves lose their warmth and become frigid, they can no longer attract the ethereal part of the soul [. . .]; it therefore disengages itself."

others in a far distance" (253–4). In this context, he quotes only two cases, one of an apparent death of a young boy and, almost entirely, the report of Schwerdtfeger. Even though he does not discuss the case more thoroughly, it becomes clear that he takes the report at face value. Leaning on a Christian basis that tends toward Esoteric metaculture, Passavant is convinced that such reports must be seen as true examples of a "liberated soul," which overcomes the limitations of time and space, as in the case of the invisible, bypassing power of the *magnetiseur* (cf. 254).[25] Recent instances, he adds, may even be found in individuals not being close to death. To adduce further evidence, he points to the examples of the Brahmans in India, whose "inner activity of the soul reveals true clairvoyance"—"Djogis," as he calls them, who are "fully enlightened" and "fully united with God [*entheoi*]," and who "see God, *as a very white, lively and ineffable light*" (261–2; italics in orig.).

2.2.10 OPIUM EXPERIENCES AND THE CONFIGURATION OF THE LIFE-REVIEW FEATURE: COLERIDGE AND DE QUINCEY

Significantly, in the beginning of the 19th century we may also notice the first narrative configuration of the life review and other near-death features in the context of drug experiences. In European intellectual circles of that time, opium (especially as *laudanum*, mixed with alcohol) became a fashionable, and not yet illegal, exotic drug. In consequence, drug experiences were increasingly reported—predominantly by poets and literary critics such as Samuel Taylor Coleridge (1772–1834). In 1817, Coleridge published a two-volume work with "Biographical Sketches" in which he also analyzed recent reports and his own experiences of "imperishable," though usually "blocked," thoughts and memories. Coleridge reasons that sensations "may exist for an indefinite time in a latent state, in the very same order in which they were originally impressed." Evidence for this emerges, he claims, from cases of a "feverish state of the brain" in which a person may remember long-lost impressions. Coleridge (1817, II, 115; italics in orig.) continues: "[I]f the intelligent faculty should be rendered more comprehensive, it would require only a different and apportioned organization, *the body celestial* instead of *the body terrestrial*, to bring before every human soul the collective experience of its whole past existence." Even though he ponders on this extraordinary quality of an externally stimulated revival of (theoretically all) hidden memories in a hypothetical manner, his thoughts are obviously based on an interpretation of reports of unusual experiences within life. Nevertheless, by ascribing this quality in pure form to the "body celestial," he builds a bridge into the afterlife, commenting that this—the collective experience of the past—might be "the dread book of judgement, in whose mysterious hieroglyphics every idle word is recorded! Yea,

---

[25] In his revised edition, Passavant (see 1837, 98–9) adds further cases of "somnambules," who were able to review their lives almost completely.

in the very nature of a living spirit, it may be more possible that heaven and earth should pass away, than that a single act, a single thought, should be loosened or lost from that living chain of causes, to all whose links, conscious or unconscious, the free-will, our only absolute *self*, is co-extensive and copresent" (I, 115–16).[26] Significantly, Coleridge links the topos of the revived copresence of impressions buried in memory to the biblical image of the recorded deeds in the "book of judgement" (cf. Rev. 20: 12–15). This topos reappears in the *Confessions of an English Opium-Eater* by the writer Thomas de Quincey (1785–1859), first published in 1821. De Quincey, who had an intimate knowledge of the work of his fellow opium-eater Coleridge, published a broadly received report linking directly drug-induced experiences and experiences near death (quoted, e.g., in Moody 1977a, 74):

> I was once told by a near relative of mine, that having in her childhood fallen into a river, and being on the very verge of death but for the critical assistance which reached her, she saw in a moment her whole life, in its minutest incidents, arrayed before her simultaneously as in a mirror; and she had a faculty developed as suddenly for comprehending the whole and every part. This, from some opium experiences of mine, I can believe; I have indeed seen the same thing asserted twice in modern books, and accompanied by a remark which I am convinced is true; viz., that the dread book of account which the Scriptures speak of is in fact the mind itself of each individual. (de Quincey 2013 [1821], 38)

Actually, de Quincey agrees with Coleridge's idea that there is in principle no forgetting—a fact that for him becomes obvious by the reappearance of these "secret inscriptions" in accidents.[27] The same, he argues, holds true for opium experiences. In a most vivid description of how he could enjoy an opera performance, he describes how opium increased certain activities of his mind. And it led to an impressive "intellectual pleasure": As in the immediate copresence of an elaborate woven carpet, de Quincey says, it amounted to an awareness of "the whole of my past life—not as if recalled by an act of memory, but as if present and incarnated in the music [. . .]; the detail of its incidents removed or blended in some hazy abstraction, and its passions exalted, spiritualized, and sublimed" (46–7).

Obviously, de Quincey conceptualizes his opium experience in religious terms. It is a dream-like state that, however, most potently triggers in the opium consumer hidden riches—most prominently a certain feeling "that the divine part of his nature is paramount" and the "great light of the majestic intellect" prevails—feelings that de Quincey,

---

[26] These ideas prefigure the later idea of the human mind as a filter for the realm of thoughts, as subsequently discussed.

[27] "I feel assured, that there is no such thing as FORGETTING possible to the mind; a thousand accidents may and will interpose a veil between our present consciousness and the secret inscriptions on the mind; accidents of the same sort will also rend away this veil; but [. . .] the inscription remains for ever" (de Quincey 2013 [1821], 69).

in his initial enthusiasm,[28] calls "the doctrine of the true church on the subject of opium: of which church I acknowledge myself to be the only member" (43). A crucial element should be noted—the involuntary, displeasing "flash-backs" in dreams or wake states: a "theatre seemed suddenly opened and lighted up within my brain," a theater that came along with lucid daydreams and immediate content shifts between dreams and waking states, accompanied by anxiety and melancholy. Here again, he reports of flashes of memory:

> The minutest incidents of childhood, or forgotten scenes of later years, were often revived: I could not be said to recollect them, for if I had been told of them when waking, I should not have been able to acknowledge them as parts of my past experience. But placed as they were before me, in dreams like intuitions, and clothed in all their evanescent circumstances and accompanying feelings, I RECOGNIZED them instantaneously." (69)

Significantly, de Quincey returned in a later work (1845) to the incident of drowning previously quoted (1851, 234). By now an old lady, he says there, she is still living, and had become "religious to asceticism." He recounts the story again, this time adding that at a certain stage, "a blow seemed to strike her; phosphoric radiance sprang forth from her eyeballs; and immediately a mighty theater expanded within her brain." Interestingly, he reframes the vision in the "theater" imagery of his own drug experiences. Finally, he parallels the vision, including the life review, with the revelation and conversion of Paul: "Such a light fell upon the whole path of her life backward into the shades of infancy as the light, perhaps, which wrapt the destined apostle on his road to Damascus" (234; quoted, e.g., in Moody 1977a, 74–6).

De Quincey's reports do not imply blatantly that near-death-like states of opium-intoxicated consciousness may prove any mystical or religious belief. Still, the religious framing of the revelatory quality of the drug-induced, dream-like experiences and the experience near death is obvious. But precisely the more modest, nondenominational nature of his religious insights that the only member of the true church of opium discloses was taken as a strong case in later Spiritualist literature. Here, de Quincy will be quoted extensively, evidencing the extraordinary capacities of the "body celestial," that is, the "astral body." Becoming such an authority may have its roots in the minimal counterintuitiveness of his visions. A decisive point is the "theater within the brain" metaphor. In general, the theater has an inherent relation to the art and techniques of memory. Already in antique mnemotechnics, the role of "active images" [*imagines agentes*]—compared to actors of a play—had been stressed. Nina Bolzoni (2006, 795) observes that from its very origins,

---

[28] However, he soon suffered from disadvantages of an addicted consumer that he reported frankly in his *Confessions*, moving from the pleasure to the pain of opium.

"the art of the theatre exerted a considerable influence on the techniques of memory. The mind could be thought of as a stage on which a play was being presented," and it seems that it is especially the "light" that is turned on, to mark the beginning of the stage performance, that has been taken as significant by de Quincey. Moreover, theater implies the perspective of a somehow distant, often uninvolved guest witnessing the performance that seems to be a prominent metaphorical element alluded to here. Some two decades later, the connection of ecstatic drug experiences and those near death will be, with explicit mention of de Quincey, prominently taken up again, strengthening their commonality.

2.2.11 HASHISH-EATERS OUT OF THEIR BODIES: CAHAGNET, LUDLOW, AND RANDOLPH (1850–1860)

In the meantime, the practice of eating hashish spread in Europe and was especially celebrated in French intellectual circles. Wouter Hanegraaff (2013; 2017) deserves the merit to have sufficiently shown that psychoactive substances played a vital role from the early 19th century onward up to modern Western esotericism in the 1960s. Hashish, however, was introduced into Egypt in the 13th century and was widespread when Napoleon conquered that country in 1800. French physicians and psychiatrists "returned to France with news of a hashish extract so potent that a user, as novelist Theophile Gautier wrote, could "taste the joys of Mohammed's heaven" (Siegel and Hirschman 1984, 72). Most famous was the Parisian "Club des Hashischins," whose "séances" were visited by writers such as Charles Baudelaire, Gautier, or Alexandre Dumas père.[29]

Attracted to the study of somnambulism, the French adept of Swedenborg, Louis-Alphonse Cahagnet (1805–1885), published various books on his experiments with "somnambulists" and the spirit communications that they received. In his *Sanctuaire au Spiritualisme* (1850), translated as *The Sanctuary of Spiritualism* as early as 1851, he also reports of experiments with hashish that he practiced together with his mediums. Indeed, as Ronald K. Siegel (2005, 166) observes, "these subjects documented visions of death and the afterlife, experiences identical to those known as 'Near-death experiences'"—including a transmundane quietness, disembodied journeys,[30] encounters with departed, a heightened mental lucidity, the panoramic life review,[31] or

---

[29] Among its members was the psychologist Jacques-Joseph Moreau (1804–1884), who was the first to devote a scientific study to the broader effects of hashish consumption that appeared in 1845, putting emphasis on the lucidity and rapidity of memory images as is the case the life review (cf. Moreau 1845, 64–6), but also on the "mental alienation" (i.e., delirium, manic states) that may occur in drug intoxication, advancing thereby perspectives of the Naturalist metaculture.

[30] In Cahagnet's book (cf. 1850, 80–1 [1851, 49–50]), there is also testimony for the emerging autoscopic interest. Cf. also Hanegraaff 2016, 115.

[31] Remarkably, in this case, is the technical description of a "panorama," reminding the reader, again, of theater installations. Cahagnet (1850, 108) continues that it was followed by the view of "a vast panorama in which all

the regret and return.[32] Among the experiences described, there is also a case in which an experience out of body is combined with the cognition of death—now knowing what it is like to be dead—but, significantly, alluding to the Spiritualist–Occult element to have witnessed also a second body:

> I saw myself dying; my body was lying on a bed, and my soul was escaping from all parts of it like a thick, black smoke; but instead of dissipating in the atmosphere, this smoke condensed two feet above my body and formed a body exactly like the one it had just left. Oh! How beautiful it is, I exclaimed. Alphonse, my friend, I have just died. I understand death. I understand how one dies, and why one dies. Oh! How sublime it is. Then I went into a state of which I have no memory at all. (76; cf. 1850, 121)

In fact, Cahagnet was highly interested in an outcome that "hashish-ecstasies" would corroborate Swedenborg's experiences, taken as universal truths that the soul realizes in a state of rapture. Therefore, he "also debriefed" his experimenting subjects "with a series of structured questions and gave them copies of Swedenborg's works to compare with their own experiences" (Siegel and Hirschman 1984, 75). And, what will not astonish us, a spiritual medium of Cahagnet is reported by the latter (cf. 1850, 126–32) to have identified in the hashish experience elements of Swedenborg's visions, finally, however, disclosing that the visions are still granted and allowed by the ever-present God.

However, experiences with hashish were also reported by other protagonists of Esoteric, Spiritualist, and Occult cultures.[33] In his autobiographical work *The Hasheesh Eater* (1857, 50), the American author Fitz Hugh Ludlow (1836–1870), explaining the "nature of this thrill," assumed that "the nearest resemblance to the feeling is that contained in our idea of the instantaneous separation of soul and body. Very few in the world have ever known before absolute death what state goes with this separation, yet we all of us have an idea distinct of that which it must be when it arrives" (50). On various occasions, he experienced the state as "floating out" of his physical body:

> In the course of my delirium, the soul, I plainly discovered, had indeed departed from the body. I was that soul utterly divorced from the corporeal nature, disjoined,

---

that I had been able to see, think or know in my life was represented by the most brilliant colours, in the form of transparent tableaux, like venetian blinds illuminated from behind by an incomparable light. This panorama unfolded all around me, turning with such vividness, presenting such an immense variety of these images, that I would need a whole book to describe what I have seen in a few hours" (cf. Hanegraaff 2016, 115). Cahagnet adds that, in this revelatory experience, he was now fully certain to be "a universe in miniature," and that he realized how "a clairvoyant could be in Egypt or in China without having to pass through any trajectory" (108).

[32] Cf. Cahagnet 1850, 102–9; 1851, 28, 67; cf. Siegel and Hirschman 1984, 76–80.

[33] For further cases, e.g., the hashish experiment in 1884 by American novelist Mary Hungerford, see Siegel and Hirschman 1984.

clarified, purified. From the air in which I hovered I looked down upon my former receptacle [. . .]. I scrutinized the body with wonderment; it seemed no more to concern me than that of another being. I do not remember, in the course of the whole experience I have had of hasheesh, a more singular emotion than I felt at that moment. (74)

In fact, Ludlow's description is the first instance in which an autoscopic interest in the body, now viewed from above, can be grasped more clearly. It is highly enlightening that this interest, namely, to scrutinize one's own body in a manner uninvolved, as if in the mood of a casual bystander observing the scene, emerges from a drug experience. Ludlow continues:

Through the Avails of the room I was able to pass and repass, and through the ceiling to behold the stars unobscured. This was neither hallucination nor dream. The sight of my reason was preternaturally intense, and I remembered that this was one of the states which frequently occur to men immediately before their death has become apparent to lookers-on, and also in the more remarkable conditions of trance. [. . .] A voice of command called on me to return into the body, saying in the midst of my exultation over what I thought was my final disenfranchisement from the corporeal, "The time is not yet". I returned, and again felt the animal nature joined to me by its mysterious threads of conduction. Once more soul and body were one. (74–5; cf. Carrington 1912, 317)

Reviewing his experience while still *in* the experience (!), he draws a comparison to experiences near death. Being aware of pertinent reports, it seems, he points to the cognate lucidity and heightened mental presence. Finally, he reports of a command to return from the realm of death—an element well known from medieval deathbed narratives and more modern experiences near death alike. What is more, Ludlow holds that his experiences with hashish granted him a "vision of celestial glory" (cf. 34–6). Interestingly, he mentions also, though not in explicit reference to his experiences previously quoted, the "panoramic display of internal images" (227). As I subsequently show, the feature of a "panoramic review" had only shortly before, in the 1840s, been introduced into near-death discourse. In other words, Ludlow was obviously well read in the respective literature elaborating on those experiences. His account clearly includes conceptions and insights of the Gnostic–Esoteric metaculture. "Forever rid," Ludlow discloses, "of the intervention of pulsing air and vibrating nerve, my soul, dilates with the swell of that transcendent harmony, and interprets from it arcana of a meaning which words can never tell. I am borne aloft upon the glory of sound. I float in a trance among the burning choir of the seraphim" (36). These quotations from *The Hasheesh Eater* provide sufficient evidence that the words, in which experiences with psychoactive, hallucinogenic substances are clad here, co-evolved with reported experiences near death.

To adduce further evidence for this connection, we may turn to the American medical doctor and occultist Paschal Beverly Randolph (1825–1875), who used hashish for exactly the same purposes.

In 1860, Randolph gave an elaborate description of an experience, called an "experiment" made in 1859: "I have experimented with Hashish upon myself, in order to reach through the gloom toward the light [. . .]. I gained more light in any two of these experiments than from all the 'spiritual' experiences of my entire life—real, positive, genuine, unmistakable light—nor has my soul ever parted with one jot of that light to this day" (Randolph 1860, 8). Being desirous of entering the clairvoyant state, but having no magnetizer at hand, Randolph narrates, he took a pill of hashish. Feeling at first no effect, he spins a gyroscope, "when suddenly, as if a stream of light had burst the walls of the house, the terrific thrill of death seemed to pass over me. I was frightened at the tremendous unveiling. 'Ah', said I, 'this is Hashish!' 'No, it is Soul!' said a voice in my ear. I turned. No one was near me. The thrill passed off" (8). He laid himself down on his bed, and a second experience unfolded: "And now a tremendous experience followed; and *on this* experience I predicate my immortal nature, and of course that of all other human beings; for to me it passes belief—it is KNOWLEDGE. I lay flat upon by back, as the shock ran through my body" (8). He experienced, the report continues,

> a sense as if my head was gently, yet rapidly, *separating at the crown*. This continued for perhaps ten seconds, when I became conscious of being entirely free from the body, and with folded arms stood calmly looking at the body on the bed. I saw it distinctly! I watched the pulses through its heart; I saw it gently breathing; and for the first time became aware of a very common physiological fallacy. Up to that moment I had supposed that the heart alone was the organ that sent the blood through the body; but now I saw that every vein and artery of *itself* contracted and expanded. (8)

Here, the autoscopic interest is more than obvious and is combined with an almost professional external interest in the physiological functions of one's own body.

Randolph, however, describes it as a "grand discovery," namely, that man and his body have but a "slight relationship," so that "he might do almost anything with it" (8). Then, he "*felt* a sweet, low, silvery voice" breathing the words, " 'Paschal! doubt no more' "—a voice that seemed to be a benevolent "aerial spirit" acting in God's name. As the drug experience unfolded he assumed, moreover, a transparent body, and flew over the city; now able to look, though not to pass, through walls, and so forth. Back in his room, other experiences followed—for example, a heautoscopic perspective of being "perfectly conscious of two separate and distinct selves, *both pacing up and down that chamber floor!*—and each perfectly conscious of the presence of the other" (8), "telegraphing," as he says, its sensations to the other. A "heautoscopic" experience, as described here, does not only encompass a visual encounter with the body, but develops into a fundamental, psychological and emotional identification with the alter ego, or the second self. Far from ecstatic, the appearance of a conscious duplicate was, for Randolph, a very dreadful experience, an omen of death. Still more duplicates appeared in the room, leaving him to think that he was "about to die." But, finally, the discomfort and the duplicates disappeared. Further experiences follow, including a deceleration of time. Trying to go to the table, he had to realize that it took him "over *one thousand years* to reach it" (8).[34]

Nevertheless, the whole experiment led to lasting insights. First, Randolph achieved certainty about the survival of death—noteworthy is the dialogue with a heavenly voice. Describing his insights with hashish, he clads his experience nevertheless in well-known biblical imagery. He ate hashish, the "forbidden fruit," he says—but to him, it turned out to be the fruit of the "Tree of Life": "I ate—and know that I can never truly die" (8). "Hashish," he declares, is an "agent especially ordained by God himself, to aid man in his search for light on the nature of the human soul" (8).[35] And again, he repeats the opinion that "Mahomet derived all his knowledge and power from its use" (8). In an attempt to adjust his worldview to what he had experienced, he broadens the scope and reasons that matter is only a form of life, and death therefore is a "misnomer." Finally assuming a celestial perspective, he ends with a mystic cosmovision that "systems of suns are but organs of one vast brain; worlds are but the cells of that brain; and human souls are but the globules floating in God's blood, sent out to the surface, and returning to the centre, to be re-charged, and sent out again" (8). Here, his hashish-triggered, disembodied perspective on his body's physiology is transposed to a metaphysical view on human souls. It offers a foothold for an esoteric physiology of an all-encompassing brain anticipating later theories of a transindividual consciousness being "filtered" into single human brains. Finally, in a later work, Randolph ([1866] 1868, 80) discusses experiences near death, informing us that he nearly drowned as a young boy, experiencing blissful states, magnificent visions, and "delicious strains of music."

It has already been mentioned that spiritual expectations of the protagonists were a key factor that made the drug experiences so meaningful. Siegel and Hirschman (1984, 84) conclude convincingly that, in such "ecstasies" as reported by Cahagnet, the Swedenborgian "spiritual set and setting" were important determinants that undoubtedly influenced "hashish-near-death-experiences." The authors, however, do not point to the historical coevolution of drug-reports and near-death reports, but argued instead that there is still an "inherent difference" between both *as* experiences: In near-death experiences, they hold, subsequent "stages" can be distinguished more clearly, whereas

---

[34] In Randolph's fictional *Rosicrucian's Story* (1863, 58), the experience found a literary echo: "What are these strange experiences of soul [. . .] while under the accursed spells of Hashish? The soul flying back over unnumbered centuries; scanning the totality of the Present, and grasping a myriad Futurities—sweeping the vortex of unborn epochs by the million! and all in an instant."

[35] Randolph (see 1861, 117; 1867, 35–9) developed only shortly thereafter a much more critical attitude toward hashish.

drug-induced near-death experiences unfold along a continuum of ongoing changes of the perception of reality (cf. 84). According to my view, different stages are clearly described in drug experiences too, as could be seen in the example of Randolph given previously. In sum, the most interesting element is again the curiosity of the disembodied soul, directed first and foremost to its own body. As it seems, the "high" soul is not only elevated and interested in the realization of celestial harmonies—it also scrutinizes its body with the detached interest of a modern scientific subject, engaged in an "experiment with experience." Whereas some topoi originated in the discourse on experiences near death and merged with the reporting of drug experiences only later, the autoscopic element—as in Ludlow's drug-induced "delirium"—seems to have evolved in close interaction of both, as becomes clearer in the following sections.

2.2.12 MORMON EXPERIENCES NEAR DEATH

Among the religious traditions founded in the 19th century, there is one that has ever since been most receptive to experiences near death, namely, the Church of Jesus Christ of Latter-Day Saints, or Mormons, founded by Joseph Smith (1805–1844). Indeed, several more recent (post-Moodian) contributions by scholars of the Latter-Day Saints have argued that near-death experiences support their doctrines—for example, their descriptions of what to experience in raptures and revelations, the "inhabited" spiritual world. Already the founding father described in 1838 how he had experienced a "first vision" in 1820, in which he had a personal encounter and communication with God. He saw a "pillar of light" over his head, and "two personages," one of whom advised him not to follow any of the "sects" of his time, "and many other things did he say unto me which I cannot write at this time" (Pratt 1850, 54). His vision ends with the words, "When I came to myself again, I found myself lying on my back, looking up into heaven" (54). I will not argue that this "revelation" should be construed as an out-of-body experience, as Smith does not say explicitly that he left his body. However, his son reported of a later incident in 1832, in which Joseph Smith closely escaped death. A mob, "antagonists of the Mormon religion," had gathered to kill him. They had beaten him up so severely that, according to his son, he had reported an experience out of his body. He was "beaten into insensibility, tarred and feathered and left for dead. A strange part of this experience was, that his spirit seemed to leave his body, and that during the period of insensibility he consciously stood over his own body, feeling no pain, but seeing and hearing all that transpired" (Smith ed. 1893, 98). It may be added that the *Book of Mormon* (Alma, 11:42–3; cf. Nephi 9: 13–15) describes a "temporal death" that includes a perfect and "bright recollection of all our guilt" (quoted in Top 1997, 214). The positive evaluation of rapture, and the conception that authentic revelation is still possible, had a lasting effect on Mormons up to the present. Accordingly, visionary near-death experiences are held in high esteem (cf. Lundahl and Widdison 1983).

In addition to mesmerist and spiritualist circles, cases of near drowning were quoted by philosophers as evidence for a death-surviving soul. The pan-psychic philosopher Gustav Theodor Fechner (1801–1887), for example, published the book *Das Büchlein vom Leben nach dem Tode* (1835), translated as *On Life After Death*. "At a glance," Fechner states therein (1906 [1835], 77), man

> will be able to survey all that is in him, his various ideas in their relations of agreement and contradiction, of connection and separation not confined to one particular direction of his thoughts, but looking into every direction at once. There are instances of persons approaching such a state of inward illumination, even in this life, in cases of approaching death, as by drowning, or in somnambulism, or narcosis, and such like.

Years later, in 1853, Fechner published a German translation of Beaufort's testimony, obviously still engaged with the reported phenomena.[36] The French Spiritist Jean Dupotet de Sennevoy (1796–1881), whose *Introduction to the Study of Animal Magnetism* would become a classic, joins Fechner and others in combining descriptions of extraordinary clairvoyance and memory in cases of near death, disease, and somnambulist states, quoting extensively Coleridge and de Quincy (Dupotet 1838, 131–6).[37]

It is indeed in the mesmerist context that we encounter for the first time cases near death in which a "disembodied" observer claims to have taken an autoscopic perspective toward his own, "old" body. The case is reported in a letter quoted by "magnetizer" Thomas C. Hartshorn (1800–1854):

> A sudden blow or shock has been known to throw persons into a sort of somnambulic state; and before I relate the next case, I will give the relation once made to me by a carpenter. He was at work on a building; he fell from the staging to the ground. *"As I struck the ground,"* said he, *"I suddenly bounded up, seeming to have a new body, and to be standing among the spectators looking at my old one. I saw them trying to bring it to. I made several fruitless efforts to re-enter my body, and finally succeeded!"* [Hartshorn in Deleuze 1843, 367]. Though there dawns an autoscopic interest on the side of the "new body," we should note that the observer seems to be not truly interested in viewing his old body. He simply finds himself among the group of spectators gathered around the site of the accident, though he seems to witness his resuscitation.

---

[36] Additional cases of visions of near drowning, with special mention of the life review, are provided by Fechner (1853, 43–7, 623, 774), quoted, e.g. in Evans-Wentz 1911; Carus 1846, 207; and Haddock 1851.

[37] For this established cluster of references, see for example Du Prel 1885 [1884], 77–9.

In the same mesmerist context, an even more expressively "autoscopic interest" of the disembodied soul can be found in a letter of American writer and political activist Lydia Maria Child (1802–1880). In the same year as Hartshorn's report appeared (1843), she published a volume of collected letters, containing one describing her opinions of "recent phenomena in animal magnetism, or mesmerism" (cf. Child 1843, 118–24).[38] Generally impressed by the evidence for these phenomena, she refers to a story disclosed in Thomas Taylor's treatise on Proclus, the latter quoting Clearchus's *Treatise on Sleep* to the effect that the soul may depart from the body, as has been demonstrated by a man using a "soul-attracting wand" that could "draw out" the soul, leaving the body lifeless and rigid. The soul, however, could by means of the wand be led back into the unharmed body (cf. Taylor 1825, 113).[39]

This story leads over to a remarkable narrative, providing early evidence for the disembodied soul's interest not only in the old body, but also in the resuscitation measures taken by the doctor. Child (1843, 121) narrates that the demonstration described in Clearchus reminds her "of a singular circumstance which happened to a venerable friend."[40] Her friend had told her that she had suddenly fallen ill and fainted. "To all appearance, she was entirely lifeless; insomuch that her friends feared she was really dead." A physician was sent for, trying to reanimate her. "She herself was merely aware of a dizzy and peculiar sensation, and then she found herself standing by her own lifeless body, watching all their efforts to resuscitate it. It seemed to her strange, and she was too confused to know whether she were in that body, or out of it" (121). To all present, she was "to all appearance dead." Yet, "when the body revived, she told everything that had been done in the room, every word that had been said, and the very expression of their countenances. The soul had stood by all the while, and observed what was done to the body" (121). The conclusions drawn by Child are, in short, that it is time to approve the evidence for "magnetic" states in which the spirit may leave the body—time for a "new science of spiritual philosophy" (122),[41] even though explanations for the phenomena may still be lacking. Equally, they shall not be encountered with fear: "Men would not be afraid to see spirits, if they were better acquainted with their own. It is because we live so entirely in the body, that we are startled at a revelation of the soul" (124). Most important in the narrative provided is, of course, the pioneering feature of a clear autoscopic interest in combination with the curiosity in which one's own resuscitation is watched. Actually, it will become a standard topos, as we will subsequently see in section 2.2.16, some decades later.

---

[38] Letter XIX: "Animal Magnetism. The Soul Watching Its Own Body. Anecdote of Second Sight" (vii).

[39] See the discussion of the example in Blavatsky 1877, 365–6.

[40] The following story is quoted in Denton [1871] 1874, 19.

[41] In the same work, Child (1843, 257) points to Swedenborg and Coleridge, disclosing that, as she grows older, "these glimpses into the spiritual" had become clearer; "all the visible stamps itself on my soul, a daguerreotype image of the *invisible*, written with sunbeams."

2.2.13 "AS IF IN PARADISE": THE NEAR-DEATH ACCOUNT OF METHODIST
PREACHER ADAM CLARKE

Around the 1840s we may also note an upsurge of interest in experiences of the dying from a point of view of what was called Naturalist metaculture in previous sections. A significant case, marking the emergence of this perspective, is the one of British Wesleyan Methodist preacher and theologian Dr. Adam Clarke (ca. 1760–1832), reported in his biography to appear shortly after his death (1833).[42] As a young man, Clarke had bathed one of his father's mares in the sea, where he suddenly was caught in a swell and nearly drowned (cf. Bulmer 1833, 81). In a discussion with Dr. Lettsom, a physician from London arguing that from the cases of near drowning known to him, he "never found one who had the smallest recollection of any thing that passed" while under water, Clarke replies—and Bulmer quotes Clarke's "own words"—that he knew a case, namely, his own:

> "I was once drowned"—and then I related the circumstances; and added,—"I saw my danger, but thought the mare would swim, and I knew I could ride; when we were overwhelmed, it appeared to me, that I had gone to the bottom with my *eyes open*. At first, I thought I saw the bottom clearly, and then felt neither apprehension nor pain;—on the contrary, I felt as if I had been in the most delightful situation: my mind was tranquil, and uncommonly happy; I felt as if in *Paradise*, and yet I do not recollect that I saw any person; the impressions of happiness seemed not to be derived from any thing *around me*, but from the state of my mind; and yet I had a general apprehension of pleasing objects; and I cannot recollect that any thing appeared *defined*, nor did my eye take in any object, only I had a general impression of a *green colour*, as of fields or gardens; but my happiness did not arise from these, but appeared to consist merely in the tranquil, indescribably tranquil, state of my mind. By and bye, I seemed to awake as out of a slumber, and felt *unutterable pain* and *difficulty* of *breathing* [. . .]. How long I had been under water I cannot tell: it may however be guessed at by this circumstance: —when restored to the power of reflection, I looked for the mare, and saw her walking leisurely down shore towards home, then about *half a mile distant from the place where we were submerged*. Now, I aver, 1. That in being drowned *I felt no pain*; 2. That I did not, for a simple moment, lose my *consciousness*; 3. I felt indescribably happy, and, though dead as to the total suspension of all the functions of life, yet I felt no pain in dying; [. . .];—5th. That animation must have been totally suspended from the time I must have been under water [. . .]; 6. Whether there were anything preternatural in my escape, I cannot tell; or whether a ground swell had not, in a merely natural way, borne me to the shore [. . .], I cannot tell. My preservation must have

---

[42] Published also in *The London Literary Gazette* (1833), 837, 65–7.

been the effect of *natural* causes; and yet it appears to be more rational to attribute it to a superior agency. Here then, Dr. L., is a case widely different, it appears, from those you have witnessed: and which argues very little for the modish doctrine of the *materiality of the soul*" (81–83).

One might first be struck by the fact that Clarke—at the time of reporting, after all, a Methodist preacher—does allude to paradise, yet a paradise strangely devoid of any specific characteristics. For Clarke, it appeared to be nothing but a state of mind, an inner tranquility. The apparent absence of any pain, terror, or "angst," if not a deep happiness, is in sharp contrast to any vision of a "court of justice," or "hellish" experience, both being parts of traditional Methodist beliefs. Neither an out-of-body experience nor a "panoramic review" of childhood memories is mentioned. Nevertheless, Clarke comments that he had actually been dead—in the sense of a total suspension of all life functions. This view, of course, attracted a lot of attention by scholars aiming either to prove or to refute the postmortem existence of the soul. To provide just two antagonistic examples: Fully convinced of the theory of the materiality of the soul, a British surgeon, Walter C. Dendy (see 1841, 390–2) recounts Clarke's report and asserts that "if animation were totally suspended, consciousness would have been suspended also" (392). The American Presbyterian minister and theologian Robert W. Landis, in contrast, argued in his book of 1859, "The immortality of the soul and the final condition of the wicked carefully considered," against the extinction of soul and consciousness at death.[43] In contrast to supernatural explanations of his resuscitation, Clarke himself concludes that his survival can be explained by natural causes, thereby mirroring again the absence of Christian afterworld imagery.

2.2.14 THE FORMATION OF THE LIFE REVIEW NEAR DEATH: FROM DE QUINCEY TO BINNS AND BEAUFORT

A significant report that includes various features of Moody's near-death experiences but only occasionally references Christian metaculture is the one by Scottish physician Edward Binns (?–1851), communicated in a work on the "art of sleeping." After a vivid description of general characteristics of the causes of death through drowning, Binns moves on to the question whether death from drowning is to be considered painful, answering, "We should say not," and reports a personally conveyed experience:

---

[43] Championing Clarke's report, Landis (1859, 350–1) argues that the "soul may exist separately from the body," evident "from the fact that its conscious existence is not necessarily suspended by swoon, coma, drowning, etc." Similar and "equally well-attested facts," Landis declares, have been "abundant in all ages."

We are acquainted with a gentleman, who being able to swim but little ventured too far out and became exhausted. His alarm was great [. . .], then sunk as he supposed to rise no more. The noise of the water in his ears was at first horrible, and the idea of death, and such a death! terrific in the extreme. He felt himself sinking as if for an age—and descent—it seemed—would have no end. But this frightful state passed away. His senses became steeped in light. Innumerable and beautiful visions presented themselves to his imagination. Luminous aerial shapes accompanied him through embowering groves of graceful trees, while soft music, as if breathed from their leaves, wooed his spirit to voluptuous repose. Marble colonnades, light-pierced vistas, soft-grass walks, picturesque groups of angelic beings, gorgeously-plumaged birds, golden fish that swam in purple waters, and glistening fruit that hung from latticed arbours, were seen, admired, and passed. Then the vision changed; and he saw, as if in a wide field, the acts of his own being, from the first dawn of memory to the moment when he entered the water. They were all grouped and ranged in the order of the succession of their happening, and he read the whole volume of existence at a glance; nay, its incidents and entities were photographed on his mind, limned in light—and the panorama of the battle of life lay before him. * * * From this condition of beatitude, at least, these were the last sensations he could remember; he awoke to consciousness, and consequently to pain, agony, and disappointment. We have often conversed together upon his feelings on this occasion, and his account has never varied, so intensely were the visions graven on his memory. (Binns 1851 [1842], 271–2)

It is here that we for the first time encounter the fully established life review. The presentation of the event is enlightening. In the terms of Christian metaculture, there is still a faint allusion to the book of deeds as "volume of existence." Most distinctly, however, the claim is articulated that the whole life was entirely present. Although emerging as single images in successive order, it could be viewed in copresence. For the purpose of communicating the experience, the metaphor of "photographic" images that emerge from memory is used here for the first time, too. This metaphor, obviously drawn from the invention of daguerreotypes and other photographic means that became increasingly popular around the mid-19th century, will from now on be a constant companion in descriptions of the life review. The panorama metaphor deserves special mention. It had been coined in 1789 by Irish artist and inventor Robert Barker originally for paintings on a revolving cylindrical surface, but assumed quickly the meaning of a "spectacular view."[44] Certainly, new achievements in arts and technology, such as the panorama, the

---

[44] Here, it is more precisely a panorama depicting the "battle of life," the latter being a metaphor of increasing popularity already in the 1830s before it became standardized by Darwin's use in *On the Origin of Species*, 1859, as a synonym for the "struggle for existence."

"diorama" (invented by Louis Daguerre in 1822), or the life-world experiences of train travel, etc., form an important backdrop of the emergence of such metaphors in the texts (cf. Bremmer 2002, 102).[45]

In less than a decade, the panorama became a fixed coin in descriptions of experiences near death, especially mediated through one of the few 19th-century reports that have been well received in modern research, namely, the one of Irish hydrographer and admiral Francis Beaufort (1774–1857). It had been published in 1847, but the incident presumably had happened to him already around 1795. Beaufort, famous for his contribution to standardizing a scale for wind force, had addressed his letter to his friend Dr. William Hyde Wollaston, probably in 1825. It was published by a certain John Barrow (1847, 398–402), an English statesman, who included it in his memoirs, quoting it, it seems, in full. As a young man, not being able to swim, Beaufort reports, he fell into Portsmouth Harbor and sunk below the surface. But, in contrast to his agitation, he reports,

my mind had then undergone the sudden revolution which appeared to you so remarkable—and all the circumstances of which are now as vividly fresh in my memory as if they had occurred but yesterday. From the moment that all exertion had ceased—which I imagine was the immediate consequence of complete suffocation—a calm feeling of the most perfect tranquility superseded the previous tumultuous sensations [. . .] [N]or was I in bodily pain. On the contrary, my sensations were now of rather pleasurable cast [. . .]. Though the senses were thus deadened, not so the mind; its activity seemed to be invigorated, in a ratio which defies all description—for thought rose after thought with a rapidity of succession that is not only indescribable, but probably inconceivable, by any one who has not himself been in a similar situation. The course of those thoughts I can even now in a great measure retrace—the event which had just taken place—the awkwardness that had produced it—the bustle it must have occasioned [. . .]—the effect it would have on a most affectionate father—the manner in which he would disclose it to the rest of the family—and a thousand other circumstances minutely associated with home [. . .]. They took then a wider range—our last cruise—a former voyage, and shipwreck—my school—the progress I had made there, and the time I had misspent—and even all my boyish pursuits and adventures. Thus travelling backwards, every past incident of my life seemed to glance across my recollection in retrograde succession; not, however, in mere outline, as here stated, but the picture filled up with every minute and collateral feature; in short, the whole period of my existence seemed to be placed before me in a kind of panoramic review, and

---

[45] Bremmer (2002, 102) holds that these technologies themselves "enabled people to see a fast succession of scenes as they had never been able to do before." Although this is highly plausible, we must still abstain from speaking of the content of the experiences themselves; emerging in the reports, however, the panorama and other concepts are to be treated as metaphors.

each act of it seemed to be accompanied by a consciousness of right or wrong, or by some reflection on its cause or its consequences; indeed, many trifling events which had been long forgotten then crowded into my imagination, and with the character of recent familiarity. May not all this be some indication of the almost in-finite power of memory with which we may awaken in another world, and thus be compelled to contemplate our past lives? Or might it not in some degree warrant the inference that death is only a change or modification of our existence, in which there is no real pause or interruption? But, however that may be, one circumstance was highly remarkable; that the innumerable ideas which flashed into my mind were all retrospective—yet I had been religiously brought up—my hopes and fears of the next world had lost nothing of their early strength, and at any other period intense interest and awful anxiety would have been excited by the mere probability that I was floating on the threshold of eternity: yet at that inexplicable moment, when I had a full conviction that I had already crossed that threshold, not a single thought wandered into the future—I was wrapt entirely in the past. The length of time that was occupied by this deluge of ideas, or rather the shortness of time into which they were condensed, I cannot now state with precision, yet certainly two minutes could not have elapsed from the moment of suffocation to that of my being hauled up. [. . .] My feelings while life was returning were the reverse in every point of those which have been described above. One single but confused idea—a miser-able belief that I was drowning—dwelt upon my mind, instead of the multitude of clear and definite ideas which had recently rushed through it—a helpless anxiety— a kind of continuous nightmare seemed to press heavily on every sense [. . .] and it was with difficulty that I became convinced that I was really alive. Again, instead of being absolutely free from all bodily pain, as in my drowning state, I was now tortured by pain all over me. (399–402)[46]

To summarize, it is with de Quincey's, Binns's, and Beaufort's reports that we see the birth of the life-review feature, which becomes in the second half of the 19th century a prom-inent feature of psychological research. With the formulation, however, that his whole past existence was placed before him in a "panoramic review,"[47] Beaufort insinuated an instantaneous and simultaneous view of the "whole life at once"—moreover, each deed accompanied by its moral quality. This description, followed by musings on the infinite

---

[46] From 1849 onward, this report was repeatedly reprinted and translated into all major European languages.

[47] Andrew J. Davis, whom I discuss in Section 2.2.16, even speaks of a "panoramic existence." Drawing on the tra-ditional post-Platonic distinction between a "corporeal" and an "internal and spiritual" memory, Davis (1853b, 162) says, "The former is a tablet whereon the world of matter and sensuous objects write the evanescent impressions of their panoramic existence; the latter is the soul's *sanctum sanctorum,* wherein are deposited, as imperishable jewels in a casket which none but the possessor can open, the *spirit of things,* of all impressions, of all useful experiences!"

powers of memory once the soul "awakens" in "another world," still mirrors Christian deathbed narratives. Once the worldly entanglement of the human "gnosis" is taken away, the soul will be able to function unimpeded, with the consequence that the soul will realize anything, including the past, all at once. Worth mentioning, on the other hand, is the prefiguration of the life review in the Christian culture of "self-examination" and the practice of keeping notebooks for personal experiences—emerging, according to Mascuch's observations, in the early modern period (cf. 1997, 71–96). For example, we read in the "Happy Death of Mr. John Angier" (Heywood 1685, 74) under the heading of "His review of his life": "Not long before he fell sick, he said to one [. . .], when I lye waking in my Bed, I sometimes run through the course of my whole life; and if a Pen-man were ready by me, I could relate may observable passages of Gods Providence about me: his friend said, Sir, you may do well to write them down as they come into your thoughts."

The more religiously "neutral" metaphor of a panorama, which now amends the imagery of the written book of life, will later, in the 19th century, be adapted as the common designation, reinforced in Moody's systematic description in 1975. Nevertheless, only shortly thereafter, Noyes and Kletti (1977a) pointed to the great diversity in life-review reports of the second half of the 20th century, which, for them, makes the panorama metaphor problematic.[48] We should be alerted by this observation to study the description of the life review in 19th-century documents as closely as possible, so that we may become aware of its subtle narrative differences.

An early instance, however, of the reception of the life-review feature is from physician and psychologist Maurice Macario, *Du sommeil des rêves et du somnambulisme dans l'état de santé et de maladie* (1857). In his treatment of healthy and pathological states of mind, Macario (cf. 1857, 47) includes the feature of the "acceleration of thought" in "someone passing away, or being in imminent danger." In the moment of dying, he explains, some people "see before them unfolding the picture [or painting, *tableaux*] of their entire life, of which they overlook all the details in one instant, verifying as such the passage of the Scripture: 'At the hour of judgment, all your actions are retraced in the blink of an eye'" (47; trans. mine). And Macario continues by reporting: "I know this phenomenon from my own experience. One day when I bathed in the Seine I thought I would drown. In this supreme moment, all actions of my life displayed themselves as if for cheering up my mind in his frightened sight." Finally, he ends his report with a remark of French

---

[48] Stevenson and Cook (1995, 456) will in the mid-1990s voice the opinion that "the popular picture of the 'whole life' being seen all at once (panoramically) is false as a generalization about these experiences. Some subjects do indeed have this kind of experience, but the majority do not." One group reported that distinct life memories encompass only a few images, whereas others spoke of countless images, depicting their entire life in a rapid flow. Differences, moreover, pertain to the impression of a simultaneous display versus a successive row, and to the chronological order—either starting or ending with childhood, or unsystematic.

physician Alfred Maury to the effect that the brain "is like the heart: emotion accelerates movements" (47; trans. mine).

On the other side, Beaufort's report has been diligently read and commented on in esoteric and spiritualist–occult circles. To provide one of the earliest examples: British surgeon and mesmerist Joseph W. Haddock (1800–1861)[49] reproduced in his second edition of *Somnambulism and Psychism* (1851 [1849]) Beaufort's entire account and commented from his Spiritist point of view that "the Admiral's case is another illustration of the state of trance, and of the higher mesmeric state, being analogous to partial death" (Haddock 1851, 215).[50] Indeed, it is around 1850, Alvarado (2011, 68) assumes, that cases of life review in people who were nearly drowned "seemed to have been common knowledge," entering also the sphere of journals, magazines, and fictional literature.[51] An example of the appropriation of the panoramic life review in spiritualist circles is the *Narrative of the Experience of Horace Abraham Ackley*, a surgeon in Cleveland who had died in 1859 of pneumonia at age 49. The account was "received" from the deceased by spiritist medium Samuel H. Paist and published in 1861.[52] Ackley communicates from the beyond[53] that the first lesson to be learned is the fact that there is no "consciousness of suffering" in dying and death. At the moment of death, he could not leave his body immediately, but only gradually. After full cessation of the bodily functions, Ackley is reported to say, "I was raised a short distance above the body, standing over it by what power I was unable to tell. I could see those who were in the room around me, and knew by what was going on that a considerable time must have elapsed since dissolution had taken place" (quoted in De Morgan and De Morgan 1863, 149).[54] Although this may count as an example of the narrative later to be called out-of-body experience, one should notice that it is not an autobiographical report in the usual sense, and, moreover, that there is on the side of the separated soul no explicit autoscopic perspective on the body, but an elevated view of the whole situation. The mediumistic communication continues:

> As consciousness returned to me, the scenes of my whole life seemed to move before me like a panorama; every act seemed as though it were drawn in life size and

---

[49] Haddock's use of a clairvoyant medium ("Emma") for diagnostic purposes was later praised by Annie Besant (cf. 1909, 77).

[50] Haddock's book (translated into German in 1852) helped significantly to popularize the report of Beaufort.

[51] As to literature, Alvarado (2011, 68) quotes from the *Scenes of Clerical Life* (1858) from George Eliot (1858, 151): "The drowning man, urged by the supreme agony, lives in an instant through all his happy and unhappy past: when the dark flood has fallen like a curtain, memory, in a single moment, sees the drama acted over again."

[52] Instead of the original print of 1861, unavailable to me, the edition of 1863 is used.

[53] Although I personally opt for this report being literary, it claims to be autobiographical. Being a borderline case, I included it for its importance.

[54] In their work, British Spiritist couple Augustus and Sophia De Morgan (1863, 176–81) quotes and discusses Beaufort's report, too.

was really present: it was all there, down to the closing scenes. So rapidly did it pass, that I had little time for reflection. I seemed to be in a whirlpool of excitement; and then, just as suddenly as this panorama had been presented, it was withdrawn, and I was left without a thought of the past or future to contemplate my present condition. I looked around me, and I thought, if there is a possibility of spirits (for I seemed half-conscious now that I was a spirit) manifesting themselves to those still in the form, how gladly would I now do so [. . .]. I had heard the spiritualists say that the newly-born spirits were always received in the arms, and welcomed by kind and loving guardian spirits; finding none around me [. . .], I concluded this was not true. Scarcely had this thought passed [. . .], when two, with whom I was unacquainted, but toward whom I was attracted, appeared before me. (149).

Along with the noteworthy reappearance of the panorama in the text, it is equally worth mentioning that the "deceased" reports of his doubts in regard to what he had heard of spirit encounters in the afterlife. Obviously, this aims at lending plausibility to the actual encounter shortly thereafter. Taken together, this all amounts to the impression that Paist's description of Ackley's report should be contextualized within a Spiritualist metaculture. The report highlights an open access to mediumistic communication with the beyond, and, moreover, training practices in life are described that aim to (prepare for) a "projection" of the spiritual body, resulting in a final metamorphosis of the "resurrection body" at death (cf. De Morgan and De Morgan 1863, 123–4, 197). The intentionally induced "magnetic sleep," in which the soul is conceived as leaving the body, is seen as "similar to death," as Paist argues with his informants. "In the somnambulic state, however, the soul has gone out and shut the door of its dwelling. For this reason I now see you and myself as a third person does a group. I am at your left, and am looking at you and at my own body" (132)—the only difference being that in death, the departure will preclude any return (see 132–3).

2.2.15 TOWARD A NATURALIST INTERPRETATION: FORBES WINSLOW (1860)

In contrast to straightforward religious interpretations, an example for the emerging Naturalist metaculture is the work by British psychiatrist Forbes B. Winslow (1810–1874), *On Obscure Diseases of the Brain* (1860). In chapter 17 on the "Psychology and Pathology of Memory," Winslow (1860, 345) proposes the by now well-known view of the "indestructibility of ideas," in short, "that no impression made upon the mind is ever destroyed."[55] "The subjoined singularly interesting facts *illustrate*, if they do not

---

[55] One might hypothesize that this theory is a "secularized" version of the "eternity of conscience" theory, argued for by American theologian and legal writer Francis Wharton (1820–1889). Referring to the case of Adam Clarke, Wharton (1859, 22) presents a Christian metaculture interpretation of the report, commenting that even if we do not note the moral quality of a deed while executing it, this quality will be resuscitated in

demonstrate, the truth of this theory" (351).[56] Winslow holds that these "morbid phenomena" might, in the future, be explained "as the result of a closer study of mental dynamics as well as of chemico-cerebral pathology" (351).[57]

After pointing to de Quincey's *Confessions*, Winslow relates the following case (without further reference):

> A gentleman fell accidentally into the water, and was nearly drowned. After being rescued, he continued in a state of apparent death for nearly twenty minutes. After his restoration to consciousness, he thus described his sensations whilst in the act of drowning: "They were the most delightful and ecstatic I have ever experienced. I was transported to a perfect paradise, and witnessed scenes that my imagination never had, in its most active condition, depicted to my mind. I wandered in company with angelic spirits through the most lovely citron and orange groves, 'Roseate bowers, Celestial palms, and ever-blooming flowers', basking in an atmosphere redolent of the most delicious perfumes. I heard the most exquisite music proceeding from melodious voices and well-tuned instruments. Whilst in this world of fancy my mind had recalled to consciousness the scenes and associations of my early life, and the memory of the companions of my boyhood. All the knowledge I had acquired during a long life recurred to my mind. Favorite passages from Horace, Virgil, and Cicero, were revived, and pieces of poetry I had been fond of repeating when a boy, came fresh to my recollection." (357)

Here, religious imagery is to be identified in the angelic companions and the "paradisiacal" description that, however, seem to owe their imagery also to romantic and classical poetry, as the quotation of Alexander Pope ("Eloisa to Abelard," 1717) reveals.

By presenting and grouping the cases under the heading of a psychology and pathology of memory, Winslow, not astonishingly, comes to a purely naturalist explanation. "Persons," he explains, "in the act of drowning (I presume during the *asphyxia* caused by the circulation of *venous* instead of *arterial* blood in the brain, consequent

---

conscience, especially in the moment of dying: "Clarke tells us that, when near drowning, his memory recalled, in a moment, all the scenes of past guilt," which, however, misrepresents Clarke's thoughts.

[56] The theory of the "indestructible character of psychical impressions," Winslow argues (1860, 355), is established by referring to "abnormal mental and disordered *cerebral* conditions," which include, (1) mental states of "*asphyxia*," (2) of "*the mind as exhibited previously to death*," and (3) resulting "*from injuries inflicted upon the brain, or to follow particular types of encephalic disease*."

[57] The cases Winslow (1860, 356) presents begin with an example from his own practice. An individual had hanged himself, but was cut down. He recovered, but "often related to me the strange mental visions that floated before his mind during the few minutes, or (in all probability) seconds" while unconscious. They include the topoi of being "most pleasing," the life review and the extraordinary acceleration of memory pictures, reviving obliterated scenes—yet, not as a continuous projection. Significantly, Winslow abstains in general from discussing the impact of religious imagery or content (cf. 365–7).

upon the suspension of the respiratory process), have had presented to their minds, whilst in the agonies of death, a series of striking *tableaux* of the most minute and remarkable occurrences of their past lives!" Childhood events, Winslow continues, were recalled and presented to the mind "like so many exquisitely executed artistic photographic representations" (355). Here again, the metaphor of photographic images is used; notably, Winslow alludes to the *tableaux vivant*, that is, the artistic arrangement of costumed figures in special, theatric poses (sometimes imitating famous paintings), which were staged as entertainment, and often taken as photographs. In the early 20th century, the metaphor will be replaced by the then most innovative "film projection" imagery. Winslow, to repeat, does not include, or even name, reports that allude to classical Christian or Esoteric elements of otherworld journey. It seems to me that in the first half of the 18th century, the naturalist perspective progresses to "emancipate" itself from religious accounts of deathbed visions. As it were, the latter were no longer included in the medico-scientific discourse, because professionalized psychiatrists could draw on their own sample of patient narrations. Now, the emerging Naturalist metaculture specializes in psychological, physiological, and pathological explanations for only some elements of what a century later will be called near-death experiences, while, at the same time, Christian deathbed narratives still continue to flourish in other circles. As a consequence of these developments, it was highly unlikely for the Naturalist metaculture to arrive at a generalized perspective of experiences near death, because they continued their discourse largely without including obviously religious (near-) death visions, for example, Christian and Esoteric narratives of transcendent landscapes, final judgment, or a being of light.

To continue our historiography of near-death narratives, a prominent example of Christian metaculture is to be found in the book with the programmatic title *Man All Immortal* (1864) written by Davis Wasgatt Clark (1812–1871), American bishop of the Methodist Episcopal Church. Discussing the topos of memories of near drowning, Clark (1864, 390) holds that "in many instances of this kind the memory seems to have been so astonishingly quickened, that the whole past life—even its long-forgotten incidents—rushed back upon the soul, so as to appear in clear and distinct view upon the broad field of its vision." Right before the case of Admiral Beaufort (quoted in its entirety, 391–3), Clark reproduces a case of an individual of his personal acquaintance, describing the topos of the life review.[58] Clark comments that "in that future world memory shall run

---

[58] Again, the metaphors used include events that were hung up, "painted on canvas, before the broad glance" (Clark 1864, 391), but also of the whole past life "reflected as from a mirror." Another interesting case is retold, in which a man, nearly drowning, could remember an important action which had been blocked in memory. Among the single pictures he saw in the life review, was himself hiding a banknote in a book. After recovery, "the first thing he did" was that he took the "long-lost note and handed it to a friend who was present" (394), which is, of course, a very convincing narrative "anchoring mechanism" (Davidsen) that succeeds in lending credibility to his whole account.

back over the history of our past probationary being and call up all its events, however much we may desire to bury the past in utter oblivion. If such be the developments of the memory, when the mind is acted upon by extraordinary circumstances, what may we not expect when this *terrestrial* body shall be exchanged, and the soul be clothed upon with its celestial body?" (395). Significantly, Clark interprets the life review in anticipation as a moral judgment that will urge the individual to review his "probationary existence," although the individual would like to suppress any confrontation with these deeds. Therefore, it is an essential element of his depiction that it turns the life review into a moral obligation that shall be actively pursued in those situations. Indeed, the "keen vision" of the eye, he continues, "shall sweep along the entire range of our past being" (395).

2.2.16 CLAIRVOYANT VISIONS NEAR DEATH IN AMERICAN SPIRITUALISM

It is of special interest for the development of near-death discourse to determine the historical moment at which out-of-body experiences were gaining prominence, as they form a core element of systematized near-death experiences of the 1970s. An important step to include them was made, as it seems, by American Spiritualist Andrew Jackson Davis (1826–1910). Embracing the ideas of somnambulism and animal magnetism as a young man, he became increasingly convinced that he possessed clairvoyant powers, using them to diagnose diseases. Influenced by ideas of Swedenborg, Davis, a prolific writer, published more than 30 books, including *The Great Harmonia Concerning the Seven Mental States* (1853). Therein, a chapter called "Lecture Concerning the Philosophy and Principles of Somnambulism" outlines the "mental science" of clairvoyant spiritual states, placing somnambulism in the context of "vital magnetism," which had replaced former explanations of magic and witchcraft (cf. Davis 1853a, 234). "It has been asserted by several very honest persons, that they have experienced a consciousness of being out of the body," Davis continues with a "vital magnetist" interpretation of an "internal man," and comments on the testimony of Clarke (see Section 2.2.15) with the words that "during the period of apparent unconsciousness, he felt a new kind of life" (248–9). With this description, Davis prefigures the technical use of out-of- [the-] body experiences that will become standard in the first decade of the 20th century. In a later work, *Death and the After-Life. Three Lectures* (1866), directed against, among others, a "supercilious class—I might say a *super-silly* class" of persons, who, in their materialistic logic, are critically minded in regard to "spiritual questions," Davis (1866, 1) departs skillfully from a reflection of Apostle Paul's positive assertion of a "spiritual body." It should be accepted not only as a Christian truth, but also as a truth "in harmony with the perfect system of Nature" (5). Here, Davis argues that "the concurrent observations of all seers, sensitives, and mediums" confirm that this spiritual body is made of finer, white, and shining substances, a "silvery body," and inside this body there is ultimately an "immortal 'golden image'" (6–7)—yet, a body of substance, weight, and force, and occupying space. Less humble, Davis adds that he has possessed the "peri-scopic and clairvoyant ability to see through man's iron coating" for the past 15 years and has, in addition, "stood by the side of many death-beds" (14). The term "periscopic" is noteworthy here, adducing further evidence for the close interaction of technology-mediated ways of seeing used to communicate extraordinary experiences.

Davis's report is a major step for the inclusion of the out-of-body feature. Yet it is not a first-person witness report of an experience near death, but somehow the quintessence of various experiences received by a clairvoyant observer. Describing an "emanation" extracting itself out of the dead body, but still connected to the (faculties of the) brain by means of a "life thread" takes up currents of the Christian and Spiritualist–Occult metacultures. However, as indicated, it is important to notice that it is not (yet) the experiencing individual himself who reports a view "from above." Davis introduces the description with "Suppose the person is now dying." While the body slowly grows cold, the clairvoyant "sees right over the head what may be called a magnetic halo—an ethereal emanation, in appearance golden, and throbbing as though conscious." The emanation ascends "higher in the air," and continues to expand. While the death coldness "steals over the breast and around on either side," the emanation "has attained a higher position near the ceiling. The person has ceased to breathe, the pulse is still, and the emanation is elongated and fashioned in the outline of the human form!" (15). However, Davis discloses, the "emanation," golden in color, is still connected by a "very fine life-thread" to the brain below. The brain, he says, is still "internally throbbing—a slow, deep throb—not painful, like the beat of the sea," and rational faculties are still present. The golden emanation "extends up midway to the ceiling," being but a "perfect prototype, or reproduction," bright shining, yet still attached by the tread to the old brain. "The next thing," he describes, "is the withdrawal of the electric principle. When this thread snaps, the spiritual body is free! and prepared to accompany its guardians to the Summer-Land. Yes, there is a spiritual body; it is sown in dishonor and raised in brightness" (15–16).[59] Finally, the clairvoyant witnesses the departure of the spiritual body—in parallel to mesmerist practices, still "sleeping." The observer sees how it silently moves through the air, "surrounded by a beautiful assemblage of guardian friends. They throw their loving arms about the sleeping one, and on they all speed to the world of Light! Clairvoyants and mediums see this; and they know it is true" (17). The "Summer-Land," which is elsewhere extensively described by Davis (1867), bears marks of paradise, but also of a utopian society (cf. Kellehear 1996): "The Summer-Land is vastly more beautiful than the most beautiful landscape of earth. Celestial waters are more limpid, the atmosphere more soft and genial, the streams are always musical, and the fertile islands there are ever full of meanings" (Davis 1866, 21; cf. 26–78). Interestingly, Davis holds that "persons always

---

[59] Cf. the religious frame of the story "A Soldier's Sensations on the Battle-Field" (dated 1864), mediumistically received by Hudson Tuttle (cf. subsequent discussion), quoted in Hardinge 1870, 526–7.

take places in the Summer-Land in accordance with their moral *status*, and not in accordance with their intellectual tastes, inclinations, or social condition" (20), which continues a Christian narrative of postmortal judgment.

One step farther in that direction, American Spiritualist Hudson Tuttle (1836–1910) reported of his "own clairvoyant experience," in which he left his body, accompanied by his "guardian," to visit the spirit world. Returning to his body, he saw it "cold and motionless, rigid in every muscle and fibre" (Tuttle 1864, II, 159). In this situation, Tuttle discloses, he endeavored to reenter the body and to regain "possession of it," but failed repeatedly to do so. He became alarmed, full of anguish and agony, but finally succeeded. Although it is again only a description of an intentional spiritual practice, Tuttle himself draws a significant comparison to experiences near death: "It was like that which is used to describe death, or which drowned men tell us of when they at length recover" (159).[60] In a mood similar to the drug experiences previously described, he looked at his body "as any other foreign substance" (159). We will not be too speculative if we hypothesize that the description of drug experiences was crucial for this new narrative element in clairvoyant experiences. Actually, pointing elsewhere to strikingly similar effects a narcotic such as hashish and "the magnetizer" produce,[61] Tuttle refers immediately after his own description to Cahagnet's séances to prove how closely "super-clairvoyance approaches death" (159). Tuttle holds that memory will be highly active on the verge of death and remembers all occurrences of life (cf. 63). His senses being unimpaired, the disembodied spirit will see, Tuttle confirms with earlier Spiritualist–Occult scholars, his spiritual friends or a guide (cf. 189).

In the following decade, it is especially the life-review feature that emerges in American mediumistic reports of "deceased." In 1874, a deceased reports to an automatic-writing medium in a spiritist séance, among other paranormal features, a life review as part of his sensations when dying (cf. Wolfe 1875 [1874], 388),[62] as has been reported by American doctor and Spiritualist Napoleon Bonaparte Wolfe. In the same year, John W. Edmonds (1816–1874), judge and politician, published a very similar automatic-writing account of a deceased. After the loss of his wife, Edmonds had sought the help of Margaret Fox— one of the famous Fox sisters, the pioneering "media" of American spiritualism—to get into contact with his dead wife. Finally, he left his profession to become himself an influential spiritualist medium. In this function, he communicated with a former colleague, Judge Rufus P. Peckham, who had died in a sea accident. Again, of prominence in Edmonds's mediumistic report (1875 [1874], 303) of Peckham is the life review: "In the

---

[60] Cf. Tuttle's description (1864, II, 192–8, 216–22; 1871, 241–3) reminiscent of the life review, and the whole report of a clairvoyant excursion at the brink of death, leading to the transformation of formerly atheist views.

[61] Tuttle (1864, II, 141) indeed argues that there is "little distinction" between "magnetizing" and "the operation of narcotics, especially hashish, or Indian hemp, which the Hindoos used to produce the ecstasy in which they communicated with the gods, and learned the course of future events."

[62] Quoted in Bozzano 1931, 80–1.

dying moment I lived my life all over. Every scene, every act passed before me as vividly as if written on my brain with living light. Not a friend that I had known in early or later life was forgotten." Finally, so the report continues, he had been lifted out of the water by his deceased parents and had been welcomed in the "realms of the life immortal" by other deceased friends. Peckham's spirit, however, mentions a presence of angels, but no personal encounter with God, apart from a general remark that love "makes us to rejoice in our Great and All-wise Father" (303).[63]

Experiences out of body, reported more properly with an autoscopic interest of the disembodied consciousness, are discussed by American Spiritualist William Denton (1823–1883) in his small work *Is Spiritualism True?* (1871). Arguing in general for a soul with retained bodily senses that will exist beyond the body, Denton discusses several cases near death.[64] For Denton, the basis of Spiritualism is therefore true and had been advanced in the mesmerist tradition—in contrast to the self-conceptualization of recent "modern" Spiritualism. He emphasizes that the ability to allow magnetized others to leave their body had been with mesmerism for a long time. Denton (1874, 18) refers to Thomas C. Hartshorn (see previous discussion), a magnetizer who said "of a friend, whom he had magnetized, 'I can send him forth instantly through the thick darkness of night into distant lands, and cause him to bring us tidings of our absent friends [...]'. This is no exaggeration, as my own experience with clairvoyants has repeatedly demonstrated. Before the advent of modern Spiritualism, I had, on numerous occasions, sent mesmeric subjects on distant journeys."[65] Denton, however, argues forcefully both against "materialism" and "Adventism," the former being ignorant of the "all-controlling spirit within," whereas

---

[63] Another influential account of 1878 was reprinted in the *New York Times*, Dec. 8, 1878, under the title "A Maine Editor's View of Death." Probably H. K. Morrell reports here that his horse had run away while he still hung in a wheel. In his distress, he called for his "spirit friends," and yes, shortly thereafter he saw "crowds of spirits" around him, known and unknown ones, hovering around the wagon. Although in danger, he felt neither fear nor pain. Of the usual near-death features, he explicitly mentions that he had not experienced the life review so "often heard." Yet, he had thought of deeds done or left undone. Finally, reflecting on the supernatural aid crucial for his survival, he adds: "I do not feel of sufficient consequence to merit God's special providence, but that loving friends from the other sphere," he says, may have sustained him, does not lessen his idea "of the goodness and greatness of the Creator" (quoted in Francis 1900, 301–2). Both the summoning of the spirits as well as the acquaintance with the life review and his conclusion on what had helped him show how certain preexistent expectations had been present, if not fulfilled in the experience (as reported).

[64] For example, the cases reported by Child or Peckham, or the accident reported by Hartshorn (see Denton 1874, 17–19; cf. also Oxon 1876, 117–18).

[65] "John O. Wattles of Kansas," Denton (1874, 18) says, a well-known activist in the antislavery cause, "informed me, that, on one occasion, he accidentally discovered that his spirit could leave the body, and return. He found, afterward, that this could be done at will; and he frequently looked down as a spectator upon his body lying in a death-like trance, and then roamed at pleasure over the earth, and returned again. Psychometers have frequently the power to do this [...]. Mrs. Cridge, Mrs. Denton, and my son Sherman, travel spiritually with great ease, and describe with great accuracy distant localities never visited by them." With the term "psychometers," Denton refers to the emergent idea that individuals may make use of a hidden "picture-gallery" ("grand panoramas of the past") impressed into objects by "Nature" itself, that consists of mental "daguerreotypes" (see Denton and Denton 1871, 30–32; 46, 263–64; cf. Hanegraaff 2017, 20-22).

the latter invokes miracles when there is no need to do so. Emphasizing the naturalness of the death-surviving spirit, Denton articulates beliefs that we subsumed under the category of Spiritualist–Occult, namely, that it will be rather natural for disembodied souls to contact the living (cf. 32). Present are also Gnostic–Esoteric convictions, with core belief being here, in Denton's words, that in "death-trance" spiritual powers are largely increased, so that the spirit becomes aware of its spiritual nature, remembers to see "formerly unconscious" things, and so forth (cf. 31–2).[66] Evidencing these facts, he quotes F. Beaufort's and other cases that encompass a life review, but also a report in the strand of deathbed narratives, in which a critically ill young girl reports after her "apparent death" of having been to heaven and having met deceased relatives there, including one whose death had so far been unknown (cf. 28–31).[67] Although Denton abstains from any traditional religious framing of Spiritualism, he deals with it as a doctrine parallel to other religions. Doctrines, Denton holds, do not become true through the number of believers or by ancientness,[68] but by their central truth of the soul's survival. In that respect, current "spiritualism," he concludes, is superior to any kind of orthodox doctrine: "Man *is* a spirit: he is not to become one. Nature knows no favored saints, who are to be spiritually created for the barbarous heaven of a half-Jewish, half-Christian mythology, while the rest are left to sink into nonentity; but she has given to all freely [. . .] that spirit which can smile at death, and soar triumphant when the lifeless body sinks to the dust" (21).

A significant contribution, first published in 1877, can be seen in the essay "Peak in Darien" by Irish writer and feminist social activist Frances Power Cobbe (1822–1904). Cobbe adapted the title from a poem that describes the surprise of Spanish conquerors in Darien (Panama), who, climbing a hill, had expected to see another continent but saw instead another ocean—the Pacific. She collected personal narratives of deathbed scenes in which the dying "seemed *to see something*; or rather, to speak more exactly, to become conscious of something present (for actual sight is out of question)" (Cobbe 1882, 287). For Cobbe, it is this facial expression of astonishment, attested, she says, by many, that seems to point to the fact that the dying might experience an "utterly-unexpected but instantly-recognized vision" (288), which is instantly followed by the soul's departure. In

---

[66] Denton (1874, 28) argues, when "the circulation is stopped," and "the pallor of death overspreads the countenance, and death itself is so well counterfeited that it is hardly possible to distinguish the one from the other, the spirit asserts its superiority and independence; it hears, sees, feels, and obtains knowledge, that, out of this trance-state, the individual is unable to obtain."

[67] Arguing for the released soul's capability to have all its past present, Denton (1874, 30) introduces new metaphors for explaining the life review, namely that "the arterial blood" seems to be "converted into black venous blood," rendering "man as unfit for action as a locomotive with the fire out, and the water in the boiler changed to ice. If we found a locomotive going at the rate of a thousand miles an hour under such circumstances, we should conclude that it ran by some other motive-power than steam," that is, the spirit.

[68] If this would be the case, earlier religious tradition should be reinstalled—arriving, finally at "Buddhism" that says to Catholicism, " 'Out, you baby of yesterday!' but, scarcely seats itself in the temple, before it is unceremoniously ejected by hoary Paganism, the son of the ages" (Denton 1874, 3).

some of Cobbe's cases, the dying reported "seeing" departed relatives. Cobbe assumes, within the Gnostic–Esoteric metaculture, that the soul of man begins "at the very instant when the veil of the flesh is dropping off, to exercise those spiritual powers of perception" (300). And she goes on to argue that an "eternity of solitude" would be an "absurd hypothesis," so that, in consequence, the soul may at once recognize its "future companions," probably waiting on the threshold. Cautiously arguing that these assumptions may be verified in the actual experiences reported, she nevertheless denies that these reports, on their part, may count as proof of life immortal. This belief, "faith in Immortality," will have to ground, as Cobbe alludes, directly in God (cf. 278; 302). In more recent literature on near-death experiences, her model of unexpected sightings of the dying has been, however, enriched with an additional assumption that was originally only an element of one of Cobbe's cases—namely, that a dying lady could recognize among her deceased brothers another brother assumed to be still living in India, whose death was confirmed later. In more recent discourse, "Peak in Darien" cases[69] are specifically those in which experiencers see recently deceased persons not known to have died, so that an illusory confirmation can be ruled out.

A notable document in this current is the posthumously published book *Visions: A Study of False Sight (Pseudopia)* (1878) by American medical doctor Edward H. Clarke (1820–1877). In a chapter on the "Visions of the Dying" (1878, 258–78), Clarke discusses the "pseudopia" ("false perception") of the dying. Sensitive to the religious dimension, he declares that the subject "is a sacred one, and is indissolubly bound up with our holiest and tenderest feelings. We love, and not unnaturally, to hope and believe, when the silver cord is loosed which has bound those we love to earth, that [...] there may come a glimpse of heaven, which for an instant shall clothe the dying features with angelic brightness, and perhaps give to the departing one a momentary recognition of those who have gone before. Such is the conviction of some, the faith of many, and the hope of most" (258–9). But then Clarke argues more in naturalist ways: It is unnecessary, he argues, to "examine the foundation of such hopes, and almost cruel to destroy them" (259). Arguing for the painlessness of dying, he explains that visions of the drowning, the "revival of past images, thoughts, and memories," "glorified visitors," "voices of angels," "friends waiting for the newcomer," an "unearthly light" and the like, represent the workings of an "anaesthetic" provided by nature, administered, for example, as "the asphyxia of drowning." Thus these visions are to be explained as a physiological effect, a sign of disintegration, a "last flashing of cerebral fire" (272). Clarke comments that saints, "who have mortified the flesh till their anaemic brains, rapidly disintegrating and highly sensitive, are brought to the eve of dissolution, present the most favorable conditions for the production of subjective, ante-mortem pseudopia" (271). Subsequently, Clarke's argument takes an unexpected turn:

---

[69] See Murphy 1945.

Probably all such visions as these are automatic. But yet, who, believing in God and personal immortality, as the writer rejoices in doing, will dare to say *absolutely all*? Will dare to assert there is no *possible* exception? If life is continuous, heaven beyond, and death the portal, is it philosophical to affirm that no one entering that portal has ever caught a glimpse, or can ever catch a glimpse, before he is utterly freed from the flesh, of the glory beyond? (272)

I may note in passing that "to catch a glimpse from afar" of spirits, of the judgment of others, and so forth, is a common element of Christian medieval visions of heaven and hell (cf. Easting 2006, 79). The way Clarke speaks of glimpses here shows obvious familiarities with Christian teachings. Quoting extensively visions of the dying from Cobbe (1877), he argues once again that testimonies in which the departed were seen can be explained by the fact that these faces were still familiar impressions: "Their hieroglyphics had been laid away in the cerebral cells of the dying individual, and were consequently capable of being revived with greater or less fidelity" (278).

Those cases, however, in which the dying did not report of any persons or objects, but found themselves as realizing a "radiant glory," seem to be different. Adducing such instances, including one he personally witnessed (and in which he felt something departing from the body), Clarke concludes that in these cases, "the ineffable expression of transfigured humanity" appears "upon the features of whoever gets a sight of heaven, before he has left the earth" (279). Even though the prominence of naturalist scientific attempts to explain visions near death may not be overlooked, it is obvious that Clarke finally relativizes his own physiological explanations; he does not doubt that authentic visions of the beyond are possible: "If ever a scene like this occurs, who will dare say that the explanation of it may not come from a height inaccessible to our imperfect physiology?" (279). In respect to the evolving naturalist discourse, Clarke's explanations are highly significant in presenting a physiological explanation of the visions of the dying (which are, therefore, not taken as evidence of life after death), while, at the same time, the belief is upheld that there *is* life after death. The "transfigured" facial expressions of certain dying individuals bear witness to the fact that they saw something inexpressible that can, for exactly its inexpressibility, not have been a hidden earthly impression in their mind.

2.2.17 THE CONFIGURATION OF A NEW GENRE: THE COLLECTION OF NEAR-DEATH REPORTS BY FRANZ SPLITTGERBER (1866)

Characterizing discursive elements of experiences near death in mid-19th-century Germany, I now turn to the influential account of Franz Splittgerber, a Protestant Prussian preacher at the garrison of Kolberg (today Kołobrzeg). The overall aim of his treatment of *Schlaf und Tod* (Sleep and Death), published in the same year as Davis's work, is, as Splittgerber (1866, xi) emphasizes from the outset, an apologetic one: to provide objective evidence that the human soul is of an eternal, transcendental nature against the "dissolving principles of modern materialism." Within the framework of "apparent death," which had in the meantime lost its danger of resulting in "premature burial" (cf. 310), Splittgerber assembled reports of those who returned from these and other life-threatened states (including, next to early Greek, Roman, and early medieval examples, the testimony of Schwerdtfeger, cf. 354–5). In a protoscientific mood, he assumes the duration of "psychic life" in these events, and defines "apparent death" as the continuation of "latent consciousness" (cf. 313). In his case collection, he narrated various case reports of survivors of apparent death—cases that include the description of indescribably wonderful, heavenly landscapes; experiencing loud noises; seeing deceased people; meeting a guide; being clothed in brightest white; and being judged before God, confronted with the book of one's deeds, and sent back to life (317–18, 331, 334–7). In the context of dying and real death, he discusses the "prophetic distant vision (of the future)" (354, 360), the "ascent to the light," "clairvoyance," and "remote viewing," and the "clear memory" visible in the "panoramic review" [*panoramischer Ueberblick*]. For the latter, he referred to Admiral Beaufort. Still, while recounting a large number of what later will become essential elements of Moody's account, there is, again, one significant element still missing. As Michael Nahm (2009, 91) observes, there are several reports of "veridical knowledge," as he has it, of the "Near-death experiencer" about "what was happening around the apparently dead corpse during the time of bodily unconsciousness. Yet, Splittgerber gave no explicit references regarding out-of-body experiences." Actually, he did include reports of "Doppelgängers" (body doubles),[70] a phenomenon defined by him as "real local dislocation of the soul." Yet, he is suspicious in respect to the "objectivity of all cases of this genre," and grants them credibility only if attested to by others to whom these souls appeared (as "a certain impression of proximity and presence," 388–9). Therefore, in contrast to Engmann (2014, 44), who argues that Doppelgänger is "a term we could refer to today as out-of-body experiences or autoscopy," I actually miss important elements of the disembodied, autoscopic view, namely, to see one's own, dying or dead body—surrounded by doctors or relatives—from above. The only case quoted by Splittgerber that shows a certain allusion to experiences out of the body is the one of a certain Erhard Veit, who, according to the report,[71] suffered from a serious thorax illness. In Splittgerber's words, "a supernatural figure reassured him that he must stay in bed a bit longer, because his inner body should be aforehand refined as bright as the sun. But then he saw in the same vision [*Gesicht*] *his old, earthly body separated from the internal* [body], so that it appeared to him as if *two bodies* laid in bed. A hand pulled down the linen cover from his

---

[70] Referencing two works, namely, Horst (1830) and Perty (1861).
[71] Quoted from Seelbach (1864, II, 37).

breast and said: 'Look, your future body will be like this' " (388, emphasis in orig., trans. mine). In modern terms, this narrative might be characterized as "heautoscopic" in the sense that the observer oscillates or alternates between the observing body and a second, perceived phantom double (cf. Marsh 2010, 121–2).

All these reports, however, are molded in Splittgerber's traditionally Christian conclusion (1866, 339) as to which all accounts converge: They provide clear evidence that "in the beyond a retributive justice reigns," and that the soul, if fully retracted from the body, is of eternal essence. Furthermore, in regard to any idiosyncrasies or inconsistencies, he recommends that the teachings of the Scripture should be taken as the unmistaken scale of reference. Only the Bible, the word of God, will allow us to distinguish between objective truth and "subjective outfitting" of the "ecstatic visions" (339). To conclude, Splittgerber argues within Protestant Christian constraints, but, in the wake of psychology, integrates "strange examples" in narratives of death and dying, for example, second sight, Doppelgänger, and other occult phenomena, which to him are more often than not examples of rampant superstition. As his work draws from sources ranging from antique authors to medieval mystics and contemporary witnesses, it closes a gap between the medieval mystics and the modern psychological interest in near-death accounts. In addition, it seems to be at least in part the first specimen of a new literary genre: an encompassing collection of case reports near death.

Another crucial account that attests the impact of near-death reports within Christian metaculture is the work of British physician William Munk (1816–1898), *Euthanasia: or, Medical Treatment in Aid of an Easy Death*. Being a forerunner to modern end-of-life care, it had been written to serve "the medical management of the dying" (Munk 1887, v). Although interested in "euthanasia," understood as "a calm and easy death" (5), Munk turns in his introduction to the cases of Admiral Beaufort, who had reported of his calm feelings, and de Quincey's descriptions, attesting the same (2–18). The main conclusion Munk draws from these reports is that "the immediate act of dying is in no sense a process of severe bodily suffering." To him, this misunderstanding emerged from false theories on the nature of death, confounded with the painful symptoms of deadly diseases. "To the dying," Munk holds, "there is no greater solace and cordial than hope—it is the most soothing and cheering of our feelings, and if, when all hope of life and in the present has fled, the dying man can dwell with hope and confidence upon his future, it will be well for him" (22). And Munk, who had converted to Roman Catholicism in 1842, adds, "The retrospect of a well-spent life [. . .] is a cordial of infinitely more efficacy than all the resources of the medical art; but a firm belief in the mercy of God, and in the promises of salvation will do more than anything in aid of an easy, calm, and collected death" (22–3). Referring to his belief, he concludes that for the "aggressive *dis*-believer" an easy, calm, and collected death, that is, euthanasia, is simply impossible.

2.2.18 THE LIFE REVIEW AND WAKE-UP DREAMS: CARL DU PREL, SIGMUND FREUD, AND FRIEDRICH NIETZSCHE

In 1844, German philosopher Carl du Prel (1839–1899) published an influential book on various topics of "Psychic Research," *Die Philosophie der Mystik* (1884), translated into English as *The Philosophy of Mysticism* (1889). Directed against the theory of materialists, who see in all thinking only "transpiring products of the brain mash" [*Ausschwitzungsprodukte des Gehirnbreies*](du Prel 1885, 89), he refers to the phenomenon of the life review in drowning and drugging. For du Prel, the human soul "consisted in the main of a subconscious but still individual 'transcendental subject' whose foundations are not destroyed by bodily illness or death" (Nahm 2009, 92). German transcendental idealism therefore provides the backdrop of interpreting the life review:

> [N]ormal self-consciousness with its physiological measure of time is only one form of our self-consciousness. Man has a double consciousness, the empirical with its physiological measure of time, and a transcendental with another measure of time peculiar to itself. Now, that this transcendental consciousness forthwith emerges, as soon as the empirical is set to rest, is most strikingly evinced by our dreams. Since the transcendental measure of time is a characteristic incident of these, it is evident that the physiological scale is inapplicable to them. (du Prel 1889, I, 93–4; cf. 1885, 77–9)

In contrast to outright spiritualist–occultist accounts, du Prel aims to integrate somnambulism, hypnotism, and extraordinary psychic phenomena into a philosophical system of consciousness. Nevertheless, in all of these phenomena he uncovers evidence for an unbound "unconscious," the "soul."

Taking a "subconscious" turn, du Prel reformulates the distinction of a terrestrial and a celestial body, and likewise, the recollection–memory distinction, as the empirical, "normal self-consciousness with its physiological measure of time" on the one side, and the "transcendental consciousness," on the other. The "extraordinary exaltation of memory" highlights nothing less than the transcendental quality of time itself—a copresence beyond all measures of succession that reign over waking life. The liberated soul therefore will experience everything in a single now, in the mode of a "transcendental consciousness." The "simultaneity" of both the empirical and transcendental consciousness, du Prel says (I, xxiv), has actually for the first time been "suggested in Indian philosophy," and only later "recovered" by Plotinus and Kant. Indian teachings of intentional experiences in deprived states, if not states near death, for example, the technique of fakirs "who let themselves be buried alive" (163), turn Western "animal magnetism" into the rank of a "rediscovery" (cf. 163, 285, 303). Of utmost relevance in our context is, however, that du Prel directs his attention to a cognate phenomenon of the life review that he locates in dreams of a certain kind. In his famous interpretation of dreams (1900),

Sigmund Freud will subsume these dreams under the heading "wake-up dreams." In an earlier contribution, du Prel (cf. 1869, 224–31) had already dealt with these "teleological dreams" in which the dreaming individual wakes up as a corresponding reaction to an "affection of the senses" (such as a loud noise) that reaches the dreamer from the outer world. Such a dream, for which almost everybody may immediately remember an example experienced by herself or himself, is, for example, attested by psychologist Alfred Maury in his *Le sommeil et les rêves* ([1861] 1878, 161):

> I am in bed in my room, my mother at my pillow. I am dreaming of the Terror; I am present at scenes of massacre, I appear before the Revolution Tribunal; I see Robespierre, Marat, Fouquier-Tinville [. . .]; I defend myself; I am convicted, condemned to death, driven [. . .] to the Place de la Révolution; I ascend the scaffold; the executioner lays me on the fatal plank, tilts it forward, the knife falls; I feel my head separate from my body, I wake in a state of intense anguish, and I feel on my neck the curtain pole which has suddenly got detached and fallen on my cervical vertebrae, just like a guillotine knife. It had all taken place in an instant, as my mother bore witness.

For du Prel (cf. 1869, 228), however, the fact that the awakened individual himself may still be able to witness the worldly source of the wake-up trigger (e.g., the knocking on the door that the dreamer had incorporated into the dream narrative as dropping objects), points to an apparent paradox: The unfolding dream seems to presuppose the final stimulus, because the dream story develops almost naturally toward an expected "unexpected end." On the other hand, the latter and the stimulus, he holds, must be simultaneous. This paradox can be resolved, du Prel reasons, only if we assume an "ideality of time and the law of causality" (231). In other words, the whole process reveals not only how a stimulus in the outer world triggers a whole story, but that the outer world, "reality" itself, is experienced by us in an imperfect, causal manner, being only a phenomenal "appearance" as in Kant's transcendental idealism. And, quoting Shakespeare's "The Tempest," "We are such stuff, As dreams are made of," du Prel (1869, 239) regretfully comments, we may not expect ever to wake up. "Probably we are dreaming the dream of life," he ruminates, "until death bangs on the door." However, in this early contribution on the interpretation of dreams du Prel did not refer to the life review. Almost two decades later, in his *Philosophy of Mysticism*, we meet du Prel (cf. [1884] 1889, 90–6) explicitly supporting the view that the "extraordinary exaltation of memory" in dreams can be met in drug experiences and use of narcotics, but also in situations near death, quoting the reports of Beaufort, Fechner, and de Quincey.[72] Referring to the dream of Maury and numerous others, he argues again that it seems paradoxical that we have the awakening cause as a final event

---

[72] C. du Prel (1889, 96–7) applies his theory also to Mohammed's joy in heaven as a drug experience (cf. Theophile Gautier, Section 2.2.11): "There is a passage in the Koran in which Mohammed relates what might suggest the

that appears to have caused "the whole purport and course of the dream" (102). The extraordinary compression of a sequence of representations [*Vorstellungsverdichtung*], he reasons, can be explained only by a "transcendental" quality of time, hidden in everyday life, but present for the "transcendental I," convinced that the extraordinary compression of time is not dependent on the external stimulus, but a quality of all dreams (including the 'dream' that is reality). In this vein, he argues, "The brain receives a stimulus, and applies to that its own inherent law of causality, that is, constructs by imagination a corresponding cause. This cause is objectified, and through the transcendental scale of time assumes the form of a concentrated series of representations, with dramatic reference to the conclusion" (104). For du Prel, it is crystal clear that the life review near death offers proof for exactly the same—the "transcendental consciousness" with its own peculiar measure of time. Yet, he does not discuss the life review or other experiences near death more thoroughly. Nevertheless, the comparison of the life review with wake-up dreams will reappear in later interpretations (e.g., by Victor Egger, discussed in Section 2.2.20) and might indeed provide valuable hermeneutics for understanding the life review. We may therefore dwell for a moment on the interpretation of wake-up dreams as they appear in Freud and Nietzsche, each being indebted to du Prel's discussion of the phenomenon.

In his *Interpretation of Dreams* (1900), Freud (1921 [1913], 397; cf. 396–8) argues that the best explanation available of how such elaborate stories are composed in an "exceedingly short space of time," is, rather simple: "the story is already composed." Providing testimonies (e.g., the dream of Casimir Bonjour[73]), Freud explains that the complete story has already been developed, composed, and stored as a whole *before* the external stimulus occurs. The narrative, actually an articulation of a "wish-phantasy," is merely "activated" or "kicked off" by the external stimulus. In sum, such stories appear to be a spontaneous invention, yet are, in contrast, "ready-made phantasies touched off by the dream-work." Explaining the motives behind the dream imagery, he turns once again to Maury's wake-up dream of the French Revolution and, taking Maury's fascination

---

suspicion that he had substituted hashish for wine. 'It is there said that the Angel Gabriel took Mahomet out of his bed one morning to give him a sight of all things in the seven heavens, in paradise, and in hell [. . .], and after having held ninety thousand conferences with God, was brought back again to his bed. All this, says the Alcoran, was transacted in so small a space of time, that Mahomet on his return found his bed still warm.'"

[73] Cf. Macario 1857. I may note in passing that the Gananath Obeyesekere (2012, 28; cf. 30–1) has drawn on the example of Bonjour and similar accounts to argue that the "awakening" of Siddhārtha Gautama, the historical Buddha, can be interpreted as such a time-contracted "visionary experience." In the second watch of the night of awakening, the becoming Buddha could redirect, the tradition holds, his "divine eye" to the "long panorama of the passing and rising of human beings," including their individual karmic dispositions, realizing thereby the law of karma. Considering also reports of near-death experiences (see 139; 202; 433), Obeyesekere's perspective shows how European thoughts on dream consciousness are used as a phenomenological framework to interpret prominent non-Western accounts.

of revolutionary times in his country for granted, Freud interprets: "the dream-work quickly utilizes the incoming stimulus for the construction of a wish-fulfilment, as if it thought (this is to be taken quite figuratively): 'Here is a good opportunity to re- alize the wish-phantasy which I formed at such and such a time while I was reading'" (397). And, accordingly, a complete story is almost simultaneously revived. The fact that Freud mentions here a situation of reading, in which complex stories are formed, and not real-life experiences, is highly meaningful and will occupy us in its relevance for near-death narratives in the following discussion. However, for Freud, a problem remains: These dreams are highly coherent and usually well remembered. To him, this reveals the presence of a special instance at work in human consciousness that aims at rendering the chaotic contents of dreams into a coherent, intelligible succession. This instance, equally active in dream consciousness and wake consciousness, is called by him "secondary elaboration." In addition to other dream-forming factors identified in Freud's theory—for example, the censorship of disturbing unconscious content—it will influence "the whole mass of material in the dream thoughts in an inductive and selec- tive manner" (399).

In conclusion, different factors come together in the final reporting of wake-up dreams: First, the "story" is usually in essential parts precomposed. As such, it will be the subject of a final redaction by the instance of the mind that, while the dreaming person awakes (or even later), will exclude the unwanted and displeasing content of dreams. Given that Freud was especially interested in deciphering the symbolic expres- sion of unconscious wishes in dreams, he was not very fond of wake-up dreams that were obviously triggered by external stimuli. It seems to us that the combined explanation of (1) already-composed stories (to acknowledge the "acceleration" of those dreams), and (2) a secondary elaboration, that is, a process of revising dream contents, is not entirely convincing. Taken seriously, the former process, if accomplished, should not need the latter, and vice versa: If there is a thorough revision, a "secondary elaboration" of dream content, then it must follow that the stories are not precomposed. An entirely different interpretation of wake-up dreams has been, however, proposed by Friedrich Nietzsche (1844–1900). In his *Twilight of the Idols* (*Götzen-Dämmerung*), Nietzsche ([1888] 1977, 469) included the following aphorism:

The error of imaginary causes. To begin with dreams: ex post facto, a cause is slipped under a particular sensation (for example, one following a far-off cannon shot)— often a whole little novel in which the dreamer turns up as the protagonist. The sensation endures meanwhile in a kind of resonance: it waits, as it were, until the causal instinct permits it to step into the foreground—now no longer as a chance occurrence, but as "meaning". The cannon shot appears in a *causal* mode, in an apparent reversal of time. What is really later, the motivation, is experienced first—

often with a hundred details which pass like lightning—and the shot *follows*. What has happened? The representations which were *produced* by a certain state have been misunderstood as its causes. [74]

Nietzsche's analysis is much closer to Carl du Prel's interpretation. The dreaming sleeper is subject to a distinct and sudden perception such as a loud shot. The excitation must be intensive enough to peak through the stimulus threshold. However, consciousness seems unprepared to wake up immediately, probably being immersed in a dream disconnected to the outer world. Therefore the impulse has to have a certain intensity that arouses in the dreaming consciousness the prelude to initiate awakening. Although the external stimulus is primarily "overheard"—in the case of acoustic stimuli; but there may be other, and even internal, stimuli such as bodily pain—it is already present in consciousness. Yet the sleeping mind, its visual organs not in use, moves on in its activity without being able to recognize the stimulus's external origin. At this point, Nietzsche, following du Prel, argues that a new dream narrative unfolds (or the actual dream turns into a new direction), as if the end of the story is *already known* and will be expected. This process seems to be exactly the opposite of the "selective attention" in perceptive faculties. Instead of being a filter that hinders the mind—with its limited capacity of processing sensory input—from paying attention to a multiplicity of probably irrelevant information, it is a kind of "context invention" that searches for an appropriate context for only one—though very relevant—perception. Concretely, the dream narrative that now unfolds will develop a story that will end with a meaningful, often dramatic plot that includes the stimulus, now being contextualized as an inescapable consequence of the story. In Nietzsche's example, the shot is heard again, as if it happened for the very first time, and forces the mind to wake up. Taking the phenomenon as an example of a general rule, Nietzsche concludes (again with du Prel, though without reference to him) that the case highlights how consciousness—and not only while dreaming, but in its wake state, too—misattributes representations for being supposedly the original cause. Without being aware of the fact, Nietzsche argues, consciousness reverts in an incredible speed the temporal order. For the individual who—finally awoken—becomes aware of the situation, it implies the impression that a paradoxical reversal of time succession must have happened. Nietzsche, in other words, installs wake-up dreams as a heuristic tool. Generalized, they provide an explanation of procedures that, though unnoticed, are common characteristics of human consciousness. This "time reversal,"

---

[74] Nietzsche 1980, KSA 6, 92; cf. KSA 11, 156–7, 26 [35]; Summer/Autumn 1884. The way Nietzsche describes the phenomenon reveals that du Prel's explanation (especially of the *passus* in 1869, 220–1) was known to him.

he says, "takes place all the time, also while awake."[75] And Nietzsche ([1888] 1977, 496; cf. KSA 6: 92) concludes:

> Most of our general feelings [. . . . .] excite our causal instinct: we want to have a reason for feeling this way or that—for feeling bad or for feeling good. We are never satisfied merely to state the fact that we feel this way or that: we admit this fact only—become conscious of it only—when we have furnished some kind of motivation. Memory, which swings into action in such cases, unknown to us, brings up earlier states of the same kind, together with the causal interpretations associated with them—not their real causes. [. . .] Thus originates a habitual acceptance of a particular causal interpretation, which, as a matter of fact, inhibits any investigation into the real cause—even precludes it.

Most significantly, while transferring the phenomenon to the wake consciousness, Nietzsche considers an element we already got to know in Freud's interpretation, namely, the unconscious operation of remembering similar instances of the same category. These, remembered with their context, are synthesized with the actual case. In regard to the story itself, Nietzsche holds that—in general—one tends to prefer explanations that temper the fearful mind and remove all oddity or strangeness of the perceived stimulus: "That which is new and strange and has not been experienced before, is excluded as a cause. Thus one searches not only for some kind of explanation to serve as a cause, but for a particularly selected and preferred kind of explanation—that which has most quickly and most frequently abolished the feeling of the strange, new, and hitherto unexperienced: the most habitual explanations" (496). These explanations are relaxing and satisfying. They supply a well-known context that will neutralize the "unknown" for the one confronted with danger. However, oddly enough, Nietzsche does not consider the fact that the whole dream narrative serves the purpose for awaken the consciousness. Following du Prel, Nietzsche, in contrast, concludes that we are actually not living in the present, but in a "presence" that was unconsciously motivated and *allowed* to be present.

But, one may ask, what does the whole discussion of these dreams yield for the interpretation of the life review? Some more fundamental questions in regard to this will be raised in the concluding part. For the time being, I may conclude that the discussion of wake-up dreams indicates how the phenomenon of the life review, even though it is discussed by neither Freud nor Nietzsche, is increasingly interesting for philosophers and psychologists. Apart from explanations drawing on brain physiology, Freud's general theory will, moreover, become the dominant model of explaining experiences near death within Naturalist metaculture of the 20th century. In this trajectory, it was a French physician, an assistant of Jean-Martin Charcot, Charles S. Féré (1852–1907), who published in 1889 a contribution on the "Mental State of the Dying." Although he admits that the panoramic review might have historically contributed to the development of a "belief in

---

[75] Nietzsche 1980, 157; KSA 11, 26 [35]; my trans.

a final judgment,"[76] he reasons that in other cases, reviews are more or less meaningless. The "reminiscences" or revisioned episodes might be connected to a "brusque modification of cerebral circulation" (cf. Alvarado 2011, 74). In this context, he provides two significant reports that are of great importance for the discursive history of experiences near death: Féré's contribution attracted the attention of Helena Blavatsky, as we will see in Section 2.3.2. In the first of two cases of his personal practice, he treated a moribund individual suffering from an inflammation of the spinal cord. Brought momentarily back to life, as Féré reports, with ether injections, he is no longer able to express himself verbally in French. However, the patient—a Fleming, but based since his childhood in France—writes, in Flemish, on a sheet of paper that he has to repay 15 francs borrowed decades ago, and then dies. As it turns out, the process of dying could, it seems, unlock this memory. The same happened in the second case, in which an ill person remembers after an ether injection a special event before dying. The "artificial excitation," Féré comments, seems to be comparable to certain euphoric states of epileptic spasms. We can see in Féré's interpretation how the deathbed visions, including the panoramic review, got increasingly pathologized in the Naturalist metaculture. Féré (1892, 170; cf. Alvarado 2011, 74) is convinced that "circulation problems" in the brain are responsible for the hyperexcitability and the "intellectual perversions" in the dying consciousness.

2.2.19 ALBERT HEIM'S CASE COLLECTION OF "FATAL FALLS" (1892)

William Munk's deliberations, passing on the well-established topos that the act of dying itself must be free from pain and suffering,[77] prepared the ground for the most prominent collection of near-death reports in the 1890s. The cases published and commented in 1892 under the title "Remarks on Fatal Falls" ["*Notizen über den Tod durch Absturz*"] by the Swiss alpinist and professor of geography at the ETH Zurich, Albert Heim (1849–1937), have been acclaimed in later literature as the first systematic description, introduced to the English-speaking world by Bromberg and Schilder (1933), and more broadly, through the translation of Noyes and Kletti (see Martinović 2015; 2017). The incentive of Heim, the "pioneer of near death studies" (Bruce Greyson), for collecting the reports of persons who survived accidents and publishing them in the journal of an alpinist club was in a way to give comfort to friends and relatives of those mountaineers who had died in accidents (cf. Martinović 2017, 103–13). Thus, he asks in his essay "of which kind are the sensations [*Empfindungen*] of a sudden casualty in his last seconds of life?" (Heim 1892,

---

[76] "Ces réminiscences des épileptiques et des noyés rappelés à la vie ont peut-être joué un rôle dans l'établissement de la croyance à un jugement dernier" (Féré 1889, 109; cf. 1892, 171).

[77] Another testimony (cf. Heim 1892, 333) for the painlessness of dying is given by Edward Whymper (1880, 79), reporting a nearly fatal fall during his attempt to climb the Matterhorn in 1863. He was "perfectly conscious of what was happening," but, "like a patient under chloroforin, experienced no pain," concluding that death by a

327, my trans.), and he sets out to provide evidence for concluding that "death from falls is, for the subject, a beautiful death" (336).

Heim reported that in his "initial" experience of 1871, in which he rushed, slid down a slope, and fell on a snow slab, he experienced a highly accelerated speed of thought reaching into the future—he imagined, for example, how the sad news of his death would be received by his relatives, and he "consoled them" in his thoughts. After that, Heim reports ([1892] 1972, 45–52), "I saw my whole past life take place in many images, as though on a stage at some distance from me. I saw myself as the chief character in the performance. Everything was transfigured as though by a heavenly light and everything was beautiful without grief, without anxiety, and without pain." Although we can identify the element of the panoramic life review, the out-of- [the-] body experience as an extracorporeal, autoscopic experience is not fully developed here. Surely, he reports that he could see himself from a distant point of view as the "actor" within certain scenes of his lived life, but there is no autoscopic point of view in which he could see himself—in "real time"—lying there in the snow. The report continues: "a godly silence traveled like glorious music through my soul. More and more a gloriously blue sky with pink and delicate violet cloudlets surrounded me—I floated [*schwebte*] without pain and gentle into the sky and could now see, while I flew through the air, that there was another snowfield below. [. . .] Then I heard my dull thud and my fall came to an end" (Heim 1892, 335, my trans.). Again, this is no proper out-of-body experience in the later sense, because he was actually falling over a belay and "flying," parallel to a rock wall, farther down. Accordingly, he recalled that he could sense "the beautiful, heavenly representations" only "as long as I flew through the air and was able to see and think" (336). Likewise, the element of out-of-body experiences is both missing in the reports of others, and, consequently, in Heim's systematized account.[78]

Heim holds that experiences unfolding while facing a sudden, life-threatening danger are homogenous, even if made in widely different situations: falls, car or train accidents, drowning, or in combat (cf. 327). Almost as much as 95% of these experiences share according to him the following elements, namely, no grief or despair, nor any "paralyzing fright of the sort that can happen in instances of lesser danger." Instead, there was

> rather calm seriousness, profound acceptance, and a dominant mental quickness and sense of surety. Mental activity became enormous, rising to a hundredfold velocity or intensity. The relationship of events and their probable outcomes were viewed with objective clarity, no confusion entered at all. Time became greatly

---

fall "is as painless an end as can be experienced. Whymper reports a life review, referring to similar phenomena in drowning, but no disembodied experience.

[78] American judge Samuel W. Cozzens (1874, 410–2) describes a "terrible fall" in quite similar terms, depicting the "wonderful harmony," the absence of fear, the life review, but no out-of-body experience. However, there is a faint allusion to religious metaculture: "I rejoiced that I was so soon to see with my own eyes the great mystery

expanded. The individual acted with lightening quickness in accord with his accurate judgment of his situation. In many cases there followed a sudden review of the individual's entire past; and finally, the person falling often heard beautiful music and fell in a superbly blue heaven [or sky, *Himmel*] containing roseate cloudlets. Then consciousness was permanently extinguished, usually at the moment of impact [. . .]. Apparently hearing is the last of the senses to be extinguished. (328–9, trans. Noyes and Kletti 1972)

Summarizing his experience more than 58 years after the event, Heim elaborated on his experience once again in letter to a Swiss theologian and psychoanalyst, Oskar Pfister. The latter had contacted him while writing an article on "shock fantasies" (see subsequent discussion). This time, Heim wrote, "I acted out my life, as though I were an actor on a stage upon which I looked down from practically the highest [*einer höheren*] gallery in the theatre. Both hero and onlooker, I was as though doubled" (quoted by Pfister 1931; trans. Noyes and Kletti 1981, 9).[79]

Here, the autoscopic, or more precise, heautoscopic perspective on himself as an "actor" and observer comes much more to the foreground. To put it in other words, while rephrasing it in the 1930s, Heim intensifies in his report an element of "depersonalized" and "extrasensory" experience, namely, to look "out of the body" upon oneself, which were, according to our interpretation, elements that gained currency in the esoteric discourse of the early 20th century. Searching for explicitly religious and spiritual elements in Heim's collection of near-death reports on the one hand, and spiritualist or occultist on the other, there is only one report of relevance, related by a "student of theology" who survived a railway accident. Heim quotes from his report (June 1891): While falling with the train from a bridge, "*a series of images showed me in quick progression all the beauty and love that I had experienced in this world, and in between resounded as a daunting melody the sermon which I had heard that morning of Mr Obersthelfer*: God is almighty, Heaven and Earth rest in his hand; to his will we must withstand. With this thought an infinite silence came to me" (Heim 1892, 332, italics in the orig.; my trans.). Apart from that, Heim himself utilizes a religiously loaded language at the end of his essay, speaking of "heavenly music" or a "feeling of peace and reconciliation," which must have been experienced by those who actually came to death in fatal falls. Death, he concludes, is accompanied by "blessed peace" for those who were finally "falling into their own sky/heaven [*Himmel*]" (337). In sum, these statements are not attributing paranormal qualities to the experiences themselves but display rather traditional religious beliefs, actualized in—or applied to—extreme situations.

---

concealed behind the veil [. . .]. I thought I heard the sound of many voices, in wonderful harmony, coming from the far-off distance."

[79] Interestingly, Heim himself mentions that by searching actively within one's own memory regarding the original event one will be exposed to the danger of being no longer able to "distinguish clearly between thoughts, which I have now about it, and the original apparitions" (quoted in Pfister 1931, 11).

The attempt, however, to locate the beginning of Heim's interest in these experiences uncovers an important complication. Although the overall conclusions about the general content of these experiences Heim could draw were based on his own two falls in 1871 and 1872 (cf. 329, 334), it becomes manifest from his article that he had been interested in those experiences already some years earlier. For providing a broader basis for his claims of the "uniformity" of the "dying experiences," he refers to interviews focused on those experiences with wounded soldiers, which he conducted in a military hospital in Hamburg as early as 1870 (cf. 328)—the year prior to his first fall! Indeed, in 1870 Heim had studied abroad, in Berlin, and traveled afterward to Northern Germany and Scandinavia.[80] The Franco-Prussian War began in mid-July 1870, and major battles were fought in the following five months. But why had Heim, a student of geology, been interested in experiences near death already in 1870? His own first fall of 1871 had happened—in the presence of his fellow mountaineers—five days before his habilitation lecture at the ETH Zurich. Yet, there is more evidence that Heim's interest in these phenomena preceded his own fall.[81] Heim wrote in 1892 that he has been fascinated by these accounts for "more than 25 years" (328), which refers back to 1867 (being 18 at that time). Of course, several different explanations seem to be possible to solve this riddle. Heim's report could, in principle, be affected by memory failure, that is, by transience, misattribution, or suggestibility (cf. Section 2.2.20). For the time being, I should, however, follow the hermeneutics of trust and lend credibility to Heim's reconstruction. In this case, we must assume that he had knowledge of such experiences predating his own "first" experience. Therefore, it is most plausible to conclude that he had learned of these experiences *through the reports of others*. It seems appropriate to assume that Heim was, at the time of his fall in 1871, well fitted in regard to what one may expect to experience in situations in which the individual is confronted with sudden, life-threatening danger. Even in the case of Heim, who argues with his own experiences made in truly existential and critical situations, we are forced to conclude that the reception of near-death reports preceded his own experiences, which had most likely not only formed his experiences but also his reporting of these. In other words, his first-hand experience was already a complex amalgamation of expectation and fulfillment.

As becomes obvious, Albert Heim did not present reports that included important elements of the Spiritualist–Occult or Gnostic–Esoteric metacultures. Likewise, even Christian narratives are sparse. Refraining, moreover, from any psychological or physiological explanation of these experiences, Heim's report and his oral presentations of these cases attracted nevertheless a lot of attention.

---

[80] In autumn 1869, we are informed, he matriculated at the University of Berlin; from April to September 1870, he went on a study trip to central and northern Europe (Brockmann-Jerosch et al. 1952, 16).

[81] Heim's visits to hospitals are mentioned by Martinović (2017, 108), but mistakenly placed in the year 1871.

2.2.20 EXPERIENCES OF IMMINENT DEATH AS DISCUSSED IN FRENCH PSYCHOLOGY (1895–1905)

Whereas Swiss and German psychologists, psychiatrists, and philosophers began to discuss Heim's collection more intensively from the 1920s onward up to the 1950s,[82] it sparked immediately a very lively debate among French philosophers and psychologists (cf. Alvarado 2011). Even though Moody popularized the term near-death experience in its current meaning, it was already in this context that a French philosopher and psychologist, Victor Egger (1848–1909), proposed a cognate French term, *expérience de mort imminente* [experience of imminent death]. Egger, parting with scientific psychology as it emerged at the end of the 19th century, was still occupied with unusual mental states such as "mesmeric somnambulism, mediumship, ambulatory automatisms, double and multiple personality, and sensory and motor hysterical disturbances" (Alvarado 2011, 66–7).[83] In a series of three successive essays, Egger discussed, in his first contribution of 1895, the feature of time experience in wake-up dreams and the life review [*vision panoramique*].[84] In his second contribution, *Le moi des mourants* ["The I of the Dying"], which appeared in 1896, he focused almost exclusively the vivid memory or life review, whereas out-of-body experiences are not mentioned.[85] Building on Féré (1889),[86] Winslow (1860), and Munk (1887), but, most prominently, on Heim's report as communicated in a French newspaper, he argued that if a sudden awareness of impending death arises, the "paralyzed" will no longer be able to translate his "I" [*moi*] into thoughts and concepts. Instead, he will revive a more fundamental stratum of his "I" in the form of a series of visual memories (cf. Egger 1895, 30).[87] According to Egger (1896a, 37), in situations of fatal falls or near drowning, the "idea of imminent and sudden death" [*l'idée de la mort imminente et soudaine*] provokes an alert, quick, or "lively I" [*moi vif*], which exactly consists of these nonintellectualized, yet "significant and rapid images." Death, [88] Egger holds, must arrive suddenly, because it is only then that images will appear—otherwise,

---

[82] Among others, Birnbaum 1920; Bozzano 1923; Pfister 1931; Jaspers 1946, 306; Fischer 1967; cf. Martinović 2012, 36.

[83] Alvarado points especially to the impact of the work of Théodule Ribot (1839–1916), *Les maladies de la mémoire* (1881). Ribot, a central figure in the emerging French psychology, wrote on "hypermnesia," or the exaltation of memories, observable in "acute fevers, ecstasy, hypnosis, and drowning" (Alvarado 2011, 67).

[84] Egger (1895, 55) points to a close relationship between opium-induced "visual dreams," wake-up dreams (Maury), and the vivid memories of people nearly drowned. According to his hypothesis, the "idée de la mort imminente peut provoquer un sentiment très vif du moi qui va cesser d'être, quelque chose comme le *qualis arlifex pereo*! attribué à Néron."

[85] The only passage alluding to out-of-body experiences is the summary of Montaigne, "Essays" (II,13), quoted and paraphrased in Egger 1896b, 345–6.

[86] Egger quotes Féré's study (1896, 26–7), relying on his part on material of Munk's study (1887).

[87] Cf. Le Maléfan 1995.

[88] It is only through the criticism of Sollier that Egger (cf. 1896b, 337–8) included "fear of death" in his considerations. Indeed, Sollier had underlined that "Egger's cases did not involve real death but instead the belief one was going to die" (Alvarado 2011, 71).

there will be enough time for consciousness to trigger not only images, but "translate the I into concepts and into propositions" (30).

Interestingly, however, Egger argues that neither a "dying optimist," in whom the idea of death is absent, nor a mystic, "happy to be shortly released from his bodily life" (31), will experience the "lively I." For the quick images of the memories to appear, one needs to "foresee one's own death with regret, without being able to avoid it." (31). Nevertheless, Egger observes a strong connection of the phenomenon to the individual's conscience. When death arrives, Egger holds with various Greek and Roman philosophers, nothing will last but the merits the individual had acquired in his life course, and, in the case of an unjust life, in consequence, demerit (cf. 36). Therefore the soul is reduced to a certain degree of good or bad—no more than a value, a quantity: "There is nothing more common in the modern than that conception. The religious, but not the mystic, soul— the soul morally religious, skilled in judging itself through the practice of examining its conscience, considers life as a preparation for death—and death, for it, is the moment at which it will appear before a God of justice" (36). In consequence, religious spiritualism will in essence be moral, and the religious quality will be immediately present in the "I"—especially, as it seems, in the religious "I." In his third contribution he criticized Féré's conclusion that imminent, life-threatening danger will causally lead to the belief in an otherworldly judgment. Instead, "everything carefully considered, I believe with good grace that there is only a 'harmony in facts' between the natural play of phenomena of consciousness and the beliefs, or religious institutions. Religion commands and moralizes a natural phenomenon" (Egger 1896b, 353).[89] In a final reply, he reconfirmed his conclusion that the panoramic life review is not only analogous to dream consciousness, but is actually a "dream" by itself, that is, constituted by "visual images" (337). Here, Egger adapts the idea that the feeling of happiness in the "truly" or "falsely dying" (les mourants faux, i.e., people with "fear of death" only, cf. 340), a moment that Heim had repeatedly stressed, should be explained as an "anesthesia" or "analgesia": "Consciousness has an abhorrence of emptiness, and the anesthesia will provoke the rise of memories" (340).[90]

---

[89] This connection is also present in Fuller's study on *The Art of Memory* (1898, 24). Here, the panoramic life review is introduced with reference to Steve Brodie, "the noted high-bridge jumper," describing the phenomenon "while making his famous leap from the Brooklyn Bridge." The ca. 130-ft-jump, supposedly in 1886, is still a matter of controversy. Fuller holds it to be an "almost universal experience" of nearly drowning, in which memory grasps "with a marvelous vigor the deeds of the life which seems about to end." In fact, the term "deeds" points to Fuller's moral trajectory, commenting that "by some mysterious compelling intuition" the sufferer is in such situation able to realize the "right or wrong of each particular act" (cf. the quote of Fuller in Atkinson 1908, 29).

[90] A prominent example of the philosophical reception of Egger had been Henri Bergson. In his *Matière et Mémoire* (1896), he discussed it as an "exaltation of memory" of the nearly drowned, or in somnambulistic states, holding that even the "smallest circumstances" are recalled "in the very order in which they occurred" (Bergson 1911, 200; on his interpretation cf. Poulet 2011 [1963]).

In the same Naturalist metaculture of French psychologists, Henri Piéron (1881–1964) focused on a number of contributions, especially on classifying panoramic reviews in those that consisted of simultaneous and those that displayed successive and extremely fast images. A significant move of Piéron's psychology (cf. 1901, 1902, 1903) is the recognition of a "subconscious" level. Treating "illusory" sensations of dying, such as flying, may, as Piéron suggests (1902, 616), show on a physiological basis of the prolonged stretched body position, an "anesthesia of the part of the body lying on the bed." In the same and well-established framework of interpretation, French physician Paul A. Sollier (1861–1933) dealt with cases of "external autoscopy" as "hallucinations" (Sollier 1903, 20–3; cf. Dieguez 2013, 96). Equally, Sollier offered a naturalist psychological explanation of the panoramic life review.[91] In this naturalist strand, the Danish surgeon Oscar Bloch, summarizing the evidence in his voluminous treatment of "Death" (cf. [1903] 1909, II, 306, cf. 412–32), comes to the conclusion that the life review will appear only in cases in which the individual is able to reflect on the existential threat. In the majority of cases, he argues, consciousness is lost too fast, and no life review—a phenomenon of no significance anyway—appears.

Finally, noteworthy in this context is a crucial concept that became a prominent element for discussing near-death phenomena, namely, the concept of "depersonalization." This term, designating the feelings and perceptions to be detached and emotionless in a universe void of meaning, had been introduced in 1898 by the French psychiatrist Ludovic Dugas (1857–1942). According to his own testimony, he had extracted the concept from the Swiss philosopher Henri-Frédéric Amiel (1821–1881).[92] The latter had included descriptions of his feelings of alienation and apathy in a very extensive diary, in which we can read in an entry of July 8, 1880:

> My mind is the empty frame of a thousand vanished images. [. . .] I find myself regarding existence as though from beyond the tomb, from another world; all is strange to me; I am, as it were, outside my own body and individuality; I am *depersonalized*, detached, cut adrift. Is this madness? No. Madness means the impossibility of recovering one's normal balance after the mind has thus played truant among alien forms of being, and followed Dante to invisible worlds. [. . .] I am but making psychological investigations. (Amiel [1882] 1903, II, 304–5)

---

[91] Sollier (1896, 306; cf. Alvarado 2011, 71) argues that in accidents, all attention focuses "on what may cause death," a "distraction" that induces "anesthesia and analgesia," explaining the experienced bliss and well-being. However, at the same time we make a violent effort to escape death, "searching, while we bundle all our energy, that what may be conducive for survival" ("*nous cherchons ce qui pourrait nous sauver, en même temps que nous rassemblons toute notre énergie*").

[92] On Amiel, Dugas, and the concept of depersonalization see Simeon and Abugel 2008, 10–1, 128–34.

Most significantly, Amiel explains his depersonalized state with a viewpoint out of the body, yet, a reversible state of no special religious significance—though Amiel comments in an earlier entry, that "absolute disinterestedness is only reached in that perfect humility which tramples the self under foot for the glory of God" (9). I should add that Amiel also included thoughts on the life review in his diary.[93]

This concept of self-alienation and detached experience will be described only three years later by the German psychiatrist and anthropologist Erwin von Bälz (1849–1913), who took residency in Japan in 1876 and taught for many years Western medicine at the Tokyo Imperial University. In a contribution on "paralysis of emotion" ([*Über Emotionslähmung*], 1901) describing the phenomenon of depersonalization, he included a personal experience near death made during an earthquake in Tokyo in 1894. Being inside a building, he reports, everything trembled, windows broke, but instead of instantly getting out, he experienced a sudden change in his psyche: "*Every higher emotional life was extinguished*, every compassion for others, every empathy for possible misfortune, even interest for threatened family members or my own life had been, *though fully clear minded*, disappeared; it seemed to me that I was thinking more smoothly and faster [. . .] than ever before. [. . .] I felt like a Nietzschean Übermensch, responsible to no one [. . .], observing the horrible operations around me with the same cold attention with which one follows a fascinating experiment in physics. Then, as suddenly as it came about, the abnormal state disappeared and made room for my former self" (Bälz 1901, 718; my trans., italics in orig.).

The salient feature of this description is, without question, the coldness of the observer and his pathos of distance, beyond good and evil (cf. 718), to use Nietzsche's famous formulas. It seems as if the—especially Christian—taboo to show an "amoral" disengagement toward others in life-threatening situations had disappeared in the age of "nihilism." Bälz frames these reports within the Naturalist metaculture. He equals the phenomenon with epilepsy and "psycho-sensitive anesthesia;" being a temporary dissociation of emotion and "consciousness" (720). As a metaphor for this state, he uses the image of an arrested watch, starting again when the clockwork is wound up. However, his

---

[93] Taking his departure with the more traditional "book-of-life" metaphor, he finally comes to speculate on the theory of the universal copresence of personal memories at death. In an entry of 1874, we read: "Consciousness seems to be like a book, in which the leaves turned by life successively cover and hide each other in spite of their semi-transparency; but although the book may be open at the page of the present, the wind, for a few seconds, may blow back the first pages into view. And at death will these leaves cease to hide each other, and shall we see all our past at once? Is death the passage from the successive to the simultaneous—that is to say, from time to eternity? [. . .] If so, death would be like the arrival of a traveller at the top of a great mountain, whence he sees spread out before him the whole configuration of the country [. . .]. To be able to overlook one's own history, to divine its meaning in the general concert and in the divine plan, would be the beginning of eternal felicity. [. . .] We had seen nothing but our own little path in the mist; and suddenly a marvelous panorama and boundless distances would open before our dazzled eyes. Why not?" (Amiel [1885] 1903, II, 166–7; French orig., II, 172; quoted, e.g., in Bozzano 1931, 95–6).

main intention is to argue that this state is beyond morals, and even perpetrators should not be made responsible for deeds done while caught in this "abnormal consciousness" (720). Obviously, we can witness that also writers of the first decades of the 20th century began to describe protagonists hit by the paralysis of emotion.[94]

To summarize, the discussion of French psychologists and physicians shows how they struggled with physiological explanations of the life-review phenomenon. Although it was still treated separately, and not in connection to out-of-body reports, it assumed an increasingly pathological quality. Egger reasoned occasionally on the possible religious dimensions of these reported experiences, whereas Féré, Piéron, and Sollier argued that these phenomena are malfunctions of the nervous system. Therefore we may subsume this group under the heading of Naturalist metaculture.[95] Moreover, through their discussion French psychologists and physicians made the phenomena of near death ever more popular, finding their readers also in Gnostic–Esoteric and Spiritualist–Occult metacultures. The latter, however, read their accounts selectively as pointing to the "scientific" attestation of these phenomena while at the same time ignoring any "reductionist" explanation. In other words, following the "scientification" of psychology, medicine, and religion, Occultists and Spiritualists in the second half of the 19th century became increasingly aware of the persuasive power at their disposal if they could refer to the latest scientific research attesting to the existence of paranormal phenomena. Such a claim has, for example, by the famous theosophist Helena Blavatsky been laid on Féré in her work on mental states of the dying, as we will see in the next chapter.

---

[94] We may mention the literary protagonists of André Gide, *The Vatican Swindle* ([*Les caves du Vatican*], 1914); or, though later, Albert Camus' *The Stranger* ([*L'Étranger*], 1942).

[95] The same holds true for the famous psychologist Alfred Binet (1857–1911), discussing the phenomenon too (1896).

2.3

The Integration of Theosophical Narratives on Travels

of the "Spiritual Body" (ca. 1860–1905)

AS IS WELL known, the soul's departure from the body and its journeying to various realms have been reported by Christian monks and nuns in several medieval sources. However, these "travels" were usually not connected to near-death situations—they are reported to have happened in a variety of life-world situations. According to my observation, reports of "out-of-body" experiences—including autoscopic visions of one's own body, extensive spirit travels through familiar surroundings, and the often "regrettable" return into the body—were handed down in their own right, in parallel but often overlapping currents of Christian and Spiritualist–Occult metacultures. Because of their special practical importance in Spiritualist and Esoteric thought, "astral travels"—and drug experiences—slowly began to fuse with the emerging near-death discourse. On a broader scale, this confluence, as we could show in the accounts of Ludlow, Paist, Davis, and others in previous chapters, occurred—in a remarkably parallel development in Europe and North America—in the 1860s. In this chapter, it will be our task to substantiate this claim and to analyze the factors that contributed to this junction.

The dominant model of early and premodern Christian heavenly journeys does not include autoscopic elements because of a general lack of interest, if not clear "repugnance"[1] of the individual in respect to his or her own body. Zaleski (1987, 48; cf. Rau

---

[1] This same repugnance can be found in the "forced" encounter with his own body of the Irish monk Furseus (died ca. 648) in 633. Of him it is reported (*Vita sancti Fursei*, seventh cent.) that in his vision angels commanded him to "acknowledge" and reenter into his own body. He, however, "shrank back as if encountering an unknown corpse; he did not want to come closer" [*ille quasi ignotum cadaver timens noluit se idem adpropinquare*]. But

1968, 42) quotes, for example, a letter of Boniface of the early eighth century, detailing a vision of the monk of Wenlock reporting "that his departure from the body was like the lifting of a veil. From his liberated vantage point, he saw clearly that his body was alien to his spirit: 'His own body, while he was outside it, was so exceedingly horrid to him that in all those visions he saw nothing so hateful, nothing so contemptible, nothing except for the demons and the malodorous fire, that exuded such a dreadful stench as his own body.'" Boniface indeed narrates that the monk had told him that his body, induced by pain, "was suddenly deprived of its weight,"[2] and that, after the removal of earthly flesh, "the whole world had been united in his sight, so that he could survey in one view all countries, people, and oceans."[3] The letter goes on to narrate an extensive vision with various otherworldly topoi until angels command him to return into his body and to reveal all that he saw even to sceptics. Yet, the passage just quoted does not report the specific element of an autoscopic vision of the experiencer's own body from above. It is, as said, merely a general declaration of body abhorrence.[4] Boniface reports that he detested even his brothers for taking care of his abhorred body (cf. Rau 1968, 42).

To review a typical early modern example, we turn to the report of Hemme Hayen (1633–1689?), a Low German peasant and Protestant mystic visionary, who communicated a "biography" (*Levens-Loop*) replete with reports of visions. It attracted a lot of attention, especially after it had been translated from Dutch into German in 1717.[5] Hayen reported: "I was lying in bed, in the morning: it was already bright daylight and I was already fully awake. My mind lay in deep contemplation and in the rapture I thereupon experienced, my new man, as if side by side at my bedside, departed from the old one, leaving me lying on the bed like a dead log. Turning round, I therefore saw my natural body lying dead. But I myself came once again into dazzling light" (Anonymous [Hayen] 1714 [1717], quoted in Hampe 1979, 34). Hayen, as seems obvious, reports a self-induced ("deep contemplation") extraction of a "new man" now able to see his bodily counterpart as if being a dead corpse. Two things are noteworthy here: First, there is no mention of any near-death situation, and second, it is embedded in an intentional

---

then he realized that the body's breast opened, and, guided by angels, he was without further ado suddenly back in his body (Latin text in Ciccarese 1985, 302).

[2] "*corporis gravidine subito exutum fuisse*" (letter 10, Rau 1968, 30).

[3] "*conspectum universum collectum fuisse mundum, ut cunctas terrarium partes et populous et maria sub uno aspect contueretur*" (Rau 1968, 30).

[4] Shushan holds (2009, 143–4) that extracorporeal experiences in ancient texts with "corpse encounter" are thematically similar to the graphic descriptions of the fates of corpses, and second, to the shamanic feature of transformation through death or dismemberment of the body. Even though he admits that there is a difference between a "corpse encounter" in this world or in the beyond, it is analogous if we "allow for a mythologizing of the concept." Obviously, this mythologizing enables him to declare "the realization of one's own physical death also being the realization of the survival and transcendence of death" (144–5).

[5] German translation in Reitz 1717, 169–99; cf. Kanne 1842, 23.

realization of a spiritual rapture of a Protestant mystic—in other words, is part of the Christian metaculture.[6]

2.3.1 VISIONARY EXCURSIONS AND "ASTRAL PROJECTION"

A report (1860) by Scottish American social reformer and politician Robert Dale Owen, son of the visionary early socialist and entrepreneur Robert Owen, shows how descriptions of autoscopic visions by "clairvoyants" slowly began to fuse with experiences near death. Owen[7] describes, under the heading "the visionary excursion," a case of a woman who reported to have experienced the following situation in the year 1857: In one night,

> suddenly awaking to consciousness, she felt herself as if standing by the bedside and looking upon her own body, which lay there by the side of her sleeping husband. Her first impression was that she had died suddenly; and the idea was confirmed by the pale and lifeless look of the body [. . .]. She gazed at it with curiosity for some time, comparing its dead look with that of the fresh countenances of her hus-band and of her slumbering infant [. . .]. For a moment she experienced a feeling of relief that she had escaped the pangs of death; but the next she reflected what a grief her death would be to the survivors, and then came a wish that she could have broken the news to them gradually. While engaged in these thoughts, she felt herself carried to the wall of the room, with a feeling that it must arrest her farther progress. But no: she seemed to pass through it into the open air. (Owen 1860, 256)

Soon thereafter, she becomes aware that her presence is not perceived by others. A bit later, "she found herself in the bedchamber of an intimate friend," residing in another town, to whom she talks. But then her seeing and hearing cease. The next morning, she wakes up as usual. However, she and her husband, after being told of her experience, discover a few days later that her friend was able to reproduce details of the visit, bearing therefore the quality of a real "visionary excursion." Owen, however, admits that "it ought to be stated that this lady has from her childhood habitually seen apparitions" (257).[8] Yet, as previously said, this description still lacks a clear "trigger"—the "death-x-pulse." On the other hand, there is no information of any intention to actively leave the body. A most

---

[6] As seen previously, spiritual journeys, most of them unintentional, were still an important topos of Christian mystics in the 19th century. Several cases of "ecstatic journeys" are, e.g., recounted in Perty (1861) or Splittgerber (1866). Perty (1872, I, 325) quotes a "somnambule" who holds that she had been able to see that the dying in general will in some moments recall their whole life, and that the disembodied spirit will look with a "short, but shivering gaze" back to the body, filled with repugnance [*Ekel*].

[7] Strangely, Owen does not refer to other cases of drowning so common in spiritual literature of the 1860s.

[8] Cf. on Owen: Alvarado 2009.

prominent upsurge of the Gnostic–Esoteric and Spiritualist–Occult metacultures that paved the way for these innovations can be seen in Éliphas Lévi (pseudonym of Alphonse-Louis Constant, 1810–1875). After his "strong if intermittent vocation for the Catholic ministry" (Goodrick-Clarke 2008, 192), he became a dominant protagonist in magic and occultism, a prolific writer who finally popularized the term "l'ésotérisme" in France. An important feature of Lévi's portrayal of "magic" and his idiosyncratic synthesis of the Gnostic–Esoteric metaculture is the "astral light" [lumière astrale], a concept that he uses to explain the relationship of the individual to an all-penetrating essence.[9] This concept shaped, among others, Helena Blavatsky's theosophical ideas and spiritual practices connected to "astral projection"—the forerunner of what later will be called "out-of-[the-] body experience."

For Lévi, the "astral light" or "vital light" is a subtle formative fluid (derived from Mesmer's concept of an invisible, magnetic fluid, cf. Lévi [1860] 1922, 396–9) that is apprehended and assimilated by the individual according to his or her individual capability or "clairvoyant sensibility." It is, moreover, the source of all apparitions, extraordinary visions, and all intuitive phenomena that are peculiar to ecstasy or madness (cf. 18).[10] The appropriation of this "light," which is manifest also in heat, light, magnetism, and electricity, "is one of the greatest phenomena which can be studied by science. It may be understood in a day to come that seeing is actually speaking and that the consciousness of light is a twilight of eternal life in being" (18–19). However, the individual's spiritual goal should be to manipulate these forces within consciousness itself, which, in consequence, will manifest a change in the outer world. In fact, Lévi already stresses the centrality of the "will" for all magico-mental purposes. The individual can misuse magic power, but it can also be "overcharged" by the "astral light" that reveals itself as a potentially dangerous (magical) power, causing hallucinations and deceptive visions.[11] We may note in passing, that Lévi, too, mentions the ambivalent powers of hashish and opium (cf. Strube 2016, 553). By the forces of "attraction" and "projection," however, everything is created and subsists (Lévi 1861, I, 153).

In our context, the most principal elements of Lévi's concept of magic agency are his descriptions of a projection of this astral light. Astral light, as previously said, can act

---

[9] On the genealogy of this concept, cf. Strube 2016, 527–9.

[10] The astral light is "la source de toutes les apparitions, de toutes les visions extraordinaires et de tous les phénomènes intuitifs qui sont propres à la folie ou à l'extase" (Lévi 1860, 21). Cf. on the astral light Owen 2004b, 149–51.

[11] "A particular phenomenon occurs when the brain is congested or overcharged by Astral Light; sight is turned inward […], night falls on the external and real world, while fantastic brilliance shines on the world of dreams; even the physical eyes experience a slight quivering and turn up inside the lids. The soul then perceives by means of images the reflection of its impressions and thoughts" (Lévi 1922, 18). Astral Light may even form natural "whirlpools and waterspouts, so to speak, which levitate the heaviest bodies and can sustain them in the air for a length of time proportionate to the force of the projection" (127). Elsewhere, Lévi argues with the "taming power" of human "projections of the Astral Light" (61). For Lévi's ideas, cf. Baier 2009, I, 267–7; Strube 2016.

upon the individual and evoke clairvoyant and "mesmeric" visions.[12] If now the soul separates or departs from the body, Lévi discloses in his *Histoire de la magie* ([1860] 1922, 111) with reference to "kabbalist" sages, it will do so only in its "astral form."[13] The term projection, in this context, assumes the quality of a spontaneous "double," a "sudden projection of astral larvae" (cf. 230). Although Lévi uses the term projection in mesmerist contexts,[14] it had a long-standing career in alchemy, denoting the central attempt of transmuting a lower substance into a higher form.[15] Lévi stated that hallucinations and apparitions can be explained by "astral intoxication,"[16] but he neither referred to near-death situations, nor did he use the term astral projection in its later, more technical sense of emitting a disembodied spirit, or mental travel, respectively.[17] John P. Deveney (1997, 3) argued that the mid-19th-century spiritualism "totally lacked the idea," and attributed its introduction to British medium and occultist writer Emma Hardinge (1860, 2), mentioning the practice as early as 1860. However, as we can see, it was a longer process through various steps, including, for example, figurative ideas of Andrew J. Davis and others.

---

[12] In this context, Lévi (1861 [1856], 61) speaks, interestingly, of a "moving panorama of the astral light" ("*panorama mobile de la lumière astrale*").

[13] A second strand speaks of "Astral Spirits," i.e., "sensitive" or "corporeal souls" which "at death wandereth in the air, or near the body" (Webster 1677, 319–20; cf. Hibbert 1825, 413–18, Horst 1830, II, 88, 134), reaching back to antique tripartite conceptualizations of body, soul, spirit, transmitted through renaissance thinkers. Cf. the opinion of Caelius Rhodiginus (1469–1525) conveyed by John Beaumont, *Treatise of Spirits* (1705, 194; with reference), that Socrates was able to perceive his spirit not "by the Sense of his Body, but, as the Platonicks were fully perswaded, by the Sense of the Æthe-astreal Body lying hid within us."

[14] "Organised bodies are sympathetic or antipathetic to one another, by reason of their particular equilibrium. Sympathetic bodies may cure each other, restoring their equilibrium mutually. This capacity of bodies to equilibrate one another by the attraction or projection of the first matter, was called magnetism by Mesmer" (Lévi 1922, 397). Moreover, Lévi ([1861] 1959, 105) defines "animal magnetism" as "the action of one plastic medium upon another, in order to dissolve or coagulate it. By augmenting the elasticity of the vital light and its force of projection, one sends it forth as far as one will, and withdraws it completely loaded with images; but this operation must be favoured by the slumber of the subject."

[15] Projection was the designation of alchemists for the process of "throwing or strewing of the Stone powder onto a base metal, which is thereupon allegedly transmuted into gold" (Haage 2006, 17).

[16] Lévi ([1861] 1959, 113) argues: "somnambulism is slumber borrowing its phenomena from waking; hallucination is waking still partially subjected to the astral intoxication of slumber. Our fluidic bodies attract and repulse each other following laws similar to those of electricity. It is this which produces instinctive sympathies and antipathies. They thus equilibrate each other, and for this reason hallucinations are often contagious; abnormal projections change the luminous currents [...]. Such is the history of strange apparitions and popular prodigies. Thus are explained the miracles of the American mediums and the hysterics of table-turners, who reproduce in our own times the ecstasies of whirling dervishes."

[17] In that respect, Hardinge Britten established in the work *Ghost Land* (1876, 5) a somewhat stronger connection, though it is cladded into a "merely fictional" account of an unnamed author (cf. 22–6, 110–12, 185). On this work, see Deveney 1997, 8.

2.3.2 BLAVATSKY AND THE SYNTHESIS OF ASTRAL PROJECTION AND EXPERIENCES NEAR DEATH

The concrete synthesis of connecting ideas of astral projection and unintentional experiences out of the body while near death, decisive for the modern near-death discourse, seems to us to be most centrally the achievement of Helena Petrovna Blavatsky (1831–1891), who founded, together with Henry Steel Olcott (1832–1907), the Theosophical Society in 1875. As Deveney demonstrates, Blavatsky and the early comembers of the Theosophical Society were particularly interested in astral travel, which for them also meant to experiment with "magnetic" and somnambule mental states leading to these extracorporeal experiences. It became an often-expressed idea that, in the words of Hardinge Britten, with proper training, "there are no phenomena produced by disembodied spirits, which may not be effected by the still embodied spirit" ([1876], quoted in Deveney 1997, 4). Blavatsky draws in her first major work, the two-volume opus *Isis Unveiled* (1877), extensively on Lévi and other works of spiritualist and occult scholars (cf. Strube 2016, 592–3). This led her to view astral projection or the "ethereal travel" of the "double" as the essential practice, the "very last and highest possible achievement of magic," as Blavatsky said in an interview.[18] In her early works, she argued that the nature of men is threefold, possessing a physical body, an astral body (the "spiritual body," spoken of by St. Paul, cf. Blavatsky 1877 [7]), and a soul. "By the separation of the astral and the physical bodies the latter is left inert and lifeless, while the former becomes almost omnipotent" ([7]). Later on in the interview, Blavatsky not only pointed to demonstrations of "Hindoo" and Buddhist practitioners capable of this separation, but also, the reporter narrates, provided a practical demonstration of a friend's "astral body" shadow that passed across the window.

In *Isis Unveiled*, Blavatsky argues that a medium's projection of an entire "double" or "astral body"[19] does not imply that those mediums are usually "diseased." Pointing again to the capabilities of "adepts of Eastern magic," Blavatsky (1877, I, 596; cf. II, 588) declares: "An adept can not only project and make visible a hand, a foot, or any other portion of his body, but the whole of it. We have seen one do this, in full day, while his hands and feet were being held by a skeptical friend whom he wished to surprise. Little by little the whole astral body oozed out like a vapory cloud, until before us stood two forms, of which the second was an exact duplicate of the first, only slightly more shadowy." It is indeed remarkable that Blavatsky explains the astral body is an exact replica of the physical body, and visible to others as a double in every detail, even with

---

[18] In the *Hartford Weekly Times*, 1877, [7], cf. Deveney 1997, 17.

[19] Deveney (1997, 2) points to the fact that the history of astral travel has yet to be written. In his study on the respective teachings of the early Theosophical Society, he argues that astral travel encompasses four sorts of phenomena: the evocation of a "double" by another; the unwilled projection of the double in stress or dream—to which near-death cases obviously belong—, willed projection by training, and the "cohabitation" of the astral body in another person's body.

the same cloth—we may say: the astral body's late Victorian decency (cf. Wiltse 1889, subsequently quoted). Within the framework of the Gnostic–Esoteric metaculture as previously defined, Blavatsky (1877, I, 596) holds that the "materialized form" of the astral projection, the "spirit entity," will experience an increase of intellectual abilities, its perceptions being far more acute and developed. For practitioners able to enter the "astral plane," a spiritual dimension not controlled by laws of physics is reached, but at the same time, the "liberated double" may see the world as if still embodied. Far from being only a curious fact, astral projection is held to be a truly religious practice of vital importance— a "royal road" leading to encounters with other pure souls, spirits, and finally, to the liberating unification with the universal divine principle (cf. Baier 2009, I, 294). And again, it is practitioners of various sects "in China, Siam, Tartary, Thibet, Kashmir, and British India, which devote their lives to the cultivation of 'supernatural powers' "—who actually possess the power "to transport themselves from one place to another, *however distant*, with speed and facility." For Blavatsky (1877, I, 618–19), this is nothing unusual but simply "the projection of the astral entity, in a more or less corporealized form." Yet, the astral body, or the phantom double, may not simply be identified with a death-surviving soul—the true goal being yet to realize the pure, absolute spirituality beyond body confinements. Obviously, Blavatsky experienced being out of the body quite commonly, and we may add that it is well attested that in her early years, she also had made use of hashish (and an undisclosed "potion")[20] that enabled her to visit distant friends by means of projection. However, descriptions of "Occult Sciences" became, as Deveney shows (1997, 48–55), in 1876 within the Theosophical Society a matter to be kept secret.

This notwithstanding, it is in the context of a psychotropic experiment that she also describes an autoscopic and heautoscopic (*Doppelgänger*) experience. In a letter, we read what she experienced after fasting severely in order to see visions of spirits. "Suddenly," she writes, "I caught a glimpse of one of the most disgusting scenes of my own life, and I felt as if I was out of my body, looking at it with repulsion whilst it was walking, talking, [...] and sinning." In the second night, she "concentrated into a single prayer," and again, a double appears. "Suddenly this second me spoke to my body, 'Look at me!' My body looked at it and saw the half of this second me was as black as jet, [...] and only the top of the head perfect white, brilliant, luminous. And again I myself spoke to my body: 'When you become as bright as this small part of your head, you will be able to see what is seen by others, by the purified [...]. Make yourself clean'. And here I awoke" (not dated, quoted in Deveney 1997, 22). Very interestingly, we may note the flavor of abhorrence toward her own body, a typical element of early Indian and early

---

[20] In 1879, she even declared that proof of "conditional immortality" was, for neophytes in India, Greece, or Egypt, only be given in a "Great Mystery," when a "sacred beverage" enables them "to leave the body" (quoted in Deveney 1997, 55). Cf., on hashish and mescaline as facilitating out-of-body experiences in Theosophy, Owen 2004b, 151, and Hanegraaff 2017, 12–14.

Christian ascetic discourse on the body, which seem to combine in her ascetic endeavors to enter the spirit world.

For Blavatsky, "astral projection" seemed to have been largely a technique of intensive imagination (cf. Hanegraaff 2017, 14; 17). It was, however, soon common belief that astral projection may not only happen while sleeping or in a mesmerized "trance" state, but that the separation from the solid physical body may happen also under the influence of drugs or in accidents, the latter being a link to near-death reports. Indeed, as early as 1877, Blavatsky was already conversant with the narratives of the "life review." In *Isis Unveiled*, we read (1877, 179) on the phenomenon of memory, "the despair of the materialist":

> That flash of memory which is traditionally supposed to show a drowning man every long-forgotten scene of his mortal life—as the landscape is revealed to the traveller by intermittent flashes of lightning—is simply the sudden glimpse which the struggling soul gets into the silent galleries where his history is depicted in imperishable colors. The well-known fact—one corroborated by the personal experience of nine persons out of ten—that we often recognize as familiar to us, scenes, and landscapes, and conversations, which we see or hear for the first time, and sometimes in countries never visited before, is a result of the same causes. Believers in reïncarnation [*sic*] adduce this as an additional proof of our antecedent existence in other bodies.

Indeed, for Theosophy, the life review, here combined with the "déja-vu," soon became a strong corroboration for the fact of reincarnation. In their reception of Indian theories, Blavatsky and other theosophists expressed their belief that the reincarnating entity may pass after "death" through a kind of temporary heaven, called "devachan." Yet, if re-embodiment is due, it is immediately after its "birth" attracted to a physical body. This new body is entered as early as the child starts to breathe. In this context of "death" and reincarnation, the "Q&A" section of the key journal *The Theosophist* establishes a significant link to near-death narratives. An inquirer asks, "Is there not a Review of all Karma good and bad, before the disembodied entity with a balance of good passes into the Devachanic existence?" The painful review, the inquirer reasons, may probably by a hellish realm ("Narakam"), whereas a "pleasurable" review might be the paradisiacal "Swargam" of the Hindus. To this, the editors, namely Blavatsky and Olcott,[21] reply: "No. The 'Ego' cannot review all his past experiences before it obtains the state of a Buddha. At the point of death, however, a man may see all of his past life as in a panoramic view."[22]

---

[21] Olcott (1880, 265), too, emphatically advocated the practice of astral projection: "Let him study Mesmerism and master its methods until he can lounge his subject into so deep a sleep that the body is made to seem dead, and the freed soul can be sent, wheresoever he wills about the Earth or among the stars. Then he will see the separate reality of the body and its dweller." On Olcott's practice of astral projection, cf. Deveney 1997, 23–6.

[22] Anonymous 1884, 301.

The editors' reference to the Buddha's awakening is indeed remarkable—as is well known, a prominent feature of the supposedly autobiographical accounts the Buddha conveyed of his awakening implies the knowledge of his manifold former existences (alluded to, for example, in Alfred P. Sinnett's *Esoteric Buddhism* of 1883, to be discussed in the subsequent chapter).

In the *Key to Theosophy*, Blavatsky describes the life review in the still-more-emphatic terms of a Gnostic–Esoteric cognition[23] and declares that this will happen to everyone who dies. However, "very good and holy men" will see "not only the life they are leaving, but even several preceding lives in which were produced the causes that made them what they were in the life just closing. They recognize the law of Karma in all its majesty and justice" (Blavatsky 1889b, 162). Even more explicitly, in her article "Memory in the Dying," Blavatsky (1889a, 125) refers to Féré's recent deliberations on the mental states of the dying. It will need only two of Féré's examples, she adds, "to show how scientifically correct [...] the teachings we receive from our Eastern Masters" are (125). These teachings were communicated in the form of the "Mahatma-letters" (see Section 2.3.3). Quoting Féré's case of the Fleming retrieving his early childhood memories, Blavatsky rephrases: "as in a retrospective panorama, all his life, even to the trifling fact of his having borrowed twenty years back a few francs from a friend," which, she states, underscores that this memory "did not emanate from his *physical* brain alone, but rather from his spiritual memory, that of the *Higher Ego* (Manas or the re-incarnating individuality). [...] *The* EGO *is almost omniscient in its immortal nature*" (126). Although she does not mention Féré's naturalist explanation of these phenomena, she posits that these examples show how "divine insight" is awakened on the deathbed. Again, the "panoramic memory" near death—especially the accessibility of long-lost memories in these situations—and also, as Blavatsky is eager to add, in "somnambulist" states, will serve to disprove any reductionist interpretations of the brain: "If indeed the physical brain is of only a limited area," she reasons, "the field for the containment of rapid flashes of unlimited and infinite thought, neither will nor thought can be said to be generated *within* it" (128). Thus it is impossible that ideas of the infinite and absolute are "within *our* brain capacities"—they are only "projected" or mirrored in our "Spiritual consciousness" (128).

---

[23] Every man, she holds, sees at the solemn moment of death "the whole of his past life marshalled before him, in its minutest details. For one short instant the *personal* becomes one with the *individual* and all-knowing *Ego*. But this instant is enough to show to him the whole chain of causes which have been at work during his life. He sees and now understands himself as he is, unadorned by flattery or self-deception. He reads his life, remaining as a spectator looking down into the arena he is quitting; he feels and knows the justice of all the suffering that has overtaken him" (Blavatsky 1889b, 162; cf. Besant 1893, 24, describing after the quotation the floating astral double).

2.3.3 INTENTIONAL ASTRAL PROJECTION, AFTER-DEATH EXPERIENCES, AND THE RECEPTION OF INDIAN YOGA

How the founding members of the Theosophical Society experimented with astral projection can be seen in an interesting report that seems to try hard to let the exceptional event emerge from an everyday situation. According to the testimony of William Quan Judge (1851–1896), member of the Theosophical Society of New York, the following happened:

> One evening at Mme. Blavatsky's I lay down for the purpose of trying to get out of my body. In a few minutes, those present said afterwards, I snored very loudly; but with me it was different. I could not recognise any interval of unconsciousness, or moment of drowsiness. It appeared to me that I was awake and had risen up in order to go out into the hall; that there was a handkerchief over my eyes as I had placed it upon lying down. An endeavour to throw off the obstruction was unsuccessful, so out I went into the hall, in what I thought was my body, going into the kitchen, where by a violent effort I threw off the handkerchief, when immediately I found myself where I had lain down, listening to the laughter of those who had heard my unmusical snore. Now here I have to take the evidence of others: they say that while my body snored, my double, simulacrum, or *scin lecca*, or whatever you may name it, i.e. a visible counterfeit presentment of me, could be seen walking down the passage to the kitchen. (quoted in Oxon 1877, 247–8; cf. Crow 2013, 21)[24]

As Deveney (cf. 1997, 18–19) explains, the expression *scin lecca* [shining body] had been introduced by novelist Edward G. Bulwer-Lytton (1803–1873) as a designation for the double in his *A Strange Story* (1861); later in Theosophy, the astral body was, in addition, designated with the Sanskrit term *māyāvi-rūpa*, that is, the "illusion body" or "manifestation body."

In his lecture to initiated members, Judge, however, makes clear that the occultist may not only pass through the "mysterious portal at whose door we stand," but may also advance the capability to influence others and obtain highest occult powers (cf. Judge [1876], quoted in Deveney 2004, 15–19; cf. Albanese 2007, 351–3).[25] In Indian yoga, the accomplished yogi is able to advance his spiritual powers [*siddhis*], to "move his body from one place to another with the quickness of thought, to extend the operations of his senses beyond the trammels of place or the obstructions of matter" (Judge [1889] 1890,

---

[24] A German translation of Judge's (unpublished) report appeared in *Psychische Studien*, 1877, 196.

[25] If one knows the motive and the intention is pure, Judge (Niemand [i.e., Judge] 1920, 29) argues, "then going out of the body is not detrimental." One impure intention, Judge seems to allude to, is selfish love and desire expressed by means of astral projection; such a person may in certain circumstances develop a fear not to find his body. Here, we also find a weird story of inhabiting the body of a dying child ("In a Borrowed Body," cf. 99–103).

39). In their search for Indian sages and sources of occult practices, Blavatsky and other members of the Theosophical circles became increasingly aware of the teachings of yoga as a practical method that allows developing a subtle, "spiritual" body. Judge, for example, published an interpretation of Patañjali's *Yogasūtra*, an Indian classic of yoga philosophy, compiled around the fourth century CE, in which he commented on a verse with the following theosophically laden words: "From the acquirement of such power over the elements there results to the ascetic various perfections, to wit, the power to project his inner-self into the smallest atom, to expand his inner-self to the size of the largest body, to render his material body light or heavy at will, to give indefinite extension to his astral body or its separate members, to exercise an irresistible will upon the minds of others, to obtain the highest excellence of the material body" (38–9, commenting on *Yogasūtra* III.46).[26]

In fact, this assumed equal essence of theosophical ideas of spirit projection and yoga's "sublime body," sent on journeys and even into other bodies by the experienced yogin, was already in the 1880s a well-established idea. "Yoga," we read in Rajendralal Mitra's groundbreaking translation of the *Yogasūtra* (1883), is the archetype of a "modern doctrine, that of spiritualism with its occult appendage." Although the two systems may diverge in regard to the substantiality of the soul, Mitra adds (1883, xxiv; cf. xl, 151–5), which is in the yoga system "pure spirituality," their cardinal theories converge, namely, that the adept "can project his soul out of his body to any place he pleases." [27]

The broadly shared openness toward experimentation with astral "self-transport" in theosophical circles of the 1870s resonates with the attitude that there is no transcendental or anthropological restriction—there is no sinfulness (or *hubris*) in these kinds of experiments. Even after death, the fate of the disembodied soul will never be a kind of hell and punishment, because, as it will become a doctrine of theosophy, the soul in its pure subjective quality can never suffer from physically objective punishments, which are confined to a world of matter.[28] Therefore the dying soul, and, equally, the soul while traveling in a disembodied state will not encounter hellish states. "What we believe in," Blavatsky (1889b, 138) discloses later in *The Key to Theosophy*, "is a *post-mortem state* or mental condition, such as we are in during a vivid dream." Similarly, reincarnation is neither a process of decline, nor a descent into lower, more miserable life-forms, but an evolutionary ascent into higher realms. This doctrine, however, will cause problems for the

---

[26] Cf. on these early *Yogasūtra* translations Baier 2009, I, 359–60. For a fully established theosophical incorporation of the *Yogasūtra*, or, for that matter, the yogic reading of theosophy, cf. Ramacharaka 1905, 1906.

[27] Mitra (1883, 151) says elsewhere that the mental function "which is out of the body, *i.e.,* independent of it, is named the 'great incorporeal' *(Mahávideha)*."

[28] In the *Key to Theosophy*, Blavatsky (1889b: 138; italics in orig.) states, "*crimes and sins committed on a plane of objectivity and in a world of matter, cannot receive punishment in a world of pure subjectivity*. We believe in no hell or paradise as localities."

theosophical reception of the after-death visions of the *Tibetan Book of the Dead*, which is subsequently dealt with.

However, Blavatsky's aim to refer to near-death reports for justifying religious beliefs was, in the theosophical environment, shared by others who correlated astral projection with the former reports.[29] An ordained minister of the Church of England, M. A. Oxon (i.e., William Stainton Moses, 1839–1892), a close friend of Blavatsky and Olcott, joined the Theosophical Society and became "one of the most prominent late nineteenth-century British Spiritualists" (Melton 2001, I, 1057). In 1875, he published an essay on his experience near death while nearly drowning (cf. Crookall 1961, 89), containing familiar elements such as the life review. In the following years, he published two essays focusing "On the Trans-Corporeal Action of Spirit" (1876 and 1877), in which he ordered a number of cases under two headings, namely, those in which the spirit acts transcorporally "without volition" and "with volition: or, exercise of will-power" (Oxon 1876, 97–8). With these two types of astral projection, Oxon laid the foundation for the important distinction between spontaneous and experimental settings. It seems, however, that for some scholars of esotericism and occultism, astral projection retained the meaning of otherworldly journeys in heavenly realms or the underworld, whereas for "modernists," it assumed a more confined meaning of a disembodied soul traveling (flying or floating) through the known life world. This differentiation, of course, follows a new practical perspective on astral projection, which is, as Oxon argues with Hardinge Britten, essentially the view that the spirit may leave the body as the "result of culture and repeated experiment" (101). Among the cases "without volition," we do find a couple of examples of transcorporeal spirit action under "abnormal conditions" that are actually near-death reports. Interestingly, the narratives encompass most prominently experiences outside the body and paranormal appearances, whereas religious elements are almost absent.

Obviously, these practices of getting out of one's own body fulfilled various needs and functions: the prestige of belonging to the "gifted" occultist, experimental training of yogic powers, influencing others at distant places, or the achievement of "higher" gnostic knowledge. Significantly, though, they never got institutionalized in the form of clear guidelines. The astral projection, being in the eyes of many contemporaries not only a weird but also a dangerous experiment, seems to have led to an increase of the secrecy of theosophical practices. Nevertheless, the narratives of astral projection as spiritual travels of a double were an enormous success. From the 1880s onward, they were pursued by various other Spiritualist–Occult organizations, for example, the "Hermetic Order of the Golden Dawn" (founded in London 1888), and they continue to be the topic of a genre of

---

[29] For the complex history of how the position on occult practices or *siddhis* such as astral projection changed in later theosophy, see Deveney 1997, 80–4.

books up to the present day. Reported cases of such travels can be multiplied *ad libitum*, and their connection to the near-death discourse became a well-established current.[30]

As a final example for this connection, the work of Alfred Percy Sinnett (1840–1921), a British publisher and leading Theosophist who later became the president of the Theosophical Society's London Lodge, is discussed. In the 1870s, he moved to India where he lived for several years. In India, he studied not only sources of Buddhist and Hindu philosophy but received as an occult medium a number of "Mahatma letters" with spiritual teachings. After his return to London in 1883, he established close relations to various scholars of matters esoteric and occult. Among them was Frederic Myers, who had in 1882 founded the Society for Psychical Research, which is subsequently dealt with. In Sinnett's writings, "being out of the body" is a fully established term for a positive quality of liberation from the physical body, that "fleshly prison"—even if temporary, as in the case of Buddhist concepts of an intermediate state before the disembodied soul is reincarnated again. In the context of the system of Lama reincarnation in Tibet, Sinnett ([1883] 1885, 169) argues thus in his *Esoteric Buddhism*: "And, meanwhile, *in the body,* the adept is relatively helpless. Out of the body he is just what he has been ever since he became an adept." In his outline of the theory of the "Mahatmas," he explains that "the adept or Mahatma can only be such in the highest acceptation of the word, when he is, as the phrase goes, 'out of the body', or at all events thrown by special efforts of his will into an abnormal condition" (17).[31] Astral projection, which by its reality ascertains "beyond all shadow of doubt" that the occultist "really has got a soul" (17),[32] allows, moreover, an intersubjective

---

[30] A telling example and major step in this direction is a mediumistic communication of a "humanitarian spirit" reporting his "death" to American Spiritualist John R. Francis (1900, 192–3). Being sick, his breathing stopped, he heard the physician pronouncing him to be dead: "I heard the piteous moans of relatives and friends, and the pathetic words of regret they expressed. Oh! what sensations I then experienced! I was conscious of passing events." Being removed from the bed, he "realized fully" that his burial was prepared. "'Am I to be buried alive?' thought I, 'be a living witness of my own obsequies, and finally pass out of the body inattended [. . .]?' [. . .] I could not only see my attendants, but friends who had long since passed to Spirit-life. The latter held a consultation in regard to my resuscitation. [. . . A] spirit-physician present convinced them that circumstances required that I should live a little longer. I then saw them form a circle around my body, and concentrating on me a powerful influence, they gradually brought me back to earthlife again [. . .]. After this incident, I seemed to swing alternately from earth to Spirit-life, and the scenes I witnessed were surpassingly grand." However, this mediumistic "report" should again be located in a fictional narrative realm.

[31] Illustrating the growing influence of various Indian religious teachings and theories, Sinnett (1885, 27; cf. Albanese 2007, 343) equates the astral body with the "*linga sharira*" of Indian yoga that "never leaves the body except at death, nor migrates far from the body even in that case."

[32] This belief, again, relativizes death: "The astral vehicle may, and does, emerge from the body quite freely every night in sleep, but it does not draw out the etheric double with it until the period of that change commonly called death" (Sinnett 1918 [1896], 142). In passing, I may point to the key phrase of the "astral body" becoming, when out of the body, a "vehicle of consciousness" (cf. 104–42). These vehicles, which seem to allude to mythic Indian "vehicles" [*vimāna*], are elsewhere space-traveling devices, connecting to the "human family" still living on Mars. If we could visit the planet, as "some of our more advanced companions can and do, in the appropriate vehicle of consciousness while out of the physical body, we should still find the least advanced [. . .] hanging on there" (218).

communication of souls while being in the astral plane, that "extra-physical state of consciousness of which millions of crass materialists know nothing" (14). Sinnett argues that
testimonies of these higher faculties are "just as easily susceptible of collateral checks and
corroboration as any other sort" (12). His line of reasoning: Suppose a friend tells you,
"being then himself 'out of the body' and functioning on the 'astral' plane of Nature, he
saw such and such a person," and another friend discloses that he "was there at the same
time," and their descriptions converge, it will necessarily press the stamp of credence on
these reports. And even more so true if, Sinnett argues, many "observers" are able to share
a "continual familiarity"—which is "the case for many modern Theosophists in Europe,
not to speak of those in India, where pupils of the Adepts in a position to visit them out
of the body, are more often encountered" (12–13). But even in dreams most people travel,
without realizing it, out of the body (cf. 338; cf. Blavatsky 1877, I, 170). The various cases of
reports mentioned by him show very clearly how astral projection as a practice while still
in this world connects to other cases of *postmortem* existence, and finally, reincarnation
(Sinnett [1896] 1918, 329–35; cf. the possibility to travel backward in time, cf. 250), which
once again demonstrates how these matters were fused into a single doctrinal frame. In
this context, the "enlightenment" of the Buddha as described in early Buddhist literature,
championed, among other aspects, as "awakened" capability to remember innumerable
earlier lives, attracted Sinnett's attention. He argued that in the consciousness of a person
"who at the end of a given chain of beings attains Buddhahood," or who succeeds in meditation and "mystic self-development," "the scenes of all these serial births are perceptible"
(1885, 80). Accompanied by a—to say the least—very loose interpretation of Buddhist
sources (for example, Thomas Rhys Davids' translation of *Buddhist Birth Stories*, 1880),
he speculates that Early Buddhism "accords with the theory of a gradual evolution of the
perfect man," and "clearly held to a permanency of records in the Akasa, and the potential capacity of man to read the same when he has evolved to the stage of true individual
enlightenment" (80–81). This passage, outlining the idea of "akashic records," a comprehensive, planetary world memory as "impressed" in the spiritual world and "readable"
by spiritually advanced individuals, is held to be the first mention of this core concept
of Theosophy (cf. Hammer 2013, 122). In Sinnett's portrayal, we can witness how occult
and esoteric ideas of a full "revival of consciousness" at some time after the "dying brain"
(Sinnett 1885, 97) shuts down, were not only combined with the hagiographical description of the Buddha's total recall of past lives, but were "westernized" in so far as it is the
enlightened consciousness that may now read the "historical" records of the earth proper!
It will be safe to assume that here again the "panoramic life review" forms an important
backdrop against which Sinnett developed his ideas. These connections become more
visible in a letter by the mysterious Mahatma, "written to," as the theosophists prefer to
describe, Sinnett. In this letter of "Koot Hoomi" (letter 23B [ca. 1883]), the Mahatma is
depicted as sharing some insights on dying and rebirth with Sinnett. After outlining the
Hindu belief that "a person's future pre-natal state and birth are moulded by the last desire he may have at the time of death," which should be given due respect by taking care

"that our last desire may not be unfavourable to our future progress," "KH" moves on by referring to the experience of dying men, which, communicated after being brought back to life, "has corroborated our doctrine in almost every case. Such thoughts are *involuntary* and we have no more control over them than we would have over the eye's retina to prevent it perceiving that colour which affects it most. At the last moment, the whole life is reflected in our memory and emerges from all the forgotten nooks and corners picture after picture, one event after the other. The dying brain dislodges memory with a strong supreme impulse, and memory restores faithfully every impression entrusted to it during the period of the brain's activity" (Sinnett [1883] in Barker 1923, 170).

Sinnett's message is clear: The by that time well-known phenomenon of the life review is presented, with certain allusions to the model of interpretation of French psychologists and researchers (Féré, Bergson), as evidence and proof for the theosophical belief system of a general "perfect lucidity at the moment of death."[33] Added are Hindu (and Buddhist) beliefs that the last moment of consciousness beares a highly important karmic quality. In fact, Sinnett combines the latter with recommendations of how not to disturb the consciousness of the dying.[34] Cognate recommendations, we subsequently see, are given in the *Tibetan Book of the Dead*. Finally, it is disclosed by KH through Sinnett that a "'full' remembrance of our lives (*collective* lives) will return back at the end of *all the seven rounds*, at the threshold of the long, long Nirvana that awaits us after we leave Globe Z" (170). Again, KH/Sinnett alludes to the awakening of the Buddha, who had described in his awakening under the Bodhi tree that he was suddenly able to review thousands of his former lives. Sinnett's KH presents, in that respect, the fully developed theosophical theory that the "higher EGO" encompasses an integral knowledge as a quintessence of all experiences gathered in numerous reincarnations, a superknowledge that becomes accessible at the moment of death. In our terminology, this claim of a "higher consciousness" in the moment of dying displays a gnostic–esoteric element, namely, that the cognitive state of the dying is to be characterized by higher insights.[35] In a later work depicting "Actual Narratives of Personal Experiences by Some Who Have Passed on," Sinnett (1914, 13, 31, 48) will again report some after-death experiences that were conveyed to him by

---

[33] "That impression and thought which was the strongest naturally becomes the most vivid and survives so to say all the rest which now vanish and disappear for ever, to reappear but in Deva Chan. No man dies insane or unconscious—as some physiologists assert. Even a *madman*, or one in a fit of *delirium tremens* will have his instant of perfect lucidity at the moment of death, though unable to say so to those present" (Sinnett [1883] in Barker 1923, 170).

[34] In between the last throbbing of the heart and "animal heat" leaving the body, he holds, "the brain *thinks* and the Ego lives over in those few brief seconds his whole life over again. Speak in whispers, ye, who assist at a death bed [. . .]. Especially have you to keep quiet just after Death has laid her clammy hand upon the body" in order not to hinder "the busy work of the Past casting on its reflections upon the veil of the future" (Sinnett [1883] in Barker 1923, 170).

[35] The same argument can be found in "the astral traveler *par excellence*" (Deveney), Charles W. Leadbeater (cf. 1896, 63). The visitor of the devachanic plane enjoys, he holds, the advantage "of seeing all his ideas and their consequences fully worked out passing in a sort of panorama before his eyes."

persons residing after their death on different levels of the astral plane. Methodologically skilled, he includes a case of an atheist disbeliever irritated and transformed by his after-death experiences (cf. 77–82). All of these "astral biographies" represent—in terms of their description of the growing awareness of being "dead," the beyond, the encounter with deceased relatives and friends, and so forth—significant links to modern near-death reports. Here, it suffices to point to one narrative "mediated" to Sinnett, and reported by the latter to his readers. In this story, a young girl decides, after having been forced into prostitution, to drown herself. "She had passed through the change called death, but found herself back again on the bridge. Again she went through the wild desperation of her suicide, repeated all its experiences. Again threw herself into the river, again went through the sensation of drowning, sank into brief unconsciousness and then repeated the whole ghastly cycle of suffering. So it went on for what seemed an eternity. I am told the process went on for at least a year; she thought for five years" (67–8). Sinnett's informant explains, additionally, that all this had to happen because of accumulated karma of previous lives. However, finally the "Great Lord of that region" (69) informs her of being released. She finds herself in a beautiful, peaceful cottage and happily encounters "the great Master of the White Lodge" in whose arms she seeks refuge. Finally, restored to her proper place in the occult world, she is able to move freely to the lower astral planes to console the miserable there (cf. 70).

As mentioned earlier, Yogi Ramacharaka (pseudonym of William Walker Atkinson, 1862–1932) published in 1905 a theosophical–yogic guide for astral travels, in which he wrote that the "Ego," leaving together with its astral body the physical body at death, will be invisible to the ordinary person, "but may be plainly seen by clairvoyant or astral sight, and may therefore be sometimes seen by persons under certain psychic conditions" (Ramacharaka 1905, 210). And again, while this happens, "the whole life of the person, from infancy to old age, passes before his mental vision. The memory gives up its secrets, and picture after picture passes in swift succession before the mind, and many things are made plain to the departing soul—the reason of many things is discovered, and the soul sees what it all means—that is, it understands its whole life just complete, because it sees it as a whole" (212).[36] Urging persons present in such situations not to disturb the dying, Ramacharaka concludes:

> So the Ego passes on, and out from the body. To where? Let us say here that the future states of the soul, between incarnations, have nothing to do with places—it is a matter of 'states' not of places.
>
> [. . .] The soul after passing out of the body, if left undisturbed by emphatic calls [. . .] falls into a semi-conscious state—a blissful, peaceful, happy, restful state

---

[36] Cf. Atkinson 1908, 29 (life review); cf. 27–8 for unusual phonographic metaphors of a "recollecting machine." On Atkinson, cf. Albanese 2007, 358–62.

[...]. This state continues for some time [...] until the astral shell falls from it, and floats off in the astral atmosphere, and until the lower portions of that etherealized-matter which confines the lower portions of the mind gradually dissolves and also drops from the soul, leaving it possessed of only the higher portions of its mentality. (212–13)

Talking of "states" instead of "places" allows him to shift from spatial conceptions of the afterlife to inner "states of consciousness" (cf. Atkinson 1908, 28). With the latter, he can also speak of "consciousness" in between reincarnations, without presupposing gross matter.

I leave the fully established theosophical discourse here with a final comment: Once the connection had been established, it was soon a common belief, reiterated in numerous publications up to the present time, that "Near-death experiences confirm Theosophy" (cf. Siémons 1889; Bland 1996)—a belief that was not only positively reinforced by every new near-death report to appear: The belief was also continually reconfirmed in the form of cognate experiences brought forth by the devoted adept of Theosophy through experimental astral projections. In our eyes, this is a distinctly new element of Spiritualist metaculture, astral projection being praised as no longer being an elitist talent of the gifted few. Although it is difficult to find out how common the practice actually was, we will not be mistaken in assuming that this new generation of practitioners, somehow acquainted with astral travel, nourished the expectation that those experiences will certainly reappear at the hour of death.

2.4

The Advent of Parapsychology and the Figuration

of "Out-of-the-Body Experiences" (1880–1930)

THE UPSURGE OF occult and spiritualist practices and discourses in Western contexts from the 1860s to the 1880s also led to an institutionalization of "psychical research" and parapsychology, the latter being a designation given to the (often uncritical and empathic) scientific study of paranormal phenomena. The term "parapsychology" had been coined by the German psychologist Max Dessoir in 1889. In the 1920s, it became a common and internationally used expression for the psychological research on telepathy, hypnotism, apparitions, or, of interest in our context, communication with the dead, extrasensory perception, and out-of-the-body phenomena. Important societies for the study of the paranormal were founded: in 1882 the Society for Psychical Research (SPR) in London; in 1885, instigated by William James, the American Society for Psychical Research (ASPR) in New York; a year later followed the foundation of the German Psychologische Gesellschaft in Munich. In this vein, several journals were launched (e.g., the journal *Psychische Studien* in 1874; the *Proceedings* and the *Journal* of the SPR, starting in 1884). In these journals, scores of near-death reports were published.[1] For my purpose, it will suffice to quote the landmark reports of experiences near death published or reprinted in these organs, such as the well-known account of A. S. Wiltse (1889). Although some recent protagonists of parapsychology argue that their discipline no longer subscribes to occult or spiritualist agendas, it is indispensable to remark that in the

---

[1] Myers conveys that collecting "apparitions at or after death" was essential for the foundation of the SPR in 1882 (cf. Gurney et al. 1886, I, lxi).

early years of parapsychology, research devoted to the "subconscious mind," "hypnosis," and "somnambulist states" was shared with mainstream psychology. On the other hand, the aim to demonstrate examples of a materially unbound consciousness or perceptions not relying on the usual function of the senses never left the agenda of parapsychology. Seemingly neutral wordings such as extrasensory perception should, however, not hinder a thorough analysis of the essential claims connected to these concepts. A prominent part was very often the attempt to prepare a scientific basis for the assumption that the soul, or consciousness, would survive death.

In line with the general argument pursued here, the central protagonists of psychical studies and parapsychology were interested in near-death reports within the confinements of a religious agenda. Modern science—well understood, of course, and not as reductionist materialism—provides overwhelming evidence of life after death. Therefore we side with Carlos Alvarado (2003, 66) when he observes that there is "no question that much of what we call psychical research and parapsychology has been inspired by the search for the transcendental." For example, in the introduction of the two-volume work, *Phantasms of the Living* (1886), Frederic W. Myers (1843–1901), a leading scholar of early psychical research (cf. Kripal 2010, 37–91), declares once again that the "master-problem" of physical life is "the possibility of an existence continued after our physical death" (Myers in Gurney et al. 1886, I, xlix). Having said this, he outlines the relationship of this "new science" toward religion as follows: "I see no probability [. . .] that our results can ever supply a convincing proof to any specialized form of religion. The utmost that I anticipate is, that they may afford a solid basis of general evidence to the independence of man's spiritual nature, and its persistence after death, on which basis, at any rate, religions in their specialised forms may be at one with science" (liv). And he adds that the "form of religious thought" seems to change in his contemporaries—namely, that now "beliefs and aspirations" are voiced that "have been in a certain sense more independent, more spontaneous [. . .] and resemble rather the awakening into fuller consciousness of some inherited and instinctive need" (liv). It is exactly this mood that lets the emerging "new science" turn to the research of the paranormal while at the same time criticizing materialist science. Not only does Myers praise Greek and Buddhist wisdom on the survival of the soul, but in the epilogue of his seminal contribution, *Human Personality and Its Survival of Bodily Death*, published posthumously, Myers (1903, II, 288) ventures on a "bold saying," namely, to "predict that, in consequence of the new evidence, all reasonable men, a century hence, will believe the Resurrection of Christ, whereas, in default of the new evidence, no reasonable men, a century hence, would have believed it."

2.4.1 THE SEMINAL REPORT NEAR DEATH OF A. S. WILTSE (1889)

Myers and his colleagues were in *Phantasms of the Living* occupied in presenting evidence that the moment of the apparent death of a person was somehow perceived by means of "apparitions" and "phantasmal announcements" by distant others. In this context, Myers himself became aware of "apparent death" narratives,[2] as they were then called. His foremost cases are, however, the ones in which the dying or dead appear to distant others. Obsessed by the idea of verification that will render parapsychology into an outright science, he sought to track down documented evidence for the exact moment at which the individual's death had taken place. For his aim, "apparitions of the dead" were open to intersubjective verification—in contrast to cases in which the dying returns from the "gates of death" (315). Nevertheless, Myers (in Wiltse 1892, 180) expressed the belief that "we might learn much were we to question dying persons, on their awakening from some comatose condition, as to their memory of any dream or vision during that state," In this regard, one of the most interesting cases that stirred the discussion of what it would be like to experience "death" was the one by Dr. A. S. Wiltse, published in an American medical journal in 1889. The only prominent near-death narrative that Myers dealt with, it was reprinted in the *Proceedings of the Society for Psychical Research* in 1892 with additional reports of witnesses and Myers's comments (cf. also 1903, 315–323). Wiltse, reporting his experience under the neutral heading "A Case of Typhoid Fever," describes that in a feverish state of "apparent death" he had lost all power of thought or knowledge of existence. Half an hour later, his narrative continues,

> I came again into a state of conscious existence and discovered that I was still in the body, but the body and I had no longer any interests in common. I looked in astonishment and joy for the first time upon myself—the me, the real Ego, while the not me closed upon all sides like a sepulchre of clay. With all the interest of a physician I beheld the wonders of my bodily anatomy, intimately interwoven with which, even tissue for tissue, was I the living soul of that dead body. [. . .] I realised my condition and calmly reasoned thus, I have died as man terms death and yet I am as much a man as ever. I am about to get out of the body.

With scientific curiosity, it seems, Wiltse observes the "interesting process of the separation of soul and body:" "By some power, apparently not my own, the Ego was rocked to and fro, laterally as the cradle is rocked [. . .]. After a little time the lateral motion ceased, and along the soles of the feet, beginning at the toes, passing rapidly to the heels, I felt and heard, as it seemed, the snapping of innumerable small cords"; he began to retreat from the feet toward the head, and, this being accomplished, he reflects thus: "I am all the head now, and I shall soon be free." Finally, he emerged from the head and "floated up and down and laterally like a soap bubble attached to the bowl of a pipe,"

---

[2] Cf. the case of a "supernormal percipience of a man in the very article of death" (Gurney et al. 1886, II, 305–6).

until he at last broke loose from the body. Expanded "to the full stature of a man," he appeared to be

> translucent, of a bluish cast and perfectly naked. With a painful sense of embarrassment, I fled towards the partially open door to escape the eyes of the two ladies whom I was facing, as well as others whom I knew were about me, but upon reaching the door I found myself clothed [...]. As I turned, my left elbow came in contact with the arm of one of two gentlemen who were standing in the door. To my surprise, his arm passed through mine without apparent resistance [...]. I looked quickly up at his face to see if he had noticed the contact but he gave me no sign— only stood and gazed toward the couch I had just left. I directed my gaze in the direction of his, and saw my own dead body [...]. I was surprised at the paleness of the face. [...] I saw a number of persons sitting and standing about the body and particularly noticed two women apparently kneeling by my left side and I knew that they were weeping. I have since learned that they were my wife and my sister, but I had no conception of individuality. [...] I now attempted to gain the attention of the people with the object of comforting them as well as assuring them of their own immortality. [...] I concluded the matter by saying to myself: 'They see only with the eyes of the body. They can not see spirits. They are watching what they think is me, but they are mistaken [...]. This is I and I am as much alive as ever.' (Wiltse 1889, 357)

Then he walked down and realized with some satisfaction, that his "new" body was taller than his former body. Yet, suddenly he became aware that he was beyond the dreaded death, and was even more cheerful, enjoying his new spiritual, eternal existence:

> "Suddenly I discovered that I was looking at the straight seam down the back of my coat. How is this, I thought, how do I see my back? [...]. Am I like an owl that I can turn my head half way round? I tried the experiment and failed. No! Then it must be that having been out of the body but a few moments I have yet the power to use the eyes of the body, and I turned about and looked back in at the open door, where I could see the head of my body in & line with me. I discovered then a small cord, like a spider's web, running from my shoulders back to my body and attaching to it at the base of the neck, in front." He turned and walked down the street. "Then a sense of great loneliness came over me and I greatly desired company, so I reasoned thus: Some one dies every minute. If I wait twenty minutes the chances are great that some one in the mountains will die, and thus I shall have company."

He waited for company, but no one came. He mused that individuals will likely travel on their individual roads into the other world, but still hopes that "some one from the other world would be out to meet me," be it angels or fiends:

I reflected that I had not believed all the Church tenets, but had written and thought verbally a new and, I believed, a better faith. But I reasoned, I knew nothing [. . .]. I may, therefore, be on my way to a terrible doom. A great fear and doubt came over me and I was beginning to be very miserable, when a face so full of ineffable love and tenderness appeared to me for an instant as set me to rights upon that score. (356–60)

The next moment, a great and lively cloud with bolts of fire appeared, and Wiltse became aware of a "presence," a "vast intelligence," and realized, "He is not as I, I reasoned." Then "from the right side and from the left of the cloud a tongue of black vapor shot forth and rested lightly upon either side of my head, and as they touched me thoughts not my own entered into my brain. These, I said, are his thoughts and not mine; they might be in Greek or Hebrew for all power I have over them. But how kindly am I addressed in my mother tongue that so I may understand all his will" (361). Fortunately, the language is English, and Wiltse renders it thus: " 'This is the road to the eternal world. Yonder rocks are the boundary between the two worlds and the two lives. Once you pass them, you can no more return into the body." If "your work" is done, "you may pass beyond the rocks. If, however, upon consideration you conclude that it shall be to publish as well as to write what you are taught, if it shall be to call together the multitude and teach them, it is not done, and you can return into the body' " (361). Accordingly, he arrived at the entrances, but, although tempted, did not enter. Finally, and without great effort, "my eyes opened. I looked at my hands and then [. . .], realising that I was in the body, in astonishment and disappointment I exclaimed: What in the world has happened to me? Must I die again?" (363). Wiltse adds that he wrote his account, almost fully recovered, "just eight weeks from 'the day I died', as some of my neighbors speak of it" (364).

The report demonstrates how the Christian and Occult–Spiritualist metacultures may incorporate a scientific stance. Again, the disembodied spirit observes "scientifically" his own body and, even more, is willing and capable of experiments: It falsifies the ability to rotate its head like owls while still in the "experience." The body is no longer simply a static prison but something that can be viewed with a neutral, scientific attitude. Reflection on the bodily self is a crucial attitude of the emerging "autoscopic culture" of modernity. The whole report is reigned by a self-reflective spirit that is soteriologically relaxed, and in the mood to undertake experiments in his after-death laboratory. The most decisive element of Wiltse's account, however, pertains to his enactment of faith and religion. Not fully self-assured of his faith, he expects that—still in the framework of Christian metaculture!—a heavenly messenger will take him to heaven, or be doomed. Finally, an "intelligence" appears in the form of a cloud—a Christian topic, again—and, without words, Wiltse is informed that he has reached a point of no return. Moving on will irreversibly transpose him into the eternal world. However, the "intelligence," or God, reminds him of the fact that he, Wiltse, has not yet succeeded in publishing what he had been taught. In Christian words again, the personal instruction of Wiltse concludes with the call to teach the multitude, obviously alluding to the mission of Jesus (cf., e.g., Mark 4:1; Matthew 15:10). In sum, he declares that he did not adhere to any religious belief before the experience, but developed and proclaimed in its aftermath an own, "better" faith. Especially with the last-mentioned element, Wiltse's report displays the religious intention of the author, namely, to have been sent back to his body and life to fulfill a mission.

An essential element of the synthetized model of near-death experiences is the "tunnel" that we did not meet in the reports quoted so far. In the spiritualist journal *Borderland*, we find a report of an experience under chloroform that speaks, for the first time, of a "tube," though seemingly narrower than a tunnel:

> The process [...] was very painful. [...]. I screamed dreadfully, though utterly un-conscious of the fact [...]. Beyond this stage came the thought, 'Now I am alone, quite alone. If I am going to die no one in the wide world can help me'. My heart swelled and beat faster as if it would burst. 'There is God', I said to myself. 'But what and where is God?' This question was followed by intense dread, a dread I determined to overcome, and succeeded in doing so. I then found myself proceeding along a straight black tube where there seemed hardly room to move; It was not a long journey, and when I had reached the stage of oppression, when it appeared as if another second of this horrible darkness would extinguish me for ever, I was dazzled by a great brightness and discov-ered myself in my own room. (signed by Asa L'Orne, 1894, 564–5)

This report is, moreover, one of the very few in the 19th century that expands on an overall terrifying and frightening experience. The tunnel in a more explicit form will, however, appear in a report published in 1920.

2.4.2 WILLIAM JAMES'S APPROACH TO EXPERIENCES NEAR DEATH AND THE "FILTER THEORY" OF CONSCIOUSNESS

In the last decade of the 19th century, it had become a fully established practice to re-port experiences near death in spiritualist, but also, in psychological–medical circles. We get a good impression of this phenomenon by exploring reports communicated in the numerous spiritualist and psychological journals of that decade, for example, the three reports of personal experiences near death by John Lamont (1894), president of the Liverpool Psychological Society, which were published in *Two Worlds*. All these con-clude usually with the thesis of the "painlessness" of dying and the proof of survival of the soul.[3]

---

[3] This element of the painless death appears, as we saw, in numerous accounts from the 1880s onward, e.g., in Whymper 1880 and Heim 1892. Psychical researcher John Lamont (1894, 633) concludes from three personal

An important account had been disseminated by the famous pragmatist philosopher, psychologist, and researcher of paranormal phenomena William James (1842–1910) in his widely read *Varieties of Religious Experience* (1902). As one of the examples adduced to describe the structure of mystical experiences, James discusses a report of English poet and literary critic John A. Symonds (1840–1893). Of fragile health and under constant medical treatment, Symonds recorded "a mystical experience with chloroform" (James [1902] 1922, 385). In a letter (Feb. 20, 1873), Symonds himself, addressing it as a "psychological experience," reports:

On Tuesday I was put under the influence of chloroform and laughing gas together. I felt no pain; but my consciousness seemed complete, and I was occupied with the strange thoughts which you shall read [. . .]. After the choking and stifling had passed away, I seemed at first in a state of utter blankness; then came flashes of intense light, alternating with blackness, and with a keen vision of what was going on in the room around me, but no sensation of touch. I thought that I was near death; when, suddenly, my soul became aware of God, who was manifestly dealing with me, handling me, so to speak, in an intense personal present reality. I felt Him streaming in like light upon me, and heard Him saying in no language, but as hands touch hands and communicate sensation, "I led you, I guided you; you will never sin, and weep, and wail in madness any more; for, now, you have seen Me". My whole consciousness seemed brought into one point of absolute conviction; the independence of my mind from my body was proved by the phenomena of this acute sensibility to spiritual facts, this utter deadness of the senses [. . .]. I also felt God saying, "I have suffered you to feel sin and madness, to ache and be abandoned, in order that now you might know and gladly greet Me. Did you think the anguish [. . .] and this experience you are undergoing were fortuitous coincidences?" I cannot describe the ecstasy I felt. Then as I gradually awoke from the influence of the anaesthetics, the old sense of my relation to the world began to return, the new sense of my relation to God began to fade. I suddenly leapt to my feet on the chair where I was sitting, and shrieked out, "It is too horrible [. . .]", meaning that I could not bear this disillusionment. Then I flung myself on the ground, and at last awoke covered with blood, calling to the two surgeons (who were frightened), "Why did you not kill me? Why would you not let me die?" Only think of it. To have felt for that long dateless ecstasy of vision the very God, in all purity and tenderness and truth and absolute love, and then to find that I had after all had no revelation, but that I had been tricked by the abnormal excitement of my brain. "Yet, this question remains, Is it possible that the inner sense of reality which succeeded, when my flesh

---

life-threatening situations that he found himself "perfectly free from pain, and in the possession of a spirit body so facile to the will that no tongue could possibly describe the joy of existence," quoted, e.g., in Bozzano 1931, 62.

was dead to impressions from without, to the ordinary sense of physical relations, was not a delusion but an actual experience? Is it possible that I, in that moment, felt what some of the saints have said they always felt, the undemonstrable but irrefragable certainty of God?" (Symonds in Brown 1895, II, 78–80, quoted by James 1922 [1902], 385–6)

This report and its adjacent reasonings illustrate very vividly how Symonds narrates his encounter with God in terms of Christian metaculture, being, however, aware of critical response by adherents of naturalist perspectives. Symonds describes how in this situation thought to be "near death," God—without verbal communication—revealed himself and let him know that there is meaning in this situation: God entertains a relationship, he cares for him, and he can be known—overall, an ecstatic, fully positive experience. And yet, back in conscious life, he does not only berate the surgeons for reviving him—still more, he is confronted with the ambivalence that his experience might have been induced by anesthetics. Although he takes into consideration that his experience might have been errant and deluded, it is nevertheless clear that Symonds retains his conviction that there is a "irrefragable certainty of God," a formulation that must turn the concluding question into a rhetorical one. The assumption that there will be a safe place for the soul after death does not seem to be doubted.[4]

I may add here that James, fascinated by such reports, was not only an eminent psychologist and philosopher, but equally interested in metaphysical questions of human survival of death and mystic states of consciousness. In essence, they converged in his concept of human consciousness as capable of receiving a higher, supra-individual consciousness. In his essay *Human Immortality* (1898), James sets out to understand and explain such phenomena as religious conversions, premonitions, "apparitions" at time of death, clairvoyant visions, and the "whole range of mediumistic capacities." Thought, he argues here, is not only a function of the brain. Instead, the human brain has a "transmissive function," namely, that thought is mediated through the brain—the latter being comparable to a "lens," a "prism" (cf. James 1898, 14–15); or a "filter"—a "psycho-physical threshold" or "brain-barrier" that may, at times being lowered, allow us to "grow conscious of things of which we should be unconscious at other times" (24). The production theory of brain-based human thought is juxtaposed with a transmission theory, which, according to James, holds that thoughts do not "have to be 'produced',—they exist ready-made in the transcendental world. All that is needed is an abnormal lowering of the brain-threshold to let them through." Pointing to cases of conversion, mental healings, and so forth, "it seems to the subjects themselves of the experience as if a power from

---

[4] Elsewhere, Symonds (Brown 1895, I, 402) explains that after death, "if anything," then "either endless change or continuity of eternal being" awaits us. In either case, "the soul needs a refuge from the things that pass like a show, to some reality above them and beneath them."

without, quite different from the ordinary action of the senses or of the sense-led mind, came into their life, as if the latter suddenly opened into that greater life in which it has its source" (27). Predictably, the transmission theory is designed to explains facts that are rejected as paradoxical by the production theory. However, in describing it being the alternative, James relies heavily on religious metaphors such as the "mother sea" of cosmic consciousness: "The word 'influx', used in Swedenborgian circles, well describes this impression of new insight, or new willingness, sweeping over us like a tide. [. . .] We need only suppose the continuity of our consciousness with a mother sea, to allow for exceptional waves occasionally pouring over the dam. Of course the causes of these odd lowerings of the brain's threshold still remain a mystery on any terms" (26–7). The religious framing of James's transmission theory becomes more obvious as it is alluded to immediately after the portrayal of Symonds's report. Here, James is not at all interested in discussing more thoroughly the psychopharmacological impact that the chloroform may have had in forming the experience. Instead, he mentions only the general fact that intoxicants and anesthetics may produce certain states of consciousness. Those agents, he concludes, "stimulate the mystical consciousness in an extraordinary degree" (James 1922, 387) and points to his own mystical experiences by using drugs. And here again, James mentions his conviction that ordinary consciousness is only a part of larger, and probably entirely different form (or forms) of consciousness. It is an almost Hegelian "monistic insight," which for some come in the form of an "anaesthetic revelation," as James says (drawing on a book of Benjamin P. Blood, cf. 389).

The relevance of experiences near death for the transmission theory becomes clearer in James's extensive quotation of a work by the German–British pragmatist philosopher Ferdinand C. S. Schiller (1864–1937). The latter had advanced in his work *Riddles of the Sphinx* (1891) the idea of the brain as a means for the inhibition of consciousness with explicit mention of the life-review feature in the dying. Schiller argues (quoted in James 1898, 66–9) that "if the body is a mechanism for inhibiting consciousness, for preventing the full powers of the Ego from being prematurely actualized, it will be necessary to invert also our ordinary ideas on the subject of memory, and to account for forgetfulness instead of for memory." Accordingly, it is the brain itself that forgets—it will be "during life that we drink the bitter cup of Lethe," Schiller (1891, 296) says. The inhibiting brain, however, is dispensed in cases of "the extraordinary memories of the drowning and the dying generally," and "experimental psychology" informs us that "nothing is ever forgotten wholly and beyond recall." In sum, matter "is not that which *produces* consciousness, but that which *limits* it" (295). What is more, Schiller, referring to spiritualist experiments, conceptualizes a spiritual progress within evolution. We, being as humans higher animals, are capable "of *somnambulism*, which already permits us strange glimpses of a *lucidity* that divines the realities of a transcendent world" (295). Although the specific elements of the transmission theory, of a transcendent consciousness perceived individually through the filtering brain, vary to a certain degree, it will be from now on a recurrent model in near-death discourse—transmitted by Myers,[5] C. D. Broad, Huxley, Pahnke, and other proponents of "psychedelic mysticism" to, finally, Moody. The latter, for example, says in his autobiography, that in the 1960s Ritchie had explained to him: "For me, the brain is like a receiver and is not the cause of consciousness. It's just receiving consciousness from somewhere else" (Moody 2012, 63). This theory is still favored by many recent protagonists of near-death experiences (e.g., Pim van Lommel or Edward F. and Emily W. Kelly).

2.4.3 BEWILDERED VIEWS ON ONE'S OWN BODY: THE GROWTH OF AUTOSCOPIC NARRATIVES

Moreover, in the first decades of the 20th century, we can notice a growing "autoscopic interest" of the disembodied spirit.[6] Sometimes, the disembodied self does not observe the physical body but a third, ethereal body, as in the case of a certain M. J. Ramel, reporting to the famous French astronomer and spiritualist Nicolas Camille Flammarion (1842–1925):

> I had a disease of the heart, which is now cured, but which played me some nasty tricks. On one occasion, among others, I remained for a certain time plunged in a lethargy. I heard all my family talking around me, but I was not I: my *self* was beside me, standing, a white and fluid body; I saw the grief of those who were striving to revive me and I had this thought: "Of what use is this miserable cast-off skin that they seek to bring to life again?" Nevertheless, perceiving their sadness, a great longing came over me to return to them,—a thing which happened. (Flammarion 1922, II, 62; cf. 1920, II, 72)[7]

In this case, the travelling "I" declares that it would have been possible to stay in the "beyond," but decides to go back without being sent by some divine presence. The spiritually

---

[5] Cf. Myers 1903, I, 16–18.

[6] Reporting in a personal communication to Isaac K. Funk, included in the latter's *The Psychic Riddle* (1907, 183), a physician from New York described his slowly intensifying, recurrent experiences of paranormal states of body and mind, which finally enabled him to undertake distant travels of the soul, realizing, as he says, thereby the meaning of St. Paul's "in or out of the body." However, he decides to return and, immediately thereafter, becomes conscious of looking down on his own body propped up in bed. With strange feelings toward the lifeless, dead body, he obvious enjoys a new "consciousness" that can pass through matter without resistance. After two minutes only, however, he looks again at his body, tries to control it, "and in a very short time all sense of separation from the physical body ceased" (Muldoon et al. 1929, xxvii). Finally, he presents to us—as usual—of now being convinced of the continuity after death (185), a conclusion shared by Funk in his religious Spiritualist–Christian metainterpretation, his search for the key to unlock heaven's gate (cf. 216).

[7] Cf. Mattiesen 1931, I, 306.

grafted and trained individual, we may comment, becomes increasingly autonomous and acts independently of supernatural beings.

2.4.4 VERACITY FIRST: PARAPSYCHOLOGY AND THE DOMINANT INTEREST IN DEATHBED APPARITIONS

There were, however, certain methodological presuppositions that hindered the growing number of parapsychologists in 1890 from focusing on near-death reports more properly. In their search for intersubjective proof for paranormal phenomena, they took a central interest in those narratives of experiences near death that provided "testable" information—for example, in which the dying had telepathic apparitions of other dying individuals in distant places. Several other psychical researchers followed the program outlined by Myers and other parapsychologists of the first generation with their aim to ascertain the trustworthiness of deathbed visions. Examples are essays by James H. Hyslop (1854–1920) on the "Visions of the Dying" in the first issue of the *Journal of the American Society for Psychical Research* (1907),[8] Hector Durville's work on "Phantoms of the Living" (in French, 1909, cf. also 1910), Gabriel Delanne's *Materialised Apparitions of the Living and Dead* (in French, 2 vols., 1909, 1911), Ernesto Bozzano's *Psychic Phenomena at the Moment of Death* (in French, 1923),[9] or the famous works of Sir William Barrett (1844–1925). One of the founding members of the SPR in 1882, Barrett became interested in the vision of the dying as early as in the 1880s. Even though Barrett (1918, 158) remarks that "hallucinations of the dying are not infrequent" and may not be overrated in their evidence, he provides some examples of cases in which people reported that they can "see" dead relatives shortly before they died themselves. In 1926, Barrett[10] published a systematic collection of deathbed visions that included many reports published in journals and books devoted to psychical studies. Barrett, still corroborating third-person evidence of paranormal information given by the dying, included only a few near-death narratives (see, for instance, Barrett 1986 [1926], 42, 57–66). Experiences out of the body, or the life-review feature, are fully absent. Interestingly, he does not comment on occasional Christian features (the vision of angels, Jesus, etc.), but places them side by side with narratives of the Spiritualist–Occult metaculture, for example, the departing "astral body" of the dying seen by observers at the deathbed (106). Barrett, in other words, is less interested in the specific content of these visions. Whatever it is, the main aim is to collect well-attested cases as "cogent arguments for survival after death"

---

[8] In 1918, Hyslop (1918b) published further reports under the same title. There, under "class II" ("borderland cases," in which a recovery took place), experiences near death are reported.

[9] "In his book *Phénomènes Psychiques au Moment de la Mort*, Bozzano (1923) used a variety of deathbed manifestations, including visions, movement of objects, and music heard at deathbeds, to defend the concept of discarnate agency" (Alvarado 2005, 211); cf. for an overview of Bozzano's categories Siegel 1983, 196–200.

[10] Barrett was influenced by Bozzano, cf. Siegel 1983, 196.

(1), for which, as previously said, the cases of near-death narratives are more problematic than cases of telepathic information or third-party visions of paranormal events at the deathbed. Nevertheless, Barrett's book is still "widely regarded as a classic" (Fox 2003, 25). It had a considerable influence on later research, for example, by Osis and Haraldsson. Parapsychological collections in the tradition of Barrett, for example, by Alexander T. Baird (1944, 80–91), do include "Death-bed visions," but remain true to the principle of not including cases of near-death reports (cf., however, Baird 1948). A crucial step in the configuration of near-death experiences was taken in 1918 by British psychical researcher and popular writer John Arthur Hill (1872–1951). If I am not mistaken, Hill was indeed the first to introduce the term out-of-the-body experiences (Hill 1918, 70, 78; using the term also in the heading of chapter IV), thereby establishing the designation as a technical term.[11] And again, Hill referred to the close interplay of these experiences and drug use (cf. 70–1).

2.4.5 NEAR-DEATH REPORTS IN ANTHROPOSOPHY: RUDOLF STEINER

In the first three decades of the 20th century, we may witness a large number of reports that combined spiritualist exercises of astral projection with out-of-the-body experiences, visions of light, meeting of deceased, the life review, or claims of supernatural "consciousness." It is not necessary to include a large number of them here, but, to demonstrate the continuous chain in which these reports were transmitted in religious contexts, it is indispensable to provide some important examples.[12] New is the sheer number of these narratives that seems to parallel the great popularity that travels to the otherworld enjoyed, as a narrative genre, in the early Middle Ages. Finally, also in the wake of the 20th century, experiences near death are documented in cases of drug-induced states, such as those reported by the French pharmacist and occult writer Jules Giraud in his *Testament of an Hashish-Eater* (1913).[13]

One important protagonist is the Austrian founder of "Anthroposophy," Rudolf Steiner (1861–1925). Anthroposophy may be described as an offspring of modern

---

[11] In earlier works, Hill (1911, 17) still wrote nontechnically of "getting out of the body." At that time, Hyslop (1918a, 10) and others spoke of "feelings out of the body." We may remark that Ramacharaka (Atkinson 1908, 9) had used the term "'out-of-consciousness' states" already a decade earlier in his lessons of how to reach an inner consciousness.

[12] Some other examples, not discussed here, are Turvey 1909; Lancelin 1913; Larsen 1927; Pelley 1929.

[13] Giraud reports of a drug experience in which he had thought that from "all available evidence I was going to die." In implacable agony, an "appalling black void that had surrounded me up until then began to lighten a bit in a thundering downpour of insane, visionary images, such as happen to those about to drown." A "splendid serenity," however, made him forget his pain. He was outside of his body, "spreading out in wonderful flashes of light," and plunged "into the infinite, extending through all the past history of the Earth my mother, through all her geologic ages," becoming "in an exploding apotheosis of suns and galaxies" finally the "universal divinity," which is followed, however, by more depressive visions (quoted in Siegel, Hirschman 1984, 70).

Theosophy, combined with other Gnostic teachings, but also modern Western philosophy. Steiner, while still being an adept of Theosophy, explains in his *Outline of Occult Science* (German 1909; English 1914) death as a new situation of the "etheric body," now being united solely with the "astral body," while the physical body separates and decays. In this period, memories of the past life emerge: "The etheric body still being present causes that past life to appear as a vivid and comprehensive panorama. That is man's first experience after death. He sees his life from birth to death spread out before him in a series of pictures" (Steiner [1914] 1922, 59).[14] Actually, Steiner argues, in the first period of separation from the physical body, there exists in the etherical-*cum*-astral body a "certain degree of perfection of memory" (59). However, the etheric body slowly loses this faculty. It is in this context, that Steiner reflects on some "abnormal" conditions at lifetime, in which a reversible separation of the etheric body takes place, for example, in an "unusual shock" (59)—and Steiner mentions drowning or fatal accidents of mountaineers: "What is related by people who have had such experiences comes, in fact, very near the truth, and can be ratified by clairvoyant observation. They declare that in such moments their whole lives pass before their minds as though in a huge memory picture" (60). Steiner is especially intrigued by reports that speak of a "single picture" not related to their respective lives (a relation that will always be established through correct observation, he adds). Moreover, "it must be borne in mind that this can happen only when the etheric body is really separated from the physical body—when, moreover, the former is still united with the astral body. If, through the fright, a loosening of the etheric and astral bodies also takes place, the experience is not forthcoming, because then complete unconsciousness ensues, as in dreamless sleep" (66–7). This reasoning explains, for Steiner (cf. 1910, 64), why not everybody in such abnormal conditions will experience the panoramic review or memory painting [*Erinnerungsgemälde*]—a reasoning that will be taken up by Crookall in the 1960s. After a certain period, however, the astral body is released from the etheric body, too, will pursue its own way, and will open up for new experiences. I may add that Steiner ([1924] 1994, cf. 146–8) discusses the panoramic memory also as a result of spiritual practice. In "meditation," he argues, higher spiritual capacities can be cultivated that finally enable the skilled practitioner to view his life as an all-encompassing memory as a "unified tableau."

2.4.6 ASTRAL TRAVEL POPULARIZED: TRAVEL ACCOUNTS OF AMERICAN AND BRITISH SPIRITUALISTS

In 1914, Emily L. Fischer, a spiritually interested American, published a work on *A Visit to the Astral Plane*. Although she grows skeptical and casts off "all religious creeds, dogmas

---

[14] Cf. Steiner 1909, 59–65; similar ideas are expressed in [1905] 1987, 156–8. Cf. on the context of the "Akasha-chronicles" Zander 2007, 617–18; on the complex anthropology, 536; 650.

and superstitions" (Fischer 1914, 7), she gets attracted by "New Thought" and adopts practicing meditation. In one of these sessions, a guide appears who commands her to stop breathing, which she obeys. While departing, she looks back to her body, and finds that "it was to all appearance as dead as it ever will be when it is dead, and that sight will never fade from my memory" (15). What follows is a floating journey beyond the clouds into a wondrous world of the astral plane, the encounter of four "classes of people" and so forth, until she is guided back into her body and acts according to the command "breathe" (17). Interestingly, Fischer reacts to her experience with a strengthening in Christian beliefs of a "Creator" and strictly opposes theosophical theories of reincarnation (cf. 36).

Only one year later, Cora L. V. Richmond (1840–1923), a famous American Spiritualist, presented a comprehensive report of "My Experiences While Out of My Body and My Return After Many Days" (1915). We read: "It was true then: I was suddenly and finally released from my body; 'this time', I said, or thought: 'I will not have to return'. Many times, almost numberless, I had experienced the wonderful consciousness of being absent from my human form, of mingling with arisen friends in their higher state of existence.'" Richmond mentions a meeting with spiritual friends and with a "Guide," "a perception of great *Light*," and, in the current of Gnostic–Esoteric discourse, that it was granted to her "a state of *Super*-Consciousness; the awakening of faculties and perceptions before unknown, of being *aware*, almost without limitation: of Knowing" (Richmond 1915, 9). Finally, she returned to "fulfil the appointed work on Earth" (69). Although her report is composed in the style of Swedenborg and other visionaries and does not mention any life-threatening situation, she concludes the story of her "experience while out of the body" with the explanation that the possibility of leaving the body intermittently and repeatedly has been aptly demonstrated—sometimes "caused by accident, illness, states of coma induced by anesthetics, trance, either of spirit control or hypnosis," and on other occasions a "voluntary absence or activity not suspending the vital functions of the body" (71). Richmond therefore displays a vast knowledge of near- death narratives.[15]

Experimentation with self-induced trance and reports of astral travels are also the hallmark of British author Oliver Fox (pseudonym for Hugh G. Calloway, 1885–1949). In the 1920s, he published several contributions on his experiences, which were followed in 1939 by a major contribution on the subject, *Astral Projection: A Record of Out-of-the-Body Experiences*. However, already his early descriptions had been well

---

[15] "Prominent physicians," Richmond (1915, 72) says, "have recorded their experiences with patients whose bodily functions were suspended." After resuscitation the subjects of "pleasant scenes and meetings with friends long passed into spirit life. These visits to 'heaven' would be sometimes tinged with the religious bias of the subject, but this is not strange in view of the fact that spirit states are conditions of the mind and spirit experiencing them." As an illustration, Richmond refers to a fictional narrative of Elizabeth S. Phelps, *Beyond the Gates* (1883), in which the protagonist's spirit, being affected by "brain fever," leaves the body and visits the astral plane.

received by other Spiritualist authors. A decade later, psychical researcher Hereward Carrington (1880–1958) will voice his opinion (Muldoon and Carrington 1929, xxx) that Fox is the first to present the "only detailed, scientific and first-hand account of a series of conscious and voluntarily controlled astral projections which I have ever come across."

By introducing the new metaphor of the "pineal door," Fox (1920b, 256) alludes to the identification of the pineal gland as the "seat" of the soul, for example, by René Descartes. Fox (1920a, 190) analyzed his mental state in these experiences as a "dream consciousness" of a "third level," "far more vivid" than both the states of ordinary dreams and waking life. His primary interest focuses on the "ways of travelling" of the astral body, and he is able to distinguish among three types, namely, "*(a)* Horizontal Gliding. *(b)* Levitation. *(c)* Skrying" (1920b, 252). The latter may be worth explaining: "Skrying," Fox says, "is like gliding, but in a vertical direction. There is no downward pull analogous to gravity, but only the call of the body. It is done by a purely mental effort, the arms being quiet, passive, and it is characterized by an enormous velocity of ascent" (254). Although no near-death situation is described, Fox—while traveling in his astral form—experiences for the first time doubt as to whether he is still alive. Yet, willingly he can—with a "strange cerebral click"—return into his body.[16] In his descriptions it becomes obvious that his thoughts are heading to the East—not only to India, but also into a past incarnation. Scenes of a temple appear, and, most important, a new feature gains prominence, namely, the vision of a tunnel:

In April, 1916, when out of the body, I attempted to get back into a past incarnation, which had been described to me by a lady who was an unprofessional trance medium. Now if I had willed to travel to India, I should have immediately rushed off with enormous velocity; but I willed to get back into my past life, and no motion occurred. Suddenly a gap appeared in the astral scenery (as though a round hole were made in a picture) and I saw very, very far away the open door of a temple, and beyond this a gleaming statue. This scene was blurred and had the appearance of being at the other end of a very long and narrow tunnel. I willed to pass through this tunnel, but found myself swept violently away, in a lateral direction, to some other astral locality. I willed once more; again the tunnel and the temple appeared; and again I tried to travel to it. This time, however, I was hurled back to my body, and with such force that the trance was broken. (197)

---

[16] "Was I dead? I did not like it and willed to return, but nothing happened. I tried again and again, and nothing happened. Then I got frightened—the utter loneliness became dreadful—but I knew that a panic would prove fatal. I waited a little, then tried once more. Again there came that strange cerebral click, and instantly I was back in my body" (Fox 1920a, 192).

In the second article, Fox describes an unknown city in India he visited disembodied, and asks, in a significant narrative move that lends credibility to his limited knowledge, if one of his readers can help him identify the place in India.[17]

So far, near-death reports did not include the experience of passing through a tunnel, and though in this report a tunnel is present, it is not (yet) entered. However, it may actually be the first instance of a topos, while also surfacing in drug experiences and anesthesia (cf. Dunbar 1905, 75), that will feature prominently in reports from 1935 onward, as subsequently seen.[18]

Finally, Fox interprets his experiments in well-known religious terms, arguing that "in all things, exists the One Supreme Life, the One Eternal Truth. In these out-of-the-body excursions it would appear that one's powers of perception are enormously increased; and if inanimate objects seem endowed with life, how tremendously alive is the investigator himself, freed from his prison-house of matter!" (260).[19] Fox may serve as a prominent example of the by now well-established fusion of astral travels and near-death reports. Almost all descriptions or handbooks of astral travels and etheric doubles in the 1920s that I am are aware of include—the decisive element of getting out of the body taken aside—further topoi of near-death discourse, such as the life review, the ignorance of being dead in after-death planes, the presence of "helpers" and other deceased, and so forth.

2.4.7 NEAR-DEATH REPORTS IN CHRISTIAN, ESOTERIC, AND NATURALIST METACULTURES OF THE 1920S

To provide only one example of the 1920s, I may turn to the impressive, three-volume work *La mort et son mystère* (1920–1922) by Camille Flammarion that was almost immediately translated into English (*Death and Its Mystery*, three vols., 1922). In the context of illustrating the relativity of time—more precisely, his belief that "time" is merely created by the movement of the stars and the succession of things (cf. Flammarion 1922,

---

[17] In what appeared to him as "some strange Indian city," he saw "a curious fountain: a kneeling elephant, sculptured in black stone, ejected from its curled-back trunk a shower of water, which was caught in a white shell-shaped basin," which, he assures his readers, he had neither heard of, nor seen. So he asks: "Can anyone tell me if it exists upon the earth?" (Fox 1920b, 261).

[18] Van Uytfanghe (cf. 1991, 464) holds that passing quickly through a tunnel has been depicted in medieval literature, too. However, a closer look reveals that he argues somewhat phenomenologically: In these sources, he says, it is described as a "tunnel," but "named" a cavern, well, valley, etc.

[19] In the 1920s, American writer Ernest Hemingway (1899–1961) narrated, without any obvious religious interpretation, a personal war experience: "'We were in a hole with sand bags around [. . .]. There was one of those big noises that sometimes occur on fronts. 'I died then'. And he laughs a big tough laugh. 'I felt my soul or something coming right out of my body like you'd pull a silk handkerchief out of a pocket by one corner. It flew all around and then came back in and I wasn't dead anymore'" (Hickok 1927, 16). Later, he adapted it in his novel *A Farewell to Arms* (1929).

I, 267)—he provides us with a life-review report by his friend Alphonse Bué, who fell from his horse in Algeria, relating, repeatedly, "and always in the same words," that during the fall, "which could hardly have lasted two or three seconds, his entire life, from his childhood up to his career in the army, unrolled clearly and slowly in his mind, his games as a boy, his classes, his first communion, his vacations, his different studies, his examinations, his entry at Saint-Cyr in 1848, his life with the dragoons, in the war in Italy, with the lancers of the Imperial guards, [...] at the Château of Fontainebleau, the balls of the Empress at the Tuileries, etc. All this *slow panorama* was unrolled before his eyes in less than four seconds, for he recovered consciousness immediately." This is the only case we are aware of in which it is emphasized that the life review unfolded in a "slow panorama." Actually, Flammarion seems to quote his friend's testimony from memory. The way it is phrased here, it seems that Bué did not only see images, but *relived* his entire life (cf. Stevenson and Cook, 1995, 455), temporarily expanded—as is indicated by such memories of "his studies" or "his life with the dragoons." We can probably witness in this example how the report finds a new framing—either already by Bué or by Flammarion—as an example for the ontological relativity of time itself. For the latter, this relativity is not just simply a neutral fact. The chapter in which it is discussed, "Knowledge of the Future" (243–322), sets out to argue that the spirit, who exists independently of the brain and physical senses, is able to foresee future events, may know what "is passing at a distance," etc. (cf. 318–19). Again, the life review is a phenomenon that is endowed with systematic meaning for esoteric cosmovisions.

Danish theologian Hans Martensen-Larsen (1867–1929) may serve as an example of how the reports were included in Christian metaculture, too. In his book *Om Døden og de Døde* ([*About Death and the Dead*], 1925–1927; German translation 1931), we do not only see the critique of the "doctor's materialism" (Martensen-Larsen 1931, 33), but we also see a positive evaluation of the various paranormal faculties in psychical research, framed, however, by Christian faith. In this context, Martensen-Larsen discusses various near-death reports of Danish informants (cf. 91–116), and interprets these referring to Splittgerber, Bergson, and James. For him, the most prominent elements are the life-review feature in connection with a moral reappraisal of one's own deeds, seen in some reports as religious "conversion"—to have found God amid the danger (cf. 94).

Although the large majority of near-death reports are framed by comments on the survival of the soul, there are still occasionally reports in the current of Naturalist metaculture. One example can be found in the autobiographical report of Scottish surgeon Sir Alexander Ogston (1844–1929), who inscribed himself in the history of medicine by discovering the *Staphylococcus* germ. Suffering from typhoid fever during the South African Wars, he had been brought to a hospital (cf. Ogston 1919, 221; the case is quoted e.g. in Tyrrell 1947, 199–201). Describing his own condition as a "delirium," he repeatedly experienced his "mental self" leaving his body. However, although he does report that he could see through walls or could observe patients in other rooms, he abstains from any religious framework of interpretation. "Though," he discloses, "I knew that death was hovering about, having no thought of religion nor dread of the end, and roamed on beneath the murky skies apathetic and contented, until something again disturbed the body where it lay, when I was drawn back to it afresh, and entered it with ever-growing repulsion" (222). Interestingly, Ogston never conceptualized his own state as dead—actually, he says that when he heard doctors at his bedside proclaiming that he "won't recover," "it confusedly amused me, for I knew perfectly that I should get well" (223). The only, slightly paranormal element in his narrative is the third-party confirmation of his detailed description obtained as a "mental" witness of someone else's death in the hospital.

The next stage of the discursive unfolding of modern near-death discourse has been initiated by the translation of the so-called *Tibetan Book of the Dead* into English. As we will see, this important move was again initiated by a theosophist searching for the transcultural validity of near- and after-death experiences.

2.5

The Theosophical Discovery of the *Tibetan Book of the Dead* (1927)

TO SUBSTANTIATE OUR central observation that the *Tibetan Book of the Dead* played a central role for the emerging belief of cross-cultural elements of near-death experiences, and especially encouraged individuals to report out-of-body experiences, I briefly summarize the teachings of the *Book* as portrayed by Evans-Wentz in 1927.[1] For this purpose, it is not necessary to discuss in detail if the translation is appropriate in regard to the early corpus of Tibetan Buddhist teachings on "liberation through hearing in the intermediate state," which is the short title of one text within a compilation of various, originally oral, teachings (see Lopez 2011). However, the Tibetan history and context of these teachings have been widely neglected by translators and interpreters in favor of "presenting three interrelated approaches designed to fit modern Western thinking: scientific, psychological, and humanistic" (Nahm 2011, 375).

Evans-Wentz portrayed the *Book* as scientific in outlook, based on a transcultural dimension of "Symbol-codes" that can also be found, for example, in the Egyptian *Book of the Dead*, Christian "*ars moriendi*," or Greek philosophy. These "symbol-codes" prepare the ground for an esoteric–occult reading of otherworldly journeys. Obviously, Evans-Wentz could easily adapt the title *Book of the Dead*, a title that was well established

---

[1] The third edition of 1957 added a "Psychological Commentary" by C. G. Jung that had been prepared for the German edition (1935). In addition, Evans-Wentz's book *Tibetan Yoga and Secret Doctrines*, published in 1935, deals with Tibetan doctrines of dying. Other successful translations include Francesca Fremantle and Chogyam Trungpa's *The Tibetan Book of the Dead*, published in 1975.

for the Egyptian context.[2] Evans-Wentz holds that it is an outstanding example for the "Art of Dying," aiming to teach the dying to be clear-minded and calm when death approaches. In his preface to the second edition, he contrasts this "art," which was developed in various cultures, with a critical comment on what I previously called "Naturalist metaculture": "Earth-limited medical science," Evans-Wentz ([1948] 2000, xiv) argues, "has no word of guidance to convey to the dying concerning the after-death state, but which, on the contrary, frequently augments rather than ameliorates, by its questionable practices, the unfounded fears and often extreme unwillingness to die of its death-bed patients, to whom it is likely to have administered stupefying drugs and injections."[3] This Tibetan art of dying encompasses, he explains, the art "of going out from the body, or of transferring the consciousness from the earth-plane to the after-death plane" (xiv), is, he adds, known as *Pho-wa* and still practiced in Tibet.[4] In his first introduction to the teachings of the *Book*, Evans-Wentz describes it as a "mystic manual for guidance through the Otherworld" (2). It presupposes an accompanying "spiritual friend" reading passages aloud to the dying, or, more precisely, to the deceased consciousness that is imagined to be still around—outside of his former body. This manual, he says, describes how the "principle of consciousness" of the deceased enters a "trance-state" at the moment of death, "unaware, as a rule, that it has been separated from the human-plane body" (29). This is the first after-death state of three "intermediate states" (Tibetan *bar do*), which amount to a maximum of 49 days until the "consciousness" gets reincarnated. The first bardo is the "'Transitional State of the Moment of Death', wherein dawns the Clear Light" (29). In the translation, we read: "Reverend Sir, now that thou art experiencing the Fundamental Clear Light, try to abide in that state which now thou art experiencing. And also in the case of any other person the reader shall set him face-to-face thus: O nobly-born (so-and-so), listen. Now thou art experiencing the Radiance of the Clear Light of Pure Reality. Recognize it. O nobly-born, thy present intellect, in real nature

---

[2] In 1842, it had been introduced by Prussian Egyptologist Karl R. Lepsius in his *Das Todtenbuch der Ägypter* [*Egyptian Book of the Dead*]. It took only some years before becoming in all European languages the common designation for the whole genre of Egyptian hieroglyphic funerary texts portraying the deceased's journey to the underworld (cf. Lopez 2011, 101). Egyptian afterlife conceptions (cf. Shushan 2009, 53–69) are not treated here, even though they were highly important to Western Occultism, e.g., for H. P. Blavatsky. Yet, they are not particularly relevant for the emergence of modern European near-death discourse; Moody does not mention them as "parallels" in 1975. Although some take Egyptian visions of judgment, crossing to the netherworld, etc., as near-death experiences, it seems to me that they represent specimens of more elaborate mythical narratives of afterlife journeys.

[3] This critical evaluation of "dying" in the West is further advanced. In America, Evans-Wentz ([1927] 2000, xv) holds, "materialistically inclined medical science" makes every effort "to postpone, and thereby to interfere with, the death-process. Very often the dying is not permitted to die in his or her own home." Dying in a hospital, "probably while under the mind-benumbing influence of some opiate," or any other drug, injected "to enable the dying to cling to life as long as possible, cannot but be productive of a very undesirable death, as undesirable as that of a shell-shocked soldier on a battle-field."

[4] Referencing his own work, namely 1935, 169–70, 246–76.

void, not formed into anything as regards characteristics or colour, naturally void, is the very Reality, the All-Good" (95). A "Clear Light"[5] also figures as a central element in Moody's description, though Moody portrays his informants as speaking in the majority of a "Being of Light." In Evans-Wentz' translation, however, it is clearly depicted as the dying's experience of reality itself.

For the one who is not able to stay focused on the "Clear Light" (Tibetan *'od gsal*), the second bardo emerges, the "Transitional state [. . .] of Reality" (Tibetan *chos nyid bar do*). Here, negative karma, heaped up through evil acts committed in a lifetime, will produce "hallucinations": "thought-forms, having been consciously visualized and allowed to take root and grow and blossom and produce, now pass in a solemn and mighty panorama" (29). Now the deceased, becoming aware of his death, develops a desire to possess a body again. Finally, if the wandering consciousness fails to recognize reality in the second bardo, the third, the "bardo of mundane existence" (Tibetan *srid pa'i bar do*), will dawn. The description of the third bardo comprises lively visions of punishment and judgment. The significant impact of these visions on the formation of the near-death discourse of the 1970s is subsequently discussed. It ends with the search for a new body. Propelled by past karma, consciousness takes rebirth in one of six spheres of existence: the realm of gods, demigods, humans, animals, hungry ghosts, or, most unfortunate, in hell. In a highly suggestive manner, the *Book* describes the departing of the deceased through the words of a well-informed narrator (i.e., the Tibetan Buddhist author[s]). Vividly appellative, descriptions of the dramatic postmortal events come as advice ("You, the dying and soon-dead, shall behave so and so") *and* as accounts of a third-person perspective. In fact, the narrator serves, as Evans-Wentz observes, as a "guide for initiates" (lix). With this comment he aims, of course, to underscore the structural similarity of the Tibetan "guide" with guides described in early Mediterranean milieus of esoteric mystery cults. However, these appellative instructions that the *Book* advises giving to the departing consciousness are in themselves a noteworthy feature. Implicitly, they presuppose first-hand knowledge of the process of dying and the after-death state on the side of the *Book*'s authors and reinforce the weight that after-death matters shall be seen (by the departed, but also by the peers) as advised by the reciting guide. For Evans-Wentz, as he discloses in 1959 (2000, v), these claims are based on insights grounded on the "unequivocal testimony of yogins who claim to have died and re-entered the human womb consciously"—they are therefore "truly scientific and yogic." Nevertheless, though deemed "scientific," there is, for example, no clear determination of the exact point at which the *Book* holds that "death" takes place.[6] Like other premodern musings on death and dying, its authors were simply not interested in this question. However, there is a

---

[5] Cf. on the "Clear Light" also Evans-Wentz's *Tibetan Yoga* (1935, 223–31).

[6] As in other descriptions of death and dying, this seems to be an outcome of the attempt to combine external description (of what happens if one dies) with internal perspectives (of what the dying sees and experiences), and the combination of both (namely, external signs which allow to deduce the latter).

moment at which the consciousness principle leaves the body—and sets forth on a way that is, in the *Book*, in principle an irreversible process that is only successively realized by the "deceased." Having realized his "death," there is no return for the consciousness into the body. Despite this important difference, which does not equate to a near-death experience, but, more properly, to an after-death experience,[7] the *Book* seems to have vitalized visionary imaginings of out-of-body experiences. In Wentz and Samdup's translation, we read, "When the consciousness-principle getteth outside [the body, it sayeth to itself], 'Am I dead, or am I not dead?' It cannot determine. It seeth its relatives and connexions as it had been used to seeing them before. It even heareth the wailings" (98). For the consciousness of the deceased, still in the "second bardo," the following forecast is given: "About this time [the deceased] can see that the share of food is being set aside, that the body is being stripped of its garments, that the place of the sleeping-rug is being swept; can hear all the weeping and wailing of his friends and relatives, and, although he can see them and can hear them calling upon him, they cannot hear him calling upon them, so he goeth away displeased. At that time, sounds, lights, and rays—all three—are experienced. These awe, frighten, and terrify, and cause much fatigue" (101).

2.5.1 TIBETAN BUDDHIST AFTER-DEATH EXPERIENCES READ AS EXPERIENCES NEAR DEATH

This Tibetan deathbed scene, viewed from an after-death perspective, is indeed highly interesting. The consciousness principle, now disembodied, becomes slowly aware of the situation through observing the actions of others—reactions that presuppose "it" has left their (intersubjective) world. The peers do not react to the communicative attempts of the "dead." In the consciousness principle, the awareness dawns that "it" still observes, but is no longer perceived by others. Finally, it departs in a depressed mood. This description shares in fact some elements with out-of-body experiences. Nevertheless, it is important to notice how Evans-Wentz strengthened the concept of the "body" in the text in order to make the "art of going out of the body" (previously quoted) a deliberate practice (as "Casting of a body," cf. xxxiii; 92).[8] In contrast to a reversible out-of-body experience, the Tibetan Buddhist framework speaks of an irreversible "out-of-the-life-world" situation. To designate it as an out-of-body experience is rather misleading. The most prominent difference is the lack of the autoscopic element in the Tibetan description, namely, to look down at, or on, one's own body. Instead, the *Book* highlights the initial phase of the

---

[7] The German translation, *Das Tibetanische Totenbuch*, was supplemented in the 1958 edition with the subtitle: "Die Nachtod-Erfahrungen auf der Bardo-Stufe." Although marked by an important semantic difference, "*Nachtod-Erfahrungen*" [after-death experiences"] foreshadows, as a term, the word formation "*Nachtod-Erfahrungen*" [near-death experiences].

[8] Later, Evans-Wentz (cf. [1927] 2000, 100) equates the Tibetan Tantric Buddhist concept of an "illusory body" (Tibetan *sgyu lus*) with the astral body of Theosophy.

dying process predominantly in terms of social reality: The departing consciousness of the deceased is still in a social relationship to its friends and relatives. The relatives "bind" the departing with their "inadequate" behavior of moaning and lamenting. The deceased, on his side, is not interested in his body, or—still less so—in getting back into his body. Later, in the third bardo, it is actually explicitly mentioned that "seeking a body" is a most unwanted procedure (cf. 165)—the Buddhist salvific goal being exactly to escape from karmic rebirth in the world of suffering.

The departing consciousness does observe a social situation signifying the acceptance of being dead. The former body is stripped of its clothing. The body itself is, in terms of epistemic interests or identity formation, no longer of interest. Thus, if the experience should be designated with a concept at all, which is not done on the emic level in the *Book*, it would be, rather than speaking of an "out-of-body experience," more adequate to call it something like "leaving one's life-world situation." From the Tibetan Mahāyāna Buddhist framework of understanding, the body has no higher meaning for the individual. It is produced through *karma*, and therefore, in most premodern Buddhist traditions, negatively connoted. Leaving this worldly body at the moment when the consciousness principle retracts from the body is therefore not connected to any interest in autoscopic self-assurance of any soul that might experience its postmortal freedom by looking at "its bodily counterpart." Taken with its Buddhist corollaries, the narrative rests on the assumption that there is a consciousness principle surviving death, but "death"— or, more precisely, the after-death state—is believed to end almost always with another "rebirth," that is, with a subsequent bodily existence as a "new" sentient being, and rarely with a rebirth in some kind of heavenly realm or, even more rare, with final liberation.

2.5.2 LOUD NOISES AND THE JUDGMENT SCENE

Without question, an important element of the teachings of the *Book* is the mention of loud noises on the side of the disembodied consciousness. For example, it will perceive in the second bardo "piercing whistling sounds," "a palatal sound like a crackling [and] a clashing sound, and a rumbling sound as loud as thunder" (137). In the third bardo, "hallucinations of being pursued by many people likewise will come; [and] sounds as of mountains crumbling down, and of angry overflowing seas, and of the roaring of fire, and of fierce winds springing up." According to Evans-Wentz, these sound impressions are "the psychic resultants of the disintegrating process called death" (162).

This explanation has been picked up by the author of studies on Indian tantrism, Sir John George Woodroffe (1865–1936, equally famous as an author under his pseudonym Arthur Avalon), who contributed a foreword to the first edition of the *Book*. Woodroffe ([1927] 2000, LXVIII) comments that the noises mentioned in the bardo descriptions "call to mind the humming, rolling, and crackling noises heard before and up to fifteen hours after death, which, recognized by Greunwaldi in 1618 and referred

to by later writers, were in 1862 made the subject of special study by "Dr. Collingues."
Unfortunately, Sir Woodroffe offers no reference for "Greunwaldi" and "Collingues."
A pertinacious search unearthed that the latter can be identified as Léon Collongues,
who wrote a book in 1862, *Traité de dynamoscopie*, a treatise on diagnostics using the
patient's finger muscles. There, on page 3, "Greunwaldi" is to be identified as Francesco
Maria Grimaldi, whose *Physico-mathesis de lumine, coloribus, et iride, aliisque annexis*
(1665)[9] deals with, among other topics, "*bourdonnements d'oreille*," that is, modern tin-
nitus. Collongues, on his side, believed that the physician's body may serve as an instrument for detecting actual death. He thought that he could hear the capillary functions
of a supposedly dead person. The involuntary muscle movements of the latter's finger,
should, if the patient is still alive, create a buzzing noise if placed in the physician's ear.[10]
To summarize, the *Book* could contribute to the narrative of hearing displeasing and
painful sounds—in contrast to descriptions of beautiful, heavenly music that were paramount, as previously seen, in accounts framed by medieval and early modern Christian
metacultures. Strictly speaking, the Tibetan sounds are not attributed to the moment
of "death" or the process of dying, but are experienced by the deceased while journeying
through the second and third bardos.

Another narrative to be found in the *Book* is the "judgment scene." It will not astonish
us that this narrative element of the Tibetan afterlife vision has attracted a lot of attention.
Evans-Wentz, arguing for a close relation to ideas expressed in the *Egyptian Book of the
Dead*, is so fascinated that he indulges in historical speculations on a common origin
of the judgment scene.[11] In spite of obvious differences in Tibetan Buddhist, Egyptian,
Greek, and, finally, Christian judgment scenes, the greater part of Christian "symbolism"
is for Evans-Wentz an adaptation from Egyptian and Eastern religions. He still adheres
to an inner core beyond cultural particularities. So it comes as no surprise that he can
present a "Buddhist" reading of the Platonic myth of Er, discovering "*karmic* record
boards"[12] there, or that he can identify a symbolic core in the "weighing" of the soul. This
outlook shares, methodologically, a lot with certain cross-cultural interpretations within
the tradition of the "phenomenology of religion," for example, Mircea Eliade. For our

---

[9] Sir Woodroffe confused with Collongues's Grimaldi's birth year (1618) and the publication date.

[10] Cf. Bondeson 2001, 149. Nevertheless, the phenomena described by Collongues (cf. 1862, 395–402) pertain
to a third-person perspective of diagnosing death. It is not discussed if, or how, a reanimated person would
describe these sounds that appear "on the surface of the body."

[11] Both "Judgment Scenes," Evans-Wentz (2000, 35) argues, are so similar "in essentials" that a common origin, "at
present unknown," seems certain. And he continues: "In the Tibetan version, Dharma-Raja (Tibetan *Shinje-
chho-gyal*) King of the Dead [. . .], the Buddhist and Hindu Pluto, as a Judge of the Dead, corresponds to
Osiris in the Egyptian version. In both versions alike there is the symbolical weighing."

[12] Plato, he says, describes in the myth of Er (*Republic*, 10th book) a similar judgment, in which "there are judges
and *karmic* record-boards (affixed to the souls judged) and paths—one for the good, leading to Heaven, one
for the evil, leading to Hell—and demons waiting to take the condemned souls to the place of punishment,
quite as in the *Bardo Thodol*" (36).

question, a more important aspect lies in the close connection that Moody (cf. [1975] 1976, 65) could build on Evans-Wentz's interpretation that reinforced the established link to think of the life-review feature as an element of judgment scenes. What did the *Book* contribute to allow for that connection?

First, in the *Book* there is no "being of Light"—"clear light" being the luminous quality of reality, including the real quality of consciousness. Instead, we find, in the "judgment scene" a "Lord of Death," inquiring about the consciousness's deeds in his former life: "Thereupon, thou wilt be greatly frightened [. . .] and thou wilt attempt to tell lies, saying, 'I have not committed any evil deed'. Then the Lord of Death will say, 'I will consult the Mirror of *Karma*'. So saying, he will look in the Mirror, wherein every good and evil act is vividly reflected. Lying will be of no avail. Then [. . .] the Lord of Death will place round thy neck a rope and drag thee along; he will cut off thy head, extract thy heart, [. . .] lick up thy brain [. . .]; but thou wilt be incapable of dying" (Evans-Wentz [1927] 2000, 165). In spite their vividness, these experiences are said to be unreal, because the bardo body, experiencing these terrors, is itself, according to the *Book*, not real. Evans-Wentz speaks therefore of "hallucinatory visions" in the second bardo and uses the psychological and psychiatric term "hallucinations" in the translation too (cf., 156, 167). The hallucinations are triggered by karmic forces and are therefore dependent on the individual's conscious life. The *Book* consequently "views the problem of the after-death state as being purely a psycho-physical problem; and is, therefore, in the main, scientific. It asserts repeatedly that what the percipient on the *Bardo* plane sees is due entirely to his own mental-content; that there are no visions of gods or of demons, of heavens or of hells, other than those born of the hallucinatory *karmic* thought-forms constituting his personality" (34).

2.5.3 EVANS-WENTZ, REBIRTH DOCTRINES, AND THE LIFE-REVIEW FEATURE

This brings us to the core questions that initially directed Evans-Wentz's interest to the *Tibetan Book of the Dead*. Prominent among these questions are those connected to the life-review feature, which was, as we will shortly see, acknowledged by Evans-Wentz as early as 1911. To begin with, in his introduction to the *Book*, we see this element flashing up in the following passage: "The deceased human being," Evans-Wentz explains, "becomes the sole spectator of a marvelous panorama of hallucinatory visions; each seed of thought in his consciousness-content *karmically* revives; and he, like a wonder-struck child watching moving pictures cast upon a screen, looks on, unaware, unless previously an adept in *yoga*, of the non-reality of what he sees dawn and set" (33). That his thoughts are occupied with the life-review feature becomes still more obvious in his comment on a paragraph of Woodroffe's foreword "Science of Death" to the first edition. Woodroffe ([1927] 2000, lxx) explains: "The 'reading' of that 'Book' is the recalling to mind by the dying man of the whole of his past life on earth before he passes from it," on which Evans-Wentz comments as follows: "That such a review of earth-life is experienced by the dying has been frequently attested by persons who had begun to die, as, for example, in drowning, and then been resuscitated" (lxx).

Actually, the life-review feature had attracted Evans-Wentz's attention at least 15 years earlier. In his *The Fairy-Faith in Celtic Countries*, he refers to it (1911, 469–70) in the context of spiritual travels to the "Faerie-Lands": Pointing to a physician's reporting of "patients under narcotics" that "experience events extending over long periods of time within a few minutes of normal time," he refers to de Quincey, having disclosed "dreams of ten to sixty years' supernatural duration, and some quite beyond all limits of the waking experience. Fechner [13] records a case of a woman who was nearly drowned and then resuscitated after two minutes of unconsciousness, and who in that time lived over again all her past life. Another even more remarkable case than this last concerns Admiral Beaufort," of which Evans-Wentz extracts the life review that Beaufort had traveled over "every incident of his life with the details of 'every minute and collateral feature.'" And once again, the "life review" is broadened to a "total recall" and connected to the Buddha's "enlightenment": As spelled out by Sinnett or Blavatsky (see sections 2.3.2 and 2.3.3), Evans-Wentz holds that the Buddha was able to remember his previous reincarnations: "In the case of a Buddha who on good historical authority is said to have been able to recall all past existences from the lowest to the highest, this evolutionary process seems to have reached completion" (1911, 509; cf. 382). Encountering the teachings of the *Book*, Evans-Wentz was already convinced that the life review reported by drugged and drowning individuals was highly significant and an important means to uncover supernatural lapses of time that turns, so he argues, cognate descriptions of the relativity of time (for example, time spent in "Fairyland") into a "scientifically plausible" reality (cf. 469).

In respect to the initial question of a relationship of the judgment scene and the life-review feature in the *Book*, we must come to the conclusion that the life-review feature in its usual portrayal is not present in the *Book* (if at all, a faint allusion might be seen in the mirror of karmic deeds). If one would like to link the intense visions of the second bardo with the judgment scene of the third bardo, it is noteworthy to point out that in the *Book* judgment takes place almost two earthly weeks later, whereas in Western cases "these judgments take place within a few earthly minutes, hours, or days" (Nahm 2011, 385). However, the life-review feature was already present in the minds of the *Book*'s commentators Evans-Wentz and, to a lesser degree, Woodroffe and Jung. Through their comments, they clearly established a connection between these two elements that became later so closely interlinked in Moody's model.

---

[13] Footnotes refer to Fechner 1853b, 774 [i.e., the case of Maury]; Haddock 1851, 213 [Beaufort]; and Du Prel 1889, I, 92–3.

The *Fairy-Faith* guides us to the roots of Evans-Wentz's religious foundation, which is, as said, Theosophy.[14] Indeed, Spiritualist beliefs were already of utmost importance in the work. Immersed in the stream of Gnostic–Esoteric metaculture,[15] Evans-Wentz was already fully convinced of the family ties between Eastern and Western concepts of rebirth before he got to know the *Book*.[16] Comparing Buddhist and Celtic "rebirth" doctrines, Evans-Wentz (1911, 366–7) wrote in his treatise on Celtic mythology: "We see in all this the intimate relation which there was thought to be between what we call the state of life and the state of death, between the world of men and the world of gods, fairies, demons, spirits, and shades." His examination acknowledged in conclusion that there is scientifically plausible evidence of "various dream-like or trance-like states during which ancient and contemporary Celts testify to having been in Fairyland," which, in "the eyes of science," "resolves itself into a reality, because it is one of the states of consciousness co-ordinate with the ordinary consciousness" (469).[17] All this amounts to the belief that "certain conscious states exist independently of the human nerves," and "therefore set up a strong presumption that complete consciousness can exist independently of the physical nerve-apparatus" (471).[18]

2.5.4 C. G. JUNG AND THE TRANSCULTURAL VALIDITY OF AFTER-DEATH EXPERIENCES

Our discussion on the influence the *Book* exerted on near-death experiences concludes with an interpretation of the *Psychological Commentary* by Carl Gustav Jung (1875–1961), which gained both importance for later interpretations of the *Book*" and for near-death discourse more generally. As will be shown, Jung's interpretation of the after-death states of the soul develops in close interaction with the Spiritualist metadiscourse. For Jung, the *Book* and its teachings were a protest against the marginalization of the "soul" in the

---

[14] "His parents were members of the Baptist Church of Trenton, but would break with the organized church to turn to Freethinking and Spiritualism. Young Walter also took an interest in Spiritualism, reading as a teen both *Isis Unveiled* and *The Secret Doctrine* by Madame Blavatsky. [. . . H]e joined the American Section of the Theosophical Society in 1901 [. . . and] received a diploma from the Raja-Yoga School and Theosophical University in 1903" (Lopez 2011, 22).

[15] Evans-Wentz (1911, 29) holds that the existence of " 'astral bodies' or 'doubles' " and apparitions of distant people to others, "especially in the hour of their death [. . .] is amply proven." Cf. also the "lost bride" tale (quoted on 49); "Going to the 'Gentry' through Death, Dreams, or Trance" (68); or the supernatural parallel world of the dead (194).

[16] "Death," he says (1911, 358–9), "is but a going to that Otherworld from this world, and Birth a coming back again," which, he argues, has been attested by mystic initiates or the Buddha.

[17] Evans-Wentz (cf. 1911, 465–6, 471–3) had also noticed Myers's concept of the "Subliminal Self."

[18] Alluding to various concepts of magnetism and theosophical doctrine, he summarizes (1911, 490): "(1) Fairyland exists as a supernormal state of consciousness into which men and women may enter temporarily in dreams, trances, and in various ecstatic states; or in an indefinite period at death. (2) Fairies exist, because in all essentials they appear to be the same as the intelligent forces now recognized by psychical researchers."

West, the attempt to degrade consciousness as a "merely psychological" fact, as an epiphe-nomenon. Therefore Jung's approach to the text rests on "his belief that the materialist, extraverted psychological attitude of the West desperately needs its complementary op-posite from the East" (Clarke 1994, 127).

In contrast to Evans-Wentz, Jung ([1935] 2000, xxxviii) departs from the opinion that the term "soul" [*Seele*] is an adequate framework to describe the Buddhist beliefs expressed in the *Book*. It is the soul that possesses a "divine creative power inherent in it." And he explains, "Not only is it the condition of all metaphysical reality, it *is* that reality. With this great psychological truth the *Bardo Thodol* opens." The "spiritual climax," as Jung terms it, comes therefore right at the moment of death—after that, a "terrifying dream-state of a progressively degenerate character" (li) will unfold. The *Book* demonstrates—for the well-trained, spiritually advanced initiate (cf. lii)—nothing less than the soul's ability for "perfect enlightenment," which is a paradoxical state of the conscious soul and of reality—be it termed as "void," "Clear Light," or something else. Expressed "in our own language," Jung elaborates, "the creative ground of all metaphysical assertion is conscious-ness, as the invisible, intangible manifestation of the soul" (xxxix). The views expressed within the *Book* begin, as said, with this uncompromising experience of enlightenment, but will, if not realized, decline through the unfolding bardos. Everything that happens there is an expression of "archetypes" that are universal, transcultural formations within the soul. As such, they are emerging in the death-surviving soul in the bardos too. Now, he argues, one of these archetypal thought forms is exactly one element that became later a central element of near-death experiences, namely, that the dead are initially not aware that they are dead: "If the archetypes were not pre-existent in identical form everywhere, how could one explain the fact, postulated at almost every turn by the *Bardo Thodol*, that the dead do not know that they are dead, and that this assertion is to be met with just as often in the dreary, half-baked literature of European and American Spiritualism?" (xliv).

Highly interesting is his attempt to argue that this archetype of lack of awareness of being dead—present in Spiritualism and the *Book*—is not, in terms of reception, de-pendent on earlier expressions, for which he names Swedenborg: "Although we find the same assertion in Swedenborg, knowledge of his writings can hardly be sufficiently widespread for this little bit of information to have been picked up by every small-town 'medium'. And a connection between Swedenborg's and the *Bardo Thodol* is completely unthinkable. It is a primordial, universal idea that the dead simply continue their earthly existence and do not know that they are disembodied spirits" (xliv–v). Seen that way, even this idea of the "dead" will emerge from the "*collective unconscious*" that is the realm for all "archetypes," including their individual expression as "religious imagination" in the "after-death state" (cf. li). Actually, for Jung, the *Book* has a tremendous value for his theory, because the bardo experiences reveal the overarching, life-and-death-encompassing reality of the archetypes. The *Book* had been his constant companion since 1927, Jung discloses: "to it I owe not only many stimulating ideas and discoveries, but also many fundamental insights" (xxxvi). It is far from astonishing, therefore, that Jung conveys his own near-death report (which is subsequently discussed) that became widely read from its publication in 1962 up to the present day.

The *Tibetan Book of the Dead* got almost instantly incorporated into the Spiritualist–Occultist metaculture of out-of-the-body" travels and helped to fix convictions of a transcultural prevalence of near-death experiences.[19] An important example for this reception is the work *The Projection of the Astral Body* (1929) by Sylvan Muldoon, serving as medium, and Hereward Carrington[20] as psychical investigator. In his introduction, Carrington outlines basic narratives of the *Egyptian Book of the Dead*, which are, however, to him more mythical than the more concrete "teachings" of the "Tibetan Book." Carrington, describing the latter in detail, comments, that "many of its teachings correspond, in a remarkable way, with those of Occult and Psychical Science" (Muldoon and Carrington 1929, xxii). To him, these teachings reinforce that the nature of the "death-consciousness" determines the future state of the "soul-complex" (xxiii), which gives a Buddhist twist to what had already been discussed in theosophical circles. Once established as a remarkable and "rational" correspondence to the teachings of the "Occult and Psychical Science," the *Book* will find its continuous use as a hermeneutic device for occurrences in dying and deathlike states (cf. Carrington 1937, 256–9).[21] Moreover, in Theosophical and Spiritualist–Occult discourses on the afterlife, other elements of Tibetan religious culture were introduced. Tibetan literary accounts of *delog*, that is, people who "return" (Tibetan *log*) from the "beyond" (Tibetan *'das*), especially attracted attention. The autobiographically styled narratives of what they experienced in their otherworldly journeys become increasingly important in Western near-death discourse.[22]

---

[19] Cf. on the importance of the *Book* for modern near-death discourse Rose 1980; Couliano 1991; Sogyal Rinpoche 1992; Fox 2003; Corazza 2008.

[20] In the late 1920s, Carrington had already an impressive record of Spiritualist publications, including treatments of yoga philosophy or self-help books on the development of psychical powers. Important to mention: In his book *Death. Its Causes and Phenomena. With Special Reference to Immortality* (1912, 315–17; cf. 120), he deals with the life review (on Heim's "sensations while falling," and de Quincey), ending with the final comment: "Surely this closely resembles the 'Book of Judgment' of theology!" (317). Cf., moreover, the chapter on the "Visions of the Dying" (319–27).

[21] Carrington (1937, 259) comments on a modern case of spiritualist communication: "It is, I think, of no little significance and interest that statements made by Tibetan priests, a thousand and more years ago, should have been quite independently verified by a young man living in a small Western town in the United States!" (cf. Crookall 1960, 153; 1961, 134–5). An important propagator of theosophical interpretations of the *Book*, mixing theosophical doctrines such as the silver cord and astral projection with Tibetan teachings, has been T. Lobsang Rampa (i.e., Cyril Henry Hoskin). He claimed his first work *The Third Eye* (1956) was a telepathically transmitted autobiography of a Tibetan monk.

[22] Information on Tibetan *delog* stories were, for example, included in David-Néel's mysterious and widely read account *With Mystics and Magicians in Tibet* ([1931] 1937, 33), stating that in Tibet, one may meet "delogs," "people who have been in a state of lethargy, and are able to describe the various places in which, they say, they have travelled. Some have only visited countries inhabited by men, while others can tell of their peregrinations in the paradises, the purgatories or in the *bardo*." And she continues that "Tibetans, like Egyptians, believe in the 'double," and may, if trained, effect it at will. The separation, however, is not complete, for a strand subsists, connecting the two forms. [. . .] The destruction of the corpse generally, but not necessarily, brings about

By the late 1920s, the technical use of out-of-the-body experience is fully established, as can be seen in Sylvan Muldoon's casual note (1929, v), "when my first out-of-the-body experiences occurred I was but twelve." Muldoon, however, searching not for spontaneous incidents but for "projections of the astral body" on a voluntary basis while retaining consciousness within the astral body, emphasizes that there is no objective proof other than experience—experience, in other words, *is* the proof (v–vi). Carrington, in contrast, relates that he initially encountered the phenomenon while experimenting with yoga (see xxxiv). Yet his experiments convey merely a lively interest in third-party validation of astral projection, whereas elements of near-death reports are, apart from the out-of-the-body fact as such, almost absent. An interesting comment in regard to expectations of the dying pertains to their wish to "see": "The astral body of a dying person is often projected to the presence of friends and loved ones a few moments before the physical death, the phenomenon arising from the strong desire of the dying person to see and be seen" (3). A wish that, we surmise, near-death experiences may fulfill. Muldoon, however, holds that death is quite probably a "permanent projection" (228). Overviewing the field between the extremes of the Materialist and the Spiritualist believing death to be but the beginning of a greater life, and of "an army of cults, religions and creeds" in between both that mostly regard "death as a 'curse,' " Muldoon leaves us with his final conclusion, that he sees "life as the curse": "I regret that life exists. No mortal mind can advance even the weakest argument in defence of life. I regret that the Materialist is mistaken. I regret that death does *not* end all" (232–3).

To summarize, we can see how the *Tibetan Book of the Dead* was especially acknowledged for validating claims of astral projection and the transmigrating soul on a transcultural basis. In its special theosophical reading, based on a translation already inspired by Theosophy, it offered a framework that could equally be labeled as "scientific proof" for the soul's near- and after-death experiences, as it was of use for pointing to the telling absence of spiritual care for the dying in modern Western medicine and hospitals. From early on, it was argued in a Universalist and Perennialist manner that there can be no historical dependency whatsoever between these doctrines and modern Western teachings, given the fact that the *Book* details teachings of Tibetan Buddhism of the 8th–14th centuries. Moreover, the insights provided were taken as psychological, scientific, and experiential evidence of "nonduality" that interpenetrates the disembodied mind and its "experienced" environments. Gods, after-death planes of existence, and so forth, are

---

the destruction of the 'double' in the end. In certain cases, it may survive its companion" (33). Interestingly, she uses well-established spiritualist and esoteric terminology in her account, but stays clear from a religious interpretation. "Evidently," she comments, "the *delog* is not really a dead man, so that nothing can prove that the sensations he experiences in his lethargy are the same as those felt by the dead. Tibetans, however, do not seem to be troubled by this distinction" (34)—as will neither be Crookall (1960, 85–6) in his study of astral projection, being especially interested in David-Néel's mention of a cord between the two bodies. The impact of *delog* accounts in near-death discourse is discussed in Bailey 2001.

neither an objective reality nor merely psychological artifacts, but do exist on a conventional level if somebody experiences them. In that respect, the karmic projection theory of the *Book* could be taken as evidence why, as Evans-Wentz argued, Hindus, Muslims, Native Americans, or Christians will experience the bardo states differently—according to their cultural and religious backgrounds. This idea, though prefigured, as previously shown, in Splittgerber's account (1866), could now be used to accredit the cultural variability of heavens, hells, God, or the quality of light (or "the Light") experienced, without, however, relativizing the "experiences" themselves. Finally, with his discovery and translation of the *Book*, Evans-Wentz could prove historically that there were indeed substantial Tibetan Buddhist teachings in regard to after-death states. Actually, the *Book* could be used to reevaluate the wisdom of the "Tibetan Masters," mediumistically received by the first generation of Theosophists, despite all disputes in respect to the former's existence or the latter's veracity, respectively.

Although the *Book* made its way into the near-death discourse, it may be added that in the late 1920s, further reports received broad attention. To pick out only one characteristic account here: In 1928, American Christian–Spiritualist writer and founder of the Fascist movement "Silver Legion," William Dudley Pelley (1890–1965), published an article "My Seven Minutes in Eternity" in the *American Magazine*. An enlarged version appeared as a book in 1929. In his account, Pelley (cf. 1929, 7) describes how he at night suddenly felt a strong "*physical* sensation" of being close to death—a heart attack or an apoplexy, he reasons. In consequence, he left his body and made a "hyperdimensional visitation." During his experience, he is warmly received by "friends" in a heavenly realm, becomes aware of other deceased living happily in the "hereafter," but finally, he returns with a "click" into his body—with great disappointment, as he says: "It was a tragedy, the coming back" (15). In the aftermath, described extensively, he went through a "physical rebirth" (27), being now determined to work for the spiritual renewal of America. Moreover, he claims to be permanently able to get out of the body at will, or being gifted with other supernatural talents: for example, he reports having received an extensive message "in pure Sanskrit" by some "Atlantean" voice (41). However, most significant is the general attraction that his report received. According to Pelley, the issue of the *American Magazine* alone (not counting other reprints) had appeared in more than 2.2 million copies. Given that each was read on average by at least four persons, Pelley reckons, it turned out that "something like *ten million people* had access to the narrative" (33). It actually won him immediate national fame. Tellingly, he describes at length the reactions that he received in a plethora of letters: praise by those describing similar experiences and by the majority of "Protestants ministers," whereas psychiatrists and other professionals saw in his report either a hoax, a delusion, or a drug experience (cf. 39–40)—an almost complete inventory of reactions that is still to be found today.

2.6

Consolidation of Near-Death Discourse (1930–1960)

THE THREE DECADES to follow, from the 1930s to the 1960s, saw a certain consolidation of the different currents within near-death discourse. The paradigmatic turn toward dying as an either successful or unsuccessful liberation of consciousness, as it had been described in the *Tibetan Book of the Dead* (hereafter the *Book*), can be seen in the increase of the terms "liberation" and "consciousness" in near-death discourse. Although in the 19th century some scholars had already occasionally spoken of the *inner* consciousness of the dying (e.g., Haddock 1851, 214–15), the term now assumes a broader meaning, being sometimes equated with the person's inner identity, replacing the term "soul." An early example for this discursive development is the article by Leslie Grant Scott (1877–?), "Dying as a Liberation of Consciousness" (1931).[1] While accompanying her husband to India, Burma, and Ceylon, she "died" in Ceylon, as she says, from a combination of illness and "too much sorrow" (Scott 1931, 113). It seems as if the related incident had happened some years before. Being relaxed and tranquil, but without the will to live, she reports the following experience: "Suddenly my whole life began to unroll before me and I saw the purpose of it" (113). Being still fully conscious, she sends for the doctor. The doctor, Scott reports, was unable to feel any pulse, so he hurriedly gave her a "hypodermic." At that time, she was becoming aware that she "was now conscious of what was passing on in the mind of others" (114). A second attempt to revive her failed, too,

---

[1] This case of Scott has been erroneously attributed by Crookall (1964, 86–7) to Haddock 1851; a mistake perpetuated in later literature.

and Scott started to laugh, because of the "futility" to revive her—she simply "wanted to go." Scott continues her narration: "Meanwhile my consciousness was growing more and more acute. It seemed to have expanded beyond the limits of my physical brain. I was aware of things I had never contacted. My vision was also extended so that I could see what was going on behind my back, in the next room, even in distant places!" (114). We read later in her report that she, in a somehow Bergsonian–Jamesian manner, could see the unity of things; but, Scott discloses, "I was obliged to narrow my vision so that it might fit the brain which I had to use" (116). Actually, it is the sadness of her close friends that make her, as disembodied consciousness, decide to go back: "The effort to return to my body was accompanied by an almost unimaginable sensation of horror and terror. I had left without the slightest struggle. I returned by an almost superhuman effort of will" (115). After her return, she still retains the capacity of an expanded consciousness and "the power to hear and see at a distance" (115). A very significant new element of this report is the narrative of watching, somehow emotionally disturbed, the resuscitation attempts of the doctor. Probably needless to say, that the emergence of the disembodied observer witnessing resuscitation attempts will go hand in hand with such attempts to happen in the life world. Although real-world events are, to put it in Kantian terms, not the condition of possibility of their being witnessed while out of the body, there seems to be nevertheless good evidence to think that the disembodied observer may see such resuscitation attempts if they are increasingly *practiced* (which happens in the first half of the 20th century) and therefore also increasingly *present in discourse*, guiding personal expectation of what may happen in life-threatening conditions, and so forth.

Although the narrative misses allusions to Christian narratives of the afterlife, it is noteworthy that Scott reports (1931, 117) having made "prophesies" for the doctor that came true later. She became aware, as she says, of the "plan" or "law," working with "math-ematical precision,"[2] that regulates the perfect moral justice of "what we sow, we shall reap." Moreover, she reports that in a "mental fashion" she had, while dead, been told that she could either stay or return. For her, it is, however, an experience that transformed her—most prominently, she realizes that she will be helped through her suffering. If "in-clined to doubt, to revert to her former agnosticism," she merely thinks of what she ex-perienced and "my faith and knowledge immediately return to me" (115). In conclusion, Scott holds that true life consists of the "free" and "wider" consciousness. There is, for sure, no death, and consciousness will continue after the death of the body, this "stupid prison of flesh"—probably, we read, consciousness continues as some kind of "vibration" (116). Again, her own evaluation combines elements of Christian and Gnostic–Esoteric metacultures: adducing her "little bit of evidence," as she says, but, characteristically, no proof, for "man's immortal life in an eternal universe" (117)—with which Scott's report ends.

---

[2] One might think of the European conception of "karma" here, cf. Schlieter 2013.

2.6.1 FREUDIAN INTERPRETATIONS OF THE LIFE REVIEW

In the 1930s, the reports of Heim and others also attracted new attention from psychologists and psychoanalysts. A forerunner had been the collection of "Psycho-pathological documents" (1920) by the German psychiatrist Karl Birnbaum (1878–1950), who had put together "testimonials from the soul's borderland." In a chapter on the "abnormal" and "deviant" experiences in mortal danger, he quotes the reports of Heim and von Bälz (Birnbaum 1920, 224); however, he is not inclined to attribute to these "abnormal episodes" a "higher meaning for the personality" (226).

A more important development in psychological discourse on experiences near death had, however, been initiated by Sigmund Freud (1856–1939) through his focus on "defense mechanisms" of the psyche. Freud, who did not treat narratives of the near-death discourse more thoroughly, conceptualized a human "death drive" [*Todestrieb*] in 1920, a "thanatos instinct" as opposed to the "will to live" or "life instinct." According to the latter instinct, the psyche of a person, if faced with a situation too uncomfortable to accept, will display the phenomenon of "denial," and will, against all evidence, transform the unsatisfactory situation into a satisfactory one through various substrategies including more basic ones such as "stimulus barriers" (cf. Pfister 1931, 19–21) or "minimization," as well as more advanced forms of "disavowal" and "repression."

It was a Swiss lay psychoanalyst, Oskar Pfister (1873–1956)—significantly, in his main occupation a Lutheran minister—who became aware of the reports of Heim and others and read them for the first time from the perspective of psychoanalysis. Already in the preliminary note of his contribution (cf. Pfister 1931, 3) he discloses his expectation that in situations of life-threatening danger the human psyche will likely employ one of two opposing strategies—if the life instinct triumphs, the mind will work in highest speed to find a way to survive or it will freeze the mind in shock and transport the psyche into a "beyond of autistic phantasies," designed to hinder a full awareness of the fact that the person is threatened by nonexistence.

In conclusion, Pfister argued in regard to the cases of Heim, additional reports and his own conclusive experiences that "the victims were evoking infantile fantasies in order to evade the unacceptable prospect of death" (Zaleski 1987, 99; cf. 171–2). In cases of extreme stimulus satiation, Pfister argued with Freud, that in cases such as "shocks," a "stimulus barrier" will be set up in order to prevent traumatization. Consolatory déjà-vus, or hyperactive production of lust and delight, or hallucinations of heavenly scenes, and so forth, are sufficient evidence for the strategy of the psyche to devalue the life-threatening danger. In that perspective, the life-review feature is simply a "[mental] play of consolation" ([*Trostdarbietung*]; cf. Pfister 1931, 21–5).[3] In conclusion, "nothing but the wildest, most indignant revolt against the impertinence of death was to be found. Likewise, the

---

[3] The concept of a "sweet" and "agreeable death," quoting Heim and others, reigns the entire book of George Barbarin, *Le livre de la mort douce*, which appeared in a theosophical publishing house in 1937.

hallucination of a beyond, or of reincarnation, cannot be construed as a suggestion for the wish for self-destruction" (27 [my trans.]). In other words, there is no clue for assuming a death drive at work in experiences near death such as those reported from falls. On the contrary, Pfister argues, these instances show how these mental overactivities pursue the additional aim to prevent unconsciousness or states of sleep (cf. 22). Paradoxically, both states—full awareness, but also unconscious sleep—are prevented, which shapes these states equal to daydreams.

Zaleski (1987, 172) concludes that Pfister provides "in germ the guiding principles for subsequent psychological interpretation of near-death experience; the central idea is that the mind cannot accept its death and therefore imagines itself detached from the body, fantasizes immortality, and regresses to infantile and 'oceanic' consolations." The regression into infantile states is, in Pfister's eyes (cf. 1931, 15–16), an obvious element of those life-review fantasies that revive early childhood images. Often, he holds, they are combined with memories of moral failure (embarrassing memories of conscience). The latter element is a prominent feature of a personal report that Pfister analyzes in detail. In this case, the "analysand" expressed a belief in postmortal judgment and, in this trajectory, an awareness of moral guilt and need of remission. Although he does not offer any religious interpretation, Pfister argues that we witness infantile visions of a pleasurable "paradisiacal existence," which he rejects without a more extensive "philosophic or religious discussion that would reassure a correct and thorough judgment" (24). In short, all religious content of these visions, that is, hallucinations of paradise or reincarnation—for the latter, he refers to possible influences of "theosophical teachings of phantastic reincarnation" (17)—is infantile, because in these visions, the "unconscious" is at work, not the "full developed, conscious I" (cf. 28).

Exactly in the same year as Pfister's contribution appeared, Emil Mattiesen (1875–1939), a Baltic-German parapsychologist, published a first article on the "exit of the I"; a few years later, an extensive collection of reports followed, arranged, more or less systematically, in various categories—for example, paranormal circumstances at death, telepathy, or reappearance of the dead. All of these serve as building blocks in the argument for the survival of consciousness. As previously mentioned, one section deals with the dying who experience an "anticipation of their death" ([*Vorwegnahme des Sterbens*], Mattiesen 1936, II, 296–411). Here, we find numerous experiences near death, some of them from earlier collections, for example, by Myers or spiritualist journals, but also new cases reported to Mattiesen, summing up to almost "60 cases" (II, 334). A striking fact is the significant number of instances in which narcotics and drugs are named as "triggering" the experience.[4] Many reports contain autoscopic experiences, especially of narcotized individuals in surgery, who report to have experienced themselves as looking down on their body on the operation table, witnessing the doctors with surgical instruments,

---

4 For example, Mattiesen 1936, 307, 311, 319, 325.

shouting at them and trying to stop the procedure. In other words, the more operations that are done, because of the progress in surgery and the equally prevalent aversion against "dehumanizing" practices of "materialist medicine" (which may have risen in proportion), the more prominent becomes this "original scene" of the modern out-of-body experience. On the other hand, Mattiesen groups them together with self-induced spirit excursions of the astral body. For him, it seems, it is only the reported contents that counts—the circumstances are arbitrary. Moreover, we do find in Mattiesen's collection several other features of Moody's scheme, namely, the life review, the order to return to life, encounters with spirits and a bright light, and so forth. Regarding the general argument, to prove the soul's survival of death, Mattiesen (II, 386, 412–13) concludes: The "projection," the consciousness's ability to leave the body, seems evident; however, the explanatory power of "spiritual excursions" does not prove "objectively," in the full sense of the latter, a survival of death—yet, if "self-conscious life beyond the body" is proven, it will at least prove the "possibility" of life after death—therefore, he ultimately concludes, the "spiritist thesis" must be acknowledged by psychologists, physiologists, theologians, and "scholars of the scientific study of religion" ([*Religionswissenschafter*], II, 413).

Equally open for spiritualist–occult interpretations, Italian parapsychologist Ernesto Bozzano (1862-1943), whose earlier work was mentioned in Chapter 2.5, collected a large number of earlier reports on the life review and out-of-body features as evidence for a survivalist position (cf. Siegel 1983, 196). An interesting characteristic of his principal publication on the former, *Della 'Visione panoramica' o 'Memoria sintetica' nell'imminenza della Morte* ([On the 'Panoramic Vision' or 'Synthetic Memory' in Imminent Death], 1931) is the fact that it connects questions regarding these phenomena pursued in Spiritualist–Occultist metaculture with reports and explanations that had so far been discussed in the Naturalist metaculture, for example, the French debate by Egger, Féré, Ribot, and so forth (cf. Bozzano 1931, 52–8). However, surveying the cases reported in the literature, he suggests that these belong to different categories: The first category consists of cases—ranging from Beaufort to more recent French examples—in which the "panoramic vision" occurred in imminent death or life-threatening danger. The second category consists of cases in which healthy persons in secure situations experienced the phenomenon. Crossing the border to the Spiritualist–Occult, he adds a third category comprising cases in which the dead communicate that they experienced the panoramic vision before death,[5] concluding that this phenomenon points to a Bergsonian capacity of memory to be virtually fully simultaneous if unleashed (cf. 89–90). Bozzano, again, holds this to be the case in disembodied souls. Similarly, he aims to sort the phenomenon of "bilocation,"[6] assuming that the spirit, being an "ethereal brain," able to leave the physical body as an "etheric body" (75; cf. Alvarado 2005).

---

[5] For example, the case of H. A. Ackley/Paist 1861.

[6] Ornella Corazza (2008, 25) reminds us that Bozzano based his model of survival on the idea of a bilocation. He used this term for "phantom limb sensations" by amputees, but also autoscopy, near-death experiences,

In that decade, we can also witness an ongoing discourse in Christian metaculture, though these Christian protagonists were usually declared spiritualists too. A somehow mysterious example is a small booklet, "My Death and Revival," by an alleged Russian, C. Uxkull, translated from the Russian by a certain (equally not traceable) Basil Doudine, and published in New York in 1934 (repr. 1961). It follows well-known lines.[7] Another example of Christian interest in near-death-discourse is the work of Herbert Henry Charles Thurston S. J. (1856–1939), a Roman Catholic priest and active member of the Society for Psychical Research in London. His interest had been raised, he reports in a 1935 article, "Memory at Imminent Death," by the experiences of his own father who nearly drowned.

2.6.2 THE CONSOLIDATION OF THE "TUNNEL" IMAGERY

As previously said, a new element reported as part of experiences near death is the tunnel experience. A certain prefiguration can be found in the work *The Astral Body*, in which Arthur E. Powell (1927, 232) describes a method of clairvoyance that uses an "astral current" of atoms, "forming a kind of temporary tube, along which the clairvoyant may look," somewhat like seeing through an "astral telescope," which may also include a tube of some kind "made by the mesmerizer" (233). Actually, the "tube" presents a wonderful example of how esoteric ideas are, in terms of metaphors, modernized. Leadbeater describes in his *Inner Life* (1911, II, 203–4), a "tiny microscope," projected from the "chakram" between the eyebrows, by which minute objects may be observed, using the final atom at the end as lens. Powell (1925, 1927) takes up his ideas but transforms Leadbeater's microscope into a projected telescope, a "flexible tube." The clairvoyant practitioner may direct his focused consciousness through the astral tube and see what happens at the end of it. The imagery of the tube, introduced into astral projection, shows once again how *intentional* practices had their share in shaping visionary content reported also in *unintentional* experiences near death.

---

and "a variety of luminous or cloud-like emanations that clairvoyants claimed left the body at the moment of death." With these ruminations, Bozzano could treat paranormal deathbed apparitions, being visible to external observers, and experiences near death as aspects of a uniform class of phenomena.

[7] The Russian protagonist, complaining about living in a "century of unbelief and skepticism" (Uxkull 1934, 59), reports of a serious pneumonia; suddenly, he realizes his disembodied self is standing in the room and watching with close interest the group of doctors surrounding the bed. Not being able to talk to them, or to touch his own body, he observes himself declared dead. At the same time, in a supernormal swiftness of thought, memories of the past assemble. Angels carry him away, and while in steep ascent, he hears yelling and roaring of evil spirits. A vision of bright light follows, called by him "the kingdom." Then he hears two portentous words from above, "not ready" (38). Against his will, he descends rapidly. A guardian angel commands him to return into the body already stored in the hospital's mortuary. He enters it with sorrow; followed by unconsciousness. The doctors, he reports, while admitting a miraculously fast recovery, declare his visions as hallucinations. This, less unusual in this genre, leads to a sustained disappointment in science. The author argues that his soul returned by God's will and illustrates the miracle with the biblical restoration of the life of Lazarus (cf. 53). Although Christian in its message, the report shows slight allusions to spiritualist literature, e.g., alluding to the astral body (cf. 27, 30).

In 1935, a certain Dr. G. B. Kirkland delivered a lecture on his experience while he, after a series of surgeries, "officially 'died.'" "To my surprise, *I found myself looking at myself lying on the bed.* [. . .] Then I was hurried off at great speed. *Have you ever looked through a long tunnel and seen the tiny speck of light at the far end*? It seems an incredible distance off. Well, I found myself with others vaguely discernible hurrying along just such *a tunnel or passage—smoky or cloudy, colourless, grey and very cold.*

[. . .] The others were passing me very rapidly, hurrying towards the light which was brightening" (quoted in Crookall 1964, 89). As it seems, the tunnel is not described as a modern architectural artifact, but connects—with its paradox atmosphere of smoke and frostiness—to hellish underworld visions.

In the United States, it was an Episcopal minister, Louis Tucker, who described in his memoirs, published as *Clerical Errors* in 1943, his own experience that had happened as he suffered from food poisoning in 1909. Again, as a significant element we encounter the tunnel experience. Tucker narrates that he had been pronounced dead by the doctor. Then he fainted. Regaining consciousness, he reports of a sensation that

was not quite like anything earthly; the nearest familiar thing to it is passing through a short tunnel on a train. There was the same sense of hurrying, of blackness, of rapid transition, of confused noise, and multiform, swift readjustment. Death is a very much overrated process. I have since suffered many times as much while waiting [. . .] for a comparatively minor surgical operation. I emerged into a place where people were being met by friends. It was quiet and full of light, and Father was waiting for me. He looked exactly as he had in the last few years of his life and wore the last suit of clothes he had owned [. . .]. Soon I discovered that we were not talking, but thinking. I knew dozens of things that we did not mention because he knew them. He thought a question, I an answer, without speaking; the process was practically instantaneous. [. . .] I did not want to go back; [. . .] the will to live was quite gone [. . .]. I swung into the blackness again, as a man might swing on a train, thoroughly disgusted that I could not stay, and absolutely certain that it was right for me to go back. That certainty has never wavered. There was a short interval of confused and hurrying blackness and I came to find myself lying on my bed with the doctor bending over telling me that I was safe now and would live because circulation was re-established [. . .]. I told him I knew that some time ago, and went to sleep. (Tucker 1943, 221–5, cf. Audette 1982,33)

Surely experiences of speedy travels through a tunnel will have been possible in premodern times, too (e.g., horse rides), but the modern technology of trains and tunnels will likely have contributed to form a kind of experience drawn here as the nearest equivalent. However, the tunnel feature will continuously gain prominence and plays a major role not only in Moody's description, but also in more recent near-death experiences.

More on the Naturalist side, though framed with a religious interpretation, British physician and professor of anatomy, Sir Auckland Geddes (1879–1954), reports only two years later of a remarkable experience, triggered by acute gastroenteritis, that attracted a lot of attention. In an address delivered to the Royal Medical Society, he included the following report of an experience, which is in the speech attributed to a "doctor-friend." Developing into an "acute poisoning," the illness is accompanied by the experience of a split into two consciousnesses: "thereafter at no time did my consciousness appear to me to be in any way dimmed, but I suddenly realized that *my* consciousness was separating from another consciousness, which was also me. These for purposes of description we could call the A and B consciousness, and throughout what follows, the ego attached itself to the A consciousness" (Geddes 1937, 374). While the "B consciousness"—the, of course, secondary consciousness of the body—begins to disintegrate, he experiences his "A consciousness, which was now me" to have left and to see the body. "Gradually I realised that I could see not only my body and the bed in which it was, but everything in the whole house and garden, and then I realised that I was seeing not only 'things' at home, but in London and in Scotland, in fact wherever my attention was directed it seemed to me" (374). Searching for a clue, he receives as explanation by an inner "mentor," that he was "free in a time dimension of space." "From now on," Geddes continues, "the description is and must be entirely metaphorical. Although I had no body, I had what appeared to be perfect two-eyed vision, and what I saw can only be described in this way, that I was conscious of a psychic stream flowing with life through time [. . .]. I understood from my mentor that all our brains are just end organs projecting as it were from the three-dimensional universe into the psychic stream, and flowing with it into the fourth and fifth dimensions" (375). Besides his mention of the "filter theory" of the brain, Geddes, being informed of further particularities of the fourth and fifth dimensions,[8] realizes that he is a "condensation" in the psychic stream, a sort of cloud, and is able to recognize this "psychic condensation" around the body of others as an aura in various colors. Being brought back with the assistance, as he narrates, of a physician's camphor injection, he "was intensely annoyed," because he was "just beginning to understand where I was and what I was 'seeing'. I came back into the body really angry at being pulled back, and once I was back all the clarity of vision of anything and everything disappeared." Most significantly, however, Geddes uses the same terms as Leslie Scott (1931) to describe the event, depicting it as an "experience of liberation of consciousness":

It is surprising to note that this dream, vision or experience has shown no tendency to fade like a dream would fade, nor has it shown any tendency that I am

---

[8] In the 1930s, theories of five dimensions in theoretical physics (e.g., by Theodor Kaluza, 1885–1954), aiming at a unified field theory of electromagnetism and gravitation, had gained prominence and were, as the theories of Albert Einstein, of growing—though often metaphorical—importance for modern esotericism, but also for the developing parapsychology.

aware of to grow or rationalise itself as a dream would do. [. . .], I was dead to the three-dimensional universe. If this is so and if in fact the experience of liberation of consciousness in the fourth-dimensional universe is not imagination, it is a most important matter to place on record. Since my return with the injections there had been no repetition of any sort or kind of the experience or of the clear understanding that I seemed to have while I was free from the body. (376)[9]

Although the report tries to adduce as much evidence as possible for proponents of the Naturalist metaculture expectedly present in a meeting of a medical society, there are nevertheless significant elements of an esoteric–gnostic character. The expansion of a fourth- and fifth-dimension consciousness, or a disembodied "consciousness" able to see another person's colored "cloud," should be especially noted here. As in the case of Scott, terms such as "astral body," or even "spirit" and "soul," are used with significant religious connotations. The whole report is framed by sympathetic comments on Spiritualism. The experience, Geddes explains, "has helped me to define the idea of a psychic continuum spread out in time like the plasmic net. It does more; it provides a comprehensible background for the soul-palæontology of Jung, and it seems to throw a flood of light on the meaning of soul abysses discovered by the method of Freud. It brings telepathy, clairvoyance, spiritualism and indeed all the parapsychic manifestations into the domain of the picturable" (376–7). Although Geddes does not speak straightforwardly of a death survival, his assumption of a "disintegration" of the "body-soul" implies the soul's survival (cf. 377). However, later in his speech, Geddes advances an interpretation of the "Spirit" that comes closer to Christian metaculture, though he still tries to mark a distance to official doctrines: "To me, Spirit is beyond direct reach, but I can see the effects it produces. I see it make a mock of the careful safety first attitude of body-soul. [. . .]. I see it set before a man an image of what it wants him to be and mould him to it. Do not imagine that Spirit is pious or sanctimonious. It is the reverse. The pious seek a reward: Spirit never does. One of the grandest spirits I ever knew treated official Christianity and the organised Churches with scant respect, almost as a bad joke, and yet mystically reached out across the years to the Master Spirit of the Greatest Jew, Jesus of Nazareth" (382). Although paying respect to the "God-seekers" or "mystics," Geddes pretends that he—personally—has "no experience" of mysticism. But still, he comments, "God-seeker's" bodies sometimes "suffer physical damage when their spirits go out to meet God, if that is what they do. Do not scoff at mysticism, it has wielded tremendous power in the world" (382)—a quite remarkable statement for being included in a medical journal! And finally, he reports that he "once stood beside a bed and observed the condition of a mystic following a supernatural adventure" (382–3), which "baffled" a physician

---

[9] Geddes quoted, e.g., in Tyrrell 1954 [1947], 197–9; Crookall 1960, 16–17; Audette 1982, 33–4.

present—but, so it seems, it did not irritate Geddes, being impressed by mystics and God seekers, such as Baltic-German philosopher Hermann Graf Keyserling (cf. 381).

In the 1930s and 1940s, near-death reports were also handed down in Spiritualist–Occult circles, enriched and combined with reports of intentional out-of-the body experiences or astral projections, as these phenomena were still called by Theosophists.[10] Leaving the body and heading regularly for extraterrestrial fourth and fifth dimensions seemed to have become an everyday practice in certain circles, as is understanding oneself as an investigator of human survival after death, or "survivalism," as it is now technically called. A prominent example is British medium and spiritist Gladys Osborne Leonard (1882–1968; see chapter XXI, "I leave my physical body again," in 1931, 103–9). She was also the medium through which Florence Barrett could communicate with her husband, the deceased Sir William Barrett previously discussed. Leonard included these occurrences in a book that documents the perfect correspondence of medium, method, and message: *Personality Survives Death* (1937). Here, Leonard makes use of near-death reports, for example, of Sir Geddes. Although criticizing Geddes's sharp distinction between his experience and those "spiritual adventures of the mystics," which belong to the "supernatural," she is happy to add that Geddes's "scientific" report converges with "many such authenticated records in the annals of psychic science" (Leonard 1937, 182). The quintessence of these encounters with and in the beyond may be summarized with the message Leonard receives to spread in the life world: "tell everybody—everybody that will listen—that there *is* this Other Life. It is a *real* life in a *real* world." In short, "God is here," and all "the best and most hopeful ideas that Christian religion on the earth has ever held out about a future life are poor compared to this wonderful reality. [...] We wait here for those we love" (208).

An American contribution to near-death discourse, again halfway to literary accounts, is to be found in Admiral Richard E. Byrd (1888–1957), a pioneering polar explorer and aviator. In 1938, he published the still widely read *Alone*, a diary-based account of his five-month stay at the South Pole (1934). Retrospectively, he remembers his emotions and thoughts while in a desperate situation, being the single person manning a remote Antarctic weather station. In this situation, Byrd experiences an intensity of fear never known before. "But it wasn't the fear of suffering or even of death itself. It was a terrible anxiety over the consequences to those at home if I failed to return." And Byrd continues, "during those hours of bitterness, I saw my whole life pass in review. I realized how wrong my sense of values had been and how I had failed to see that the simple, homely, unpretentious things of life are the most important." In comparison with life reviews reported in acute stress or fear-of-death situations, Byrd reports it in an unusual

---

[10] The novelist William Alexander Gerhardie (1895–1977) intended "to write a book on the subject of immortality and went to bed in a state of nervous exhaustion." In a disembodied experience, he awoke to a "higher consciousness." The long narrative of his "travel" is included in his autobiographical novel *Resurrection* (1934); quoted, e.g., in Crookall 1960, 26–31.

way. Slowly, reflectively, and, far from considering himself "a martyr to science," he is "bitter toward the whole world except my family and friends." Early on the morning of June 2, he wrote in his diary, "The universe is not dead. Therefore, there is an Intelligence there, and it is all pervading. At least one purpose [. . .] of that Intelligence is the achievement of universal harmony [. . .]. The human race, then is not alone in the universe. Though I am cut off from human beings, I am not alone. For untold ages man has felt an awareness of that Intelligence. Belief in it is the one point where all religions agree. It has been called by many names. Many call it God" (Byrd 1939, 118–22). Falling asleep, he struggles to awaken; and he reports, the struggle "went on interminably in a half-lighted borderland divided by a great white wall. Several times I was nearly across the wall into a field flooded with a golden light, but each time I slipped back into a spinning darkness. Instinct plucked at my sleeve: You must wake up [. . .]. Then the tension eased; I fell across the wall; and, instead of warm sunlight, I found myself in darkness, shivering from cold and thirsting for water" (118–22). We must take Byrd's narrative as evidence for the well-established link between situations near death—though, in his case, not of a sudden but continuous threat—and reflection on religious meaning.

In the context of explorers' and aviators' mystical experiences near death, the case of Charles Lindbergh (1902–1974) deserves mention here. Being in 1927 the first individual who crossed the Atlantic in a solo nonstop flight, he reported in his widely read *Spirit of St. Louis* (1953) of his experiences. Interestingly, in his first book (*We*, 1927), published only two months after the flight of more than 33 hours, he remained silent on these experiences. In 1953, however, he reports that during the long, "unearthly hours," being "both conscious and asleep," he (2003 [1953], 389) noticed "ghostly presences." He was not surprised, he says, by their presence. Lindbergh describes that he could see them all around without turning his head, his skull being "one great eye, seeing everywhere at once." His body lost its weight, his mind, "still attached to life," became "universal as aether." The spirits he witnessed are, he holds, "emanations from the experience of ages, inhabitants of a universe close to mortal man." As things progressed, Lindbergh became aware of being on "the borderline of life and a greater realm beyond." Experiencing a changing of "values," he asks himself, "Is this death? Am I crossing the bridge which one sees only in last, departing moments? Am I already beyond the point from which I can bring my vision back to earth and men?" (390). Similar to various other narratives, he arrives at a new insight: "Death no longer seems the final end it used to be, but rather the entrance to a new and free existence which includes all space, all time." In contrast to him, the spirits were not attached to life, and so he reports, clad in questions posed to himself, if he is about "to join these ghostly forms," and will become "a consciousness in space, all-seeing, all-knowing, unhampered by the materialistic fetters of the world." All this happened in a relaxed mood. The spirits, on one occasion termed "emissaries from a spirit world," reassured and consoled him in friendly voices, comparable to a "gathering of family and friends after years of separation, as though I've known all of them before in some past incarnation" (390). Finally, the memoir of this situation ends with him reporting experiences with faint allusions to the life-review feature: All at once, he says, he lived at different times and at different places; old associations and memories from friends, voices from distant times, and changing vistas were all around him. Certainly such extreme forms of sensory deprivation may cause such experiences. But why he did not report these experiences in the 1927 book? As it seems, to report them became increasingly important to him—somewhere over the years between 1927 and 1953. We may notice that the question he poses to himself, "am I crossing the bridge which one sees only in last moments," reveals a familiarity with near-death reports.[11] Besides, concepts referred to, such as reincarnation, emissaries, an all-knowing consciousness, or the critique of "materialistic" fetters, point to ideas of the Gnostic–Esoteric metaculture. Crucial is the expressed capacity to reflect on these experiences as having revealed a *new* insight, namely, that death is not final but an entrance into another world. Indeed, Lindbergh seems to have been in his youth not particularly religious, but, as Friedman shows, became increasingly interested in immortality, occultism, parapsychology, and the teachings of yoga (cf. Friedman 2008, 23, 109–20).

In the 1940s and 1950s, further books and numerous articles in journals of psychic research appeared—either including personal narratives or case collections—that kept the near-death discourse running (e.g., Oxenham and Oxenham 1941[12]; or the case collections in Muldoon and Carrington 1951; Johnson 1953; Hart 1954). Among these publications, there is also a monograph, *Apparitions* (1943), written by British parapsychologist and physicist George N. M. Tyrrell (1879–1952), who is nowadays held to have coined the term "'out-of-the-body' experiences" (Tyrrell 1943, 149).[13] As previously seen, it was by 1918 already in use. Most of these publications do not include new aspects; worth mentioning, however, is the concept of extrasensory perception, introduced by parapsychologist Joseph Banks Rhine in 1934 (cf. Alvarado 2003, 74–5). This concept, "ESP" for short, appears basically to be a terminological innovation. With the increasing influence of empirical psychology, positivist philosophy, and radical behaviorism in the 1940s and 1950s, claims of clairvoyance, telepathy, precognition, and so forth, had to pass rigorous tests. "Perception," of course, implies that there *is* something to be perceived. To counter criticism of metaphysical and supernatural claims, Rhine introduced, therefore, the new descriptive framework. Empirical evidence is matched with the concept perception, whereas the metaphysical dimension is presented as an innocent attribute, namely, "extra" (-sensory). Soon, the potential of the concept of ESP, as allegedly without

---

[11] The bridge has as the "test-bridge" prominence in medieval near-death visions (cf. Zaleski 1987, 29, 65–9; van Uytfanghe 1993, 148–9); yet, it is a rare topos in modern near-death accounts. Nevertheless, Lindbergh obviously refers to "crossing a bridge" that one may *see*.

[12] Quoted, e.g., in Crookall 1960, 9–10.

[13] In the *Oxford English Dictionary*, we find the entry: "*out-of-the-body* adj. 1946 G. N. M. Tyrrell Personality of Man vii. xxii. 199. These out-of-the-body cases are of exceptional interest [. . .] percipients describe the process of getting out of their bodies in almost identical terms" (www.oed.com, June 10, 2016).

presuppositions, was approved for the study of "projections" of the "double"—it is the "etheric body" that may "hear" or "see" with his nonphysical ears and eyes. American sociologist and psychic researcher Hornell Hart (1888–1967), who had published on "apparitions" from the 1930s onward, seems to be the first to apply the concept of "ESP projection," that is, the *traveling clairvoyance*, to out-of-body experiences (cf. Hart 1954, 121–2; cf. Stratton 1957).[14] Building, however, on "evidential cases" (i.e., reports mainly from spiritualist literature) and on questionnaires pointing to a broad familiarity with extrasensory experiences,[15] Hart's central aim is to ground evidence on "repeatable experiments" (135–7), which marginalizes his interest in spontaneous cases of experiences near death. In the same year, another attempt was published that tried to clad astral projection in medico-scientific terms, namely, parapsychologist James Baker's description (1954, 15–16) of the phenomenon as an "exteriorization" of the body and as a "pneumakinesis," that is, the movement of the mental body, to him an "electrical" phenomenon that may emerge in astral projection or in cases of sudden death.

Although Hart and Baker were firmly based in the Spiritualist–Occult tradition, it is in this decade that the thread of Pfister's psychological interpretation of the life-review feature is taken up again. The most prominent of these is the medico-psychological interpretation of "Mental States During Falls" [*"Über die seelischen Zustände während des Absturzes"*] by the famous Austrian neurologist and psychiatrist Viktor E. Frankl (1905–1997) and his colleague Otto Pötzl (1877–1962), published in a neurological–psychiatric journal in 1952. Viktor E. Frankl, who had invented "logotherapy," and his coauthor mention that these phenomena attract a lot of public interest. However, Frankl and Pötzl did not build on earlier research, but discussed two recent reports from Austria. Again, it is the life review that happens to raise their interest. One of their informants, surviving a fall from a scaffold, described the experience as "peaceful" and "fearless"—a "cinematic projection" of single pictures of his life, fast as "flashlights" (Frankl and Pötzl 1952, 364–6). The authors, who speak without hesitation of a "pathological" quality, attribute this to an "adrenaline rush" (367). For the explanation of the positive mood and the pleasurableness of the experience, they stick—as had been Pfister's approach (1931)—to Freud's theory, especially the concept of a "libido," taken as "the will for pleasure" (372). The second case, that of a well-known mountaineer from Vienna, however, introduces a new element. Surviving a fall in the mountains, he had, while falling 15 meters, shouted repeatedly the name of his young daughter. Asked later, he explained that he, still falling, "had experienced again the whole life of his daughter, from her birth to the day of the fall. All of his fear was only directed to the child, because he awaited his own death and assumed,

---

[14] The term "traveling clairvoyance" had already been in use in psychical journals of the 1880s (e.g., the *Religio-Philosophical Journal*, No. 23, 1883).

[15] To me, Hart's definition (1954, 121) of ESP projection of an observer that acquires consistent extrasensory information by means of an out-of-the-body location looks scientifically sober but implies, nevertheless, the existence of suprahuman sense organs.

"that the child will be left alone in the world." Frankl and Pötzl argue that this example points to a "projection mechanism" able to "elect the most beloved person" (373). An interesting aspect of their Freudian interpretation pertains to the idea that the life review does not consist of a "chain of thought" but a translation into a chain of images. Far from being a "healthy" reaction of consciousness, it is, in their view, a process of "depersonalization of the present moment" (376).

Finally, they ask if these images might uncover elements of experiences [*Erlebnisse*] that were not only hidden, but even *unknown* to the consciousness in the moment of their original experience (cf. 376). In other words, they postulate a "preconscious fraction" ["*vorbewusste Fraktion*"], probably a "repression," within the original experience, regained in the reminiscence of fast image projection. Although the authors discuss various clinical—neurological and psychiatric—aspects of the phenomenon, they finally turn to an "existential" interpretation. Quoting Nietzsche's "lust, longing for eternity" and Schopenhauer's "will to life," they conclude that the "final moment" consists of a "pretended triumphal victory of the [Freudian] pleasure principle over the [Freudian] reality principle": the "*final* moment" "comprises in itself a longing for palingenesis in the face of threatening death" (378, my trans.). Most significantly, however, the authors, even though they do not quote any parapsychological or spiritualist literature on the subject, reveal in a short sentence that they actually associate the phenomenon with these discussions: "The *final* principle leads into the transcendent, as the 'second sight' ["*das zweite Gesicht*," i.e., clairvoyance and other paranormal capacities] seems to lead beyond the individual['s] place" (378). So, even if the authors do not take sides whether "transcendence" is reached—pursuing, in that respect, a psychiatric and neurological, "naturalist" explanation—they argue with a longing for transcendence. There is a will to survive and to achieve a new existence after death ("palingenesis"). With the latter, they do not follow their naturalist colleagues who close the door toward transcendence. The contribution of Frankl and Pötzl raised further interest in psychiatry and psychology (e.g., by Noyes in the 1970s; cf. Martinović 2017, 68–70). In 1960, German psychiatrist Max Mikorey published a short note on 24 cases of life review he could gather from patients' personal reporting. According to Mikorey's interpretation, the affected individuals experience a "slow-motion" effect with direct relevance for possible survival. It should allow them "to recognize the catastrophic situation, and how to parry it." This attempt, however, must fail—and this is precisely the moment the life review, which disconnects the person from the hopeless situation, is set in motion. In sum, Mikorey (1960, 34) joins those who believe that the primary function of the life review is to offer what he calls a "euthanasia-effect."[16]

---

[16] Mikorey argues in the line of thought by Pötzl and Frankl, but with a stronger focus on coping with danger. The slow-motion effect helps to realize an unwinnable situation; it enables us "to realize most clearly the acute catastrophic situation and to parry it." Realizing the futile situation and "through the surrender into his fate, hearing and seeing elapse," interrupting the contact with the external. This inner turn "will provide the cue for

2.6.3 ALDOUS HUXLEY, THE *BOOK*, AND THE SEARCH FOR A "GOOD DEATH"

Especially regarding the latter, "euthanasia," the views expressed by widely read British author Aldous Huxley (1894–1963) are highly meaningful. Without doubt, Huxley's narratives as an intersection for the configuration of near-death experiences are of crucial importance, even though he did not discuss the features of out of the body or the life review more explicitly. Not only did his autobiographical essay on drug experiences, "The Doors of Perception" (1954), become a classic in the counterculture of the 1960s and 1970s—it shows how Huxley links his hallucinogenic drug experiences with mescaline to the postmortem visions described in the *Tibetan Book of the Dead*. As early as 1946, Huxley already drew in his *The Perennial Philosophy* deeply from Buddhist sources, focusing on the Tibetan Buddhist teachings of a "Clear Light" (Tibetan *'od gsal*) as the ultimate nature of (one's own) reality. "Mahayana Buddhism," he says, teaches the "Mind" as "Clear Light of the Void" (Huxley [1946] 1947, 30; cf. 40–2). As Lambert Schmithausen could show, Huxley was quite familiar with Buddhist teachings—not only with the *Book*.[17]

In his essay on the "Doors of Perception," Huxley recounts a personal experiment with mescaline, which he did, surveilled by psychiatrist Humphry Osmond, in May 1953 (cf. Shipley 2015, 44–6). Osmond, on his part, became famous for his coining of the term "psychedelics."[18] After various blissful experiences and insights, Huxley (1954, 45) reported that he found himself "all at once on the brink of panic," terrified by the fear of losing his "ego," which he contextualized as an encounter with the "Mysterium tremendum" described in religious literature. "Divine Light," Huxley muses, can by "unregenerate souls" be apprehended only as a frightening "purgatorial fire." This momentum leads over to his significant identification of his experiences with the Buddhist doctrine of the terrifying "Clear Light." Huxley continues that an "almost identical doctrine" is to be found in the *Book*, where "the departed soul is described as shrinking in agony from the Pure Light of the Void, and even from the lesser, tempered Lights, in order to rush headlong into the comforting darkness of selfhood as a reborn human being, or even as a beast, an unhappy ghost, a denizen of hell. Anything rather than the burning brightness of unmitigated Reality—anything!" (47). If one departs on such an "infernal road," the

---

the appearance of the picture-show of life," that is, "harmless pictures of remembered past, and, in ideal cases, a composed picture-show of life" (1960, 4, trans. mine). To my knowledge, Mikorey never published, apart from this note, his findings. Cf. on his interpretation Stevenson and Cook 1995, 457; Martinović 2017, 133–6.

[17] Schmithausen 2001, 159, note 33, with further sources. Huxley repeatedly expressed an encounter of an increasing "bright light"; cf. also Shipley 2015, 59–61,162–70.

[18] In a letter exchange following Huxley's mescaline experience in 1953, he suggested "'phanerothyme', from the Greek words for 'to show' and 'spirit', and sent a rhyme: 'To make this mundane world sublime, Take half a gram of phanerothyme'. Instead, Osmond chose 'psychedelic', from the Greek words psyche (for mind or soul) and deloun (for show), and suggested, 'To fathom Hell or soar angelic/Just take a pinch of psychedelic'" (Tanne 2004, 713).

experiencer will "self-validate" and reinforce his malevolent visions and will no longer be able to interrupt his terrifying journey. This view motivates Huxley's wife to interfere. Equally conversant with Tibetan Buddhist teachings, she asks her husband if he could in principle imagine how a person might manage to avoid these visions: " 'Would you be able', my wife asked, 'to fix your attention on what *The Tibetan Book of The Dead* calls the Clear Light?' I was doubtful. 'Would it keep the evil away, if you could hold it?' " Huxley answers, " 'perhaps I could—but only if there were somebody there to tell me about the Clear Light. One couldn't do it by oneself. That's the point, I suppose, of the Tibetan ritual—someone sitting there all the time and telling you what's what' " (47).

Then, with the rhetorical figure of reattributing a later insight to experiences already made, Huxley continues: "After listening to the record of this part of the experiment, I took down my copy of Evans-Wentz's edition [. . .] and opened at random. 'O nobly born, let not thy mind be distracted'. That was the problem—to remain undistracted. Undistracted by the memory of past sins [. . .], by all the fears and hates and cravings that ordinarily eclipse the Light. What those Buddhist monks did for the dying and the dead, might not the modern psychiatrist do for the insane? Let there be a voice to assure them [. . .] that in spite of all the terror, all the bewilderment and confusion, the ultimate Reality remains unshakably itself and is of the same substance as the inner light of even the most cruelly tormented mind" (48).[19] That Huxley opened the book at random and, of course, strikes a meaningful passage, is a telling detail of his literary account. In the Christian history of the West, the practice of opening the Bible at random and taking the verse or sentence utterly meaningful has been, for example, a key element of St. Augustine's conversion story, in which he followed the command of God to read in the Bible, "Take up and read!" (cf. *Confessions* 8: 12, 27–8). By applying this "lucky dip" method to the reading of the *Book*, Huxley's attitude displays a religiously meaningful interaction with the text. It could actually be read as an evocative quality of the text itself: It *should* be read to the dying and dead. In his appellative character ("let not thy mind be distracted," etc.), the *Book* is indeed highly suggestive and appealing. With his comments, Huxley suggests a therapeutic value of the Tibetan teachings in psychiatric settings, raising the expectation that these teachings will not only be useful in their original application, as oral guidance for the dying, but even for a schizophrenic in acute psychotic terror or psychedelic consumers on a "bad trip." It is reported that Huxley himself practiced the teachings of the *Book*—he read it aloud to his first wife Maria while she was

---

[19] In a disturbingly ambivalent vision so characteristic for Huxley, he continues (1954, 48) with an almost totalitarian thought experiment. By applying technological means such as pillow speakers, Huxley muses, "it should be very easy to keep the inmates of even an understaffed institution constantly reminded of this primordial fact. Perhaps a few of the lost souls might in this way be helped to win some measure of control over the universe [. . .] in which they find themselves condemned to live."

dying, whereas his second wife, Laura, read it to the dying Huxley, injecting him, as he had wished, with LSD as a means for a "good death."[20]

To connect Huxley's interest in these teachings to the discourse on near death, we should be aware that Huxley quotes from an essay of Cambridge philosopher C. D. Broad, "The Relevance of Psychical Research to Philosophy" (1953 [1949]), in his turn discussing, in the context of "paranormal cognition," the theory of Henri Bergson (as developed in *Matière et mémoire* with reference to the life-review feature): " 'Each person is at each moment capable of remembering all that has ever happened to him and of perceiving everything that is happening everywhere in the universe. The function of the brain and nervous system is to protect us from being overwhelmed and confused by this mass of largely useless and irrelevant knowledge, by shutting out most of what we should otherwise perceive or remember at any moment, and leaving only that very small and special selection which is likely to be practically useful'. [21] According to such a theory, each one of us is potentially Mind at Large" (Huxley 1954, 16).

Reflecting on the "urge of self-transcendence" as the great motivational force, Huxley argues that psychedelic drugs are in principle capable of undoing the filter function of the brain, which will result in a broadened awareness of reality and the mind, respectively (cf. Stevens 1987, 41). As has been shown, the filter theory had been, with certain variations, proposed by Schiller, James, and Bergson—and actually all of them had built on the life-review feature to highlight evidence for their theories. Considering the widespread reception that happened to Huxley's report, we may not be mistaken if we see in this work a suggestive blueprint for subsequent discourse. It should be added that, in the meantime, the Tibetan teachings of the *Book* had also become evermore popular, for example, through Alexandra David-Néel or Lama Anagarika Govinda (i.e. Ernst Lothar Hoffmann, 1898–1985). The latter, founder of a neo-Buddhist tradition, had published various works on Tibetan Buddhism, including *Foundations of Tibetan Mysticism* (1957 [German ed., 1956]), in which he outlined the teachings of the *Book* (cf. Govinda 1977a, 122–5). Govinda holds that "death" means to dwell on the separated "ego,"[22] so that liberation is (only) reached by those able to train the process of dying in higher meditation, because both entail the same stages (cf. 125). Therefore, the practitioner "must go through

---

[20] As it seems, this time, in 1963, the *Book* was read in Leary's rendering ("We read the entire manual of Dr. Leary based on the *Tibetan Book of the Dead*," quoted in Stevens 1987, 205). If this statement is correct, it was probably a preprint, because it appeared in 1964 (see subsequent discussion).

[21] Broad ([1949] 1953, 22) refers here to Bergson's theory "that the function of the brain and nervous system and sense-organs is in the main eliminative and not productive," which seems to enable a more "coherent synthesis of normal and paranormal cognition" than offered by a theory of the brain as "*generating sense-data.*"

[22] This idea is most clearly expressed in Govinda's later book, *The Way of the White Clouds* ([1966] 1977b, 116): "The torn and tortured human being of our time, who [...] has lost the connection with his timeless being, is like a man suffering from incurable amnesia, a mental disease which deprives him of [...] the capacity to act consistently and in accordance with his true nature. Such a man really dies, because he identifies himself with his momentary existence." Cf., in the context of experiences near death, 78, 102, 180.

the experience of death, in order to gain liberation within himself. He must die to his past and to his ego, before he can be admitted into the community of the Enlightened Ones" (125). We will see in the next chapter how this idea of an ego death, engrained, as Govinda holds, in the Tibetan Buddhist after-death teachings, influenced the reception of these teachings by Timothy Leary.

To sum up the developments in the 1950s, we saw occasionally explanatory attempts of certain features of experiences near death—especially the life review—emerging. Taken together, in the first half of the 20th century, psychological or naturalist explanations were still of marginal influence. Obviously contributors were mainly engaged in medical and psychological discussions of chronically ill, paying only occasional attention to "abnormal" abilities of low prevalence. At the same time, and in a parallel strand, collections of deathbed visions and individual reports of personal "survival" of death were still fashionable. However, the 1950s saw an intermittent decline of new biographical reports and case collections of experiences near death. In general, interest in paranormal phenomena had declined. On the one hand, scientific rationalism, philosophical empiricism, behaviorist psychology, neurology, and psychiatry collaborated in defining more strictly the healthy, "normal" psyche, refusing acceptance for parapsychology in "official" science. As an outcome, several important journals for psychic research disappeared. In the same mood, psychologists focused increasingly on the surmised absolute authority, intolerance, and dogmatism of "religious belief systems." Moreover, studies revealed that subjects who had declared to have accepted the possibility of extrasensory perception had in experimental settings higher scores of those perceptions than those who rejected their possibility—an effect demonstrated by Schmeidler and McConnell in 1958. In addition, research on psychical phenomena had turned out to be irrelevant for the prevailing political discourse on "capitalism or socialism." Finally, it seems that near-death discourse had reached a certain point of "saturatedness." All factors taken together had tremendous effects on the individual's willingness to describe "paranormal" features of his or her experiences (near death), and, in consequence, of researchers to collect and study them. However, this intermittent decline did not last very long.

2.7

The Final Configuration of Near-Death Experiences (1960–1975)

IN THE EARLY 1960s, reports of, and literature on, astral travel, out-of-body experiences, and so forth, increased again considerably. The factors that contributed to this successful reanimation will be analyzed more thoroughly in Part III. In this period, new discursive topoi were introduced, such as near-death-like visions triggered by psychoactive substances, especially LSD—equally as a bad trip or, on the side of elevated moods, as expansion of consciousness. Futuristic elements of near-death visions appeared, inspired, for example, by the US Apollo program of human spaceflight (NASA, 1961–1972). In the 1960s, cosmonautic and psychonautic visions merged in a "space-age" imagery that obviously left their trace in the discourse of experiences—Osis and Haraldsson even spoke of Moody as having created "a new myth for the space age of ours" (Fox 2003, 28). On the other hand, a growing prominence of operation units and intensive care in near-death narratives points to significant societal changes.

2.7.1 TOWARD A SYSTEMATIZATION OF EXPERIENCES NEAR DEATH: ROBERT CROOKALL

A major actor in reviving the discourse was the British geologist and botanist Robert Crookall (1890–1981). After his retirement in 1952, he turned his life-long interest in out-of-body experiences into a full profession. By the late 1970s, he had published at least 16 books on astral projection, out-of-body experiences, and psychic communications. For my purpose, it suffices to portray Crookall's approach toward reports of experiences near death in his contributions published between 1960 and 1965, which comprise his most successful books, starting in 1960 with *The Study and Practice of Astral Projection*, followed by *The Supreme Adventure* in 1961 and *Intimations of Immortality* in 1965. Crookall's books were published by The Churches' Fellowship for Psychical Studies. It was founded in 1953 with the aim of initiating an ongoing dialogue among Christian doctrines, psychical research, and mystical thought. Nevertheless, full membership was limited to church members who "held Jesus Christ as Lord and Savior" (Melton 2001, I, 288).[1]

"Pseudo-death" experiences, as he called them, convey so much the same message as experiences communicated mediumistically by people "permanently out of the body" (i.e., dead) that there is simply no need to assert any special status for experiences near death, or "communications from the so-called dead" (Crookall 1960, 151). In both ways, information will be gathered by "communicators," Crookall says. Despite some characteristic differences, understandable as an outcome of the specific emotional situation of the pseudo-dead, both categories of "communication" offer veridical testimonies. Being trained in systematic study, Crookall developed a new criteriology for sorting the accounts he could draw from earlier Spiritualist and Occult literature. Moreover, personal reports were sent to him that, Crookall notes, are "new to literature" (1).[2] Instead of the categorization of astral travels induced "at will" or made "unwillingly," Crookall prefers to distinguish between experiences of individuals "who died naturally" and others who experienced an "enforced death." Among the first, "natural out-of-the-body experiences," the case collection starts with testimonies of "people who nearly died" (cf. 1960, 3–20). Other "natural" cases were caused by severe illness and exhaustion, but also experienced by people who were quite well. Among the class of "enforced out-of-the-body experiences," Crookall lists cases caused by anesthetics, suffocation, falling, and hypnosis. Although the experiences may differ in respect to their causes, the accounts of natural and enforced "after-death experiences" are, for Crookall, "genuine" and "agree with the findings of psychical science" (1).

In contrast to earlier collections, Crookall mentions nearly all topoi listed by Moody 15 years later—tunnel experiences, spiritual beings, the life review, heaven, perfect peace, noises, and so forth. However, though Crookall provides in his *Intimations of Immortality* a nearly complete list of what will become Moody's standard model, he was still unable to develop a concept of near-death experiences. Yet, given his systematization, Crookall's importance for Moody's concept of near-death experiences cannot be overestimated. Moody, oddly enough, did not quote Crookall's studies in his early works. Similar to Moody, Crookall arranged the phenomena (experienced by pseudo-dead and

---

[1] With reference to Pearce-Higgins 1973.

[2] Alvarado's analysis (2012, 66) shows that in Crookall's studies of 1961 and 1964 almost 314 cases were described—mostly cases "from the spiritualist and psychical research literatures (40%)" and accounts "sent to the author (36%)."

ill individuals, but also in "normal" conditions) in a "general sequence of experiences."
Accounts of the natural dying process uncover the following phases:

1. It starts with a *Call* that dying persons send out to contact departed loved ones,
who shall assist in the transition. This is followed by 2., a (first) *Review of the Past
Life*. This review is impersonal and does not imply a judgment. Then, the next
experience is 3. *Shedding the Body*. Here, the dying will experience sensations of
rising out of the body, falling or floating in the air, passing through a tunnel, and
will experience an expansion of consciousness. In this phase, deceased, discarnate
friends may appear. Finally, the disembodied may see a "silver cord" that still holds
a connection to the earthly body, and will be snapped at physical death. Phase 4.,
the Sleep, will emerge shortly after death, namely, a half-conscious or fully unconscious state, a form of acclimatization to the new environment. Next, there will be
5. *an Awakening*, i.e., quite literally, to wake up in the new environment, followed
by 6., *the Judgment*. This time, it is this second "life review," emotionally charged,
and a reflection of personal deeds and responsibility. Finally, there follows 7., *the
Assignment*. In this phase, the spirit journeys toward the sphere or "condition"
of existence ("Hades" or "Paradise") that corresponds to the achievements of the
individual's consciousness.

Elsewhere, Crookall (1965, 17) summarizes the process as follows: (1) The release (or "Birth") of the Soul Body from the physical body caused various sensations,
namely, (*a*) a "click", (*b*) a mental "blackout" (or […] a dark tunnel) […]. (2) Many
reviewed their past lives. (3) Many saw their own physical bodies from the deceased
"double" […] being unseen and unheard by mortals […] and able to pass through
walls, etc. (4) The release of the double took place without pain or fear. (5) The
physical body was observed to be […] inferior to the Soul Body: hence the indiffer-
ence as to the fate of the physical body. (6) The attitude taken by a number of people
to "the silver cord" showed that it was not a mere symbol […]. (7) Consciousness
expanded […]. (8) Many saw "dead" friends, etc. (9) Many expressed reluctance to
re-enter the body and so return to earth-life. (10) The *re-entrance* […]. *This "seeing"
resulted in belief in an after-life.*

Significant is, of course, the conclusion—the new or renewed belief in an afterlife.
Crookall's sequence of events is so close to what Moody will outline that it seems hard to
believe that the latter was not aware of his forerunner. Both are, for example, in full accord
that the life review connects to the judgment. However, we may also notice differences.
For Crookall, there is a first, almost meaningless, life review at death, and only the second
life review in the after-death state will appear as "Judgment." Worthy of notice is, furthermore, the "silver cord," not mentioned by Moody, but of vital importance for Crookall
(cf. 1965, 36–8), who emphasizes its biblical mention (Eccl. xii, 6; Crookall 1960, 191;
1964, 18).

Interestingly, he argues that experiences by unimpeded persons in everyday situations are, in comparison with experiences near death, not less veridical and authentic. Seconded by his observation that most of his cases are neither those of people who have "'died,'" nor "nearly died" or were "very ill," but exactly those of the well and normal individuals, Crookall (1960, 140) stresses that "leaving the Physical Body is a natural, and not an abnormal, process." Beneath the fact that he affirms the term "astral projection," he expresses belief in cases of "objective," and not just simply mental doubles, which underlines the presence of a major Spiritualist doctrine. The same naturalness holds true to the corresponding "environments," whose ontological status is never doubted or even discussed. Crookall notes that these descriptions, though not literally true, must refer "to reality of some sort"—sometimes, the "'dead'" report of very earthlike institutions, including "lecture halls, libraries, hospitals" (5)—as its seems, especially for intellectuals a very agreeable life to come. These environments or "conditions"—namely, "paradise," "earth," and "hades" (referring to experiences with confusion, bewilderment, fog, a "heavy murky atmosphere," crossing rivers, dreamlike conditions, etc.) are drawn from religious sources of Christian and Esoteric metacultures (e.g., the Osiris cult, cf. 135–6). "Paradise conditions" are, for their part, experienced by a "super-normal consciousness." Crookall puts emphasis on the fact that communicators who "died" irreversibly, typically awoke in those paradise conditions, which they conveyed mediumistically. Furthermore, these conditions will usually be achieved without greater efforts by "true mystics" who possess a highly organized "Spiritual Body" (cf. Crookall 1961, 56). If (reversible) death happened in the "natural course," he concludes from his cases, the (nearly) dead will experience "paradise" as a sometimes earthlike, yet, in every respect extraordinarily beautiful and peaceful, environment. If dying is "enforced," the "normal" and "subconsciousness" come into play, resulting in experiences of the Hades condition (Crookall 1960, 140–2). Consciousness, however, will be "wider" and "higher" if the "projection" happens naturally. Far less than arbitrary, this observation is an essential link for Crookall's argument (1964, 136), because "the difference is inexplicable on the hypothesis that the 'double' is imaginary"—in other words, the difference must be explained based on an objective astral body.

In "enforced death" conditions, a life review usually starts immediately. Crookall holds that the "first review" is caused by the loosening of the "vehicle of vitality," or "body-veil" (the animating force within the physical body, as it seems), that encompasses memory traces. The second review, as said, is intertwined with the judgment experience. This time, the loosening of the astral body, or "soul," from the "spiritual body" will take place, as Crookall reasons with Rudolf Steiner. The judgment is done by an "Inner," "Transcendent Self," a "super-normal consciousness" that judges the works of the outer, "lower, immanent and temporary self" (163). This judgment, the second review, is at the same time the "Judgment of God" (164). In contrast to the first, it entails "emotion, a realization of motives, effects, responsibility" (166). Crookall is busy in pointing to biblical passages as confirmation of the judgment experience, while, on the other hand, dogmatics of modern theology is overruled by his trust in the veracity of psychic experiences: "Whereas our learned theologians seldom envisage the cause of the 'Judgment', and can produce no evidence for its existence [. . .], psychic communications include both these desiderata" (163).

In sum, Crookall (1960, 136) argues with a scheme of three forms of consciousness. The normal consciousness of "intellect," "reason," and the "physical world," is the source of "all our doubts about survival and immortality." Below the "normal," there is the "sub-normal," and above—in every metaphorical sense—the "super-normal" consciousness. The latter is clearly related to telepathic, clairvoyant, and "precognitive" experiences and their correlated objects of the "paradise" condition. Sometimes, a fourth consciousness appears, called the "Spirit" (with a certain Gnostic flavor, cf. 136, 144).[3] Apart from that, he uses the term "vehicle of vitality" for denoting, as it seems, the animating life force. "Astral projection," therefore, not only "assures us of survival and indicates the mechanism involved"—furthermore, it provides "definite information" on the different "after-death states," and the respective "Spiritual experiences." Crookall adds, that the "information obtained accords with that revealed in our Scriptures, but it is fuller, more coherent and it is independent of authority" (143–4).

The religious background of Crookall's interest is obvious. In fact, his system embodies all relevant religious metacultures of the West: Most prominently, the Spiritualist–Occult, as attested in his theosophical outlook and terminology, the Gnostic–Esoteric in his claims of a "super-normal consciousness," and finally, Christian metaculture in his aim to harmonize biblical teachings and mediumistic experiences. The latter is attested in Crookall's concluding words of the main part of his first work on "astral projection": "*In view of these studies, we are, in an increasing measure, 'ready to give a Reason of the Hope that is in us'* (1 Peter iii: 15)" (144). Interestingly, the King James Bible, and all other Bibles consulted, translates: "the hope that is in *you*"– Crookall prefers a plural, thereby transferring a religious, first-person claim into the plural of objective science.[4] At least to a certain extent, Crookall discloses his awareness that all testimonies, taken together, will not amount to a scientific proof of "survival." In his words, the latter is "undoubtedly true but exceedingly difficult to prove" (143). In a later work, he admits that survival "may not be 'scientifically proved'—and may not be capable of this—it is, we maintain, so highly probable as to be practically certain" (Crookall 1965, 58; cf. 73). This probability argument reminds me of an inverse improbability argument against the existence of God put

---

[3] On Crookall's system of three bodies, cf. Alvarado 2012, 67.

[4] Crookall (cf. 1961, 190–3), aware of a prevalent "mediumistic climate of thought," stresses repeatedly that some informants never read or heard of spiritualism or occultism, so that their experiences corroborate mediumistic reports.

forward by Richard Dawkins, discouraging, as is done here, the applicability of ontological proof.[5]

Yet Crookall does not only argue with authoritative texts of the Christian tradition. A second argument builds on the global convergence of religious testimonies. In general, he believes that the respective experiences are universal and were already "regarded as genuine" in the ancient cultures of Tibet, India, China, and Egypt.[6] Recent descriptions of mediumistic experiencers out of the body agree "in all essentials with those of spiritualists, Quakers, Anglicans, Buddhists, Hindus, agnostics, atheists and nondescript men and women who have claimed temporarily to leave their Physical Bodies" (Crookall 1960, 10). The inclusion of agnostics, atheists, and "nondescript" individuals is a thoughtful rhetorical move for broadening the basis of veridical reports, because the nonpartisan and nonconfessional attitude, assumed by the author, neutralizes allegations of experiences out of body as being a religious phenomenon. However, the claim of Crookall is less well attested than these passages seem to insinuate. Cases of atheist descriptions are almost absent in his collections. With a final turn to Christian metaculture, Crookall (cf. 1961, 242–3) stresses that virtually all communications convey the message that life is a chance to love—a metainterpretation of utmost importance for Moody, too.

2.7.2 C. G. JUNG'S EXPERIENCE NEAR DEATH

As Crookall did, Carl G. Jung, interested in parapsychology too, published works over four decades that show his never-ceasing interest in near-death reports. For example, in his *Naturerklärung und Psyche* (1952; English translation 1955), he explains cases of "ESP" (extrasensory perception) near death with his principle of "synchronicity," that is, events that have "no causal relation with organic processes" (cf. Jung 1955, 128).[7] His own experience near death, published posthumously in his autobiography *Memories, Dreams, Reflections* (1963 [German 1962]), he narrated as follows.

"At the beginning of 1944 I broke my foot, and this misadventure was followed by a heart attack. In a state of unconsciousness I experienced deliriums and visions which

---

[5] Dawkins (2006, 54; cf. 113) argues, as is well known, that "God almost certainly does not exist": "What matters is not whether God is disprovable (he isn't) but whether his existence is probable"; improbability, for Dawkins, "comes close to proving that God does not exist."

[6] Cf. Crookall 1960, 135, 140; cf. Appendix I, 145–6, 153.

[7] In this context, Jung (1952, 93–4, 137) provides a case personally witnessed. A parturient, suffering from a great blood loss, reported that she had left her body, observing the scene from above, and seeing herself in bed, pale, and eyes closed. While realizing she was believed to die, she becomes aware of a beautiful landscape, an entrance into another world. However, to enter this world through the portal would be an irreversible decision for death, so she returns to life. Jung comments, that in contrast to the opinion of the attending nurse, the patient, while fully unconscious, "had perceived the events exactly the way they had happened in reality." Later in the account, Jung reviews the case of Geddes (1937).

must have begun when I hung on the edge of death and was being given oxygen and camphor injections" (Jung [1963] 1983, 322). And he continues that he "had reached the outermost limit," not knowing whether "in a dream or an ecstasy." Strange things began to happen, elevating him as if he was high up in space: "Far below I saw the globe of the Earth, bathed in a gloriously blue light. I saw the deep blue sea and the continents. Far below my feet lay Ceylon, and in the distance ahead of me the subcontinent of India." However, he could still see a bit of the Mediterranean Sea and also the snow-covered Himalayas. Knowing that he was nearly departing from earth, he enjoys this sight as "the most glorious thing I had ever seen. After contemplating it for a while, I turned around [. . .]. A short distance away I saw in space a tremendous dark block of stone, like a meteorite. It was about the size of my house, or even bigger. It was floating in space, and I myself was floating in space." The stone, he comments, resembled gigantic granite blocks he had seen on the coast of the Gulf of Bengal, hollowed out and turned into temples. He enters the block temple and witnesses, to the right of the entrance, "a black Hindu" who sat "silently in lotus posture upon a stone bench. He wore a white gown, and I knew that he expected me. Two steps led up to this antechamber, and inside, on the left, was the gate to the temple." Again, he realizes that he had seen such a locality before, namely, the Temple of the Holy Tooth at Kandy in Ceylon. "As I approached the steps leading up to the entrance into the rock, a strange thing happened: I had the feeling that everything was being sloughed away; everything I aimed at or wished for or thought [. . .] fell away or was stripped from me—an extremely painful process. Nevertheless something remained; it was as if I now carried along with me everything I had ever experienced or done, everything that had happened around me. I might also say: it was with me, and I was it. I consisted of all that." Speaking of a fundamentally ambivalent experience of "feeling of extreme poverty, but at the same time of great fullness," the latter finally prevailed: "There was no longer anything I wanted or desired. I existed in an objective form; I was what I had been and lived." Interestingly, Jung's report repeatedly shows that he had certain expectations of what to experience next. He continues that something special engaged his attention, as he approached the temple: "I had the certainty that I was about to enter an illuminated room and would meet there all those people to whom I belong in reality. There I would at last understand—this too was a certainty—what historical nexus I or my life fitted into. I would know what had been before me, why I had come into being, and where my life was flowing" (323). Being in this state of a highly self-reflective expectancy, he felt that he would "receive an answer to all these questions as soon as I entered the rock temple," and to "meet the people who knew the answer." Yet, "something happened that caught my attention. From below, from the direction of Europe, an image floated up. It was my doctor, Dr. H.—or, rather, his likeness—framed by a golden chain or a golden laurel wreath. I knew at once: 'Aha, this is my doctor, of course, the one who has been treating me. But now he is coming in his primal form, as a *basileus* of Kos.' " In reaction to the appearance of his doctor as "an avatar of this *basileus*," Jung himself reckons to have now his "primal form." As the doctor stood before him, "a mute exchange of thought took place between us. Dr. H. had been delegated by the earth to deliver a message to me, to tell me that there was a protest against my going away. [. . .] The moment I heard that, the vision ceased. I was profoundly disappointed, for now it all seemed to have been for nothing"—the painful process of defoliation, not to be allowed to enter the temple, or to join his people. In consequence, he felt a "violent resistance to my doctor," for being brought back to life, but also worry for him: " 'His life is in danger, for heaven's sake! He has appeared to me in his primal form! When anybody attains this form it means he is going to die, for already he belongs to the 'greater company!' Suddenly the terrifying thought came to me that Dr. H. would have to die in my stead. I tried my best to talk to him about it, but he did not understand me. Then I became angry with him. [. . .] 'Why does he always pretend he doesn't know he is a *basileus* of Kos?' That irritated me. My wife reproved me for being so unfriendly to him. She was right." Finally, the vision ceases. In addition to its extraordinary content, Jung adds that his nurse had observed paranormal signs while his ecstatic experience had taken place, telling him afterward, " 'It was as if you were surrounded by a bright glow'. That was a phenomenon she had sometimes observed in the dying, she added" (323).

In its vivid imagery and its highly stylized, extensive storyline, Jung's experience has much in common with medieval and ancient otherworld journeys. A close comparison with this literary genre, for example, the apocryphal accounts of the visions of St. Paul and the medieval hagiographies—both of which Jung had read extensively—would be a promising undertaking. In general, the rich imagery taken from religious traditions is overt. Jung's soul, attracted by its equal interest in Indian and Mediterranean wisdom, overviews both from a bird's-eye view, searching for spiritual revelation either here or there. The reader may be reminded that already by the time of his experience, in 1944, Jung had proven his intimate familiarity with the *Tibetan Book of the Dead*. Finally, I should mention the formal coherence of the narrative with Jung's own approach of "analytical psychology." In his report, he assumes a self-reflective position toward the experienced elements while the experience still unfolds—discussing, while within the experience, for example, appearances of "primal forms." Sharing his vision, Jung made a significant contribution to the final configuration of near-death experiences, rehabilitating premodern visionary experiences by fusing narratives of Indian knowledge seekers with Christian otherworldly journeys. Moody (1976, 177) referred in his first book to Jungian interpretations of "archetypes of the collective unconscious," and points in his second book explicitly to Jung's "Near-death experience" (1977, 76).[8]

---

[8] The Jungian framework of analysis for experiences near death has stirred a continuous controversy (cf. Zaleski 1987, 201). Shushan (2009, 164–5), for example, argues that speaking of symbols of the collective unconscious denies the possibility of near-death experiences being "an objectively transcendental event," thereby replacing, however, one religiously engaged interpretation by another.

2.7.3 DEATH-BED VISIONS IN INDIA? PARAPSYCHOLOGY AND
THE "REINCARNATION" THESIS

In the early 1960s, the parapsychological research of deathbed visions saw a revival. The Latvian American parapsychologist Karlis Osis (1917–1997) began with his own research on deathbed visions, starting with a pilot survey on "Deathbed Observations by Physicians and Nurses," published in 1961. From an empirical survey of questionnaires and interviews of nurses and doctors,[9] he is explicitly interested in third-person evidence for "postmortem survival" and mystical visions. Referring to Barrett (1926), Myers, James, Hyslop, Tyrrell, and others, he acknowledges also more recent developments in society, for example, the prevalence of experiences caused by psychedelic drugs (Osis 1961, 9–10). His claim that so far only a few "psychical researchers" had been concerned with the "experiences of dying persons themselves," but instead took interest in "extrasensory and hallucinatory experiences of the relatives and friends of dying persons" (13), reveals how Osis's approach emerges from traditional research but introduces a new, more empirical perspective. Osis notes—as he says, with "surprise"—that his study revealed an "elevated mood" of the dying, whereas only a few reported visions with some "disagreeable kind of imagery which Aldous Huxley calls 'Hell'" (30). In several cases, he says, patients either "temporarily or permanently revived from a death-like state," offered as a "characteristic" response: "'Why did you bring me back, Doc? It was so nice there'" (30). The general aim of his study is, again, to uncover deathbed visions that offer evidence for postmortem survival—for example "Peak in Darien" cases, in which, as Osis explains, spirits of dead relatives come and aid the dying in their passing to the other world (cf. 16). For that purpose, he compares visions reported by terminally ill with those made in normal conditions of health. His general conclusion: "healthy persons hallucinate predominantly the living; terminal patients [. . .] the dead; visions and hallucinations of religious figures are much more frequent in our sample of the dying than in the samples of healthy individuals" (39). Regarding their content, Osis grouped the visions as follows: "(a) Traditional religious concepts (Heaven, Hell, Eternal City, etc.); (b) Hallucinations of scenes in brilliant colors, resembling those under hallucinogenic drug intoxication" (85). Although Osis speaks throughout of hallucinations (e.g., of spirits helping the dying), he entertains—in line with protagonists of Spiritualist–Occult metacultures of the 19th century—an idiosyncratic definition of hallucination. It insinuates that something real may have caused the hallucination. In this train of thought, hallucination is an external observation from a third-person perspective: Some people *appear* to be "hallucinatory," whereas the individuals themselves have "visionary experiences" (cf. 27–8).

The "predominance of the dead" in hallucinations of the dying, Osis comments, "is easily explainable by the survival hypothesis, i.e., the dead have an interest in the patient's

---

[9] I should add that, though based on questionnaires and interviews, the quality of Osis's work is methodologically poor—for example, direct quotations from interviews are lacking.

transition to another world" (68), and the closer the relationship had been, the more often they appear. In other words, the survival hypothesis is treated as an operational category for further analysis.[10] Of importance to Osis is his observation that hallucinogenic factors such as medication with morphine or a high fever did not generate an increase of deathbed visions—on the contrary, as Osis summarizes retrospectively, impaired states even suppressed "survival-related phenomena" (Osis and Haraldsson 1977, 238). In sum, "*deathbed patients see apparitions more often when fully conscious and having proper awareness and capability of responding to their environment*" (Osis 1961, 49, italics in orig.).

In respect to the "life-film rapidly unrolling," Osis explains that it might be "an extension of hallucinatory reliving of past memories" (76). However, in response to a question about the "life-film" in the questionnaire, only few reported an acceleration: "We received only two cases where acceleration of subjective time was indicated. One was an anesthesia case in which the memories flashed childhood experiences. The other was the self-observation of a nurse when nearly drowning" (76). If, as it seems, the life review is facilitated by a distinct trigger (or "death-x-pulse"), then I am inclined to conclude that such situations were largely absent in Osis's sample of people dying in hospitals. In respect to the religious dimension of the reported visions, Osis draws from his material that only "religious patients"—defined as "patients affiliated with churches"—"had visions" (31), the majority of whom believe in life after death. Osis offers two explanations of this "very pronounced" trend: "(a) the religious people expect visions and the expectation is the cause of them; or (b) people who practice religion have developed sensitivity to a transcendent reality which emerges into consciousness via traditional imagery" (31). Elsewhere, too, Osis points out that individuals might experience visions according to their expectations,[11] yet he shows no sensitivity to the problem that the reporting parties could compose conventional accounts based on what they felt as being expected of them.

However, Osis declares "religious apparitions" to be of relevance, unfashionable as it may be to the current "philosophy of science." Still, a number of philosophers and scientists "admit the possibility that in the religious experience one makes contact with a reality, with some aspect of the universe that does not manifest itself to the five senses." Osis grants that possibility, too, if patterns in the empirical data point to "this transcendental reality." However, he discourages taking the "anthropomorphic idea of one patient in our survey who 'shook hands with the Lord' (an ultra-Americanized bit of religious behavior!)" (39; cf. 59) at face value. In other words, Osis sees in anthropomorphic

---

[10] Osis (1961, 87) explains that the dying may not have adequate "forms of images, concepts, 'hypotheses', etc." for their "experiences of a transcendental nature," and might therefore provide " 'borrowed' " forms. Moreover, they are "utterly unprepared by past experience," and so overwhelmed that they "either grasp it with inadequate but available anthropomorphic images, or meet it with the unstructured emotion of a child seeing a Christmas tree for the first time." Although this reasoning is "speculative," which, he says, holds true for "psychiatric explanation" too, his reasoning at least arranges "hallucinations of the dead" into a "meaningful pattern."

[11] This, the "non-survival explanation," Osis says (1961, 68), builds on "cultural inheritance"; that is, "patients 'see' what they *expect* will happen at death."

visualizations of certain religious traditions a subjective vision, influenced by cultural backgrounds. Imagine, he asks, how hallucinations of an atheist, expecting "death to be final for his existence," will differ from those of "an Orthodox Jew or a devout Catholic who believed in saints." However, "if deathbed experiences vary entirely with individual cultural background, beliefs and expectations, we have something purely subjective to deal with" (14). Although his study *strongly suggests a close relationship between being religious and seeing apparitions during terminal illness,* he denies that there are no- table differences between religious confessions: "Protestant and Catholic patients 'saw' living, dead, and religious figures in about the same proportions," while even 20% of the "nonreligious" (according to the preceding definition!) patients " 'saw' religious figures in their hallucinations" (59–61). In consequence, Osis concludes that deathbed visions offer a general, transreligious, and transcultural insight, namely, the importance and "in- fallibility" of one's experience: "Thousands of years of history indicate that religion can easily be 'proved' or 'disproved' according to a skilled disputant's previous convictions. Introspective experience is the best ground for a mature decision for or against religion" (87). So his study ends with the appeal that experience only shall be the judge (cf. 90). In the following decades, Osis published extensively on out-of-body experiences, deathbed visions, and extrasensory perception, his most prominent publication being *At the Hour of Death*, published in 1977 together with Erlendur Haraldsson (born 1931).

Although this study appeared after Moody's book, Osis and Haraldsson could draw from their empirical research that had started in the 1960s. The book's aim was to com- pare deathbed visions in the United States and in India. The Indian cases, however, were to a considerable extent based on information provided by Christian nurses (cf. 24–5). In 1977, the authors were already aware that Moody's book had at an astonishing pace established an authoritative blueprint for near-death experiences. As Mark Fox (2003, 28) observes, Osis and Haraldsson saw in their first edition of 1977 their findings "in agreement with Moody's, in the *second* edition they went on to highlight some inter- esting differences," especially in regard to the low prevalence of the life review and the being of light. Intriguingly, Osis and Haraldsson (1997, xv) concluded, "Maybe Moody created a new myth, or provided a newer, more attractive vocabulary for describing re- ligious figures in this space age of ours." Obviously, the authors expressed their wish to be in line with earlier parapsychological research on deathbed visions and their meth- odological premise, namely, to provide third-person evidence for "hallucinations." Seen from that perspective, they were slightly suspicious of the value of Moody's collection of first-person narratives that were in part made by healthy persons in situations of sudden danger ("fear of death").[12] "Stress," or the "expectation to die," Osis and Haraldsson (2012, 188) argue, does not cause "afterlife-related deathbed visions" (188). A closer look into *At*

---

[12] Accordingly, they describe their project as the "first truly scientific research into the experiences of the dying at the hour of death" (Osis and Haraldsson 2012, 2).

the Hour of Death reveals that the authors were especially attracted by "Peak of Darien" narratives, namely, that a considerable number of the dying will "see" relatives waiting for them and guide them into the sphere beyond death (cf. 184). Although Osis and Haraldsson occasionally touch upon religious differences in the dying experience (e.g., the Hindu "messenger of death," cf. 176–9), they argue that "on the surface it appears that religion, to some extent, shapes the phenomena" (118). Interestingly, they note that Hinduism might inhibit and Christianity might enhance "religious emotional reactions" (118). However, it is a vital element of their argument that experiences near death "often do not conform with *religious afterlife beliefs*"—for example, they stress that basic Hindu ideas of the afterlife, for example, reincarnation, a "formless God" such as Brahma, or "Vedic 'loci' of an afterlife" were "never portrayed in the visions of Indian patients" (191). Instead of pointing to the Christian embedding of their informants, they argue astonishingly that the "concept of Karma" may have been "vaguely suggested by reports of a 'white-robed man with a book of accounts'" (191)—though this imagery barely conceals its Christian origin.

Referring to Schmeidler's research (1959) on the enhanced performance of "believers" (i.e., "sheep") in "extra-sensory perception" (cf. 119), they never express any principal doubt—"core phenomena of the dying experiences," they say, are "not much affected by individual, national, or cultural factors" (98). The religious interest of the authors therefore can be grasped as an attempt to interpret their data—testing the "survival thesis"—as conspicuous proof for the adequacy of the dying's elevated mood in confronting one's own death: "Nearly all the American patients, and two-thirds of the Indian patients, were ready to go after having seen otherworldly apparitions with a take-away purpose. *Encounters with ostensible messengers form the other world seemed to be so gratifying that the value of this life was easily outweighed*" (185). Osis and Haraldsson's own religious preconceptions become most clear in the "Epilogue" of their work. Here, they present their findings in form of a narrative: Suppose, they say, a "modern Lazarus" were to rise up and talk to us. His advice "might go like this: 'When your heart stops and the hour of death comes, you will not break up and disintegrate like ice in the rapids of a river. Instead, it will be like diving in a new kind of reality,'" and weariness, pain, and sadness, "all will be left with sheets on the hospital bed" (209). A "religious figure" will come in brilliant light, the presence of "sacred, light, love," and so forth. And Lazarus offers answers to Hindus, too: "If you are a Hindu, you will most likely experience the same things, but you may be received by a Yamdoot rather than by the 'professional' himself. But don't despair; you will be brought to the man in the white robe, and he is always a benign ruler with an aura of sacredness" (210). For Mark Fox (cf. 2003, 27), 20th-century research that comes closest to that of Moody is to be found in the work of Barrett (1926) and Osis and Haraldsson—we can see, however, that all of them were embedded in a continuous stream of significant contributions.

In this decade, another influential scholar made his appearance in research near death, namely, Canadian psychiatrist and parapsychologist Ian Stevenson (1918–2007), founder of the "reincarnation research." In his first book *Twenty Cases Suggestive of Reincarnation* (1966), he collected cases in which individuals purportedly remembered facts from earlier lives. In this context, he also presented a case in which a boy survived an "apparent death," recovered, but was now in possession of someone else's memories, attested—Stevenson claimed ([1966] 1974, 34–52)—by various witnesses. With reference to out-of-body experiences, Stevenson argued that in some cases such "reincarnation memories" might come close to "projections of a double."[13] Again, empirical evidence for reincarnation was sought for within narratives of the Indian tradition.[14] In the decades to come, Stevenson published several further contributions on near-death experiences, always insinuating a "survivalist" conclusion.

In addition to these contributions of Esoteric parapsychology, a more hardheaded contribution, halfway to strict empirical research, had been published by the British parapsychologist Celia Green (born 1935). It is probably the first study of out-of-body experiences by way of an opinion survey. In her work *Out-of-the-Body Experiences* (1968), supervised by philosopher Henry H. Price (cf. 1953; 1968) and published by the (former) Institute of Psychophysical Research, Oxford, she based her findings almost exclusively on interviews and questionnaires. Individuals had responded to an appeal (by means of press and radio) for "first-hand accounts" of experiences in which things were observed from an out-of-body perspective (Green 1968, 13). Instead of "out-of-the-body experiences," Green prefers to speak of "ecsomatic states" and distinguishes two forms—"asomatic" states, in which the subject is unaware of a body, and "parasomatic" states, in which an association with a "seemingly spatial entity"—a "parasomatic body" parallel to the physical body, is felt (cf. 17). Although she did not classify a subgroup of the experiences as made near death, there is a chapter on "stress" as an important prerequisite of those experiences (cf. 25–30). Especially "single," nonrecurring, ecsomatic experiences are often made in situations characterized by some form of stress such as physical trauma, illness, or accidents. Nevertheless, she notes that in a considerable amount of single-occurrence cases, stress had a psychological origin. Although subscribing to the perspective of a Scientific–Naturalist metaculture, Green does not propose a straightforward explanation of these ecsomatic experiences as hallucinatory, arguing that "no evidence has yet emerged that the information about the subject's environment which is conveyed by his visual experiences in a 'single' experience of the ecsomatic state is misleading" (54). Green, in sum, does not rule out the possibility of "ESP" or "travelling clairvoyance," though

---

[13] "In nearly all cases with claim of memory of a previous life, the subject identifies himself with the images of the claimed memory," remembering "himself as an actor in them. But in a small number of cases, the images are projected so that the subject sees his previous self as another person external to himself whom he watches, somewhat like instances of seeing one's own body or double" (Stevenson [1966] 1974, 352).

[14] The Buddha, Stevenson ([1966] 1974, 130) argues, is not only attributed "the capacity to recall previous lives," but also "offered some instructions for others who wished to do this." There are "numerous cases of persons who claim to remember previous lives" in Buddhist countries from Ceylon up to Tibet, providing "some continuing empirical support for the beliefs of Buddhism."

she frames the relevant reports with "the subject claims . . . " (127). From the reports, Green could extract the element that subjects look in states out of the body at themselves impersonally, without concern, or with a certain "academic" curiosity. Green subsumes these experiences under the notable category "detachment" (94–9), which reminds us of Bälz's observation of a "paralysis of emotion" (Bälz 1901). In the chapter on "Relaxation and Meditation Practices," however, we read, "A number of occurrences of the ecsomatic state have resulted from the practice of relaxation exercises, sometimes in conjunction with meditation practices. Although these exercises were deliberately undertaken, the induction of an ecsomatic state was sometimes an unexpected by-product" (Green 1968, 56). It seems that these individuals practiced some form of yoga (e.g., "I was standing in my room at home and concentrating on raising the level of my consciousness into the 'spirit', when I found I was looking at my body from outside it" (108; cf. 56–7). Green, however, does not reflect on the fact that these subjects induced their experiences as a part of systematic practice (cf. 109–12). One yoga practitioner is quoted as saying, "one is supposed to have deep religious experience but instead this strange thing happened to me and I became separated from my own body" (58). Others report—in that respect, more successful—an illumination, mental clarity, all-powerfulness, being wide awake, heightened senses, or an intense concentration (cf. 72, 83, 113). One individual comments that "the only feeling I had was one of being higher than anyone else (like God)" (78–87). Further experiences include a physical "click" while returning into the body (91, 113)—the latter being, as we saw, a characteristic element of exercises in astral projection. Even in Green's chapters of "travelling clairvoyance" and "telepathy and precognition," in which reports contain many specific terms of Spiritualist–Occult metacultures (e.g., "I decided to project my conscious self some distance away from my body"; 129), Green only once refers to a work on astral projection (namely, Oliver Fox). Conceivably, this abstention will have contributed to the fact that her work was received with some reservation in the final phase of the emerging discourse on near-death experiences, criticizing her apparent proposal to explain out-of-body experiences as mere "hallucination" (which she did not, at least in her early work). Most significantly for her approach, however, Green abstains from discussing or quantifying the impact and meaning of Christian, Gnostic–Esoteric, or Occult metacultures. This is astonishing, given the fact that her informants' reports disclose clearly that to them these religious meanings are of crucial importance. Although out-of-body experiences are treated by Green as "ecsomatic states," being a distinct feature with different subtypes, there are testimonies that clearly fulfill the blueprint of the hospital setting of near-death experiences.[15]

---

[15] "I was in hospital having had an operation for peritonitis; I developed pneumonia and was very ill. The ward was L shaped; so that anyone in bed at one part of the ward could not see round the corner. One morning I felt myself floating upwards, and found I was looking down on the rest of the patients. I could see myself; propped up against pillows, very white and ill. I saw the sister and nurse rush to my bed with oxygen. Then everything went blank. The next I remember; was opening my eyes to see the sister bending over me." Later, she is able to

2.7.4 THE INTIMATE RELATIONSHIP OF PSYCHEDELICS
AND EXPERIENCES NEAR DEATH

Of decisive importance for the vibrant atmosphere of the 1960s and early 1970s that influenced the finalization of near-death experiences was the encounter with hallucinogenic, "psychedelic" drugs, especially the broader use of LSD, but also more traditional anesthetics and narcotics. Psychotropic substances with their backside of bad trips were certainly experienced by some as a threat to their own life. Drug-induced visions of "losing oneself," but also of a life review were, as we saw in Section 2.2.10, part of the hashish and opium reports of the literary avant-garde in the early 19th century. On the other hand, several reports of the late 19th century included "mystic experiences," or had likened levitation out of the body to drug experiences. In the following, I aim to show that near-death reports of the 1960s and 1970s have a strong relation to reports of drug-induced "altered states of consciousness," as they—but also experiences near death—were designated after Charles T. Tart and Arnold M. Ludwig (1969) had successfully introduced the term.[16] The more those drugs came into use—in addition to the increase of the medical use of general anesthetics such as chloroform—the more individuals reported cognate experiences near death. In the case of LSD, mescaline, and some other psychoactive substances, a well-known phenomenon contributed to the convergence of both, namely, that drug experiences may return—sometimes after months!—in the form of "flashbacks," that is, as recurrent hallucinogenic episodes without a repeated ingestion of the substance (discussed by Mardi Horowitz as early as 1969).

Paradigmatic is a report by American minister and psychiatrist Walter N. Pahnke (1931–1971). A researcher of psychedelics, he became immediately famous after the publication of his (in various respects controversial) "Good Friday Experiment" (1962), where he had, in short, claimed to have induced with psilocybin "mystic experiences," indistinguishable from the usual "religious experiences," of church attendants. Pahnke (cf. 1963, ii) had realized this experiment under the auspices of Timothy Leary (1922–1996), who had also helped to conduct the experiment. In his PhD dissertation, Pahnke discussed not only the psilocybin experiments, but discussed extensively, and emphatically, the literature on "spontaneous mysticism" (e.g., of William James and W. T. Stace), including, of course, Huxley's essays. However, in 1964—the year in which David Solomon edited the influential book *LSD: The Consciousness-Expanding Drug*—Pahnke undertook a self-study with LSD that he described in a protocol as follows:

---

describe in detail a patient she had seen while looking down (Green 1968, 121; on similar cases cf. 122–4). The accounts quoted by Green, Mark Fox (2003, 24–5) comments, bear indeed "significant parallels" with many contemporary claims, "particularly in the subject's concern to present information as confirmatory proof that the experience was no mere hallucination."

[16] Tart got increasingly interested in out-of-body experiences and published several studies (cf. Tart 1967, 1969).

The most impressive and intense part of this experience was the WHITE LIGHT of absolute purity and cleanness. It was like a glowing and sparkling flame of incandescent whiteness and beauty [. . .]. The associated feelings were those of absolute AWE, REVERENCE, and SACREDNESS. Just before this experience I had the feeling of going deep within myself to the Self stripped bare of all pretense and falseness. This was the point where a man could stand firm with absolute integrity—something more important than mere physical life. The white light experience was of supreme importance—absolutely self validating [. . .]. The white light itself was so penetrating and intense that it was not possible to look directly at it. It was not in the room with me, but we were both somewhere else—and my body was left behind. Later [. . .] I had a vision of absolute DIVINE love. It was like a flowing spring of silvery white liquid overflowing upward and was very beautiful to watch and feel. The feeling was of love and compassion toward the Divine and toward all men. I had the insight that all men had this same potential and worth within themselves. All men were equal in the sight of God and to my own feelings at this moment. I realized how I had not taken this enough into account in my past actions. (Pahnke 1964, [1])

Two years later, Pahnke published together with William A. Richards ([1966] 1969, 404) an article discussing the "Implications of LSD and Experimental Mysticism," in which his report is, though anonymously, quoted again. Here, it is subsumed under the heading "sense of sacredness," and framed with Rudolf Otto's category of the "*mysterium tremendum*" (cf. 403–4). We may detect in Pahnke's description well-known elements of near-death reports: An experience out of the body is envisioned, and a "white light," which, the way it is described, seems to me in line with the bright light of the *Tibetan Book of the Dead*. This is not a too far-fetched conclusion if we take into consideration that Timothy Leary and Ralph Metzner (born 1936), both advisers and close collaborators of Pahnke, were (together with Richard Alpert) already in 1962 working on a psychedelic adaptation of the *Book* (cf. Ram Dass, 2010, 29), which, as is reported, had been advised by Aldous Huxley, whom Leary had met.[17]

In 1964, their version of the *Book* saw the light under the title *The Psychedelic Experience. A Manual Based on the Tibetan Book of the Dead*. Obviously, Leary and his collaborators paralleled the after-death experiences, described in the book, to their own psychedelic experiences. Being aware of the ambivalence of LSD experiences as "consciousness-expanding," but also—for the "uninitiated" as potentially threatening experience of "ego loss" or "ego death,"[18]—Leary emphasized that a user's experience of psychedelic drugs is highly dependent on the (mind) "set" and the "setting," that is, the social and

---

[17] Metzner (2010, 51) states that Huxley had, among others, recommended them to study the Book.
[18] On the "ego-death" in the *Book* and LSD: cf. Metzner 2010, 34.

physical environment.[19] To make the parallel structure apparent, however, Leary et al. (1964, 11) explain that the "dead" is not really the addressee of the *Tibetan Book*—it is the living that shall "regard every moment of his or her life as if it were the last." Physical death, they say, is nothing but an "exoteric façade," and, far from "being an embalmers' guide, the manual is a detailed account of how to lose the ego; how to break out of personality into new realms of consciousness; and [. . .] how to make the consciousness expansion experience endure in subsequent daily life" (22). Exactly with this insistence that the *Book* is addressed to the living, its teachings are no longer explanations of a transmigrating "consciousness" but describe a "pre-mortem-death-rebirth experience" (22)—which brings us in fact closer to what a decade later will be called near-death experience.

Moreover, Leary had described in 1963 to a journalist of the *Saturday Evening Post*, John Kobler, his first trip on psilocybin mushrooms that had taken place three years earlier in Mexico. Undoubtedly, the report Leary gave to Kobler bears the signature of an experience near death: "I realized that I had died, that I, Timothy Leary, the Timothy Leary game, was gone. I could look back and see my body on the bed. I relived my life, and re-experienced many events I had forgotten. More than that, I went back in time in an evolutionary sense to where I was aware of being a one-celled organism. All of these things were way beyond my mind" (Kobler 1963, 31–2). The general conviction that these psychedelic near-death experiences are essentially experiences of liberation becomes a standard feature crystallized in the formulation that the "game"—that is, the conditioned daily routines of life (cf. Shipley 2015, 123–5)—has ended: "There was no visible evidence that the twentieth century existed. I listened. No sounds of machinery. Bird cries. The rustle of the breeze across the garden. The crowing of cocks. The Timothy Leary game now existed only as a memory. I was liberated" (Leary [1968] 1995, 333).

Without question, Leary, who was raised as a Catholic in a pious family but had dissociated himself from Catholicism (cf. Ram Dass 2010), was still intensively moved by the question of religious and mystical experiences—he even went so far as to write a small handbook on how to *Start Your Own Religion* (1967). Leary's endorsement of a non-partisan Christian-mysticist position becomes obvious in his explanation of the *Tibetan Book*, too. There, Leary and his coauthors explain that the "White Light" of the first bardo "may be interpreted as God the Creator": "Persons from a Judaeo-Christian background conceive of an enormous gulf between divinity (which is 'up there') and the self ('down here'). Christian mystics' claims to unity with divine radiance has [sic] always posed problems for theologians who are committed to the cosmological subject-object distinction. Most Westerners, therefore, find it difficult to attain unity with the source-light" (Leary 1964, 53). Therefore, returning into the meager reality of "social games" is

---

[19] Leary et al. (1964, 11) hold that the drug does not produce the transcendent experience but "merely acts as a chemical key—it opens the mind, frees the nervous system of its ordinary patterns and structures," but the experience itself "depends almost entirely on set and setting."

inevitable, whereas persons of an advanced spiritual development may, at the "moment of ego-death," gain full liberation. Indeed, Christian imagery is evoked in other parts of their explanation of the *Book*, too. For example, they argue thus in respect to the Tibetan Buddhist Judgment Visions: "A judgment scene is a central part of many religious systems, and the vision can assume various forms. Westerners are most likely to see it in the well-known Christian version. The Tibetans give a psychological interpretation to this as to all the other visions. The Judge, or Lord of Death, symbolizes conscience itself in its stern aspect of impartiality [. . .]. The 'Mirror of Karma' (the Christian Judgment Book), consulted by the Judge, is memory" (87). The overall assumption is, again, that there is a deeper level of consciousness, to be found cross-culturally and chiefly independent of historical circumstances. The religious foundation is much more than a subtext—it is almost programmatic. Leary's self-description (1995 [1968], 28; cf. 301) as "we are high. High Priests" evoked severe criticism on the side of theology (cf. Benz 1972, 3), but also in social theory (cf. Roszak 1969, 165).

In line with earlier thought of the brain as a limiting factor of consciousness, Leary could elaborate elsewhere on the "filter theory," quoting, again, Huxley's theory of "reducing valves" (cf. Baier [in press]). In the context of the final configuration of near-death experiences, an influential term of Leary deserves special mention, namely, the "reality tunnel."[20] Leary had coined it in the context of his version of the "filter theory." As previously shown, the imagery of a "tunnel" had over the decades gained importance in descriptions of experiences near death. In the 1970s, it was already an almost indispensable feature of descriptions that depict the passage to another realm.

To summarize, as in earlier decades, the framework of the *Tibetan Book of the Dead* helped to provide a scheme for near-death experiences. For Leary and his coauthors, the scheme of rebirth, the system of postmortal bardo planes, and other Tibetan Buddhist beliefs can be dismissed for its central, this-worldly message: Authenticated by the high spiritual accomplishment of its visionary Tibetan authors, it does not voice after-death experiences, but *premortem ego-death experiences* that call for just one thing: the mystic expansion of consciousness and, in consequence, a renewed awareness of the sacredness of life. In this strand, Pahnke published in 1969 a key essay that explored the value of the "psychedelic mystical experience" in the context of the "human encounter with death." Discussing the situation of terminal cancer patients, Pahnke (1969, 5) refers to Huxley's novel *Island* (1962), which described "the all too common situation for the dying cancer patient," characterized by increasing pain, isolation, anxiety, morphine addiction, and so forth, in short, by "increasing demandingness, with the ultimate disintegration

---

[20] It seems that initially Leary (1977, 2; 28) spoke of a "tunnel reality"; Wilson, however, popularized it as "reality tunnel." German philosopher Thomas Metzinger (2009, 9) recently borrowed the term, explaining it thus: Moving through the "outside world" and "objective reality," "we constantly apply unconscious filter mechanisms," constructing unknowingly our "own individual world, which is our 'reality tunnel.'" It must not astonish us that Metzinger deals in this book extensively with out-of-body experiences (cf. 75–113).

of personality and loss of the opportunity to die with dignity." Immediately after this statement, Pahnke introduces his LSD experiments as a successful attempt "to alter this dehumanization in the course of events prior to death" (5)—namely, to apply LSD as a potent means that helps people cope with dying. Pahnke even thinks of institutionalized psychedelic hospices (cf. 20)—an idea that will be taken up by Stanislav Grof.[21]

According to Pahnke, "dramatic effects came in the wake of a psychedelic mystical experience": "Most striking was a decrease in the fear of death. It seems as if the mystical experience, by opening the patient to usually untapped ranges of human consciousness, can provide a sense of security that transcends even death" (12). Invoking the brain-as-a-filter theory,[22] Pahnke explains that if "an individual brain is damaged, disintegrates, or dies, this Larger Consciousness does not cease," and that his LSD patients with psychedelic mystical experiences, "who previously knew nothing of this transmission theory are supplying data which precisely fit this hypothesis. Their threshold seems to be lowered so that they directly experience this Vaster Consciousness in an Eternal Now [...]. Again and again we are told that this experience subjectively occurs 'out of the body'" (16). The latter proves how reports of psychedelic experiences encompass elements of experiences near death—a connection that is further strengthened by Pahnke in his comment that the psychedelic helpers may induce the best relief if there is "complete surrender to the ego-loss experience of positive ego transcendence, which is often experienced as a moment of death and rebirth" (15).

2.7.5 ROBERT A. MONROE AND THE REVIVAL OF ASTRAL TRAVEL

Although autobiographical accounts of psychedelic experiences with near-death-like characteristics flourished in the late 1960s, we can note a parallel resurgence of more theosophical practices and narratives. An important author in this context is American businessman Robert A. Monroe (1915–1995), who published a widely received book on astral projection in 1971 under the title *Journeys Out of the Body*.[23] Monroe not only published further books on astral journeys, he also founded an institute that offered guided "journeys" and developed several other programs of spiritual and cognitive enhancement. Monroe's successful book, however, made the term "out-of- [the-] body experience" truly popular. In his introduction to the first edition, Charles T. Tart[24] is

---

[21] Even after the use of LSD had become illegal in the United States, the *Book* was still popular in end-of-life care. In 1975, Stephen Levine and Richard Alpert (now Baba Ram Dass) initiated the "Living/Dying Project" in San Francisco. Now, without LSD, the dying were escorted according to the *Book* (cf. Lopez 2011, 9).

[22] The physical brain as a filter of consciousness transmits only a part of the "Vaster Consciousness of Reality," like a "partially opaque glass allowing through a few rays of a super solar blaze" (Pahnke 1969, 16).

[23] Monroe, Fox (2003, 24) explains, "discovered an apparently latent ability to project spontaneously whilst at rest. His first experiences took place in the 1950s and [...] he later learned to project at will, visiting a range of different realms or locales varying widely in their similarity to the physical Earth." Taking the "journeys" as experiences, Fox follows Monroe's self-presentation.

[24] Tart actually did research on Monroe's claimed abilities—cf. Couliano 1991, 28–9.

eager to define these experiences, though they had been "termed traveling clairvoyance, astral projection," with this "more scientific term," arguing that an "OOBE" implies that "the experiencer (1) seems to perceive some portion of some environment which could not possibly be perceived from where his physical body is known to be at the time; and (2) knows at the time that he is not dreaming or fantasizing" (Tart in Monroe 1971, 7). Therefore, the "experiencer" retains his critical faculties and knows that he is not dreaming. Apart from that, Tart once again invokes the belief that reports of OOBEs of "housewives in Kansas [...] closely resemble accounts [...] from ancient Egyptian or oriental sources," and, again, it is finally taken as "usually one of the most profound experiences of a person's life, and radically alters his beliefs. This is usually expressed as, 'I no longer believe in survival of death or an immortal soul, I know that I will survive death'" (8).

We may not indulge in Monroe's extensive reports of how he was able to visit with his "Second Body" distant friends, to report of equally distant events that he could witness, or his claim to have explored not only the "Locale I," the "Here-Now," but also a "Locale II," a nonmaterial environment, inhabited, as it seems, by ghosts and spirits, and even a "Locale III," a parallel world to ours, though with certain differences in technology and culture. Obviously, this is new wine in old wineskins. It exchanges classic descriptions of theosophy with new imagery of science fiction, human space travel, and post-Newtonian quantum mechanics, while keeping basic ideas of astral travel. Monroe, however, does not quote classical theosophists. He does not even mention the plain source of so many of his topoi. Declaring himself to be innovative, he contributed to the widespread impression that he was in fact the first modern experiencer to have drafted reports of out-of-body experiences. Of crucial relevance are those passages in which Monroe (cf. 1971, 205) describes the training of experiences in his "Second Body" as a systematic practice to overcome the "fear barrier" of death and his general conclusion that recommends them as generating new religious certainty. Monroe asks for the consequences if "sophisticated man" would establish research journeys as common practice and would accept the reality experienced therewith: "What then? First, man will be freed of all uncertainty of his relationship with God. [...] He will know, rather than believe, whether death is a passing or finality." Moreover, "religious conflict will be impossible. Quite probably, Catholics, Protestants, Jews, Hindus, Buddhists, et al. will still retain much of their individuality, knowing that each has its place in Locale II" (270). But not only that. He expects also serious effects on the current practice of medicine, criticizing their mechanical and materialistic method of treatment, which highlights the opponent of his spiritual therapy: the soulless modern biomedicine and its practices. I may finally add that in a post-Moodian book on the same topic, *Far Journeys*, Monroe (cf. 1982, 266) argues that his journeys and near-death experiences are identical, if one subtracts the "high-stress ambience" and the "anxiety" of the latter.

2.7.6 JOHN C. LILLY AND THE FIRST MENTION
OF A NEAR-DEATH EXPERIENCE

Whereas Monroe's contribution to the final configuration of the near-death discourse has been acknowledged in more recent near-death studies (cf. Couliano 1991, 28–9; Fox 2003, 23–4), the work of John C. Lilly (1915–2001) is, astonishingly, scarcely mentioned. As I show in the following discussion, his impact has been essential. Lilly, a polymath covering research areas such as dolphin communication, psychoanalysis, or the search for extraterrestrial intelligence, became increasingly interested in the study of consciousness. He pursued the latter with his famous "Samadhi-tank," as it is known today, an isolation tank he invented in 1954 for the study of experiences under conditions of almost total "sensory deprivation." Moody (1976, 175) quotes Lilly's book *The Center of the Cyclone: An Autobiography of Inner Space* (1972), "a spiritual autobiography" in which, according to Moody, Lilly showed that experiences he had under conditions of isolation are "real experiences of enlightenment and insight, and not 'unreal' or 'delusional' at all." And he adds that Lilly "recounts a near-death experience of his own which is very much like the ones with which I have dealt, and that he puts his near-death experiences in the same category with his isolation experiences" (175). Indeed, Lilly points to LSD experiences and Shamanism, but also to James, Monroe, and Tart. Prominently, he refers to Buddhist, Hindu, and Western mystical descriptions of the "highest states of consciousness" that interest him most. The theosophical translation of Patañjali's Yoga Sūtras by I. K. Taimni, *The Science of Yoga*, published in 1961, deserves a special mention, as Taimni's categories of consciousness were closely adapted by Lilly (cf. 1972, 149).

The impact of his religious expectations become immediately clear if we read in his autobiography of the effects of his LSD ingestion:

> The whole experience had first been programmed and stored in my very early youth, when I was a member of the Catholic church serving at Mass and believing, with the intense faith of youth, in everything that I was learning in the church. I moved with the music into Heaven. I saw God on a tall throne as a giant, wise, ancient Man. He was surrounded by angel choruses, cherubim and seraphim [. . .]. I was there in Heaven, worshiping God, worshiping the angels, worshiping the saints in full and complete transport of religious ecstasy. (10–11; cf. 16).

Crucial is his notable continuation of Catholic faith and imagery. Later, the experience continues with a relived childhood, reaching as far as his birth, the "wonderful" safe place of the womb, and him being egg and sperm. Yet, the second time he took LSD, not everything went so well. Lilly reports that a combination of negative factors, being occupied with duties resulting in a feeling of being "under pressure" and an unsanitary self-administered antibiotics injection, led to a horrendous experience. Lilly discloses that he "almost died," being "in a coma for approximately twenty-four hours," and had "been blind for two days" (22). Later, Lilly became aware that he had gone through a "close-to-death experience" (23; Lilly uses also the plural, speaking of "one of the close-to-death experiences," 17), which is, later in the book, termed a "near-death experience." Here, he reviews his second encounter with LSD with the words "I found in the near-death experience of 1964, when I thought I was finished, that I had gone straight to –6 and then the two guides had brought me to the +6 level" (147). This precedes Moody's technical use of the concept by three years. The second chapter narrates extensively this second vision, triggered by grief, anger—and guilt (24). Although close to death, Lilly reports, "I remember very well the inside experience that occurred while I was in the so-called coma" (25). He had been transferred from his hotel room into a hospital. What now follows encompasses major elements of Moody's classification—he leaves his body, meets two guardians, communicates without words, sees an exceptional bright light, timelessness, experiences (other being's radiated) love and overwhelming power, and at one point the two guardians communicate *"that if I go back to my body as I developed further, I eventually would perceive the oneness of them and of me"* (27). Evoking a well-known element of Gnostic metaculture, Lilly describes the final moment of this experience as higher insight, surveying even the future: *"I am in a state to perceive them when I am close to the death of the body. In this state, there is no time. There is an immediate perception of the past, present, and future as if in the present moment"* (27). It seems clear that both the near-death experience and his interest in spirituality never ceased. In a later work, *Simulations of God* (1975), Lilly, pointing to his own "close scrapes with death," indicates that he even took a more professional interest and "collected many firsthand accounts of close brushes with death," asking specifically "about the inside experiences" (Lilly 1975, 80). After summarizing again well-known elements, including the idea that a person's memory might not be his own but part of the "central, universal store in which such information is carried through the centuries and the millennia" (82), he argues that such experiences contribute to the belief in endlessness, that one can no longer feel that one "ceases to be" when the "body dies," subscribing to a "much broader view than the egoistic, solipsistic, body-centered belief system common in the human being" (82). Death, therefore, can be accepted with "dignity, love, and with compassion" (83).

2.7.7 "I DIED AT 10:52 A.M."—VICTOR D. SOLOW

I should not miss including in this chapter at least one example of many individuals who reported experiences near death without becoming interested in them in a scholarly fashion. One testimony that reached scores of readers was the report of Victor D. Solow that appeared in several newspapers in 1974[25] and was eventually published under the telling

---

[25] Among others, in the Bowling Green (Kentucky) *Daily News* (May 26, 1974); quoted by Grof 1977 or Zaleski 1987.

heading "I Died at 10:52 A.M." in *Reader's Digest*. On March 23, 1974, Solow had suffered from cardiac arrest while his car was stopped at a red light. Picked up by an ambulance and carried to a hospital, several reanimation measures taken had no effect—for almost 23 minutes, Solow was "dead by all available standards," an attending doctor is quoted as saying. Solow reported that, for him, the moment of transition from life to death was easy. "There was no time for fear, pain or thought. There was no chance 'to see my whole life before me,' as others have related." He was "moving at high speed toward a net of great luminosity. The strands and knots where the luminous lines intersected were vibrating with a tremendous cold energy. The grid appeared as a barrier that would prevent further travel. I did not want to move through the grid." He slowed down, and then he "was in the grid." While he made contact with it, a "vibrant luminosity increased to a blinding intensity which drained, absorbed and transformed me at the same time." Words, he says,

> only vaguely approximate the experience from this instant on. The grid was like a transformer, an energy converter transporting me through form and into formlessness, beyond time and space [. . .]. This new 'I' was not the I which I knew, but rather a distilled essence of it, yet something vaguely familiar, something I had always known buried under a superstructure of personal fears, hopes, wants and needs. This 'I' had no connection to ego. It was final, unchangeable, indivisible, indestructible pure spirit. [. . .] 'I' was, at the same time, part of some infinite, harmonious and ordered whole. I had been there before. The condition 'I' was in was pervaded by a sense of great stillness and deep quiet [. . .]. But there is nothing further to tell except of my sudden return to the operating table. (Solow 1974, 178–9)

We can at once identify the well-known, Gnostic–Esoteric content in his report. Besides, recent features of the late 1960s appear, for example, the vision of an energetic, somehow electrified, luminous "grid"—a new metaphor, it seems, of a barrier—or the mention of a "superstructure." Finally, the author, pretending to be somewhat skeptical, conveys that this experience indicated a transformation: "since my return from that other condition of being, many of my attitudes toward our world have changed and continue to change, almost by themselves. A recurrent nostalgia remains for that other reality, that condition of indescribable stillness," namely, that "memory softens the old drives for possession, approval and success" (179). In addition to these comments, Solow's postscript shows many literary similarities to conversion narratives, namely, to be now aware of the incredible richness of life.[26]

---

[26] The "Postscript" reminds us intensively of conversion narratives. Solow says (1974, 182) here: "I have just returned from a pleasant, slow, mile-and-a-half jog. I am sitting in our garden writing. Overhead a huge dogwood moves gently in a mild southerly breeze. Two small children, holding hands, walk down the street absorbed in their own world. I am glad I am here and now. But I know that this marvelous place of sun and wind

2.7.8 COLLECTIONS OF NEAR-DEATH REPORTS IN THE 1970S

Besides reports of experiencers such as those of Solow or Ritchie, the 1970s also saw
new publications collecting various older and more recent reports, again with a religious metainterpretation—for example, in the United States, Jess E. Weiss's *The
Vestibule*, published in 1972, or, in Germany, Jean-Baptiste Delacour's *Aus dem Jenseits
zurück*, published both in German and in English translation (*Glimpses of the Beyond*) in
1973.[27] The collection by Weiss, *The Vestibule*,[28] perfectly illustrates the function of such
publications. The author skillfully combines eight accounts of experiences near death
with excerpts of Swedenborg, contemporary Christian reasoning on "revelation" or the
"beyond," and advice on how to develop one's spiritual potential. Of special religious significance is the conversion narrative "I was an atheist until I died" by Rev. Burris Jenkins,
included in Weiss (1972, 21–9). In the last chapter, Weiss narrates how he himself had
survived in World War II a mortar explosion close by. Hospitalized for over a year, he had
been finally discharged with a paralyzed arm. Searching for answers, he found in 1954 "an
open door": Christian Science. Experiencing a "growing spirituality within," Weiss (cf.
1972, 126) reports, and even wonderful "healings" happened, for example, his arm was
no longer paralyzed. His fear of death passed away, but he still searched for purpose,
praying regularly. His praying was answered. In 1970, there came a message: "Be patient,
be willing, listen, write a book" (127). And it is exactly the "Vestibule experiences," he
concludes, that should solely form the basis of a reasoning on how to follow the "good,"
which starts with the "willingness even to believe that life continues"—held to be the
"beginning of the realization that Eternal Life is our life" (128).

In that respect, Weiss' book achieves a perfect harmony of form and content: His
own experience near death initiated a search for reports by kindred souls. The latter,
published together, form the basic contents of a kind of "lay theology," attesting to the
reality of "near-death-induced," spiritual growth in "new born" religious subjects—a
lay theology that finds its final expression and dissemination by the divine command
to write exactly this book that shall guide others to draw from their—or other's—
experience the same conclusion (including, of course, to write a book, if they happened

---

[...], this murderous place of evil, ugliness and pain, is only one of many realities through which I must travel
to distant and unknown destinations. For the time being I belong to the world and it belongs to me."

[27] Delacour (pseudonym of Egbert Pies), however, presents in his book (besides various factual mistakes) several
untraceable and dubious accounts (cf. the "Tibetan" case, German ed. 1973, 167–77). Yet, some narratives—for
example, by a certain Mrs. Francis Leslie—follow closely the established narrative. Suffering from heart failure,
she was brought back with repeated adrenaline injections, which she reports as having experienced as cold, iron
needles piercing her brain while experiencing the "Light" and paradisiacal music (see 19–22). Delacour's book
has been widely read, cf., e.g., Grof 1977.

[28] The title refers to the Mishnaic tractate *Pirkei Avot* (4.16). There, Rabbi Ya'aqov is quoted as saying, "This
world is like a vestibule before the world to come; prepare yourself in the vestibule, that you may enter into the
banquet hall" (quoted and explained in Bar-Levav 2014, 10).

to hear that command). This genre-typical framing of experiences near death that could be paraphrased with the words "Now I know! I should write a book—has it not been commanded?—I should share my experience!" deserves further attention. The reader should, in this context, be reminded of the famous divine command to write a book in the first chapter of Revelation in the Bible, namely, "I am Alpha and Omega, the first and the last: and, What thou seest, write in a book, and send it unto the seven churches" (Rev. 1:8)—the "Revelation" being, as previously said, the most influential source for Christian near-death narratives. Thomas Welch, a Pentecostal evangelist, for example, reported in the 1960s an experience near death (which happened in 1924) that had become the basis for his "conversion" and "vocation" for "preaching the Gospel." It was published as "Oregon's Amazing Miracle" in the 1960s and reprinted in 1976 as a booklet by the evangelist publisher "Christ for the Nations." Welch, working the first day in a mill, had fallen 55 feet onto floating logs in a pond, and was nearly drowned. Found after an hour of search, he was inanimate, with broken ribs and head injuries. According to his report, "he was dead as far as this world is concerned," but "alive in another": "The next thing I knew I was standing near a shoreline of a great ocean of fire. It appeared to be what the Bible says it is in Revelation 21:8: 'the lake which burneth with fire and brimstone'. This is the most awesome sight one could ever see this side of the final judgment" (Welch [1960s] 1978, 8; cf. Rawlings 1978, 102–7). While standing at the shore, he could remember every detail and moment in his life. He saw another boy he had known years ago and who had died young, also staring speechless at the lake of fire. Welch reports that he thought by himself that the only way to escape this "prison" is by "Divine intervention." "I said to myself in an audible voice, 'If I had known about this I would have done anything that was required of me to escape coming to a place like this'. But I had not known" (9). Suddenly, he becomes aware of a man approaching and realizes that it is Jesus. Speaking to himself, Welch reasons "If He would only look my way and see me, He could rescue me from this place because He would know I never understood it was like this." And so it comes. Just before Jesus passes out of sight, "He turned His head and looked directly at me. That is all it took. His look was enough. In seconds I was back and entering into my body again" (9).

That the look of Jesus is enough to transfer him back into his body emphasizes as a narrative plot that Jesus will not only intervene in the beyond. The reader will become aware of Jesus's transformative power already in this world and put trust in him before disastrous postmortal punishment will happen. In passing, I may note that the power of God's look described here fits well to recent Cognitive Science of Religion's emphasis of the prosocial functions of a supernatural observer–God. Crucial is Welch's framing of his memoir. He continues his description that he was in hospital for four days, "in constant communion with the Holy Spirit," and it was in this time that he received the command of God to tell the world what he saw and how he came back to life (cf. 11). For that purpose, he boasts to be healed miraculously of his more severe injuries. He left the hospital after only four days. Being asked by others to relate his experience, he disclosed on Sunday before a large audience in a schoolhouse what he had seen, and to warn "of the judgment to come and tell them of the love of God for man that he might escape it" (14). However, we are informed in his booklet that Welch, an orphan, had arrived in Oregon only the year before, following friends who had "suddenly become very religious" (7). According to the latter's witness, included in the booklet, Welch had not been a (true?) Christian before the episode (cf. the report by Mabel Brocke, 15–18). We are told that these friends were, while Welch was unconscious, praying relentlessly for him being saved by God, and it is they who received the first report of his experiences in the hospital. Their praying, we read, was rewarded not only by the miraculous healing. A subsequent conversion resulted, finally, in Welch becoming shortly thereafter an evangelist preacher. In sum, the whole report illustrates in an exemplary fashion how Welch had already been attracted by the new faith of his peers. He emphatically embraced God's revelation in his experience near death to substantiate a call that, I assume, perfectly resonated with the expectations of his peers.

2.7.9 "GOLDEN JUMPS": ROSEN ON NEAR-DEATH EXPERIENCES IN ATTEMPTED SUICIDE

Resuming with a key step toward the final introduction of the term near-death experience, the 1975 article of psychiatrist David H. Rosen on survivors of suicidal jumps from the Golden Gate and Oakland Bay Bridges deserves mention. As did Lilly, and equally preceding Moody's publication, Rosen (1975, 291) speaks, this time already as a generic term, of near-death experiences. Of the six survivors interviewed, five reported an "apparent slowing of time"—a phenomenon, Rosen explains with reference to a preprint article of psychiatrist Russell Noyes and psychologist Roy Kletti (1976a; cf. 1974), that has been frequently reported by persons "undergoing sudden accidental near-death experiences (falls or near drownings)." However, a life review in its more distinct sense was reported by none of the survivors (Rosen 1975, 291); most prominent, however, is the spiritual dimension that followed, or even preceded, the jumps. One individual reported that he had not intended to kill himself, but that the jump was an outcome of spiritual longing to enter the "Golden Doors," which he commented " 'My jump has more to do with parapsychology than with psychology' " (291). The majority of the survivors reported that the fall was accompanied by transcendental experiences. One reported that his survival initiated his transformation from agnosticism to "fully Christian"; several others renewed their belief in a benevolent God in heaven, or felt "chosen" to disseminate the message of love (cf. 292–3). In his concluding comment, Rosen points to an interesting difference that he observed in regard to life-threatening accidents analyzed by Noyes (1971; 1972). Whereas Noyes could in the latter group outline three phases of experiences—"resistance" (against death), "life review," and finally, the phase of "transcendence"—Rosen finds among his survivors just one: transcendence. "Most reported a feeling of submission or surrender, as if they were guided or controlled by God or a higher power. [...] All the subjects reported in varying degrees spiritual rebirth experiences which are similar to previous reports of religious and transpersonal experiences" (293). Referring to Grof (see end of this section), Rosen is convinced at having collected corroborating evidence that people who have experienced an "ego-death," that is, "a feeling of total annihilation," move on to a more spiritual view of human existence. "The suicide survivors' death-rebirth experience represents both an ego-death [...] and a rebirth (with feelings of love and salvation)" (293). Actually, Rosen adds, in one of his cases an individual had taken LSD before jumping from the bridge, which makes his cases, so he says, even more comparable to Grof's LSD therapy as a method to reduce patient's fear of death.

2.7.10 NEAR-DEATH EXPERIENCES IN PSYCHOLOGICAL RESEARCH: RUSSELL NOYES AND ROY KLETTI

Rosen, as we saw, drew from interpretations of American psychiatrist Russell Noyes (professor emeritus at the University of Iowa), who had begun to study the experience of dying in late 1960 (cf. Martinović 2017, 23–6). Collecting reports of experiences near death from his patients, Noyes became increasingly aware of earlier work on those reports, especially the collection of Heim, but also the interpretations of Pfister, Frankl, and Pötzl (cf. Noyes 1971, 30–2). In collaboration with his younger colleague, clinical psychologist Roy Kletti, Noyes started empirical research on survivors of experiences near death, but prepared also an English translation of Heim (published in 1972), which contributed significantly to the formation of near-death research in the United States.

Although Noyes and Kletti followed in their collaborative research the trajectory of psychological explanations of "depersonalization" and "escape of reality," it is well worth mentioning that Noyes's early interest (cf. 1971, 25) in these experiences near death was significantly shaped by William James's and other scholars' interest in "mystical states of consciousness." In this early contribution, Noyes quotes extensively from the reports of Beaufort, Heim, and Jung, but also the works of de Quincey, Clarke, Munk, Hyslop, Barrett, Hunter (1967), and others. Noyes, pointing moreover to recent research with LSD as "experimental mysticism" (37–8), believes, nevertheless, that religious deathbed visions have declined since the 19th century (35). Many patients, he says, die nowadays while asleep or unconscious. Even though the potential for "mystical states" to unfold is still there, it is rare. Making classical secularization theory his own, Noyes believes "Affirmation of a spiritual reality is rather foreign to Western culture, at least since the industrial revolution" (38). However, Noyes acknowledges the general mechanisms of expectation and suggestibility—a psychedelic drug user will through his expectations "modify the effects of the drug upon him." In short, users seeking insights tend to find them: "The person who desires a religious encounter and believes that it will be forthcoming tends to have an experience he interprets as religious" (37). Although this explanation seems to outline a naturalist interpretation, Noyes still believes in a central value that mystical experiences near death do have. Consequently, he demands that the dying person "must be informed about mystical experiences" (39)—so that the respective expectation may rise. Distinguishing a "religious" from a "mystical" content, Noyes argues that a "religious follower" may experience the "direct presence of God," whereas "immediate experience" of the secularized dying may bring the latter "face to face with death," which may even renew or deepen "faith in some cosmic force" (38). Noyes, in that respect, believes that religious and mystical experiences will prepare one for death. In what reminds us of Kübler-Ross's terminology, Noyes speaks of an initial stage of "resistance" that will end if "acceptance" is reached. The latter, it seems, is the precondition that the life review unfolds, which in turn will trigger the essential insights (cf. 29). For systematic reasons, Noyes, however, does not speak in this early contribution of "near-death experiences." He underscores that dying is a highly individual act and in most cases the respective experiences remain "uncommunicated" (40); Noyes, therefore, while still arguing in favor of mystical experiences, hesitates to declare from a normative point of view that the evocation of these experiences is the only acceptable way in which death shall be encountered.

Noyes continuously contributed to the discourse on near-death experiences, though he was neither emphatic about the new designation nor enthusiastic in respect to the (economic) success of books describing near-death experiences as a spiritual awakening (cf. Martinović 2017, 193). For example, he and Kletti stressed that near-death experiences are often "fear-of-death" experiences, that is, experiences that do not belong to the dying process more properly but emerge from encounters with life-threatening danger. Of special interest to Noyes was the "panoramic memory," but not the bundle of experiences that Moody had put together, of which Noyes remained skeptical. From a number of interviews, Noyes and Kletti saw in the life-review feature (or, in their words, the "panoramic memory") a pacifying strategy of the mind, attempting to escape life-threatening danger (cf. Zaleski 1987, 120). Among the overall group of their cases of life-threatening danger, almost a third reported descriptions of panoramic memory. For the authors, in line with the psychological and psychoanalytical theories that had emerged in German-speaking countries, the effect of the life review is obviously a psychological function: "Clearly, the review of memories served as an escape from the reality confronting victims of life-threatening danger" (Noyes and Kletti 1977a, 189).

In the Freudian tradition of Pfister, Frankl, and Pötzl, they argued for a double strategy of a consoling escape and a depersonalized self-observation. The threatened personality, they reason, "appeared to seek the safety of the timeless moment. There death ceased to exist as the person immersed himself in his experience. For that purpose, past experiences of a relatively timeless quality were restored to consciousness, especially blissful ones. Such moments were drawn largely from early childhood, when life was experienced with greatest intensity [. . .]. This retreat toward the moment stands in striking contrast to a second mechanism used by the depersonalized individual to defend against death," namely, as an out-of-body experience: "Through a split into an observing and participating self the person (observer) removes himself from the endangered participant and watches as though a disinterested third party. The intense involvement in memories appears to be the opposite of such detachment" (Noyes and Kletti 1977a, 192). To conclude, Noyes and Kletti can count as the most prominent voices in the final constituting phase, remaining somehow faithful to a more orthodox psychological interpretation. Accordingly, especially Noyes was, in his later work, interested in developing therapies of "near-death trauma" and other phenomena of "depersonalization," which made him less responsive to their assumed quality of religious self-transformation (cf. Martinović 2017, 197–200). Nevertheless, the early work of Noyes and Kletti on the life review still argues with the psyche's search for "meaning," which transgresses a purely naturalist explanation.

2.7.11 LSD, THE *BOOK*, AND EXPERIENCES NEAR DEATH: STANISLAV GROF

A final contribution that we may deal with here is the mentioned work of Czechoslovakian psychologist and psychotherapist Stanislav Grof (born 1931), who, in collaboration with anthropologist Joan Halifax (born 1942), investigated the value of psychoactive drugs—especially LSD—in therapy for dying patients. Grof had started his career initially as a psychiatrist with psychoanalytical interests. In this context, he had explored the efficacy of LSD therapy in Prague, Czechoslovakia; in his continuation with LSD therapy in the United States in the late 1960s, he became with his new environment increasingly aware of the limitations of his rather conventional half-Catholic, half-Marxist–Materialist background—the latter at that time being the official doctrine in large parts of Eastern Europe. In his new American environment of the late 1960s and early 1970s, however, he enthusiastically subscribes to the "transpersonal" and "transcendental" dimensions of death and dying. Although the work *The Human Encounter With Death*, published in 1977, appeared after Moody's seminal contribution, Grof and Halifax (1977, 154; cf. 1976) note it was by then nearly finished. Indeed, the "rebirth experiences" quoted and analyzed by Grof and Halifax have, as Zaleski (1987, 100) already observed, "much in common with current accounts of near-death visions." The work shows in an exceptional manner how the different strands of near-death discourse were now tied together in order to present a homogeneous whole—integrating out-of-body experiences and the life review, psychoanalysis, parapsychology, LSD and rebirth experiences, and Kübler-Ross's system of the stages that lead to an acceptance of death—aiming, finally, at demonstrating the importance of supraconfessional mystical visions of the world's religions for strategies for facing death. Grof and Halifax are aware of a larger number of earlier contributions, quoting extensively the reports and interpretations of Beaufort, Heim, Jung, or Solow, but also E. Clarke, Cobbe, Hyslop, Barrett, Pfister, Hart, Huxley, Hunter, and Osis. In addition, they mention Pahnke, with whom they collaborated in their LSD research in the late 1960s, but also Noyes, who drew their attention to "the phenomenology of near-death experiences" (1977, xii). In her introduction to the work, Kübler-Ross surveys the emerging field of "thanatology," to which this book belongs. Grof, she adds, takes us through various fields, including "near-death experiences associated with drownings and accidents" (vi). Most important, she criticizes the attitude in modern medicine to sedate patients prior to death, instead of helping them to open up to more blissful states of death transition. It is in this context that Grof conceptualizes an authentic encounter with death—facilitated not only by (LSD) psychotherapy, but also enabled through insights of "Comparative Religion" (cf. 7–8).[29] Placing a bold statement on the decline of "religion," Grof and Halifax explain: "Religion, which can be of great help for the dying, has lost much of its significance for the average Westerner. A pragmatic life orientation and philosophical materialism have replaced religious fervor. With some exceptions Western religions have lost their function as vital forces in life." Indeed, they miss not only the function of religion for guidance and ease for the dying—equally, they say, do contemporary philosophy and "medical science" fail to offer something (cf. 7). Indeed, it is the contemporary approach of medical care to simply delay dying "by all means"—"electric pace makers, artificial kidneys," and so forth—while "religion offers no help" (Grof and Halifax 1976, 182). Therefore, they emphasize that it is not the traditional religiosity— offered by the "mainstream" tradition—that should be sought by the dying. The "mystical branches," as incorporated in Christian mysticism, Kabbalah, Sufism, or Buddhism are harboring the wisdom Grof is looking for. In line with a transcultural interpretation of a common core of experience within these mystical traditions, Grof emphasizes that LSD experiences may as such tap on unconscious resources that were not part of the individual's culture or socialization: "Frequently the psychedelic experience involves elements totally alien to an individual's own religious tradition [. . .]. Thus a Christian or a Muslim can discover the law of karma and generate a belief in the cycles of reincarnation, or a rabbi may experience a conversion to Zen Buddhism" (1977, 29; cf. 1976, 190–3, 195).

This amazing quality of LSD experiences can be found in near-death experiences too. Grof and Halifax (1977, 112–13) state that various reports of both experiences show intimate similarities, for example, the life review, telepathic communication with deceased persons, and so forth. However, what makes this study special is the way in which its authors combine comparative religion with mysticism and psychedelics, which is used as a template to integrate the more technical psychological literature on the life-review feature. The authors, as previously indicated, quote extensively Albert Heim's study (cf. 131–5, 147–8), which had in the meantime been translated by Noyes (1972). Finally, the authors refer to Moody's work. Although they see great similarities, they find one

---

[29] Halifax was a student of Joseph Campbell, whose work on the transcultural pattern of mythical journeys (1949) had become highly influential.

essential difference worthy of notice. Moody, they say, "emphasizes the lack of mythological elements in these new concepts of death [...]. In our experience concrete archetypal images of deities and demons were equally frequent as the occurrence of the divine or demonic entities without form" (156). In consequence, Grof and Halifax deal extensively with afterlife conceptions of religious traditions that are said to reemerge in current psychedelic research. In contrast to Moody, they elaborate extensively on the *Tibetan Book of the Dead* (cf. 167–70, 175–7) and other sources, and they repeatedly argue that these "visions" are also seen by those "unsophisticated individuals" unacquainted with this literature (cf. 177).

Likewise compatible with Jungian "universals" of the collective psyche and Campbell's "monomyth," they still account for the specific religious "framework" in which these experiences of transcendence and spiritual rebirth may appear. "Death-rebirth sequences can be experienced by some individuals in a Biblical framework as identification with Christ's suffering, death on the cross, and resurrection. Others, however, identify at this point with Osiris, Dionysus, or the victims sacrificed to the Aztec Sun God [...]. The final blow mediating the ego death can also be experienced as coming from the terrible goddess Kali, from Shiva the Destroyer, from the Bacchants, or the Egyptian Set" (177). This seems to be a comprehensive list of mostly historical religious traditions. In the view of the authors, it may confirm the fact that ego death and spiritual rebirth are, as such, features that transcend individuals and cultures. Significantly, they also report of a case in which the *Tibetan Book* has been read as a guide to a dying cancer patient in a hospital setting, to whom LSD had also been administered therapeutically (69–77). Once in the LSD therapy, "he became convinced that he had died, and God appeared to him as a brilliant source of light telling him not to fear and assuring him that everything would be all right" (76). Again, we may notice the close entanglement of LSD and near-death experiences. Finally, the authors narrate, in a situation of sudden deterioration of his health, the instructions of the *Book* were read to him, namely, that he shall move to the light without being afraid. It seems something unexpected happened in that situation: The surgeons decided to operate and had the patient transported into the operating room. Grof and Halifax report that "all the persons in the room were shocked by what appeared to be a brutal intrusion into an intimate and special situation" (181). During the operation, he experienced two cardiac arrests, "clinical death," as the authors say, but was successfully resuscitated. But still, as he reported later, he had been able follow the advice of the *Book*, which merged into a near-death experience with many of Moody's characteristics:

> The initial darkness was replaced by brilliant light, and he was able to approach it and fuse with it. The feelings he described on experiencing the light were those of sacredness and deep peace. Yet, simultaneously, he saw a movie on the ceiling, a vivid reenactment of all the bad things he had done in his life [...]. While this was happening he was aware of the presence of God, who was watching and judging

this life-review. Before we left him that day, he emphasized how glad he was that he had had three LSD sessions. He found the experience of actual dying extremely similar to his psychedelic experiences and considered the latter excellent training and preparation. (181–2)

The latter description fulfills, for sure, an important function for Grof and Halifax. It is a personal narrative of the victory over the dehumanizing practices of biomedicine—a victory facilitated by accustomed psychedelic experiences.

The narrative, moreover, amounts to the conclusion for Grof and Halifax that (1) experiences unearthed in psychedelic therapy sessions, (2) those described in the *Book*, and (3) near-death experiences are basically the same (cf. 153–4): hearing unpleasant noises, roaring, or majestic music; peace; passing through a tunnel; out-of-the-body phenomena; pure consciousness; a Being of Light; a second body; encounters with other beings; a longing for return into the physical body; and so forth. However, Grof, being firmly involved in the psychoanalytical study of "birth" and rebirth adds that, though not "specifically mentioned by Moody, one finds in these accounts many indirect allusions to the birth process," for example, "sliding down head first" (154).

2.7.12 ALBERT HOFMANN'S FIRST LSD EXPERIENCE: AN EXPERIENCE NEAR DEATH

In the context of intertextually related reports of experiences near death with and without LSD, we may substantiate this correlation that was already by the late 1960s a well-established discursive topos by turning to the autobiography of its inventor, Swiss chemist Albert Hofmann (1906–2008). Appearing in 1979, its first English translation *LSD: My Problem Child* (1980) had been endowed with a telling subtitle: *Reflection on Sacred Drugs, Mysticism, and Science*. There, he described his first fully intentional self-experiment with the psychedelic substance of LSD that had happened in April 1943—after the unintentional discovery that led to his hallucinogenic experiences on a bicycle ride home (the famous "bicycle day" as it is nowadays called and sometimes even celebrated by psychedelic enthusiasts). The description, included in the chapter "How LSD Originated," had already been presented on several occasions, including an international conference dealing with "Hallucinogens, Shamanism and Modern Life" (San Francisco, 1978; cf. Hofmann 1979b). Actually, by the time he wrote his autobiography, Hofmann looked back on more than two decades of close contacts with various important protagonists for the coming-together of "transformative" experiences near-death dealt with in previous sections—Huxley, Pahnke, Grof, Leary, to name but a few. From his short notes taken after the experiment, Hofmann ([1980] 2013, 20) described his experiences thus: "Even worse than these demonic transformations of the outer world, were the alterations that I perceived in myself, in my inner being. Every exertion of my will, every attempt to put an end to the disintegration of the outer world and the dissolution of my ego, seemed to be wasted effort. A demon had invaded me, had taken possession of my body, mind, and soul." The "demonic possession" mentioned here does not only invoke a religious framework of the altered mind; moreover, regarding the fear of losing touch with reality and the ego, we may also think of the famous thought experiment that René Descartes described in his *Meditationes* (1641). Descartes started his experiment of systematic doubt with the hypothetical assumption that a "malicious demon" may have placed him into a complete and all-encompassing illusion of the world, including the illusion of his and other minds.

Hofmann, however, continues his narration that he "was seized by the dreadful fear of going insane," his body seemingly "without sensation, lifeless, strange. Was I dying? Was this the transition? At times I believed myself to be outside my body, and then perceived clearly, as an outside observer, the complete tragedy of my situation. I had not even taken leave of my family [. . .]. Would they ever understand that I had not experimented thoughtlessly, irresponsibly, but rather with the utmost caution, and that such a result was in no way foreseeable?" (20) With the psychological aid of an attending doctor, Hofmann finally overcomes the fear of death and starts to "enjoy" the hallucinogenic show. Obviously, this description evokes experiences of out of the body or the probability of "transition" beyond death, prominent elements of near-death discourse. Most significant is the way Hofmann introduces the aftereffects:

> Exhausted, I then slept, to awake next morning refreshed, with a clear head, though still somewhat tired physically. A sensation of well-being and renewed life flowed through me. Breakfast tasted delicious and gave me extraordinary pleasure. When I later walked out into the garden, in which the sun shone now after a spring rain, everything glistened and sparkled in a fresh light. The world was as if newly created. All my senses vibrated in a condition of highest sensitivity. (22)

Without question, this report reminds us of well-known portrayals of conversion and spiritual awakening.

Indeed, the spiritual dimension of psychedelics-triggered experiences had attracted Hofmann's interest from early on. This included, for example, a search for blissful moments of childhood stored in memory. "I had come with the hope that in the [. . .] inebriation I could manage to allow certain images from euphoric moments of my childhood, which remained in my memory as blissful experiences, to come alive" (166; cf. 3–4). Although the first phase of his trip turned out to be bad, he reports that he finally achieved what he had sought, being again an example of how reported experiences may develop according to expectations. In his autobiography, he outlines the necessity of existential experience for understanding reality and the "innermost self": "The true importance of LSD and related hallucinogens lies in their capacity to shift the wavelength setting of the receiving 'self', and thereby to evoke alterations in reality consciousness. This ability to allow different, new pictures of reality to arise, this truly cosmogonic power, makes the cultish worship of hallucinogenic plants as sacred drugs understandable" (144). Consequently, the work ends with the statement on the true importance of his "sacred drug," as he says, namely, that LSD provides "a material aid to meditation aimed at the mystical experience of a deeper, comprehensive reality" (153). A sacred drug, however, not for the masses (as Leary had propagated in the 1960s), but, as Hofmann says repeatedly, for some chosen few. In this regard, he shared the elitist opinions on drugs with his friends Ernst Jünger and Rudolf Gelpke (cf. Baier [in press]).

To summarize the interrelations between LSD and near-death experiences in the 1960s and 1970s, we can easily see that they form part of an overarching discourse of authentic mystical experiences. In his study of *Psychedelic Mysticism*, Morgan Shipley (2015, 220) shows how the agenda of the use of psychedelics as "entheogens" (Gordon Wasson), that is, as means "generating the divine within," was meant to renew a cosmic spirituality and altruistic oneness. Shipley concludes: "To understand psychedelics as entheogenic sacraments is to engage the 1960s not as an expression of a world gone wrong, but as an attempt to carve out space for the revival of *homo religious*." Most of the researchers were, as "scholar–practitioners," interested in three interrelated aspects of these experiences: First, they were personally interested to open up a "mystical" experience of self and reality. Second, they were interested in scientific proof of the capacity of psychedelics to transform attitudes toward reality, including the reduction of fear of death. Finally, they aimed to develop a psychotherapy that could make use of these assumed transformative powers of psychedelics and hence to usher in a more humane, altruistic society.

What is more, we can see how LSD directly "induced," as it seems, both frightening and blissful experiences seen as similar or even identical with near-death experiences. At least some LSD users had in fact actively searched for such experiences, as, for example, is obvious in survivors of Golden Gate jumps. Others experienced them in the aftermath of LSD intoxication as flashbacks—a phenomenon that had already been reported by the opium users in the 19th century. Being faithful to the methodological approach favored here, we may, however, not argue that LSD actually "caused" these experiences. Dealing, again, with reports of experience, we must confine our observation to the contents and forms of these reports. Regarding the latter, we can but only notice that both assume in some cases an almost indistinguishable conformity. This may be the outcome of shared expectations of what was to be found in both. Narratives of LSD experiences influenced the reports of near-death experiences, and the other way around.

2.7.13 MOODY, GREYSON, AND THE STANDARDIZED SCHEME OF NEAR-DEATH EXPERIENCES

Having accomplished the historical genealogy of the different topoi and strands that were bundled by Moody with the generic term near-death experience, we should take a final look how the religious elements in them have been accounted for in the early phase of their standardization. In addition to Moody's standardized narrative (see Chapter 1.3.), I may provide a list of the headings under which they figure in his work (cf. Moody [1975] 1976, 19–107):

1. Hearing being pronounced dead (or: "hearing the news").
2. A strange noise.
3. The Dark Tunnel.
4. Out of the Body ("out of body," travel of the "spiritual body").
5. Watching (emotionally disturbed) resuscitation attempts.
6. Becoming aware of a supra-empirical "powerful" body.
7. People of Light (or "meeting others"): deceased friends, relatives, and "spiritual guides."
8. Ineffability.
9. The Being of Light.
10. The (panoramic) Review; evaluation of everything ever done.
11. The Border and reluctance to return.
12. Intense feeling of joy, love.
13. Feelings of Peace and Quietness.
14. Coming back.[30]

This list combines, as we saw, very different experiences, transmitted in various strands and contexts that often did not belong to experiences emerging from life-threatening situations. Nevertheless, Moody was convinced that all of them belong in one and the same category. In his second book, Moody (1977a, 9–28) added further elements such as the "vision of knowledge" (which was categorized here as Gnostic–Esoteric topos), "cities of light," or a "realm of bewildered spirits." Various later attempts tried to reorganize its "core elements"; even different formalized ratings for these have been proposed (cf. Ring 1980, 275–9). For my final purpose (Parts IV and V), namely, to uncover their function within the religious discourse, I may point to the fact that only eight years later, psychiatrist Bruce Greyson (born 1946), one of the most prominent researchers in the field, developed scale of 16 items to measure the "depth" and centrality of reported experiences. Actually, the "Greyson scale" (1983), based on Moody's elements, assumed the distinction of being the standard scheme in empirical research (cf. Parnia 2014).

In the final form of the scale, Greyson (1983, 373) identified four "components." First, a cognitive component, which is explored with the following four questions: "1. Did you have the impression that everything happened faster or slower than usual? 2. Were your thoughts speeded up? 3. Did scenes from your past come back to you? 4. Did you

---

[30] It is not fully clear which elements count as the 15 that Moody could identify—they are never listed as such (cf. Moody 1977a, 3, 9).

suddenly seem to understand everything?" Second, there is an "affective component," which, however, encompasses not only feelings of peace, joy, and happiness (5, 6), but also "harmony" or the light: "7. Did you feel a sense of harmony or unity with the universe? 8. Did you see, or feel surrounded by, a brilliant light?" The third component is termed "paranormal": "9. Were your senses more vivid than usual? 10. Did you seem to be aware of things going on that normally should have been out of sight from your actual point of view as if by ESP [extrasensory perception]? 11. Did scenes from the future come to you? 12. Did you feel separated from your body?" (373). Last but not least, there is the "transcendental component," again explored with four questions: "13. Did you seem to enter some other, unearthly world? 14. Did you seem to encounter a mystical being or presence, or hear an unidentifiable voice? 15. Did you see deceased or religious spirits? 16. Did you come to a border or point of no return?" (374).

Greyson, however, takes the disparate categories of these four clusters or components as "psychologically meaningful,"[31] and does not discuss the concept of transcendent or paranormal more thoroughly. In my eyes, it might well be worth arguing that a sudden understanding of everything (question 4) belongs to the "transcendental." The same holds true regarding "universal harmony or unity," or the "bright light" (7, 8). A vision of a "deceased spirit," on the other hand, may well be subsumed under the heading of paranormal (and not transcendental).[32]

Greyson's scale, however, avoiding the category "religion" or "religious," brings to light an understanding that already permeates Moody's presentation. Scrutinizing Greyson's scale from the perspective of the history of religious ideas reveals that it amalgamates topoi under the heading of paranormal or transcendent that can be identified as visionary narratives within religious traditions, that is, Christian or Buddhist discourse. Glossing over the problems of expectations and reporting, he takes the authenticity of individual experiences for granted. Furthermore, the categories used display the motive of separating experience from literary topoi of religious traditions. This amounts to the effect that traditional religious narratives of the reports, such as, say, from persons describing the "light of heaven," will become, in their religious contextualization, insignificant. "Light of heaven" may score as an answer to question 8 as a weighted response of 2, "Light clearly of mystical or other-worldly origin"—in other words, as an "affective component." A vision of Jesus, in contrast, will be transcendental (question 15). Finally, elements of spiritualist, parapsychological, esoteric, and mystic beliefs are categorized side-by-side with emotional, affective, or cognitive states. This, again, may not happen unintentionally. Looking tentatively from Greyson's scale retrospectively on Moody's systematics highlights that already in Moody's various testimonies these currents of paranormal and

---

[31] Greyson's four clusters (1983, 371) were "empirically assembled based on inter-item correlations," and retrospectively designated as reflecting a Cognitive, Affective, Paranormal, and Transcendental Component.

[32] Especially if the "Weighted Responses," given by Greyson (cf. 372–3), are considered.

transcendent form an essential part of the accounts. In contrast to the palpable influences in Moody's collected testimonies, he himself insinuated that he became aware of esoteric "parallels" only *after* collecting the accounts: "[M]y surprise has been compounded as over the years I have come across quite a number of striking parallels to them. These parallels occur in ancient and/or highly esoteric writings from the literature of several very diverse civilizations, cultures, and eras" (Moody [1975], 1976, 111). Already in the introduction, Moody declares to be "not broadly familiar with the vast literature on paranormal and occult phenomena," but to "feel confident that a wider acquaintance with it might have increased my understanding of the events I have studied. In fact, I intend now to look more closely at some of these writings to see to what extent the investigations of others are borne out by my findings" (3–4). It has been already observed by Mark Fox (2003, 23) that in spite of this disavowal of any knowledge of parapsychological literature, "it is clear that *Life After Life* fitted chronologically and developmentally into an ongoing, widely shared [. . .] concern to detect empirical evidence of both the existence of the human soul as distinct from the body and that soul's ability to survive the body's death." This concern, for which I see overwhelming evidence, presupposes a better knowledge of the corpus of literature on the paranormal and occult than Moody admits. Apart from the technical term out of the body, Moody uses the even more specific term of the panoramic review—introduced by Beaufort but well established in pertinent near-death literature. Regarding his own religion in 1975, Moody characterizes his background as an encultured Methodist, but, in terms of belief, as a concern for the supradenominational truths of religion.[33]

Despite the obvious religious inheritance of certain elements reported by Moody's informants that, in consequence, became part of the composite description previously quoted—for example, the weighing of the life lived, the Being of Light, the encounter with Jesus or with deceased relatives and friends, and the impression of an overwhelming, oceanic feeling of bliss—Moody insisted that the phenomenon described has significance beyond religion. Although he admits that these experiences "seem to be to some extent" shaped by religious beliefs and backgrounds, he argues that, on the contrary, none of his reporting individuals experienced "a heaven or a hell [. . .] like the customary picture to which we are exposed in this society. Indeed, many persons have stressed how

---

[33] On his "religious upbringing," Moody comments ([1975], 1976, 4), that he and his family attended the Presbyterian Church, "yet my parents never tried to impose their religious beliefs or concepts upon their children," resulting in a nondogmatic understanding of religion as "a concern with spiritual and religious doctrines, teachings, and questions. I believe that all the great religions of man have many truths to tell us." In "organizational terms, I am a member of the Methodist Church." However, Moody's autobiography of 2012 depicts a quite skeptical father: "My father had been raised an atheist and was dubious about religion, to say the least. The notion of an afterlife was not a live option for him. In fact, he would become agitated at the mere discussion of religion, calling it institutionalized superstition, or worse" (33). Oddly enough, Moody reports of his father who got to know Ritchie in the Army: "My father called Ritchie a 'legend' and said that he was an honest man who 'didn't let religion get in the way of being fun' " (57).

unlike their experiences were to what they had been led to expect in the course of their religious training" (140). With such words, Moody even encourages individuals to report of experiences that are in stark contrast to experiences that conform to orthodox beliefs of the Churches and denominations. In the late 1970s, Peter L. Berger will argue in the same vein, but from a theological perspective, that, recently, religiosity has now conformed to a "heretical imperative": Modernity with its characteristics of "religious uncertainty," will almost necessarily produce "heretical" deviations on a broader scale. "Picking" and "choosing" are, he says, no longer an occasional rupture—a position now occupied by "orthodox" religious affirmation—but common ground: "Indeed one could put this change even more sharply: For premodern man, heresy is a possibility—usually a rather remote one; for modern man, heresy typically becomes a necessity" (Berger 1979, 28). Instead of a "heretical imperative," we may use, however, a less theology-laden language and speak of an "imperative of individual experience" (cf. Chapter 3.5).

Looking back on the enormous success of his first book, Moody (2012, 96) explains that it filled a "vacuum": "Up to this point the subject had been considered one that belonged to the world of religion, and therefore it had received little if any examination by medical science. Hence, there was no real scientific examination of the possibility of life after life." Describing his work as "scientific" (but sometimes also as "not scientific"; cf. 101) discloses that Moody at least halfway believes that patients' reports on experiences dealing with, carefully termed, "life after life" (cf. 100), can be dealt with from a "scientific" perspective. Reassuring his religious neutrality,[34] Moody was forced to realize, as he comments, that "religious people and New Agers" had begun a battle "over exactly what it was I had discovered in near-death experiences. Both of these groups believed the same thing—that near-death experiences are proof of life after death. And members of each group wanted me to publicly agree with them" (101). Moody, again, treats the reported experiences as a "discovery," and assigns "religion" to being merely one interpretation of this discovery. In the final chapter of his autobiography, we are informed, "I have a relationship with God and talk to him all the time. But what I really don't know, from a rational point of view, is whether life after death is in his plan or not. And it may well be that God has something in mind for us that is even more remarkable than a life after death." And Moody adds, "I love God," "but he hasn't told me anything yet about an afterlife" (245–6). For us, such statements make it obvious that Moody is surfing the waves of current spirituality, adjusting his statements strategically to what he expects his various audiences want to hear.

Having outlined the coming-together of the generic term of near-death experiences, I refrain from pursuing an intellectual history of the more recent near-death discourses, spanning from the 1980s to the present. In general, prominent Spiritualist and Esoteric

---

[34] "I wanted to stay neutral on the question of religion. I felt that the notion of life after life extends to all people, even atheists. I didn't want anyone to think that I came at this subject with a religious bias" (Moody 2012, 95).

strands were still influential in the decades following the 1970s. Outlining the roots of "New Age Spirituality," Robert Ellwood (1992, 62), for example, argued that the "progressivist strand of Spiritualism," characterized by an optimistic eschatology and a sympathetic stance toward scientific progress, has much in common with certain influential books on near-death experiences. Discussing the examples of Michael Gross, *The Final Choice*, or Ring's later publications from *Heading Toward Omega* onward, he shows how the latter even championed testimonies that turn predictions received near death into full-blown "near-death prophecies" (cf. 63–7; cf. Kinsella 2016). Interestingly, and in line with Zaleski and others, Ellwood does not consider a historical continuity and dependency between what he calls "parallels between nineteenth century Spiritualism and twentieth century New Age" (62). Instead, he acknowledges a compact set of parallel themes, for example, a monistic absolute, intertwined spirit and matter, astrology, occult practices, or the inclusion of the latest science. In the case of New Age, this has been especially quantum physics, which, I should add, still plays a prominent role in contemporary near-death discourse, for example, in Pim van Lommel's work. As seen in the previous sections, there is good evidence to assume an uninterrupted current that connects 19th-century Spiritualism with 20th-century Esotericism and, finally, New Age. Instead of portraying the subsequent historical evolution of reporting or systematizing near-death experiences of the five decades after Moody, I aim to show in Part III how the crucial developments in modern biomedicine contributed on their part to the skyrocketing reports of near-death experiences in the 1960s and 1970s.

PART THREE

"Near-Death Experiences" as Religious Protest Against Materialism and Modern Medicine in the 1960s and 1970s

3.1

Introduction

ꙮ ──

SO FAR, THE focus has been on reports of near-death experiences (Part I) and their religious framing (Part II). In this part, I still deal with discourses that contributed to the emergence of those reports, but I place them within their context of societal changes of the 1960s and 1970s. As we saw in the preceding chapters, a discursive topos that gained momentum in near-death discourse has been the description of the "primal scene" of modern out-of-body experiences. The body in the surgical theater of a hospital, surrounded by doctors and medical personnel, connected to monitors, transfusion tubes, and heart–lung machinery—very often a critical situation, a balance on a knife's edge. While attending doctors work heavily to increase the chance of survival, take measures of reanimation, and so forth, the disembodied observer—depicted as soul, spirit, or consciousness—surveys the primal scene from above, moved by ambivalent thoughts and emotions: for example, being already "through" and at ease. Determined to leave irrevocably, the disembodied observer feels discontented with the reanimation measures and responds to the doctor's attempts sometimes even with aggression. In the introduction, I suggested reading the reports of near-death experiences as a stream of narratives, being fed by three different religious metacultures. As we saw, it was in the late 1960s and early 1970s that these narratives and topoi were acknowledged as a homogenous whole of consolidated elements. What had happened in the meantime that led to a multiplication and systematic collection of these reports? Surely the use of psychedelics or the resurgence of esotericism, yoga practices, and other spiritual techniques had their share (cf. Pike 2004, 67–88). Yet we may still ask: Which expectations had spurred such experiences in the surgical theater that, as the reports show, express a critical attitude toward the latest practices in modern hospitals? Which factors contributed to the heart-felt need for the spirit's self-assurance of its nonmaterial nature?

In the following, I take a short look at how substantial changes within Western society of the 1960s and 1970s contributed to an intensification of near-death discourse. Reaching out to clarify these factors, I remain true to our methodological approach and continue to analyze these societal changes mainly as they are reflected in discourses on these changes. Occasionally, however, I point to inventions, medical innovations, or institutional changes in the medical sector. Essential factors that pushed reports of near-death experiences were, as I argue, the following. A long-term development that took place on a global scale was the successful institutionalization of certain biomedical practices: the spatially inclusive and comprehensive introduction of intensive care units (ICUs), rescue services, and the improvement of resuscitation technology. What is more, the 1960s and 1970s saw an intensified trend to transfer the dying into hospitals, especially because of the growth of the cohort of the very elderly in biomedically advanced societies. Equally, in the second half of the 20th century, there is a trend to loosen strong family ties. Taken together, this implied a corresponding increase in the risk of dying in isolation. This trend is mirrored in a critical discourse on the uncomfortable dehumanizing anonymity of dying in institutions, the full surrender into the hands of medical specialists, or the dominating presence of medical apparatuses. What kind of repercussions did this discourse have on what patients in critical condition formed as expectations when transferred to a hospital?

Conspicuously, these two decades are rocked by heated discussions of how to define death, coma, but also the "locked-in syndrome," or the "persistent vegetative state." An additional factor that contributes in the 1960s and 1970s to a societal discourse on the horrors of dying in helpless situations is the fear of "depersonalization." The threat to die a "social death" before dying, included being a family confronted with the decision of whether doctors should terminate artificial life support, or being personally diagnosed with a poor or terminal prognosis, pronounced with a high probability and certainty. The fear of losing the ability to communicate—in a society in which verbal communication is of utmost importance—deserves special mention. This fear seems unassuaged by the increasing willingness to administer pain medication in terminal care—a development that Japanese bioethicist Masahiro Morioka (2005) has summarized as the trend of modern society to achieve a "painless civilization," taking its rationale in not only treating emerging pain, but in preventing pain experiences before they occur. Another distinctive factor was psychotropic effects of medication (narcotics, opioids, etc.) during surgery or postsurgery, or in palliative care. Finally, in the 1950s, potent antipsychotics were developed in order to treat schizophrenia, psychotic hallucination, and so forth. In the 1960s and 1970s, their use—in fundamental opposition to mystical interpretation of the visionary significance of hallucinations—was criticized by the "Anti-Psychiatry movement," holding that schizophrenia could be a life-enhancing and meaningful experience. The importance of all these debates, mostly neglected in the field of near-death studies, were emphasized by Jelena Martinović (2017, 18, 28–62) in her study on Russell

Noyes, pointing to the "taboo" of dying in modern medicine. In my view, the debates were especially spurred by new techniques of organ transplantation, which, for their part, called for a new definition of death. This process that was finalized, though not settled, with the introduction of "brain death." The importance of the general discussion of brain death and the ethical status of the comatose for the discourse becomes immediately visible if we turn to Moody's work that is one of the first, but certainly not the last, to discuss the new definition of brain death in the context of near-death experiences.

Taken together, the interest in those experiences seems closely tied to these developments. First, and rather simply, the absolute number of persons surviving—and being able to report from—situations "near death" increased.[1] Second, certain narrative strands of near-death experiences allow the conclusion that these reports can be read as comments on the situation previously described—for example, the disembodied consciousness witnessing from above the body being declared dead. Third, the narrative of being brought back to life against one's will, a topos prevalent even in the earliest strand of Christian deathbed reports, seems to express the wish to die fast and without existential struggle. Montaigne had already expressed this wish. In his *Essays*, he declares that he wants "death to find me planting my cabbages, but caring little for it, and even less about the imperfections of my garden."[2] Seen in this way, a significant number of near-death reports may probably be read as an appeal to let people die with dignity, without violent attempts to keep the body alive. It is especially this strand that was upheld by protagonists of the three religious metacultures, believing that death is not the end. Dying is declared to be merely a journey to the other world, which, additionally, will likely happen without pain or struggle—even though it is an open question if these experiences may grant insights into what people may experience while dying of multiple organ failure.

---

[1] Moody ([1975] 1976, 145) had already pointed to the resurgence of near-death reports and resuscitation technology, though only in quantitative terms. Moody holds that near-death experiences have been "vastly more common in the past few decides than in earlier periods" because of "advanced resuscitation technology." This is indeed a well-attested fact. According to the study of Pim van Lommel et al. (cf. 2001, 2040–1), the number of cardiac arrest survivors with "(core) Near-death experiences" has been given as 18% (12% with core experience, $n = 344$). As a caveat, we must remark that the study speaks of "experiences," not of "reports."

[2] "Je veux [. . . . .] que la mort me trouve plantant mes choux, mais nonchalant d'elle, et encore plus de mon jardin imparfait" (Montaigne [1580] bk. 1, ch. 20; cf. 1842, 30). A study (survey in 2006, $n = 289$) by Matthias Hoffmann (2011, 1) on the fear of "social death" revealed that an 80% majority of the German sample expressed the wish to die "sudden and unexpected," and only 20% wished to die "prepared for death."

3.2

Pushing Near-Death Experiences (I)

PRIVATIZED DEATH

ALAN KELLEHEAR (2007, 173) observed that in the 1970s and early 1980s there was a "growing critical tide of dissatisfaction with modern scenes of dying, death and bereavement." Indeed, a broad alliance of different actors such as French historian Philippe Ariès, American Swiss psychologist Elisabeth Kübler-Ross, Jewish philosopher Hans Jonas, sociologists Barney Glaser and Anselm Strauss, or the Austrian critic of modern medicine, Ivan Illich (1974, 1976), published in this period crucial works on essential aspects of the modern biomedical framework of death and dying. To illustrate the general impact this discourse exerted on the emergence of the composite description of near-death experiences, I explore two major actors, namely, Kübler-Ross and Ariès. Both authors offered systematic descriptions of attitudes toward death, being from the outset, and to a significant degree, moved by what they felt to be the latest developments of the "dishonorable" biomedical treatment of the dying. Quoting from their works, written in the 1970s, follows a double intention: First, these descriptions represent first-hand observations of certain changes in society.[1] No less important, they are in a second respect discursive events that by themselves had a tremendous effect on public depictions of dying in hospitals.

To publish interviews of dying persons was by every means a pioneering approach of Elisabeth Kübler-Ross (1926–2004). In doing so, she did not only break a taboo: Most important, she raised a large-scale awareness of the psychological needs of the dying

---

[1] On the approach of Ariès, see the literature discussed in Kellehear 2007, 172–6.

(1969; cf. Ariès 1981, 589). In a way, she outlined an ethical imperative: Listen to what dying have to say. Analyzing the attitudes of dying individuals, she distinguished five interrelated stages—originally as stages of the experiences of the dying: denial, anger, bargaining, depression, and acceptance. The final phase, "acceptance," of course is the most meaningful. It is the only straightforward "positive" stage, though not a happy one in collective understanding. "Acceptance should not be mistaken for a happy stage. It is almost void of feelings. It is as if the pain had gone, the struggle is over, and there comes a time for 'the final rest before the long journey' as one patient phrased it" (Kübler-Ross 2009 [1970], 92). At this stage, ideally, fear and despair have passed away. To realize that a patient has fully accepted his fate should also be the moment in which medical specialists should no longer pursue prolonging life by all means (cf. 93). This does not mean, as Kübler-Ross points out, that all hope is gone (cf. 113). However, to describe acceptance as ideally the final stage, it means that all parties involved—patient, family and friends, and physicians—have accepted dying. This is a message, as we read it, not only to the patient, relatives, and friends, but also for the doctor—a message that reveals itself in Kübler-Ross's depiction of "modern dying."

Just as Ariès did a few years later, Kübler-Ross diagnosed a recent change in attitudes toward "death," which she designated as a "flight from facing death calmly": "One of the most important facts is that dying nowadays is in many ways more gruesome, more lonely, mechanical, and dehumanized; at times it is even difficult to determine technically when the moment of death has occurred" (6). Most significantly, she portrayed the situation of an "imaginary patient" in the emergency room: "Well, our imaginary patient has now reached the emergency ward. He will be surrounded by busy nurses [. . .], a lab technician perhaps who will take some blood, another technician who takes the electrocardiogram. He may be moved to X-ray and he will overhear opinions of his condition and discussions and questions to members of the family. Slowly but surely he is beginning to be treated like a thing. He is no longer a person [. . .]. If he tries to rebel he will be sedated, and after hours of waiting [. . .], he will be wheeled into the operating room or intensive treatment unit and become an object of great concern and great financial investment. He may cry out for rest, peace, dignity, but he will get infusions, transfusions, a heart machine, or a tracheostomy" (7).

This imagined scene is equally prominent in first-person accounts as it is part of the respective literature dealing with near-death experiences. Kübler-Ross herself described a patient's experience near-death to underscore her perspective. In an article on the "experience of death" (1972, 52), she refers to the one and only case among her 500 interlocutors whom she and her research team considered to have been truly "dead." Suffering from internal bleeding, "Mrs. S." had been hospitalized and was in a critical condition when the resuscitation team arrived. Observing the scene from above (and to remember minute details later), she had only "one desire"—to tell the physicians "to let go." "She also knew that she would not be able to communicate her feelings of peace and acceptance to them." Later, she did not speak of her experience, fearing to be labeled "psychotic." Kübler-Ross adds that the medical team and students alike had termed it "depersonalization," or "delusion" (cf. 53). In her later career, Kübler-Ross took a more explicit interest in near-death experiences and deathbed visions, ever more religiously interested in the paranormal's significance for survival after death (cf. Kellehear 2009, x–xi) that had already formed the backdrop of her earlier studies.

Kübler-Ross's topos of a "flight from facing death" found a strong resonance in a famous study on the Western history of attitudes toward death by French historian Philippe Ariès (1914–1984). Modern society has, Ariès holds, banished death—the well-known hypothesis of a "Denial of Death" (cf. Becker 1973). In the early 20th century, death in the Western world was still largely a public event, and, accordingly, it was in the majority of cases followed by certain reactions of a social group (cf. Ariès 1981 [French orig. 1977], 559). Dying and death was not only public—it was also perceived as the appropriate scene and situation for a collaborative review of the moribund person's life and for farewells (cf. 583). According to Ariès, the general change of death attitudes became in Western countries fully manifest in the 1960s. It was propelled by the "medicalization of death," combining advances in "surgical and medical techniques" only "fully effective in the hospital." The modern hospital possesses even "pharmaceutical laboratories and rare, costly, and delicate equipment," giving it "a local monopoly on death" (584). Institutionally, the change was termed as the growing "hospitalization" of death. Patients with severe illnesses are now usually confined to the hospital, which also offers a sufficient elimination of pain. A tube, Ariès continues, runs from the dying man's mouth "to a pump that drains his mucus and prevents him from choking. Doctors and nurses administer sedatives, whose effects they can control and whose doses they can vary. All this is well known today and explains the pitiful and henceforth classic image of the dying man with tubes all over his body." Although the focus of Ariès' study is on medieval and early modern times, it seems beyond doubt that it is reigned by a grave concern regarding the latest developments of "medicalized and hospitalized death," indicated by the newly established criterion of "cerebral death," by which "Death became an instant." "The old signs, such as cessation of heartbeat or respiration, are no longer sufficient. They have been replaced by the measurement of cerebral activity." Brain death, or "medicalized death," Ariès holds, borrowed "time from this life, not from beyond," lengthening dying (585). Ariès delegates a lot of responsibility for the emergence of the new situation to biomedicine and its newly arisen attitude to prolong "bare" life as far as possible, and to "delay the fatal moment." Prolonging of life sometimes become "an end in itself, and hospital personnel refuse to discontinue the treatments that maintain an artificial life." With the invention of life-supporting technology, the time of death has become a matter of personal decision, which increased the powerful positions of biomedicine and the doctors in charge.[2]

---

[2] "The time of death can be lengthened to suit the doctor. The doctor cannot eliminate death, but he can control its duration, from the few hours it once was, to [. . .] even years" (Ariès 1981, 585).

In conclusion, Ariès draws a picture of dehumanizing practices of "alienated dying" (589) in modern hospitals. However, he could already foresee the first dawning of a countertrend. He notices attempts for the restoration of the dignity of dying—for example, in the hospice movement of Cicely Saunders[3] or in the work of Kübler-Ross.[4] In effect, with the spread of artificial life support in terminal care, a new fear arose in society: the fear to become actually "comatose" or "brain dead."

This fear harbored a second fear, namely, to be diagnosed "brain dead" while being alive. It is well worth considering that this fear perpetuated the earlier cultural anxiety of being buried alive.[5] An important part of both situations is the fear of losing the ability to communicate. The modern clinic, Ariès argues, has become an "asylum" for families, in which they may unload the unbearable burden of terminal illness, in a way sacrificing them while pursuing their own lives in the mood of "business as usual." Providing the institutional setting for this kind of behavior, the modern hospital, Ariès argues, assumes the role of a coperpetrator of lonesome, anonymous dying and death. In this sense, it expresses a general fear of dying a "social death" before dying. In contrast, Kellehear has argued (cf. 1996, 48–50) that near-death experiences uncover a "crisis," similar to the experience of shipwreck or being a castaway. Therefore experiences near death include a loss of control, an absence of help, loneliness—or, in his words, "an experience of social death" (51). Astonishingly, he does not acknowledge the role of fear—a fear to die a social death that had, at least in the 1960s and 1970s, a dominant impact on what people reported after experiences near death. To summarize: These two situations—(being) a person in the emergency room, resuscitated back to life, and (being) an artificially respirated, comatose person, whose disconnection from life-supportive treatment is purely a matter of a doctor's decision—seem to be primary scenes in the imagination of "death" and "dying" in the early 1970s,[6] forming a specific expectation on the side of patients, building on the "fear of the unknown" (Pahnke 1969, 3).

By and large, this development, however, connects to the growing "individualism" in Western societies since the 18th century, diagnosed already in classical sociology. "Death," sociologist Luhmann (1995, 277) observes, "became privatized," and in consequence, the

---

[3] Saunders founded the St. Christopher's Hospice near London in 1967 (cf. Ariès 1981, 585).

[4] Ariès, for that matter, is speculating if there will reemerge a new sensitivity for the manner of dying, comparable to public discussion of abortion, in a not-too-distant future. The image of "another person dying in a tangle of tubes all over his body, breathing artificially, is beginning to break through all taboos to galvanize a sensibility that has long been paralyzed" (593).

[5] Ariès 1981, 396–406; cf. Bondeson 2001, 72–87; Royle 2003, 142–70.

[6] In fact, some images appear earlier. For example, the movie "A Matter of Life and Death" (1946), portrays a whole post-mortem court case that takes place while the protagonist, an Air force squadron leader, undergoes brain surgery. The court visits the patient in the operative setting for interrogation, and he, the protagonist, leaves his body to serve as a witness. The operation is successful. The case being decided for him, he finally returns to the lifeworld.

individual "was also—if only by the conspiratorial silence of his doctor—distracted from his own death. Even if this did not succeed, he was expected not to communicate about it. Attempts to do so were felt to be distressing and found little resonance." I now explore in greater detail the impact of certain medical innovations, the changes that they brought about, and their effects on cultural imagination.

Once upon a time a patient died and went to heaven.
but was not certain where he was. Puzzled, he asked
[. . .]: "Nurse, am I dead?" The answer she gave him was:
"Have you asked your doctor?"
—ANONYMOUS, circa 1964 (Glaser and Strauss 1965, vii)

3.3

Pushing Near-Death Experiences (II)

REANIMATION, "COMA," AND "BRAIN DEATH"

AS SAID IN Chapter 1.3, Moody was aware that the survivalist notion of near-death experiences inevitably rests on the respective definition of death. The central question to be answered is, hence, according to which criteria of "death" the experiencers' states will be described. Moody ([1975] 1976, 147) observes that this question is so "confusing and difficult to answer" because of the unresolved semantic question of "the meaning of the word 'dead.' The still heated controversy surrounding the transplantation of organs reveals that the definition of 'death' is by no means settled." Criteria of death, he says, "vary not only between laymen and physicians, but also among physicians and from hospital to hospital. So, the answer to this question will depend on what is meant by 'dead.' " It is by no means insignificant that Moody mentions the organ-donation controversy in connection with the unsettled dispute on the newly introduced criteria of death *as* brain death.

Moody discusses three definitions of death: first, the traditional definition of death as absence of any observable "vital signs," second, as an absence of brain activity, and third, as irreversible loss of vital functions. According to the first definition, Moody declares, many "near-death experiencers" were "clinically dead"—because of the absence of vital signs. However, he adds, this definition has been recently being replaced by the second, defining death as the "flat EEG." Moody seems to be perfectly aware that a flat EEG over a certain period will result in a state that surely precludes any further reporting on the side of the affected individual (to avoid the term "death" here). In consequence, he argues that in the near-death cases that he collected, there had been, given the urgency to start reanimation, no EEG recorded. But even more principally, so he argues, the EEG criterion may not be overrated, because "'flat' EEG tracings have been obtained in persons who were later resuscitated" (148)—though Moody concedes that there might also be technical failures in measurement. In a final, rhetorical move, Moody defies the value of EEG measurement for the question of near-death experiences, because it cannot be proven whether the latter are made within the period of a flat EEG or shortly before, or after, this period. This, of course, presupposes that a person may survive a (longer) period with no observable EEG traces (cf. 149). We must conclude here that for Moody any definition of death as absence of electrical brain waves will miss something essential. His critical stance toward the introduction of "brain death" becomes more obvious in his discussion of the third definition, death as "irreversible loss" of vitality. According to the latter, none of the persons who were resuscitated could be declared (temporarily) dead, even if a flat EEG had been recorded. Applying this definition, Moody concedes, will rule out all his cases, because "all involved resuscitation" (149).

Finally, Moody expresses that he would agree with the third definition, but it becomes obvious that he does not accept it as "irreversibility," but rather as a metaphorical "point of no return." Not too astonishingly, for the introduction of this point at which a final separation will take place, Moody switches to a new descriptive framework, defining death as "a separation of the mind from the body, and that mind does pass into other realms of existence at this point" (151). Now he argues that any precise definition is "pointless." Death is most probably a "point of no return" that "may well vary with the individual" (151).

If one considers Moody's entire argument, several aspects are noteworthy. In sum, Moody does not offer a precise distinction between the *definition* of death, the *criteria* that allow us to decide if a person is dead, and the *technical media or devices* that enable observations that determine if these criteria are fulfilled. Moody is aware that only a definition of "clinical death" as "heart death" and "respiratory arrest" (*apnea*) allows qualifying the reporting individuals as having been temporarily dead. In consequence, he must oppose the newly introduced definition and the respective criteria of an irreversible brain death. Yet this is not done in a straightforward manner. It is Moody's goal to campaign for the recognition of the reported experiences in the medical sphere too. Therefore, while declaring to be in line with EEG diagnostics, he adduces various arguments that aim to show the impracticability and unreliability of EEG measurements that allow him to switch finally to a nonmedical framework of defining death.

It is very telling indeed that the essential steps of innovative medical practices were closely followed by certain discursive patterns of expectations, fears, and philosophical as well as psychological reorientation. To begin with, an overview of some essential events:

In 1952, the Danish anesthesiologist Bjørn Aage Ibsen invented the positive-pressure mechanical ventilator (with intubation) and established in 1953 the first "Intensive Care Unit" (ICU) (cf. Jonsen 1998, 236). Artificial respirators allowed sustaining "brain-dead" patients for a much longer period, now covering not hours, but months. As early as 1957, leading anesthesiologists approached Pope Pius XII to encourage their definition of death as cessation of brain functions and to consider a patient "dead" if only artificial respiration upholds life. Although the Pope said, as Jonsen summarizes, that the medical definition of death is an open question and "does not lie within the competence of the Church and cannot be deduced from any religious or moral principle" (237), he took a more liberal stance concerning the obligation of doctors to use in hopeless cases extraordinary "resuscitative interventions" (quoted in Belkin 2014, 21). In the early 1960s, it had already been widely acknowledged that myocardial infarction was a major source for morbidity. Accordingly, in the 1960s the total number of ICUs was constantly growing, adding up to around 100 in the United States (cf. Lock 2002, 61). Cardiopulmonary resuscitation (CPR) and, in the late 1960s, defibrillation became standard measures taken in the majority of cases of sudden cardiac arrest. For the United States alone, an estimation of the 1980s reckoned with at least annually 400,000 cases of deaths that were due to sudden cardiac failure; in the 1970s, however, almost all in-hospital patients and a growing number of outpatients with cardiac arrests received prompt treatment—though the survival rate, especially out of hospital, was still low (cf. Hemreck 1988). This led to a widespread use of cardiac monitoring in ICUs, especially for patients after heart attacks. Accordingly, a large number of patients who reported near-death experiences were, because of repeated heart failure, already more or less familiar with certain procedures while being brought to the ICU a second time. Already in the early 1980s most studies were drawing from a "majority of patients" interviewed after they had been "resuscitated from cardiac arrest" (Sabom 1982, 20).

In 1959, two French physicians, Pierre Mollaret and Maurice Goulon, defined for the first time a condition termed "irreversible coma" [coma dépassé], in which they saw the brain damaged to an irreversible degree by the lack of oxygen (cf. Belkin 2014, 149–50). However, the concept of "coma" began its international career some years later, in the mid-1960s. Obviously, the observation of this state has been made possible, or at least facilitated, by the invention of artificial respiration, which, in consequence, made death a decision, namely, the decision to turn off the respirator. It introduced a major ambiguity over the exact point at which death "happens," and, Belkin comments, "that ambiguity needed to be addressed, and growing unease over when death occurred can be read in medical journals especially in the latter part of the 1960s" (20).

In 1966, Fred Plum and Jerome Posner (New York) introduced the term "(total) locked-in syndrome" depicting a condition in which a patient suffers brain-stem damage, while being awake and usually aware of his situation and neither able to move nor to communicate verbally. In a state of an almost complete paralysis of voluntary muscle movement (tetraplegia or quadriplegia), the affected person is mostly able to move only his eyes voluntarily (cf. 184–8). One year later, in 1967, Dr. Christiaan Barnard performed the first human-to-human heart transplant

(Cape Town). Together with other transplants from brain-dead organ donors done in Western countries, it stirred the already heated debate on the definition of death. In 1968, the Ad Hoc Committee of Harvard Medical School (Boston), which included 10 physicians, a theologian, a lawyer, and a historian of science, published a milestone paper that successfully "redefined" death as "irreversible coma," followed by a routinization of organ procurement from brain-dead donors (cf. Lock 2002). In 1972, Bryan Jennett (Glasgow, UK) and Fred Plum introduced the term "vegetative state" for patients "awake but without awareness." In 1975, Moody published his book with cases chiefly collected in the early 1970s, and soon thereafter, in 1977, the Association for the Scientific Study of Near-Death Phenomena was founded. Most tellingly, the title of one of its periodicals, a quarterly newspaper first published in 1981, was *Vital Signs*—obviously alluding to the then still polarized debate on the criteria of (brain) death.

These innovations in medical technology and decision-making had a tremendous influence on bioethics and the public discourse. It caused considerable irritation. In an article of *The Nation*, Desmond Smith declared, "For some time thoughtful men have been increasingly troubled by the present attitude in the medical profession: 'You're dead when your doctor says you are'" (quoted in Lock 1996, 575). Margaret Lock, however, having completed comparative ethnographic fieldwork of biomedical settings in the United States and Japan, observed in the American context an astonishing quietness regarding the adoption of brain death as irreversible coma: "a brain-dead entity clearly lurks on the margins of life and death, culture and nature, and person and machine. Nevertheless in North America [. . .], we have stayed remarkably silent about this particular technology, whereas turmoil has erupted in Japan over the past twenty-five years around this particular domain of technoscience" (579). In comparison to the heated discussion in Japan, the silence in the United States is indeed astounding. Nevertheless, the "silence" as such may also be an artifact of the observer, based on the traditional academic distinction of cultural spheres, researching mostly either biomedicine and (theological[1]) bioethics *or* spiritual and religious imaginaries. Given the prominence in which near-death experiencers reflect on the body and soul in modern medicine, comment on materialism of brain-based definitions of a person, or the doctors dishonorable or faint-hearted behavior of artificially prolonging the "life" of the "brain-dead," we should hold that these developments are indeed an important factor that led to reports of near-death experiences raising a voice against the "silent consent" to brain death.

For the intellectual history of "death," the report of the Harvard committee was, as previously said, a milestone. The committee set the following criteria of "death": (1) unreceptivity and unresponsivity, (2) no movement or breathing, (3) no reflexes;

---

[1] See the affirmative theological discourse on brain death summarized in Veith et al. 1977; yet, among critics of brain death were theologians too.

(4) flat EEG (discussed and contextualized in Belkin 2014, 63–85, 198–200). In the 1970s, the definition of brain death was adopted almost worldwide, and even in Japan a person may nowadays provide for their own criteria of death, whether he or she will be declared dead by the criteria of cardiac death or brain death (Bagheri 2007; cf. Asai et al. 2012). Symptomatic are the two motives for introducing the brain-death criteria that were named by the Harvard Ad Hoc Committee: "(1) Improvements in resuscitative and supportive measures," the report discloses, have sometimes "only partial success so that the result is an individual whose heart continues to beat but whose brain is irreversibly damaged. The burden is great on patients who suffer permanent loss of intellect, on their families, on the hospitals, and on those in need of hospital beds already occupied by these comatose patients. (2) Obsolete criteria for the definition of death can lead to controversy in obtaining organs for transplantation" (Ad Hoc Committee 1968, 337).[2]

The Harvard report,[3] Jonsen (1998, 239) observes, mixed "two distinguishable situations, 'irreversible coma' and the abolition of function at 'brain-stem levels.' Its very title confuses 'irreversible coma' with 'brain death.' It is never clear whether 'stopping life support to allow death' or whether 'stopping respiratory support on a dead body' is the issue." The purpose of the Harvard criteria was to set up the diagnosis of "irreversible coma" as criteria of death. Nevertheless, by defining these criteria, the influential bioethicist Robert M. Veatch argued in response that the report did not provide an argument that irreversible coma was identical to the death of a person (cf. Veatch 1977, 1978). In other words, by its answer, the report suppressed the question of the meaning of death (cf. Belkin 2014, 72–7). In the same vein, philosopher Hans Jonas stated that the purpose of institutionalizing brain death was to propose a definition that allowed for organ donation from human bodies—an intention freely admitted in the report, as we previously saw. As early as 1969, Jonas criticized the pragmatics behind the redefinition of death. In other words, transplantation medicine, not at least an economic venture, urged for a more permissive definition of death, even though any straightforward "harvesting" of organs was, as Belkin (cf. 2014, 220–2) shows, not the intention of the report's authors. However, by judging the continuation of a mere "vegetative existence" to be pointless, Jonas (cf. 1987, 224) argued, the committee's report did not define death in the strictest sense. To summarize, Jonas diagnosed a disquieting moment in the adoption of this new definition of death, namely, to justify the permission "not to turn off the respirator, but, on the contrary, to keep it on and thereby maintain the body in a state of what would have been 'life' by the older definition (but is only a 'simulacrum' of life by the new)—so as to get at his organs and tissues under the ideal conditions" (Jonas 1969, 243–4). It

---

[2] Astonishingly, Belkin (2014, 6) shows how the second element, a suitable definition for securing organ donation, came into the report, but neither quotes nor discusses it thoroughly.

[3] Cf. the detailed study of the report and its authors in Belkin 2014, 165–75.

remains to be added, however, that prominent voices against brain death in this early phase of the debate—such as Jonas, Veatch, or Daniel Callahan, Catholic intellectual and cofounder of the Hastings Center, a world-renowned institute for bioethics—belonged to scholars with a strong background in religious traditions, criticizing what they saw as a move toward neo-utilitarian ethics.[4]

Opposition toward the introduction of the brain-death criteria came also from within the medical establishment. A cardiologist in Denver, Colorado, Fred Schoonmaker, claimed in an article that appeared in *Anabiosis* (cf. Audette 1979) to have a large number of near-death cases in which patients were for quite some time lacking any electrical brain activity—that is, were brain dead—but recovered in the end (cf. Zaleski 1987, 161). Significantly, Schoonmaker was chiefly interested in visionary experiences near death. As it seems, he never published his findings in a medical journal but communicated his results in interviews well received by scholars of near-death experiences, convinced of now having reliable information on the survival of (brain) death (cf. Habermas and Moreland 2004, 160).[5] In the early history of transplantation medicine there were indeed problematic cases in which organs were explanted from only the "virtually dead" (cf. Jonsen 1998, 238).

Although the medical establishment has ever since denied the possibility that, if brain death is diagnosed correctly, a person may regain consciousness or other higher brain faculties, or even more basically, to survive in that state,[6] protagonists in the public discourse hold a dissenting view, which—and this is essential—stirred doubts. In his study *Buried Alive*, Bondeson (2001, 270) argues convincingly that the outbreak of a "renewed fear of apparent death and premature burial" in the 1970s can be linked to the "introduction of a new definition of death." Mistrust and fear emerged in the public that occasionally, even cases of euthanasia cannot be ruled out. Movies such as "Coma"[7] contributed to the broader public concern. Since the ethical dimension of terminating life of the comatose and extracting their organs breathed the oxygen of publicity, near-death scholars discussed brain death and the practice of organ transplantation.[8] In conclusion, we can substantiate the observation by Kellehear (1996, 15) that near-death experiences emerge "in a cultural milieu where anxieties about

---

[4] Veatch graduated from Harvard Divinity School; Jonas and Callahan "sought to extend the relevance of moral theology in an increasingly secularized world" (Belkin 2014, 77).

[5] Commenting on Schoonmaker's findings, Zaleski (1987, 161) holds that because "misdiagnosis, faulty EEC readings, or simple tampering with the data cannot be ruled out, this finding is unlikely to disturb the medical establishment."

[6] Cf. the controversy on Alan Shewman's studies discussed in Belkin 2014, 211–13.

[7] "Coma" (MGM, USA), directed by Michael Crichton, 1978, based on the novel by Robin Cook, 1977.

[8] A latest example is the Dutch cardiologist and near-death-researcher Pim van Lommel (cf. 2010, 301–2, 330, 340–2), discussing critically in his "survivalist" work *Consciousness Beyond Life* the permissive attitudes toward organ transplantation based on brain death.

social change meet within a broad range of social institutions." But we can be more precise here. Ever since the 16th century, experiences near death were reported without interruption. Therefore we should correlate the introduction of the systematic concept of near-death experiences to a cultural milieu that was indeed reined in by fears and suspicion regarding social change, but especially directed to modern biomedical practice and hospitalized death.

3.4

Pushing Near-Death Experiences (III)

LSD- AND OTHER DRUG-INDUCED EXPERIENCES

ALTHOUGH THE SIMILARITIES between the experiences near death and LSD use are "stressed throughout" (Fox 2003, 178; cf. Fischer and Mitchell-Yellin 2016, 161–9), we may go a step further in providing evidence that the consumption of morphine, hashish, and especially hallucinogens in the 1960s and 1970s are to be identified as a major component of the emerging discourse on near-death experiences in the 1970s. This, of course, does not mean that a certain number of near-death experiences in these decades can be causally explained by drug experiences. There were several different ways in which drug experiences contributed to the near-death discourse: First, actors' narratives display structural similarities, or even shared beliefs, of drug use in esoteric contexts and reported experiences near death. In that respect, there is an intersection not only of drug users who reported experiences near death with the same mystical, gnostic, or esoteric content; there is also a shared interface of expectations of what to experience in life-threatening situations. Second, especially the more potent hallucinogenic drugs such as LSD, mescaline, or psilocybin, were held by various users to be responsible for dissociative states that included experiences out of the body, frightening visions of "being dead" and "bad trips," or "flashbacks" and perception disorders that followed from habitual use but were not directly the outcome of recent ingestion. Finally, there are also nonintentional drug experiences in medical contexts, especially anesthetics or narcotics in surgery or dental care that reportedly triggered experiences near death. However, surveying the evidence for the impact of drugs, I refrain from concluding that drug experiences are directly responsible for certain elements of the experiences reported. Even though an individual may report a deep, existential impact while under influence of a psychoactive substance, it is still the report that we "have" in the first place. It is communicated meaning that the affected individual bestows on its experience and its heterogeneous elements. Any kind of monolinear causality—between drug and experience, or likewise between drug and near-death experience—would do harm to the multifaceted factors that influence the reporting of experience. Evidence that therapeutic and intentional drug experiences had an impact in Moody's sample can be unveiled at various places in his initial work of 1975. Arguing against any "drug-based" view of the hallucinatory nature of near-death experiences, Moody ([1975] 1976, 157–8) himself grants that he had collected "a few accounts" from people under anesthetics who had identified their experiences "as hallucinatory-type visions of death." In general, the use of anesthetics will surely have been in several cases of critical health an accompanying factor of the "experience" that cannot be simply "subtracted." Yet, for Moody crucial differences remain. Therapeutic drug experiences, of which he quotes an example that includes several topoi of his systematized experience (185–9), are of a different kind. They are held to be unreal by most experiencers. In consequence, they are declared to be irrelevant to afterlife beliefs. In the case quoted by Moody, the experience had been described as in accordance "with religious training" (159), whereas in near-death experiences, people stressed how their experiences were in stark contrast to "what they had been led to expect in the course of their religious training" (140). In other words, therapeutic drug experiences may reconfirm expectations, whereas "real" experiences usually run counter to intuitive views. Significantly, while downplaying experiences made as side effects of administered narcotics, Moody offers a much more positive interpretation of experiences resulting from the intentional use of psychoactive substances. He introduces this aspect by arguing that the opinion has found resonance in the "great mass of laymen in our society," that psychoactive drugs directly cause hallucinatory, delusional episodes. This opinion, he says, should not be accepted unchallenged. In his reply, Moody displays an understanding of psychoactive drugs that unties the knots between hallucinogens and their hallucinatory mental effects. "Through the ages," he explains, "men have turned to such psychoactive compounds in their quest to achieve other states of consciousness and to reach other planes of reality" (162). In line with Esoteric interpretations, Moody continues with the religious use of peyote (mescaline), "ingested in order to attain religious visions and enlightenment," and concludes that this intentional drug use—assuming the belief of drug-induced means of a "passage into other dimensions" held "valid"—is just one "pathway" of discovering or "entering" an otherworldly realm. The "experience of dying" could be also such a pathway, which would finally help to explain their resemblance (cf. 162). Obviously, Moody shared (and quoted) John C. Lilly's emphatic view of mystical states of consciousness achieved through hallucinatory drugs, and the "close call with death" (175), being one of several ways of entering new realms of consciousness. In sum, Moody was not only well conversant with the beliefs of the 1960s and 1970s "drug culture" but saw, in addition, his systematized near-death experience as a parallel way to enter a higher realm. This attitude, however, goes against the grain of reporting an individual's "therapeutic" drug experiences declared to be largely unreal and hallucinatory. Taking this into consideration, it is less astonishing that Moody's main distinction is defined neither by the setting (therapeutic or experience seeking) nor by the experienced content. Instead, it is defined by whether drug experiences contain revelatory, "breaking news" of the other realm. The only criterion for the latter is, again, how the experiencing individual reports his or her experience and reacts to it. This effect, however, is usually itself part of the autobiographic narrative that the individual reports. I will subsequently return to this element, the narrated changes of life orientation, famously installed by William James as a "test" for the validity of religious experience.

In general, even Moody acknowledged the impact of both the esoteric interpretation of drug experiences and the nonintentional triggering of cognate experiences in therapeutic settings. Moreover, we saw in the historical genealogy that important innovations of near-death discourse were achieved in close interaction of individual reports of drug experiences. As early as 1817, Coleridge described the copresence of collective experience of all memories triggered by opium and ascribed this capacity to the celestial body in after-death states, too. The prevalence of unhindered lucidity, the life review, and so forth, in both drug experiences and experiences near death was taken up and further established by de Quincey (1821), Cahagnet (1850), Ludlow (1857), and Randolph (1860). It seems safe to assume that a lot more of the reported experiences from the early 19th up to the 20th century were directly or indirectly connected to voluntary or nonintentional drug experiences, even though the experiencers either did not want to include their drug use in the report or did not see a direct connection. Further reports of experiences near death as triggered by drug use have been shared by Symonds (in Brown 1895), Sollier (1903, 29, cf. Alvarado 2011, 72), or Hill (1918). Experiences of levitation, of distant observing out of the body, or the life review, including more classical religious topoi, are especially prominent features of these reports. As previously discussed, in the counterculture of the 1960s, however, the use of psychedelics for mystical purposes, prepared by the influential writings of Aldous Huxley, became much more common. In 1966, Allen Ginsburg, Beat poet and protagonist of eclectic Buddhist spirituality, could urge that "every American aged 14 and above should take the mind-expanding drug LSD at least once" (quoted in McLeod 2007, 124).

In the 1970s, many instances of drug-induced experiences near death are reported in Hampe (1979, 81; cf. 33, 80), who concludes that "through drugs, healthy young people of today want to visit prematurely the land of the dead, where they as yet have no business to be," and it was, as shown, a dramatic experience with drugs that led Lilly 1972 to the notion of a near-death experience. In addition to the popularity of psychedelics in the 1960s, the invention of ketamine was crucial, synthesized by American chemist Calvin L. Stevens in 1962 and officially patented and used as medication from 1966 onward. It soon became clear that ketamine was not merely a potent anesthetic, but may also cause side effects such as trance-like states, bodily lightness, and hallucinations (cf. Marsh 2010, 179–83). Only shortly after the introduction of the concept of near-death experiences, studies appeared that argued for ketamine as responsible for the majority, if not all, such experiences. Already in the early 1970s, studies (e.g., Collier 1972; Johnstone 1973) reported ketamine-induced experiences near death. After the introduction of Moody's systematic concept, other studies appeared that, comparing the "phenomenology" of both experiences, argued for a very close correlation or a common core. Evidence was adduced that significant elements of systematized near-death experiences can be triggered by ketamine in experimental settings (cf. Grinspoon and Bakalar, 1979). A close connection of drug and near-death experiences has been established in recent research too.[1] Surely a common psychopathological explanation of near-death experience will find an appealing foothold in these studies, and, far from astonishing, religious scholars and theologians who despise the "supernatural insights" of those experiences, such as Hans Küng (1984)[2] or Michael Marsh (2010) do, are much in favor of such an explanation.

Summarizing various more recent studies on the empirical prevalence of "out-of-body or ecsomatic experiences," Engmann holds that the phenomenon occurs in round about 50% of consumers of certain drugs, which leads him to a skeptical reflection. Given that "the same or even a greater proportion of out-of-body phenomena occur in people consuming drugs than in people who have survived a clinical death," he asks, "Does this not mean that out-of-body experiences would be better regarded as a symptom of drug consumption than as a characteristic of a survived clinical death?" (Engmann 2014, 53). This reflection—justified as it might be in respective research on the neuropharmacological basis of out-of-body experiences—neglects the essential characteristics of near-death discourse. As previously shown, in the Spiritualist–Occult metacultures of the 19th and 20th centuries out-of-body experiences were often intentionally sought after—comparable to drug experiences. Moreover, the reports of what had been experienced under drugs or near death emerged in close interaction. To put it in terms of text transmission, drug reports contaminated near-death reports, and vice versa.

According to a common assertion shared by a significant group within the more empathetic near-death research, a coherent psychopharmacological theory of near-death experiences must fail, because drug-triggered experiences vary considerably whereas near-death experiences are held to be more uniform (cf., in addition to Moody, Zaleski 1987, 165). Shushan (2009, 174), for that matter, argues that despite some similarities of psychedelic drug experiences on the one side and near-death experiences and "afterlife mythologies" on the other, the former "do not have anything like their regularity and consistency; and similarities are largely to do with highly general elements such as feeling

---

[1] In their study of near-death states reported by more recent ketamine misusers, Ornella Corazza and Fabrizio Schifano (2010) could show a strong correlation of ketamine intake and the reported occurrence of near-death states (using the Greyson scale).

[2] Hans Küng (1984, 28) comments, "If the phenomena associated with drugs, narcosis, suggestion, brain operations, etc., cannot be understood as evidence of a 'hereafter', why can the phenomena connected with experiences of resuscitated people be so understood?"

of oneness or spirituality." In addition, it is often argued that even in cases in which the phenomenology of the experienced content is the same, individuals will usually not react to their drug-experience with fundamental changes in life-orientations (cf., for a more recent example of this argument, van Lommel 2010, 115–17). This, however, builds on a rather conventional view of how drug experiences are perceived. Far from taking the hallucination as meaningless, individuals often ascribed especially their first experience with hallucinogens life-transforming and "entheogenic" qualities.

Significantly, the whole discussion of the assumed or disputed similarity or identity of psychedelic drug experiences and those near death focus on experiences, and not on reports of experiences. Moreover, occupied with (disputed) truth claims of both, researchers did not ask for the historical genealogy of the narratives that were offered as the individual's meaning making of drug experiences, which were, to a significant extent, shared by reported experiences near death.

In sum, side effects of the medical use of ketamine and other anesthetics and the intentional use of psychedelics contributed as general push factors to the considerable increase of reported experiences near death. Much earlier than in the 1960s and 1970s, but doubtless peaking there, receptive individuals were prepared to experience the extraordinary by any means, *and* willing to combine these experiences with existential interpretations in line with their religious background assumptions.

3.5

The Imperative of "Individual Experience"

INSTITUTIONAL CHANGE OF RELIGION

IN THE 1960S AND 1970S

AN IMPORTANT BACKGROUND—though not a push factor as were the three factors discussed so far—for near-death experiences in becoming broadly reported, is the institutional change, and the general transformations, in religious belief and practice that became an important trend in the 1960s and 1970s. As Kellehear (1996, 92) notes, near-death experiences had, in this climate of religious change, "a great appeal for those in alternative and quasi-religious circles because it seemed to deemphasize the importance of traditional indicators of spirituality: church attendance, doctrinal knowledge, rituals, public asceticism." In this chapter, I outline some of these developments in these two decisive decades, though it is important not to fall into the easy trap of narratives of the "great decline," or too-general secularization theories. In fact, it is exactly the uninterrupted stream of reports of experiences near-death, ranging over at least 200 years that should warn us against any theory of a general religious decline. Surely, the discussion of the "grand theories" in the background of an assumed long-term secularization, such as modernization, functional differentiation, or rationalization, cannot be taken up here. These processes are often held responsible for the decline of institutionalized religion. For my purpose, it suffices to name some of the general dynamics that are of importance for understanding an obviously strongly felt need of individuals not only to share their near-death experiences, but to assign far-reaching religious significance to them.

The general observation seems to be unquestioned that, in the 1950s, Western countries saw themselves usually as "Christian" nations, in which the Christian churches as de facto increasingly powerful institutions had a significant role in community life. Almost all individuals were at least formally members of religious denominations. However, already in the late 1950s, a polarization of positions on how to practice "true religion" within present society can be witnessed—probably best to be described as a formation of "conservative," "liberal modernist," and "radical reformist" movements within (and also outside of) the major traditions. In the United States, these debates were especially intense—nourished by the political activism of the Civil Rights Movement, Liberation Theology, and the counterculture (Roszak), but also by Christian "Fundamentalism," Pentecostalism, and the Charismatic Movement. I subsequently argue that it was especially in radical reformist, to a lesser extent in modernist, and only occasionally in conservative circles, that near-death experiences were of special importance. These movements gained traction in the 1960s and 1970s, though not only to a very different extent, but also with considerable differences regarding age cohorts, the urban–rural divide, and the respective Western country.

In his analysis in *The Religious Crisis of the 1960s*, Hugh McLeod (see 2007, 124–39) identifies four major strands that highlight the changes in religious practice and attitudes—namely, (1) the rise in "alternative spiritualities"; (2) the change of self-perceptions of Western societies—from "Christian countries" to secular, pluralist, and post-Christian societies (cf. 216–26; cf., however, Field 2017, 152–3); (3) a weakening of socialization into membership of religious institutions (cf. 46–51), initiating a dramatic generational divide of church attendance (cf. 201); and (4) a rise of ecumenical thought (cf. 246–7). The shift that led people to describe their nation and society as post-Christian, religiously pluralist, and increasingly secular had a significant effect on the increasing necessity to affirm religious experience in an "authentic way" (cf. Taylor 2007, 473–504), disengaging classical forms and media of religious discourse—such as catechisms, dogmatic treatise, conventional sermons, praying the full rosary, or the like. Instead, in the 1960s and 1970s, the laity increasingly emancipates itself from expert knowledge—that is, the knowledge that religious experts such as priests and pastors offer to make lay experiences "meaningful." The crisis of the churches and traditional belief was, in addition, catalyzed by radical avant-garde Christian theology declaring the "death of God," Rudolf Bultmann's program of demythologizing traditional supernaturalism, or the more outright atheism of Marxist, Nietzschean, or Freudian origin—the latter criticizing the sexual morals, dogmatism, and authoritarian structures of the churches. In his widely read book on *Counter Culture*, Theodore Roszak (1969, 212) spoke of a "sweeping secularization of Western society," ushered in by the deification of "objective science" and merciless scientific progress, but in essence brought forth by "Christianity's reliance" on "a precarious, dogmatic literalism." And he reasons, "Such a religious tradition need only prick its finger in order to bleed to death" (212), anticipating, at the same time, a change from the "In-Here," a "warm and lively sense of the sacred" (273).

In that respect, the rise of ecumenical activity of institutionalized Christians and the increase of multiple religious identities (or "eclecticism," as it has been called from the mainstream point of view), can be seen as a response to the call of radical reform. The Second Vatican Council (1962–1965), intended as a renewal of the Catholic Church (cf. 82-4), may serve as the most prominent example here. Interestingly, according to quantitative data of church attendance and communal activity, the decline of institutional religion seems to have stopped in the United States around the mid-1970s, when measurable religiosity consolidated. However, these developments had one central effect in Western countries that McLeod (2007, 265) condensed in the final sentence of his study: "As Christianity lost a large part of its privileged position, the options in matters of belief, life-path, or 'spirituality' were open to a degree that they had not been for centuries."

As previously seen, the radical reformist movements—under which we may subsume Gnostic–Esoteric and Spiritualist–Occult currents—were the most fertile ground in which the discourse of near-death experiences could flourish. Yet, liberal modernist movements could also accommodate and integrate the respective discourse. Lay followers within this movement especially could articulate a position that takes individual experience seriously. The respective reports of the experience do not subscribe to any exclusivist claim of ontological truth or abound with private revelations and paranormal topoi such as telepathy or to fanciful travels of the astral body. But still, liberal theological experts continue to express difficulties in a systematic appraisal of near-death experiences (e.g., Marsh 2010). This is far from astonishing, given the fact that they were up to the 1970s transmitted in occult and esoteric discourses or by Christians with often strong inclinations in the respective discourse.

Probably the greatest difficulties with individual accounts of experiences near death are expressed in the conservative milieu. Although there are, to my knowledge, no book-length treatises of the topic, there are many short evaluations of mostly single accounts of near-death experiences. The strictest representatives of this milieu, however, subscribe to a view that experiences have found their once-and-for-all expression in revealed texts and neither need, nor can be amended by, individual experience. Others, such as Maurice Rawlings (1978, 88), even went so far to argue that these experiences might be demonic deceptions, quoting, for example, "for Satan himself masquerades as an angel of light" (2 Cor. 11:14). Moreover, exclusivist and ahistorical positions will usually despise the "pluralizing force" of modernity, which is obvious to them in "eclectic–syncretistic" examples of near-death experiences. In sum, being still in possession of religious certainty, they are not tempted by the precarious situation of modernity, in which, as Peter L. Berger has argued, religious faith becomes a matter of choice. Describing the situation in theological language, Berger (1979, 25) holds, "*heresy typically becomes a necessity.*" Instead of a "heretical imperative," I would, especially for the 20th century, prefer to speak of an "imperative of experience" that finds expression in near-death discourse. However, near-death experiences have been more sympathetically met with in those conservative traditions and communities that in one way or another see certain accounts in line with their basic teachings. Most prominently, Mormons (the Church of Jesus Christ of the Latter-Day Saints; cf. Lundahl et al. 1983; Top 1997), but also spokespersons of Eastern Orthodox traditions may serve as examples.[1]

Having said this, I may summarize that, in the 1960s and 1970s, the imperative of resorting to the privileged, first-person experience reached a new peak. This imperative is also reflected in Lutheran theologian Gerhard Ebeling's discussion of what he observed in the 1970s as the "complaint of the experience-deficit in theology" (cf. Ebeling 1975 [1974], 15–16). Next to the decline of organized Christianity, the obvious trend of disallowing official religious specialists of the major traditions to *authoritatively* interpret each and every lay experience—"private revelations," in certain Christian theology—prepared the ground for individuals to report their near-death experiences, idiosyncratic in religious terms as it may be. Yet the general democratization of esoteric traditions (cf. Hammer 2004, 402)[2] and the growing prevalence of psychiatric, psychopathological, and psychoanalytical explanations of religious experience made it necessary to frame the latter not simply as self-evident revelations. In terms of plausibility, they gain enormously if emerging from biographically verified, existential situations. Surely narratives of having been close to death served this purpose perfectly. In that respect, near-death experiences could smoothly connect to earlier "imperatives of individual experience" advanced by experiencers of mesmerist states of somnambulism, clairvoyance, astral projection, Indian yogic and Buddhist meditation, and, finally, psychedelic drug experiences.

---

[1] For example, the report of Uxkull 1934; cf., however, Rose 1980; Fox 2003, 93–4.

[2] Cf. the growing impact of paranormal and reincarnation beliefs attested in Gallup polls of the 1960s (cf. Field 2017, 141–7, 214).

PART FOUR

Wish-Fulfilling Expectations, Experiences, Retroactive Imputations

IN SEARCH OF HERMENEUTICS
FOR NEAR-DEATH EXPERIENCES

4.1

Introduction

⌒ _____

PART II REVEALED an almost uninterrupted chain of textual transmission, being most likely only the tip of the iceberg of an oral transmission of narratives of respective memoirs of experiences near death. If we look at the experiences as a process that culminates in the report, we can identify a fourfold scheme:

(A)   the individual social and conscious life before event "x,"
(B)   the event "x" identified by the affected individual as a situation near death— and its conscious content,
(C)   the phase that follows the event, culminating in, and terminated by,
(D)   the reporting (of a memoir).

For the near-death reports to "work," it is necessary to identify the conscious content of (D) with an experience made in (B) while, at the same time, reassuring the recipient that no significant influence of thoughts, experiences, expectations, or third-hand knowledge apprehended in the preecstatic or postecstatic phases (A) and (C) had been exercised both on the experience (B) and the report (D). Overviewing these four phases of the near-death narrative, it becomes obvious that they have—in terms of structure or their script—conspicuous elements in common with a certain type of autobiographical conversion narratives. Both the experiencer and the convert aim to solve—by means of communication—a problem of reference, namely, to declare retrospectively that a personal and authentic experience in (B) has been the single cause of the radical change in life orientation in (C) that followed the event. As has been shown in regard to conversion narratives, they often possess a threefold scheme: first, the preconversion life culminating, usually, in a biographical crisis; second, the conversion; and third, the postconversion phase in which existential problems have been resolved, adducing therefore indirect proof of the success that came along with the conversion. The conversion narrative, Bernd Ulmer holds (see 1988, 31–2), conveys an intersubjective description of the biographical crisis that could not be solved by other means. As an effect, it articulates an experience in the center of the conversion that establishes the inner world of the convert as an essential domain of the personality. The conversion itself appears as a discovery of an inner world, a catalyst that can be conceptualized only if the preconversion phase will be described as a life lived with erroneous goals, in absence of conscious awareness, and so forth. In consequence, converts describe, for the sake of a convincing structure of the whole, the preconversion phase as often utterly devoid of religious orientations or experiences. As we previously saw, numerous experiences near death share aspects of mystical experiences that form also the heart of sudden conversion, according to William James. As is well known, James (see [1902] 1922, 243–9, 380–1) characterized mystical experiences as brief (transient), overwhelming, and ineffable, and argued, in addition, for a characteristic "noetic" quality. In those experiences that include cases of conversion, the individual is often convinced that the experience imparted cognitive insights— illuminations, revelations, or other insights into reality. In the reconstruction of the discursive history of experiences near death, we could also identify the element of the "ineffability"—for James so central to mystical states of radical spiritual transformation and therefore also peculiar to experiences of sudden conversion.

Reviewing the four-phase process, we must, however, become aware of the fact that in all phases certain cognitive errors may emerge: misapprehensions, misattributions, invented memories, and so forth. In 1909, Guy M. Whipple had already raised awareness for the often autonomous nature of reports of "experience" in general: "We fail to keep in mind that the observer not only observes, but also reports, and that it is not only possible, but practically certain, that the report is only a partial, often misleading statement of the real experience" (Whipple 1909, 153). For matters of convenience, it should suffice to enumerate the "seven sins of memory" as described by psychologist Daniel L. Schacter. These include "transience," that is, the decrease in accessibility of memory over time [which is most relevant if there is a long time period between (B) and (C/D)], "absent-mindedness," that is, the various forms of lapses of attention, operating both when a memory is encoded and when accessed (in the retrieval stage); "blocking," that is, if stored information is temporarily inaccessible; "suggestibility," that is, the incorporation of misinformation into memory; "bias," that is, retrospective distortions that are produced by current knowledge or beliefs (a "sin," as will be shown, of utmost importance in our case of near-death reports); "persistence," that is, unrelenting, intrusive memories that people would like to forget, but are unable to; and "misattribution," the attribution of memories to incorrect sources or the belief in an event that did not happen or did not happen that way (cf. Schacter 2001). Applying these categories to the preceding schema, there are numerous gateways of memory failures and cognitive misattributions. First, there is the prefiguration and influence of expectations, religious orientations, and conscious experiences made in phase (A). What had an individual already been found or formed as an answer to the questions, "What will it be like for me to be dead?" and, "What will it be like to my surviving peers?" Whatever these answers may be, they cannot be declared as an outcome of a particular situation, but as quintessence of a life lived so far. Yet, for existential answers to become prominent, it seems to be an intensely felt psychological necessity to identify an "existential" situation in which they emerged. To focus on the near-death situation of phase (B) serves not only as a strategy of legitimizing corresponding experiences, but also as a means of coping with a situation in which the individual has been actually "close to death." Hence the surviving individual is also in need of an explanation for *what* had happened, and especially, *why* one has survived. The event, we may argue with Kellehear (1996), is, in most cases, a crisis. As a *survived* crisis it may induce the individual to conclude that a kind of "vocation" or "preordination" was at play in its return to life. As in comparable cases of careers and callings (e.g., a near-death experience resulting in a vocation to follow a career of a spiritual healer), it may additionally lead the individual to report of the event as a turning point. In respect to the reporting and report (D), the narrative memoir consisted mostly of a distinct episodic story that, in respect to the form it usually assumes, may be called with Asprem and Taves (2017, 51) an "event narrative." A typical feature of memoirs is the strong reflexive focus on the author as the experiencing individual. In many cases, these memoirs are still close to an oral form, but we could also witness examples that assumed a highly stylized form (for instance, the report of Wiltse or C. G. Jung in previous chapters). A stylized form originates in the process of telling and retelling, but, most important, in the process of (creative) writing. Reports of experiences near death, however, do not simply report a life-world situation in regard to which they entertain a mimetic and stable relation. From the experiencer's point of view, the memoir was often declared to be nothing but the honest report of an experience, pursuing therewith no hidden intentions. In addition, several reports included—as scripts—interpretations by the individuals to the effect that the experience changed their lives, reensured their belief that death is only a transition, and so forth. Thonnard et al. (2013, [4]) observed that near-death experience memories have more characteristics than memories of real or imagined events, which they take as an outcome of their "emotionality and consequentiality," but also the predominance of "self-referential information" in near-death experiences (which they take, finally, as "flashbulb memories of hallucinations," [4]).

We may take these observations—including the experiencer's self-referential comments on the experience and their aftermath—as highlighting the religious functions of the reported memoirs. Their function "is not to inform but to evoke," as we may say with Jacques Lacan (2004, 84). Communicating the experience searches for empathetic responses in significant others, which has, in general, been acknowledged as a specific strategy of storytelling more generally (cf. Keen 2007). Many near-death reports did not only describe autobiographical episodes of the past, but justified changes in religious life orientation. Ideally, the reports will transform the worldviews of the recipients, too—so the experiencers declare. Although this evocative intention varies in scope and content according to the respective religious metacultures, the reported experience is usually meant to encourage the recipients to see their lives as meaningful, to conceptualize dying as a peaceful transition, and to trust in the efficacy of moral self-cultivation.

In addition, it seems crucial to acknowledge that the experiencers position themselves with their reported experiences in a field of expectations. Therefore we should perceive their reports as documents within a social field in which several factors lead to intentional or unintentional alterations of the communicated content. Persons may forget essential content, may skip or conceal elements, invent or misattribute others, as an attempt to render a singular experience meaningful to themselves and others. Reports, as is well known, often adapt to social expectations. Event (B) will, if fully incomprehensible to the experiencing individual, necessarily be integrated into some kind of interpretative work—a work that will also integrate changes of lifestyle and attitudes developed in (C). In other words, all that changes for the individual in (C) will be evaluated in (D), too.

As Marsh observed in respect to most studies in near-death research, "qualitative descriptions of the experienced phenomenology abound," which are, quite often, the result of suggestive interviewing. The oral narratives, obtained from those individuals willing to speak about their experiences, are often "stylized, rehearsed accounts of retrospectively experienced phenomena, and then subsequently interpreted and incorporated by each of the authors into their respective texts. The opportunity to ask subjects individually not simply what they remembered, but what meaning they thought the NDE had offered them, appears to have been passed over without due concern by all authors" (Marsh 2010, 242). However, even Marsh is guided by the idea that individuals may have a direct grasp on visionary experience, ideally delivering "true eyewitness reportage of the experiences undergone" (53). I subsequently discuss the shortcomings of such a perspective.

In the 1970s, it quickly became common to sense how others view situations of near death, so that experiencers got accustomed to play up to these expectations.[1] There are two sides to it: To match social expectations, that is, to long for the recognition of others by way of narrating near-death experiences; and second, to be prepared and ready for actually "experiencing" these according to preconceptualized prototypes. The latter should not be a too-demanding task, given their uninterrupted omnipresence in the respective religious metacultures. Quite often, report (D) is communicated or published many years, if not decades, after the event (B) portrayed as the original setting of the experience took

---

[1] That people usually sense how others view them and exhibit behaviors according to the stereotypes that are projected onto them has been aptly demonstrated in social psychology, e.g., in the famous experiment by Mark Snyder and colleagues (Snyder et al. 1977). They could show in a complex study how women conformed in conversation to the stereotype men projected on them.

place. This was the case in Montaigne, Beaufort, Heim, Jung, or Ritchie, to name but a few. In these cases, specific processes will influence the form and content of the report. First and foremost, memory fades. Equally powerful, the experiencer's repetitive oral presentation in (C) will reorganize the account. For example, in terms of logical succession of reported "inner experiences" additive structures of narration—simple enumerations—are replaced by subordinate structures with logical dependencies (cf. Ong 2002 [1982], 37–51). I regard this process as extraordinarily relevant because the account reports inner experiences that have no other foothold than subjective memory. This creates serious problems for the narrator, as becomes obvious in Ludwig Wittgenstein's famous private language argument. And finally, reports will, especially if years or decades have passed since event (B) happened, in phase (C) be enriched by third-person comments, and, what is more, be harmonized with near-death reports of others. This may even happen in the very final drafting of the report for example, by journalists, editors, or scholars that include these orally communicated reports in their studies. The latter processes especially have often been ignored by scholars of near-death experiences. Long and Long (cf. 2003, 24) tried to find out if there are differences in "experiences" before and after 1975 (that is, the publication of Moody's book), but, astonishingly, based their study not on *the time of reporting*—all descriptions were past-Moodian, submitted between 1999 and 2002 by means of a Near-Death Network—but on the year the "experience" is said to have occurred! The gratefully received result that there are "virtually no differences" (29) between near-death experiences that occurred before and after 1975 is far from astonishing. As such, it follows directly from an approach designed to reconfirm the researcher's bias of the ubiquitous nature of the experiences.

Taken as narratives, they are, in addition, influential prototypes for new reports, if not—raising expectations of what to experience—for the experiences themselves. This is even more the case in those elements of the experience that were also part of intentional training practices such as astral projection as a blueprint for nonintentional experiences out of the body. Having gathered sufficient evidence for that, one could reasonably stop here. However, I think it is worth considering if we might develop an interpretation that may account for at least some of the narratives' content of what is experienced near death. In the general introduction (chapter I.1), I suggested that at least a number of near-death narratives can be conceptualized as being dependent on a sudden trigger within consciousness that brings forth the possibility of its own nonexistence, that is, death—a trigger I propose to call "death-x-pulse." It consists of a sudden, impelling thought that prompts a highly vivid conscious activity searching for thoughts, images, and even whole narratives that will be useful to contextualize and explain this most existential, unknown, and highly critical situation. In Part IV, I now explore more in depth if there is a hermeneutics available that could help to determine if and how certain reported topoi and the narrative structure of experiences near death may actually be viewed as emerging *in* the concrete situation near death. In principle, the two other possibilities are, as mentioned, that certain elements, and even reports as a whole, are either precomposed or retroactive imputations. However, these three possibilities are not mutually exclusive. We should be open to account for a variety of combinations of preexperiential expectations, experiential content emerging in the situation near death, and the subsequent reworking.

As previously stated, I will resist assessing the ontological claims made by "near-death experiencers." There are no criteria at hand that allow us to decide whether "heaven is real," whether there is a *light* or a *Light*, or whether the experiences themselves reveal a soul immortal or consciousness surviving death. In this part, the objective is a more modest one: Is there any hermeneutics at hand that helps us to describe how some of the prominent experiences near death are based in the structure of human consciousness? Namely, is their meaning in the experience as narrated, given there is meaning for the individual's consciousness to survive in the critical situation? For this purpose, some hermeneutics observable in common life-world situations (which are, in existential and epistemological terms, less precarious) would be of help. It should allow gathering evidence regarding the question if there are topoi of the reported experiences that can be seen as directly emerging from the situation near death. Ideally, it would enable us to rule out other explanations, namely, reported experiences as an outcome of expectations (especially wish-fulfilling ones, if we follow Freud), or as an outcome of postexperiential revision processes. Regarding such an ideal hermeneutic potential, I must, however, dampen exaggerated expectations. The reported experiences in question are simply too heterogeneous. Yet the hermeneutics will be of help in strengthening evidence for the observation that certain distinct experiences may, if of a certain quality, trigger whole narratives *while still unfolding*. The hermeneutics should finally be evaluated in its potential for explaining the religious functions of the experiences near death, which will be the aim of Part V.

4.1.1 ASSEMBLING AN EXPERIENCE: THE "REVISIONIST" INTERPRETATION OF NEAR-DEATH EXPERIENCES

Before I present the hermeneutical model, I may shortly discuss the "imputationalist" explanation, namely, that the visions, excursions of the soul, and so forth, are falsely attributed by the individual to the core "experience" itself, while being experienced in the crucial moments *returning* from unconscious or comatose states. An even stronger claim will consist in the argument that the moment in which the experience is formed will occur even later. Although it has been occasionally mentioned, for example, pertaining to out-of-body experiences, that subjects "probably stabilise their memories of them soon after the event by repeated narration or mental examination" (Green 1968, 14), it was especially the psychologist Robert A. Kastenbaum who argued for this view. Underscoring his position that experiences near death tell us nothing about death, he invokes a lively picture of the existential turmoil in which an individual may find himself or herself after the experience. After "the worst of the stress and disorganization" in acute crisis is over,

Kastenbaum (1984, 30) argues, "intense feelings and images have been generated, but these do not add up to an integrated memory." Therefore the latter will not be accomplished in the actual moment of crisis—instead, "memory starts to develop *on the way back*" (30). The central nervous system will now process residual feelings, the raw tensions produced, and so forth, and will transform them into "a kind of 'story' in which all the parts more or less fit. At a more remote point in time, the survivor will then be equipped with what he considers to be a mental record of the specific experiences he went through at a specific time." Having fleshed out a sufficient version of what has been experienced, the survivor will come to an integral narrative that does not only include "what was experienced during the crisis itself. The memory conforms, then, to the general principles of mental organization [. . .]. But it does not necessarily correspond to what the person experienced during the peak of the crisis" (30).[2]

The theory by Kastenbaum that near-death experiences might be formed "on the way back," in a mind regaining its ability to memorize and to reflect, has recently been seconded by Michael N. Marsh (2010).[3] Depicting out-of-body and near-death experiences as "extra-corporeal experiences" (ECE), Marsh (2010, xvi) argues that these "are likely to be generated by metabolically disturbed brains especially during the period when they are regaining functional competence." In an elaborate model, Marsh distinguishes an "early phase ECE," in which the mind is increasingly functionally impaired, encompassing the absence of pain, sensation of floating, or seeing a light, whereas in the late phase, the "re-acquisition of full conscious-awareness," pain is perceived, real voices are heard, or moral imperatives—for example, to return, are becoming dominant again (cf. 88). Although the model certainly has its advantages, there are at least two problematic assumptions at play here. First, not all reported experiences are extracorporal, e.g., the life review. Second, if disturbed brains are held to be responsible, the question of meaning can no longer be addressed. It will always be only a "phenomenology" of experienced contents, Marsh holds with common psychiatrical language, that can be assessed. In consequence, he describes these experiences as illogical, bizarre, and banal, comparable to "dream-state modes" (xix; cf. 79–80). This evaluation allows him to posit rational theological reflection based on revelation against the experiencer's claim to original insights into an otherworldly domain. Marsh mentions that there is a risk, if not an inevitability, that "every account will become stylized, stereotyped, and edited in its subsequent tellings and re-tellings" (30; cf. 49), and he points, moreover, to the familiarity of the experiencer's reports with usual forms of "ecclesiastical iconography," "totally dependent" on common illustrations of Jesus present in so many experiences (83; cf. 235). But, being faithful that these are accounts of experiences—because otherwise it would make no sense to discuss

---

[2] Obviously, this interpretation conforms to certain elements of Freud's interpretation of wake-up dreams—especially the wish to sort out displeasing or disintegrating content.

[3] Marsh, however, was obviously unaware of Kastenbaum's research. Fischer and Mitchell-Yellin (cf. 2016, 17, 20) argue for a postexperiential corroboration, too, though in the form of an "experience."

various pathological brain-based mechanisms—he turns a deaf ear to his own warning.[4] Interestingly, and somewhat inconsistently, he still asks why "model apprehensions of the hereafter" are so often reported. And he reasons that these "will already have been synthesized from subjects' imaginations, past experiences, impressions based on vicarious religious and other secular influences, [. . .] attendances at funeral services, and their overarching constructions about the future afterlife," that will be "subconsciously unfolded, being directly recalled from memories already implanted in the brain" (93). But still, he refrains from calling these experiences "religious" (126), speaking instead of "neurophysiological constructs of sick brains" (206).[5] All this finally allows Marsh to deemphasize the "experiences," and to disavow from "several features of NDE testimony which militate against an authentic eschatology." In contrast to the Christian theological account, Marsh argues, the narratives "reveal subjects in a passive role; there is a noticeable absence of expressed repentance or penance; and there is no implied resurrectional transformation whatsoever" (211). Reporting individuals, in other words, fail to acknowledge that end-time judgment will be collective, not individual, and a willed choice (cf. 213–7, 266). Nevertheless, postexperiential subjects develop, attested by their peers, a new concern for others, the ability to listen, empathy, and so forth. This noble growth of personality, Marsh argues, can "be seen as important manifestation's of God's grace permeating through various means, including the experiences of the NDE subject" (254). Moreover, such postexperiential changes attest to, at least, the human "will towards transcendence" (263). Marsh, in conclusion, sees the primal value of these experiences not in themselves, but in the aftereffects they may initiate, maintaining that the tangible outcome "is the measurable qualitative alteration in subjects' behavioural profiles towards themselves and, importantly, to others" to which, and not to the experience itself, he attributes the quality of being occasions of "divine grace and hence of revelation" (265).[6] As such, Marsh attempts to defend central elaborated Christian doctrines of revelation, eschatology, and trinitarian theology against effervescent claims of "new age spirituality" on the one hand, and a common believer's naïve soul and afterlife conceptions on the other hand.

To summarize the "revisionist" interpretation, it seems worth noting that it cannot be ruled out that essential elements of the reported experiences are made in the final phase of the whole event. Especially in the case of comatose and other unconscious states, they may only later be "backdated" by the individual to exactly the most critical phase

---

[4] Occasionally, Marsh (cf. 2010, 253) grants that relevant neurophysiological mechanisms that correspond to abrupt postexperiential alterations in life attitudes are still poorly understood.

[5] Yet, Marsh (cf. 2010, 255) counts on God's manifestation even through "aberrant" brains, as in the case of Hildegard von Bingen.

[6] Marsh's position bears certain similarities with a central Mahāyāna-Buddhist idea, namely, the application of a "skillful means." It allows the superhuman Bodhisattva to guide the individual on the right track to liberation, even though the "expedient means" is ultimately an illusion.

while being unconscious or even comatose. The same holds true for Kastenbaum's theory that extends the phase of "reworking" beyond the immediate recovery phase. Certainly, reworkings will take place, in one case or the other, but we are in principle unable to figure out to what extent this happens. Kastenbaum's theory is all the more relevant if we acknowledge with Freud that at the moment individuals verbalize and conceptualize their personal inner experiences (be it for themselves or for others), a "self-censoring" will almost certainly happen. It will interfere with some elements and alter others. Besides the difficulty to ascertain the real extent of it, some kind of "censorship" will highly likely take place. In fact, it seems a usual procedure in communication—communication with others or, in internal verbalization, even with oneself. In sum, it is not only consciousness near death, but also the post-near-death consciousness that is prone to order the chaotic multifariousness of "life images" or "life events"—at least in those cases in which this has been not achieved in the first phase. However, those reworkings can be combined with the assumption of a "death-x-pulse," at work in certain experiences "near of death" and "in fear of death," to which I shall now turn.

4.2

Excursus

THE "DEATH-X-PULSE," OR: HOW TO IMAGINE THE
UNIMAGINABLE?

IN THE FOLLOWING excursus, I deviate to some extent from the perspective assumed so far. As said, in its most radical version, "revisionist" and, even more so, neurobiological theories deny—though in different methodological frameworks—that the reports refer to any veridical experience at all. In contrast to such trajectories, I may pick from the various different phenomena subsumed under the heading of near-death experiences the life-review feature in order to ask if this phenomenon reveals a more general insight into human consciousness in search of meaning. To ask this question implies, of course, shifting attention from the history of near-death discourse to a theory of consciousness itself. Being aware of this difference in perspective, I may flag this chapter explicitly as an excursus. However, I hope that the benefit of this more philosophical discussion will become visible in the concluding part that will ask why near-death experiences became a major source of religious meaning.

4.2.1 THE "DEATH-X-PULSE," THE ATTEMPT OF CONSCIOUSNESS
TO IMAGINE ITS NONEXISTENCE

Various philosophers argued aptly that the question "what is it like to be dead?" is in principle unanswerable. "No one can experience his own *death*," says Immanuel Kant in his *Anthropology* (1797), "for life is a condition of experience." And he continues: "So the fear of death that is natural to all men, even the most wretched and the wisest, is not a horror of *dying* but, as Montainge rightly says, horror at the thought of *having died* (being dead); and the candidate for death supposes he will still have it after his death, because he thinks of his corpse, which is no longer himself, as himself lying in a dark cave or somewhere else" (Kant [1797] 1974, 44 [VII, 167]). Indeed, the astonishing continuity in which reports of experiences near death emphasized that "dying" had been a pleasurable, peaceful experience may substantiate that Montaigne's and Kant's views have been largely shared. Conspicuously, Montaigne's insight was most probably a direct outcome of his experience near death. In the discourse previously described, the horror of being declared dead while still being alive, or the imagination of being declared irreversibly comatose and one's body becoming the source of multiple organ retrieval, may be the dramatic climax of this fear. Forerunners to this specifically modern horror can be seen in the fear of apparent death and being buried alive, or, in the early years of anatomy and forensic medicine, being dissected while still alive.[1] To continue with Kant's principal argument, the horror of "being dead" is rooted in the illusion of consciousness to be still present in the corpse. According to Kant, we "cannot get rid of this illusion because it belongs to the nature of thinking, insofar as thinking is talking to and about oneself. The thought *I am not* simply cannot *exist*: for if I am not, then I cannot be conscious that I am not [. . .]. [W]hen we are *speaking* in the first person, it is a contradiction to *negate* the subject itself, so that the subject annihilates itself" (44). Must we conclude, then, that any conscious experience of being dead is impossible? Will the question, "how is it like to be dead?," be in principle a malformed sentence in Wittgenstein's sense: A sentence that includes signs without attributed meaning? To draw on the famous analogy by Thomas Nagel here—interestingly, published in the crucial mid-1970s—it is already impossible to answer the question "what it is like to be a bat?" Even though one might be able to imagine how it feels hanging upside down in a cave, being able to fly, or navigating with sonar signals, "it tells me only what it would be like for *me* to behave as a bat behaves," but not, "what it is like for a *bat* to be a bat. Yet if I try to imagine this, I am restricted to the resources of my own mind, and those resources are inadequate to the task" (Nagel 1974, 439). In fact, unable to cope with imagining being a bat, human consciousness seems even more unable to imagine itself as "dead." Nagel discusses in *The View From Nowhere* (1986, 42) whether one can imagine oneself surviving the death or destruction of one's brain, or if it is not imaginable at all. It is the crucial structure of individual consciousness to continue and to accept no boundaries. At least, in imagination. "The desire to go on living, which is one of our strongest, is essentially first-personal" (223). Death, defined as an irreversible loss of consciousness, poses therefore the most perplexing task to consciousness. Nagel muses that "the appropriate form of a subjective attitude toward my own future is expectation, but in this case, there is nothing to expect. How can I expect nothing *as such?*" (225). I follow Nagel's assumption that in response to the absence of an adequate "form of thought" about one's own death, consciousness adopts either "an external view,

---

[1] See the example of apparent death in Splittgerber 1866, 313.

in which the world is pictured as continuing after your life stops, or an internal view that sees only this side of death—that includes only the finitude of your expected future consciousness" (225). Nevertheless, Nagel holds that "there is also something that can be called the expectation of nothingness, and though the mind tends to veer away from it, it is an unmistakable experience, always startling, often frightening" (225). Yet, there is still a significant difference between the expectation of how it might be to be completely unconscious and to be dead, "when I as a subject of possibilities as well as of actualities cease to exist" (226). In sum, "the subjective view does not allow for its own annihilation, for it does not conceive of its existence as the realization of a possibility" (227), and the encounter with its own mortality must therefore come as a "rude shock" for the individual's deep-seated self-apprehension as an autonomous "universe of possibilities." Although it is certainly highly likely that a philosophical premeditation of death will have a substantial effect on how dying will be experienced, it seems, however, structurally impossible to know in advance.[2] Famous narratives of a premonition training, or self-cultivation in the thought of death, as, for example, in the case of Socrates, divert from those near-death experiences that have a sudden onset, and finally, even the premonition of the wise, facing death from a distance, may prove to be insubstantial in the actual encounter with death. Nagel's argument can be further substantialized with the sociological Systems Theory by Niklas Luhmann. He defines consciousness as "autopoiesis," that is, self-reproduction, and argues accordingly that one can imagine one's own death as the end of life, but not as the end of consciousness. Pointing to classical studies of the experience of dying, namely, by Elisabeth Kübler-Ross (1969), Karlis Osis and Erlendur Haraldsson (1977), and Moody (1975, 1977), Luhmann (1995, 276 [1994, 374]) observes:

> All the elements of consciousness are concerned with reproducing consciousness, and this and-so-forth cannot be denied without their losing their character as elements in the autopoietic nexus. No futureless element, no end of the entire series can be produced in this system because such a final element could not function as an autopoietic element, that is, could not be a unit and thus could not be determinable and, largely with the permission of society, it consequently attributes eternal life to itself, only abstracting from all the contents it knows. Any termination that it can foresee is the termination of an episode within consciousness, and in this sense one understood "life on this earth" to be an episode. Death is no goal. Consciousness cannot reach an end; it simply stops.

As has been argued by Nagel, Luhmann holds that consciousness is destined to reproduce itself endlessly and to do so as "self-reference"—yet, it still has something "other"

---

[2] "Death," Nagel (1986, 229) says, "is the negation of something the possibility of whose negation seems not to exist in advance."

to refer to, an external reference, be it "life" or the "body." To function as consciousness, it needs to have future states of itself because it is itself essentially just this: an ongoing process of getting prepared for the future. In this respect, every future state itself has to be one that can—again—be aligned to a third, also reproducible future state, and so on.[3] Consciousness is, moreover, in fear-of-death and near-death situations deprived of its possibility to act—action being another way to conceptualize and "realize" the future. In consequence, it has to reassure us that there are always possible future states.

4.2.2 THE DEATH-X-PULSE

It is therefore precisely this "rude shock"—which I call "death-x-pulse"[4]—that consists of an awareness emerging in consciousness that its own activity (to reproduce itself) is essentially threatened. This shock itself seems to be the trigger of various sorts of narratives, memories, and imaginations that fill the void of consciousness's expected nonexistence. This general structure of death-x-pulse-triggered experience causes a sudden increase of lively, imaginative visions that—for the respective individuals—seem to emerge, without any context or genealogy, in the situation itself. As is indicated by the "x" of the death-x-pulse, the impact is incomparably forceful because it presents itself within consciousness as possible annihilation of the continuity of reproducing itself. Consciousness, as previously said, is indefinitely capable of projecting itself into the future, imagining possible future states of itself, and, as self-consciousness, reflecting on its conscious content and processing it in almost infinite ways. There is only one content (and form), the "x," that cannot be represented: the nonexistence of its representing activity. Although one may argue that consciousness grapples also in vain with its unimaginable beginning, a threatening sudden end of its own self-reproduction—designated as "x"—is much more dramatic. To function as consciousness, it needs to have future states of itself because it is as such an ongoing process of getting prepared for the future. In this respect, every future state itself has to be one that can—again—be aligned to a third, also reproducible, future state, and so on. Moreover, embodied consciousness immersed in such situations is largely deprived of its possibility to act. Acting, for that matter, can be seen as an alternative way to conceptualize and "realize" the future. This possibility being blocked, too, it has to try hard to envision possible future states on any expense. The "x" has no context, but in order for it to be processed, it needs a context. Therefore, driven by the wish for survival, consciousness explores as quickly as possible memories stored in order to contextualize the death-x-pulse, propelled by the final existential wish to reproduce itself,

---

[3] In an almost Hegelian move, Luhmann (cf. 2013, 34–5) argues in the same vein that death cannot be a limit or border—it is a "limit experience," yet in contradiction to the idea of a "limit," because that would presuppose the other side. In consequence, every meaningful interpretation of the "other side" will necessarily be a religious interpretation, operating with the scheme of transcendence/immanence.

[4] Cf. Schlieter 2018.

namely, to find a way out of the situation. Most prominently, the narrative of the pano-ramic life review bears witness to the phenomenon, but we subsequently explore whether other topoi of near-death experiences might also be understood in this way.

To summarize the argument: There is only a state or situation for which consciousness is not equipped—the existential wake-up call, or death-x-pulse. In consequence, it will search for meaning, a context for the "x," and this will lead to a highly accelerated activity of consciousness, resulting in mental presence and, we hold, the life review. If conscious-ness is finally forced to contextualize the "x"—that there may be no future state—it seems to react in certain ways of which we found traces in the reports: It searches within all conscious content stored in memory for already experienced situations that may help the individual to understand this fully incommensurable state (this may, in fact, be a very fast search motivated for actual survival—in real life, even the 10th of a second may make a difference). Threatened by the prospect of its own nonexistence, it refers to its own history, its existence as embodied consciousness, from an already detached perspec-tive. One of its consequences might even be to look at its own life from the outside. In our view, this may explain the predominance of reports that speak of the life review as a "spectacle," a noninvolved "spectator perspective," that has often been reported be-fore it was conceptualized as "paralysis of emotion," "depersonalization," and so forth. "It is indeed impossible to imagine our own death," as has been argued by Freud (1918, 289), "and whenever we attempt to do so we can perceive that we are in fact still present as spectators. Hence the psycho-analytic school could venture on the assertion that at bottom no one believes in his own death, or, to put the same thing in another way, that in the unconscious every one of us is convinced of his own immortality." Although I follow Freud in assuming a spectator perspective toward one's own death, I am less convinced of his second conclusion, namely, that one is unconsciously convinced of one's immortality. This assumption leads to the psychoanalytic view that there is largely a denial of death. In fact, as previously seen, various psychologists such as Egger, Sollier, Pfister, Frankl and Pötzl, or Noyes and Kletti saw the principal function of the life review and other topoi of experiences near death in a search for deceptive security, that is, an escape from reality—realized as a display of comforting memories and pervasive feelings of happiness. Kastenbaum, for example, builds on Noyes and Kletti in their view that in extreme anx-iety the mind will display an adaptive behavior that reacts with depersonalization, a state that is "thanatomimetic" in the sense that the individual may look at himself or herself as already "dead" (i.e., the autoscopic view and the paralysis of emotion), or, paradoxically, it will develop a "hyperalertness," a reaction to death fear. However, Kastenbaum (cf. 1984, 33–4) does not mention any concrete value those mechanisms may have for *actual* sur-vival. It is only an escapist adaptation: In short, for someone convinced to be inescapably dying, it may only reduce the threat of death. As previously discussed, this interpretation leaves important aspects unconsidered.

To draw some preliminary conclusions in regard to types of narratives in near-death reports: Given that consciousness is still present in near-death experiences—at least, as

Marsh (2010, 88) argues convincingly, in the early phase of loss and the late phase of reacquisition of "full conscious awareness"—the threat of imminent death can force consciousness to imagine itself without reference to its body or an external world. One might, however, raise an objection here. Why then the comparatively low incidence of near-death experiences in situations near death, as attested in more recent empirical studies? And how do we explain the even lower prevalence of the out-of-body and life-review features that are reported if experiences are reported at all? Actually, to locate the death-x-pulse as a structure that presupposes consciousness implies it will be less prominent, or even absent, in impaired consciousness. Yet, an intensive threat to one's own consciousness can also be imagined later, for example, in the shock of realizing that the strike of death has been close or in a communicative situation in which the individual describes the experienced situation for the first time. In both situations, the individual consciousness may most radically envision that death could bring about a separation of self-reference and external reference. If, moreover, an individual consciousness realizes that death would mean the loss of reference to its body and to others (imagined, again, as the end of life, not as the end of consciousness), both—to imagine itself as "eternal life," but also as "out of the body"—seem to be plausible consequences. The latter experiences especially illustrate the attempt of an individual consciousness to perpetuate a projected external reference, because only the latter will guarantee vitally important relationships to others—in those cases in which the affected individual is actually no longer able to communicate.[5] Nevertheless, at least one element of near-death experiences can be understood as an outcome of these structures of consciousness: the life-review feature, especially if combined with a moral evaluation of the life lived, that is, the attempt of consciousness to consider its "life" (external reference) under the perspective to put the past behind it. One may object that what has been said so far is merely a speculative theory of consciousness. Before I discuss the death-x-pulse and the life review, I should therefore turn once again to the phenomenon of wake-up dreams as discussed by du Prel, Nietzsche, and Freud. May these dreams provide a tool for interpreting the life review?

4.2.3 THE COGNATE PHENOMENON OF "WAKE-UP DREAMS"

In wake-up dreams, a whole dream narrative is dependent on a "wake-up call," a distinct stimulus of the external world that, being above a certain detection threshold, leaves an implicit—but strong—mark in the dreaming consciousness. It calls for immediate awakening. We should now devote ourselves to a more thorough discussion of the phenomenon as an interpretative tool for the life review. Freud argued that wake-up dreams are called forth as a complex "stock phrase," if not composed by the "postexperiential" subject

---

[5] Reference can be made here to the "sensory deprivation," e.g., Lilly's well-known experiments with floating tanks (on Lilly, cf. Chapter 2.7.).

in a "revisionist process." Yet there are two elements that are not sufficiently represented in Freud's model. First, Freud ignores the general function of the dream narrative. It conducts the dreaming consciousness into a dead-end street for the purpose of forcing consciousness to become awake. This actually goes hand-in-hand with the acceleration of mental procession. Some whole narratives seem to develop within a second. But why, then, not follow Freud in his argument that the incredible acceleration in which the dream narrative is composed points to its prefiguration and retrieval as a ready-made story?

At this point, I should stress an important aspect left unconsidered both by Freud and Nietzsche, namely, the life-world function of wake-up dreams. Rather simply and existential, these dreams are conducive for increasing the chances of survival in situations in which there is an imminent, real threat. While being asleep, consciousness is not able to relate more broadly to the external world. Still being largely devoid of perceptual capacities, coordinated bodily activities, and so forth, the dreaming individual cannot directly refer to what exactly it is that is perceived.[6] It is therefore an important function of wake-up dreams to force consciousness out of the sleep and dream states. Imagine the real-world noise of a smashed window in the nighttime, represented as the clinking of champagne glasses in a cozy, continuing dream. If it would not cause awakening, robbers, or danger by any other name, could be left unnoticed. We could therefore even go a step further and assume that the acceleration of processed content in wake-up dreams presents evidence that it is already the dreaming mind that speeds up in order to be highly alert, and, awakened, ready for action if there is an imminent danger that needs an immediate response. Probably the mental clarity reported of experiences near death correlates to this survival value of being alert. Using "wake-up dreams" as hermeneutics, we may put the explanations given by Noyes and Kletti or Kastenbaum into perspective and offer a more plausible interpretation of the life review that, in turn, yields insights into the coming-together of near-death narratives in general. However, it presents a model for the triggering of narratives emerging from experience itself. In other words, for this interpretation to work, we have to presuppose that the relevant reports faithfully report the experience. It is, to repeat, not the intention to present a single-factor theory of near-death experiences. Because we are still engaged with them as *reported* experiences of various sorts, being dependent on texts, tradition, and respective expectations, such experiences defy in principle any monocausal "explanation." Equipped with the hermeneutics of

---

[6] Wittgenstein (1975, § 676) argued that someone "who, dreaming, says 'I am dreaming', even if he speaks audibly in doing so, is no more right than if he said in his dream 'it is raining', while it was in fact raining. Even if his dream were actually connected with the noise of the rain." There is, in other words, a perception of rain, but references to it are still within the evolving context of the "dream rain." The intricacy of this situation becomes obvious. Such phenomena can be noticed by neither the dreamer inside a dream nor by consciousness immersed in everyday life. It will become visible only in the case of wake-up dreams, in which the external impulse serves retrospectively as a tool for understanding the dream story.

wake-up dreams, we aim to probe what it will yield in the case of the life review in particular and, more broadly, for near-death narratives in general.

One can easily discover parallels between most elements of wake-up dreams and the life review. In both cases, there is an abrupt stimulus that serves as a trigger (in the latter, the death-x-pulse). Moreover, both cases reveal an instantly evolving process, drawing especially on memorized events in which consciousness searches for an explanation, while a succession of images, if not a story, unfolds. One may object here that the life review has often been reported as being only "images." Given that most descriptions that we previously discussed spoke of either a retrograde succession or a succession of images in the biographical order, it seems to be more structured, and not just an arbitrary projection of images. However, according to the reports, there seem to be considerable variations in which the life review took place. Whereas some spoke of having revived, or even relived, images of the most significant experiences of their lives,[7] others reported minute details of a "tableau," whereas still others spoke of a simultaneous copresence of the life lived as a whole. However, in regard to the suggested interpretation, I should mention two crucial points of difference between wake-up narratives and the life-review feature. A first difference pertains to the emotional quality reported of both experiences. Whereas wakeup dreams are often accompanied by negative emotions of fear (because of its narrative function to induce awakening), life reviews near death were, in contrast, continuously characterized as accompanied by feelings of bliss, peace, and "cosmic unity." Actually, there are several aspects that render this difference plausible: First, the survival function of wake-up dreams previously mentioned goes along with dream narratives that require a "negative end"—life reviews, which were reported because the experiencers survived near- or fear-of-death situations, have no narrative, and consequently, can in principle have no "negative end." Moreover, actual survival in real life-threatening situations will probably override exact memorization of negative emotions (in those cases in which these occurred) and will relativize the stress suffered. This assumption allows us to refrain from more theory-laden descriptions such as a Freudian "suppression" of death, powered by a narcissistic wish for immortality, or a pathological "depersonalization." Besides, following Luhmann in his description that in death "consciousness simply ends," we are actually not equipped to hold that there is any final "wake up" in life review, that is, some kind of higher awakening to a postmortal world. To assume this would indeed require a "view from beyond" of a "soul," defined as superempirical. Accordingly, one may be able to ask but not to answer if death will take place in fatal accidents exactly at that moment when the autobiographical picture show will come to an end—when, in other words, no

---

[7] Cf. Roland Fischer's explanation of an "excitation-produced time contraction" or "increased dataprocessing" aroused by a sudden fear of imminent death. Building on several reports available, Fischer (1967, 454) summarizes that the "individual's instantaneous but futile attempt to avert catastrophe is followed by the depicting in rapid succession, at an exponentially increasing rate of a few hundred images per second, of the most meaningful past events in his life."

conscious content could be found to explain the actual situation with its death-x-pulse. Consciousness, as said, may in contrast to "escapist" interpretations still be interested in actual survival. Ignited by the death-x-pulse, it still searches for contexts that may render the situation describable, exploring final possibilities of how to parry the threatening situation. As seen, the paradox of the two antagonist reactions, the distractive "anesthetic" bliss on the one side, and the hyperalertness as a "violent effort to escape death," has usually been resolved by declaring the blissful "euthanasia" function to be the dominant. Only occasionally, for example, by Paul Sollier (1896) or Max Mikorey (1960), has the life review been conceptualized as a final search for possible action that may still help us to survive.

Stressing the death-x-pulse-triggered search for survival, another objection could be raised. As is well known, a large number of accounts do not include the life review. Seemingly, the life review is more prominent in cases of near drowning or accidents, being usually reported by 20%–30% in collections or empirical studies (cf. Blackmore 1993, 187). In the German sample studied by sociologist Hubert Knoblauch and collaborators (1999; 2001), the life-review feature had been reported by almost 40% within the sample of near-death experiences (5% of the total population), whereas the most prominent feature, reported by more than 60%, had been the item to have been mentally "wide awake" (cf. Knoblauch 1999, 127–40). Ian Stevenson and Emily Cook (cf. 1995, 454) found among 122 cases from literature or newly communicated to them that some reported distinct life memories of only a few images and others an almost infinite number of simultaneously displayed images. The authors concluded that their most important finding is evidence of a wide variety in life reviews, and the "popular picture" of the "'whole life' being seen all at once" a false generalization. In about 40%–60% of the cases, there was a succession of memories from childhood to present (anterograde), whereas 11%–15% reported to have witnessed memories in retrograde order. Stevenson and Cook furthermore sorted their reports in regard to an either "gradual" or "sudden" onset. The group of the latter consisted of cases of drownings, falls, accidents, cardiac arrests, and so forth (cf. 454), and amounted, in cases from literature, to a total of 84%, whereas in the new cases collected by the authors, a sudden onset was a characteristic of only half of the cases. Be that as it may, according to the hermeneutics of a death-x-pulse proposed here, suddenness—the realization of imminent danger—should be an essential element for the life review to take place. Yet, even a "gradual onset" may imply a distinct point at which life-threatening danger emerges, for example, in cases of surgical operations categorized by the authors as "gradual onset" (cf. 454). However, statistical data in this field are seldom comparable, because the respective studies use different criteria for inclusion as well as different settings and methods for data mining; for our purpose, it may suffice to note that there usually was a significant amount reporting the life review, though there will always be a larger group without reporting it. In these cases, there was supposedly either no death-x-pulse (for example, if the life-threatening situation had come about gradually), or individuals reacted differently to it, for example, reporting experiences out of the body or simply ignoring the impulse. Even more, the life review could also have been there, but either not remembered or not reported. Obviously, there is a large variety of possible reactions, and I do not intend to argue that the death-x-pulse shall be accountable for all.

The death-x-pulse, an existential wake-up call, can evolve in fear-of-death and near-death situations. That there is a phase of increased brain activity after the assumed death-x-pulse has been recently demonstrated by a team of researchers in animal experimentation. Recordings from electrodes implanted in rat brains were made during and after externally induced cardiac arrest (euphemistically, the rats were sacrificed for science). The research provides evidence that there is after "death"—that is, cardiac arrest—a 30-second surge of "highly organized brain activity," which the authors hold to be "consistent with conscious processing" (Borjigin, Lee et al. 2013, 14432). Although these results pertain to rats, which lack autonomous self-consciousness, the authors argue that their findings should be relevant for the study of near-death experiences: The latter will represent "a biological paradox that challenges our understanding of the brain and has been advocated as evidence for life after death and for a noncorporeal basis of human consciousness," based on the "unsupported belief that the brain cannot possibly be the source of highly vivid and lucid conscious experiences during clinical death." Presenting "evidence of highly organized brain activity and neurophysiologic features consistent with conscious processing at near-death," the authors allude, will be a first step to explain "the highly lucid and realer-than-real mental experiences reported by near-death survivors" (14436). Interestingly, Jimo Borjigin and her team could show that it is a highly organized, synchronized brain activity, especially of high-frequency gamma waves, the latter being in the eyes of some neuroscientists a possible neural correlate of higher cognitive processes of "experiencing coherence."[8] However, physiology-based scientific explanations of near-death experiences will likely not grasp why these experiences are held to be utterly meaningful by the experiencers. For that matter, I may remind the reader of the fact that many situations near death are fear-of-death situations and not bound to any dying brain. The authors put the cart before the horse with insinuating that the brain activity itself will—as a single factor—account for the conscious content of experiences near death. The results of the study may nevertheless be compatible with the interpretation of the death-x-pulse in human consciousness. Actually, in recorded cardiac arrests in humans, too, there seems to be a period of several seconds in which conscious brain activity does not simply decrease, but, on the contrary, increases. This fits well with the interpretation pursued here. Consciousness is destined to reproduce itself endlessly and does so as self-reference—yet, it still has something "other" to refer to: the animated "body." Therefore it may not astonish us that, in modernity, the disembodied

---

[8] Neuroscientist Wolf Singer argues that 40-hertz synchronicity correlates with sudden cognitive coherence and hypothesizes that it may correspond to an Archimedean *eureka*, "I have found [it]!" This synchronicity has also been detected in experienced Tibetan Buddhist meditators while meditating (cf. Lutz et al. 2004).

consciousness is still discursively tied to the body. In consequence, leaving the body in situations near death is usually not reported as, for example, a unification with some other person's disembodied consciousnesses. Only a minority reports that consciousness achieves in such situations all-observing capacities or relinquishes perspectival sense perception in total, merging with a "cosmic" consciousness. Despite some reports in the Gnostic–Esoteric metaculture, near-death narratives are in respect to the consciousness's new body—for example, the "astral body"—merely minimally counterintuitive. Usually, disembodied consciousness still possesses major attributes of its "former" body—the object of its austoscopic interest—into which it returns. To conclude the excursus, I now return to the experiences as they are reported, because this is the most solid basis for the study of their meaning.

4.3

The Survival Value of Narratives?

SEEN FROM THIS perspective, one may explore whether other topoi reported can be read as an outcome of consciousness confronted with the "death-x-pulse." The encounter with a guide—no matter if human-like, angelic, or godly—who encourages or commands the soul to return to life seems to have a certain value for the self-conception of the surviving individual too. It renders the contingency ("Why did I survive, while others die in such a situation?") into something meaningful. If an individual consciousness has developed strong religious or moral conceptions in its life before the "death-x-pulse," it comes as no surprise that it will finally also interpret this existential moment with decisive previous insights and expectations: meeting deceased; divine apparitions; feelings of peace; a heavenly court; impressions of an overwhelming certainty; and so forth. In regard to the "survival value" of the narrative ordering within the experience, we find relevant reasonings in Mark Fox's work. Building on theories of the narrative structure of human experience, Fox (cf. 2003, 190–5) focuses on the narrative structure of the "self" as advanced by Paul Ricœur, David Carr, and others. Summarizing the evidence, he holds that "the self thus (re)constituted is a plotted, *narrative* self. This much is clear from the testimonies of near-death survivors themselves: they return from death with *stories* to tell" (193). In consequence, Fox asks—though not in regard to the life review proper, but to the narrative of the "life-or-death decision"—if the "narrative ordering" itself may have some "survival value": "Could it be that the casting of the NDE into such a narrative form serves a function within the dying process itself, either by increasing the very possibility of survival or by securing some other crucial objective?" (193). Applying the narratological idea of the "self-as-story," Fox argues that "in order to live we must render intelligible the actions and intentions—friendly or hostile—of others," which "is accomplished through a narrative ordering of the events of our lives." However, he asks, does this apply to the "apparently private episodes near death"? (194). A narrative ordering of experience, he hypothesizes, might have survival value in the dying process, say, "by casting into a (familiar) narrative environment the important [. . .] decisions which need to be taken" (194). The climax of many narratives is therefore the "border" at which a life-or-death decision is unavoidable. The "plot" of the narrative actually "serves to aid choice: either for survival or for death" (195). Obviously, Fox does not consider the life review and its possible value for *actual* survival, but takes the border as an internal narrative fact. A decision within the confines of the story, the plot's benefit will be merely to highlight the existential choice: to opt for life and to return. In the speculative case of going beyond the border, it will, as I understand Fox, "*ease* the transition from life to death" (195). Although Fox's assumption of a narrative ordering both of the self and near-death reports is plausible, it seems in the case of the border more convincing to see it as a retroactive element. It assumes its position in the narrative while, or after, conscious awareness returns.[1] Admittedly, this is matter of speculation. To describe the arrival at the border as a *point of no return* parallel to the person's real survival would, however, imply that consciousness is somehow still in a position to decide over the matter of life and death. This presupposes, I am inclined to think, a "soul" that may in itself be in such a position to decide its point of departure, that is, determining its own death—an assumption that can, in principle, not be verified.

In contrast to these speculative conjectures, we should return to what we have: the reports in the form of narratives. As it becomes clear, there are three different concepts of the assumed "survival value" of narratives at stake. First, there is the narrative ordering of the autobiographical life review, which, we should remind ourselves, may in cases of "single images" also be absent. Second, there is a possible survival value of other topoi while consciousness is, or assumes to be, close to death; and third, there is the survival value of the finalized narrative of the whole experience as being considered to be true by the individual. As said, the first narrative ordering of autobiographical images may indeed have already happened while the experience is unfolding. However, although some life-review reports mention that among them were most meaningful episodes, others reported a recall of most incidental and marginal events. Given that the death-x-pulse triggers a search for survival-relevant information, it will, compared with wake-up dreams, at least in certain cases do so in a more contingent manner. Finally, in regard to the survival value of the life review, I may point to the fact that it emerged as late as the early 19th century. Therefore a historical contextualization of the survival value should

---

[1] In addition, as seen in various reports of the Christian metaculture previously, the border conceptualizes the idea of being not yet sufficiently pure to enter heaven, and often comes together with moral warnings (see Easting 2006, 79).

be taken into consideration too. It would imply that the life review as an outcome of the death-x-pulse itself is dependent on the modern self and its individualized, autobiographical self-understanding, searching for relevant information exactly because it understands itself in autobiographical terms.

In some of the reports previously quoted, religious meaning was straightforwardly created by the most recent religious admonition or edification, whether heard or read. For example, in a case reported by Heim (1892, 332), a sermon *"which I had heard that morning"* was remembered and its meaning applied to the situation: "'God is almighty, Heaven and Earth rest in his hand; to his will we must withstand. With this thought an infinite silence came to me.'" Yet, we will have to count with certain retrograde imputations and distortions. In direct comparison with wake-up dreams, individuals in situations near death will usually not immediately be able to (internally) verbalize their experiences. Especially in cases of life-threatening accidents, cardiac arrests, and so forth, a more extended phase of medical treatment and rehabilitation may follow that will also induce the probability of the well-known memory failures previously described. This being said, in these cases, the articulation of the experience, as being reckoned by Kastenbaum, will be a more creative process of meaning making, aiming at a defense against the experience's depersonalizing, centrifugal forces. However, I may augment his reasoning in that regard that also the narrative of the near-death experience as a whole should be analyzed in respect to its survival value. Seen from this perspective, the postexperiential consciousness will also have to answer questions such as "how can I integrate the experience into what I assume to be most important in life?," or "hearing my report, what will my significant others think of me, of my attitudes toward them, and of my view of life as such?" Given the existential quality of life-threatening situations, it seems almost trivial to assume that individuals will in their answers tap on resources that for them are most promising to transform the "x" into meaning, but also, to counter possible criticism that they may expect of their peers. These may include criticism of having gained an exclusive insight into the otherworldly realm, or praising an egoistic indulgence in the peace and equipoise of death.

Yet my major question in the present part, namely, to figure out to which extent near-death reports may represent experiences, remains difficult to answer. To be on the safe side, we must count with all processes previously discussed. There are surely individual expectations that in the narrative formation of the unfolding experience inextricably merge with what is actually experienced. And it is here that virtually any analysis of whether a certain element had been conceptualized before or was an unpredictable and "original" part of experience proper, will come to a grinding halt. To assume a "death-x-pulse" as a trigger of memories and equally as a trigger that accounts for a first narrative ordering of the experience while the latter still unfolds seems to be plausible—at least for those experiences in which a life review is reported. Moreover, an impact of the death-x-pulse may also be assumed in other aspects of reported experiences, for example, the ineffability. Although the latter is certainly a long-standing topos of descriptions of God, the "light," mystic experience, and so forth, that has been condensed into a fixed expectation of how to experience "mystically," we can connect the reported impression of an "inexpressible," or "ineffable" quality of the experience with a death-x-pulse-triggered search for memory-stored, autobiographical content that did not come up with any "worldly" results. In such a case, there is probably no life review triggered and reported, but some kind of "naked" or "empty" awareness. However, as previously mentioned, the qualification of inexpressible or ineffable is, in our reports, usually attributed to a "mystic light," to unconditional "love," and so forth. Thus, it builds on well-established traditions of (not) expressing the ineffable. But still, we should count with a revision process that will start immediately after the experience and will usually come to a close only when the narrative configuration through internal and external retellings of what had happened and experienced has achieved a standardized form. As seen in the case of Heim's memoir(s), it may even decades later be reported with new elements. In the concluding Part V, I reflect on the results and outline the functions of reported experiences near death in the respective religious metacultures.

PART FIVE

The Significance of Near-Death Experiences
for Religious Discourse

5.1

The Presence of Religious Metacultures in Near-Death Discourse

(1580–1975)

───

MY MAJOR TASK in the historical reconstruction has been threefold. First, the discursive development of autobiographical narratives of reported experiences near death has been reconstructed, including the aims to report these experiences. How did individuals make sense of them, and what kind of meanings did they draw from them? Second, what exactly did they report having experienced? And finally, does the claim of a large number of reporting individuals (including mediators and collectors), namely, that they were largely unaware earlier narratives of those experiences, seems in general justified, or do we have evidence to relativize this claim? In the Part V, I reflect on the results of Parts II and III, aiming to show how narratives of religious metacultures formed the main current of narratives of experiences near death. Finally, I discuss the religious functions of the reported experiences (Chapter 5.2.).

To summarize the genealogical findings, I start with some general remarks. First, and in contrast to studies that argue for a broad decline of Christian narratives of deathbed experiences in the early modern centuries, there is ample evidence of a continuous stream of Christian reports. Enlarged by a broad current of Spiritualist–Occult and Gnostic–Esoteric reports from the late 18th century onward, near-death narratives were finally, in the 1970s, subsumed under the new "collective concept" (Koselleck) of near-death experience. Transmitters of these reports were more often than not religiously interested individuals—preeminently spokespersons of non-mainstream churches and denominations such as Pietists, Theosophists, Occultists, and Spiritualists, joined, in the early 20th century, by parapsychologists. Many of them considered themselves, at the same time, to be an integral part of the Christian metaculture, whereas others can best be characterized as nondenominational seekers of religious and mystical experience. Only in the latter respect may I join Kellehear in arguing that "religious denomination" cannot be accounted for as a dominant factor in near-death experiences.[1] Nevertheless, there are considerable differences in respect to religious background, confession, or historical situation.

In addition, there is a continuous reception of the earlier reports, though quite often quoted only as "parallels," not as a tradition that might have influenced the successor's own expectations or experiences. Up to the 1970s, only a minor number of physiologists, psychologists, philosophers, and scholars of psychoanalysis developed a more academic interest in these reported experiences—and if so, they were predominantly interested in certain features, especially in the life review, the supposedly peacefulness and quietness of dying, and, to a much lesser extent, in out-of-body experiences. Only a minor subgroup within the latter strictly adhered to "naturalist" explanations of these experiences. Usually, they were treated side by side with other "abnormal," psychopathological phenomena, for example, epilepsy, personality disorders, drug-abuse hallucination, and so forth.

Among the most common elements that form a continuous, uninterrupted current within reported experiences near death, we do find descriptions of a paradisiacal realm, a "summerland"[2] of flowers and gardens. In contrast to late medieval deathbed narratives (cf. van Uytfanghe 1991, 473–7), very rarely negative descriptions prevail—from early on, "hell," I may say, is present only as a quick peek by which the "experiencer" realizes that other denizens *are* being punished (cf. de Benneville 1791). In all cases, negative experiences were resolved within the narrative, being transformed into a merely temporary discomposure. All in all, positive emotions prevail: Tranquility, quietness, and feelings of peace and joy are present from Montaigne (1580) onward.[3]

Descriptions of a border or a gate, at which the reporting individual is sent back, equally abound, either from a "voice" within or by a divine command, or by other messengers. This element could be found in Atherton's report (1680); in Schwerdtfeger (1734), but also in Wiltse (1889) and Symonds (1895), to name but a few. Although intermittently not reported, we could generally notice that meeting others, "people of light," angels, saints, and "spiritual guides," but also deceased friends and relatives, have been an element of Christian deathbed narratives, and equally of esoteric, spiritualist, and parapsychological accounts up to the 1970s. It should be mentioned, however, that meeting saints is a decreasing topos of reports that originate in 20th century—in contrast to the ever-popular mention of meeting angels and family members.

---

[1] "Rather, it seems that the religious ideas that dominate whole societies create the symbols and metaphors by which we communicate our stories about death" (Kellehear 1996, 177).

[2] The "summerland" as a paradise in which seasons seem to have disappeared may connect to an early Christian topos of the eternal spring (cf. Bremmer 2002, 61).

[3] van Uytfanghe (cf. 1991, 460) shows that this element of pleasant, calm feelings is already a common feature of medieval reports.

As it seems, the medieval Christian topos of the disembodied soul's knowledge of witnessing the postmortal fate of the recently deceased—still present in some Christian and spiritualist sources previously discussed (e.g., in Quaker Thomas Say's 1796 report)— transforms into a more general "clairvoyance at the moment of death" (e.g., Passavant 1821). Decisive here is the emergence of a Spiritualist–Occult metaculture in the 19th century, in which the knowledge of the deceased person's afterlife fate (hell, purgatory, etc.) is broadly replaced by a knowledge that now "only" knows of another person's death that had happened in the meantime and parallel to the experience near death. In addition, in the late 17th and early 18th centuries it was still held by many that seeing oneself in cases of clairvoyance, "second sight," or "deuteroscopy," was an omen of approaching death (cf. Horst 1830, II, 141). Consequently, communicating such experiences was therefore held to be inauspicious.

However, although Spiritualism systematically searched for clairvoyant or telepathic contacts into the other world and developed spiritual practices such as astral projection securing intentional "out-of-body travels" in the world of spirits and the dead, these practices were nevertheless despised as deceptive and fallacious by adherents of a more orthodox Christian theology. We could observe from early modernity up to the 20th century a continuous current of reported experiences near death in Christian metaculture, in which more exclusivist protagonists argued decidedly against the view that experiences near death entertain an intrinsic relation to Gnosticism, Occultism, Spiritualism, or Esotericism. Authors convinced of the exclusive truth of Christian near-death visions argued persistently on the basis of a negative evaluation of psychic phenomena (occult knowledge as not from God, unreliable, etc.) that experiences near death are not related to occultism (cf. McLaughlin and Malony 1984, 157). This discourse strand, that experiences near death must not be related to occultism, can be seen as a central factor that hindered the emergence of an overarching concept of near-death experiences in the 19th and early 20th centuries.

An experience of light has obviously been reported in two different modes: either as an overwhelming, nonanthropomorphic or nonpersonal bright light, or, in contrast, as a supernatural "Being of Light." Schwerdtfeger (1734), for example, speaks of an experience of God as "pure Sun," "brilliance," whereas in the report communicated by du Monchaux (1766), merely an "extreme light" is mentioned. Surely such important differences of a perception of "light" or "Light" can easily be resolved by applying either a naturalist hypothesis in regard to an underlying neurophysiological basis of all experiences of a bright "light," or, building equally on all experiences, as a numinous presence—acknowledged by some, but unrecognized by the spiritually unprepared. However, as the example of the "light/Light" shows, to identify a physiological basis will not explain why one individual will report simply of an extremely bright light, while the other is unshakably certain that it is a bright "Light" announcing the presence of God. Ritchie, for example, identifies the light with Christ: "I knew because a thought was put deep within me, 'You are in the presence of the Son of God'" (see Chapter 1.3). Applying the method established here, we are not to put the authenticity of this reported experience into question. Yet, we saw not only that the perception of a bright light as Jesus has a long history in Christian deathbed narratives (cf., e.g., the report of Schwerdtfeger, 1734)—moreover, it is also declared in Richtie's and numerous others' reports, that it is impossible to speak of this encounter or that the "presence" communicated itself only mentally, beyond words.

Genealogically significant are, moreover, those elements that clearly show decisive developments within the discourse previously surveyed. Special attention should, in this respect, be given the "dark tunnel," the "life review," and the autoscopic interest within "out-of-body experiences."

To put it bluntly, descriptions of a tunnel were, up to the 1890s, totally absent in the discourse analyzed here—in stark contrast to the ubiquitous depiction of "The Ascent Into the Empyrean" by Bosch in the milieu of near-death studies. The earliest account, published in *Borderland* (London), speaks of a "tube." Although the tube is described as very narrow, without "room to move," it is worth mentioning that the term "tube" already had currency in the late 19th century as an established designation for the London Underground Railway (the world's first metro that opened in 1863). Life-world experiences of passing through a tunnel were popularized by the increase of railway tunnels or, later, street tunnels. In addition, the "tunnel view" has been further acculturated by the view through binoculars, microscopes, and the like (cf. Kellehear 1996, 36). So it may not be too astonishing that the term "tunnel" proliferated as a concept for describing experiences near death in the 1920s, until it finally became a fixed topos of Moody's standard description.

The second element that has clearly emerged and developed in the memoirs of experiences near death has been the "panoramic life review." In the early modern deathbed narratives, we encountered reports of judgments scenes, including, as in Schwerdtfeger's account (1734), the recovery of memories long lost or the reported impression that deeds committed in the distant past were as lively as if just committed. A preparation stage of the life review can be seen in the narrative that the disembodied soul may be capable of a full recollection of its earthly life, as Jung-Stilling argued (1808). This experience— or doctrine, for that matter—is gaining traction in mesmerist accounts (e.g., Passavant 1821). Probably in close interdependence, literati began in the 1820s to express their drug experiences, in which they claimed to have experienced an absolute self, co-present and fully aware of its past. Yet this idea is still not conceived of in real, sudden situations near death—it is an assumed "heavenly body" that may remember everything (Coleridge 1817). To relate this topos of the instantaneity and co-presence of revived images of childhood with experiences near death is essentially the contribution of de Quincey (1821), who for the first time mentions the revival of hidden childhood memories during near drowning. The first narrative of a full life review, using the metaphors of photographic images and the "panorama," was communicated in Binns (1842)—only some years before the report of Beaufort (1847) popularized this narrative. It seems that it is actually this report, quoted time and again by adherents of all religious metacultures and by proponents of a naturalist grasp of the phenomenon, that had a catalytic and cohesive function for collecting reports of experiences near death.

The third element of systematized near-death experiences that evolved and changed considerably in the discourse has been the element of out-of-body experiences. As a matter of fact, a soul leaving the body has been a continuous element in the reports, though it varies remarkably in its narrative form. In many ancient and medieval experiences near death, it was conveyed in the form of an extensive "journey to the otherworld," and we could still witness some reports, in the centuries covered here, that followed the narrative trajectories of those elaborate compositions—for example, the "heavenly journey" of C. G. Jung (reported 1963) or of G. Ritchie.

In contrast to these journeys, we may differentiate narratives in which the individual reflects on the sudden experience of being an observer "out of the body." However, in the earlier reports within our corpus, as in the case of Schwerdtfeger, de Benneville, and others, the departing soul does not cast a backward glance to its own body. Examples of an autoscopic interest in the "old" body did not, as in the case of the "rapture" of Hemme Hayen (1717), form an integral part of an experience near death. An autoscopic perspective in the latter finds an incipient, yet still implicit, mention in a letter to Hartshorn (in Deleuze 1843), and, interestingly in the same year, in the narrative presented by Child.

As is the case with the life review, it is, most notably, for the first time more broadly expressed in drug experiences. Ludlow reported in 1857, as we saw, of a "delirium" in which his soul departed from his body, but turns around and scrutinizes the body from above. However, we should emphasize that the autoscopic interest here does not emerge in a situation near death.

Some years later, we encounter an out-of-body narrative, mediumistic communicated by a "deceased," in Paist (1861), and it is in this decade that the intentional "projection" of the soul, that is, the soul's mental travel out of the body, comes to the fore. Magnetic sleep, it is now argued, has similarities to the moment of death. Moreover, clairvoyant observers are able to "witness" the spiritual body (Davis 1866)—but still an explicit autoscopic interest is largely lacking (the "heautoscopic" narrative reported in Seelbach 1864 taken aside). Its explicit mention appears as late as in reports in spiritualist and occultist circles, disclosed by Denton (1871), Tuttle (1863; 1871) or in Wiltse's report of 1889. In these decades, between 1860 and 1890, the visionary excursion of the disembodied soul gets increasingly practiced as part of the astral projection, as propagated in theosophic circles. Within the revival of concepts of reincarnation, after-death states may be experienced as temporal excursions, and, as we saw in Blavatsky's accounts, reports of experiences near death were used to corroborate in-life experiences of after-death states communicated by Indian masters as well as by "somnambulists." Out-of-body experiences, though the technical term is still lacking, are, in the trajectory of Swedenborg's and mesmerist experiences, now systematically pursued and trained. Only shortly thereafter, it is in this context that the technical term "out-of-the-body experiences" is established (Hill 1918). It should be mentioned that from now on, numerous spiritualist and occultist accounts up to the

1970s will deal side by side with astral projection and near- and after-death experiences as facets of a homogeneous phenomenon. Death is nothing but a permanent out-of-body experience. The theosophical discovery and translation of the *Tibetan Book of the Dead* (1927) established further evidence to speak of experiences near and after death as a trans-cultural phenomenon. Applying the specifically Buddhist "karmic projection theory," the idea is popularized that, even though religious imagery may be culturally bound, there *is* a reality that is experienced—the nondual reality of consciousness-and-suchness. In this vein, experiences near death highlight mind-at-large, and the *Book* becomes a modern Western Buddhist and esoteric model for concrete guidance for the dying.

Descriptions of the disembodied soul witnessing reanimation attempts emerge—with the forerunner quoted in Child (1843)—as a standard element in the 1930s, evidenced in the reports of Scott (1931) or in Mattiesen (1936). It gained traction in the 1950s and 1960s. Here, the topos is formed that the soul, or consciousness, hovers above the resusci-tation scene, often in an emergency unit, hears itself declared "dead," but still tries to com-municate with the medical personnel—very often in an ambivalent emotional state of being "at peace" and discontent with the "violent" measures taken to bring it back to life. In sum, descriptions of the out-of-body experience show a crucial development, namely, the growing interest of the disembodied observer to look at his or her own "dead" body, and to examine it with an increasing exactitude. Although naturalist psychologists from the late 19th century onward portray such reported experiences as instances of "deper-sonalization," they appear, in religious metacultures, still as soteriologically meaningful. Finally, in the 1960s and early 1970s, the popularization of cognate psychedelic drug experiences lead to attempts to theorize experiences. Looking inside, Theodore Roszak (cf. 1969, 219–27) argues with Maslow, should put the illusory, alienated objectivity of science—to find a world "Out-There" which is strictly divided and detached from an "In-Here"—into question. In this context, out-of-body experiences appear to be ambig-uous: Some hold them to be an escape from reality, that is, depersonalized consciousness forced into an external (and sometimes even scientifically interested) observer position, esoteric protagonists can connect to such experiences as excursions to the "really real," as Shamanic soul travel, and so forth.

Finally, we could witness the publication of systematic approaches, especially by Crookall, that had already assembled almost all elements of near-death experiences, while still incorporating mediumistic reports by the "pseudo-dead." Although Crookall was, for the latter reason, not prepared to conceptualize near-death experiences as an independent category, but spoke, more generally, of the dying process, his influence was nevertheless formative. He had already offered a systematic sequence of what the dying may (usually) experience—beginning with the "call" by the deceased, the life re-view, the release of the "double," the tunnel experience, a judgment, etc. And again, it was reports of drug experiences, this time especially hallucinogens such as mescaline and LSD, that, in adepts of esoteric religiosity such as engrained in Western mysticism or Tibetan Buddhism, triggered experiences near death—culminating in Leary's or Lilly's more drastic reports of drug-induced experiences. Moody, in the end, could pick up Lilly's expression of a near-death experience, and, prepared by Ritchie's first-hand near-death account that included an after-death encounter with Christ, started collecting and documenting all those reports of experiences near death that were made in his direct environment—the modern clinic with its enhanced resuscitation measures.

A final observation pertains to formal changes in near-death narratives. In medieval and some early modern reports, the dying visionaries' peers provide the framing of the memoir—monks, nuns, priests, and preachers. The visions are not reported by the respective individual—often, the visionaries are portrayed as hesitant to disclose their visions in order not to boost themselves. Moreover, many of them died shortly thereafter. Therefore we do not have autobiographical verbatim accounts, but descriptions by others, most often in perfect match with expectations of the Christian deathbed genre. However, as the modern era unfolds, the memoirs are increasingly literal accounts authored or authorized by the "experiencers" themselves. This development toward individualization has important impacts on the wording of the memoir, but also on the place of the memoir in the individual biography. In modernity, the individual becomes the central agent within his own life world, and so the question becomes increasingly important of how memoirs of experiences near death can be integrated into the autobiographical narrative. In consequence, the memoir of a critical experience must no longer attest a preconceived religious cosmovision of the afterlife and the beyond, but provide an answer to the question: "What did it do to *me*?" The observations presented so far were mainly based on our corpus of reports (1580–1975). I now broaden the view and include also remarks on more recent near-death discourses as well. Doing so, allows the underscoring of how the religious significance that we attribute to reports, scripts, and memoirs of near-death experiences is equally to be found in historic examples as in most recent discourses.

5.2

The Religious Functions of Near-Death Experiences

HAVING THE DISCURSIVE history of the near-death reports at hand, I now discuss more thoroughly the functions that these reports exert within religious discourse. In principle, this function can be twofold—for the experiencers and for the audience. Various researchers after Moody have emphasized that near-death experiences have religious effects. Yet there has been no consensus reached about the form and contents of religiosity that is strengthened by or brought forth through the experience. Some collectors of relevant reports, such as Rawlings (see 1978, 158–60), were convinced that true near-death experiences will transform even staunch atheists into believers because they "corroborate" all essential Christian teachings of heaven and hell, God's love, and the reality of final salvation. Others, such as Ring (1980, 173) in his earlier publications, argued that "core experiencers" will, after the incident, undergo significant changes toward a spiritual, tolerant, and universalist worldview. They feel closer to God, are less attracted to organized religion, and, finally, "are significantly more inclined than non-experiencers to be convinced there is life after death"—in sum, they show a "*universalistically* spiritual orientation" (Ring 1984, 145).[1] In addition, they are "more likely to be open to the concept of reincarnation," and more sympathetic to Eastern religions such as "Hinduism and Buddhism" (185). Near-death experiences, Ring reasons, could signify an

---

[1] Defined by further traits such as characterizing oneself as more spiritual than religious, and that there is life after death, "regardless of religious belief"—a principal element of downplaying the impact of earlier religious discourse—or the perennialist belief in an "underlying unity of all religions" (Ring 1984, 146).

evolutionary step toward a new spiritual age.[2] Sabom (1982, 88), on his part, concluded from his interviews that there are "transcendental near-death experiences" that express a general "increase in afterlife beliefs" and saw in various reports the acknowledgment of a superior "Spirit" (cf. 254–5). In his subsequent publications, however, he argued that even though "a deepening of intrinsic faith" can be observed, a clear direction of this postexperiential development toward Eastern spirituality, New Age thoughts, or Christianity cannot be deduced from the material. The characteristics of this "spiritual deepening," Sabom (2003, part II, [2]) now declares, appear "to be influenced by factors other than the NDE itself." These general differences in interpretation that have led to "religious wars in the NDE movement" (Ring) are, given the historical genesis of the near-death discourse in Christian, Spiritualist, and Esoteric metacultures, far from astonishing. They are an outcome of methodical biases based on the different religious agendas of the first generation of post-Moodian researchers. At the same time, they emerge, of course, from the different religious backgrounds of the interviewees. The competition among Christian, Esoteric, and Universalist interpretations has not ceased over the last four decades. For the external observer, the "religious wars" confirm that all religious metacultures of Western modernity contributed on their terms to the uninterrupted stream of reported experiences up to the present day. Furthermore, they demonstrate anew the general importance of near-death experiences for attesting authentic religiosity in late modern circumstances.

Still, the function of the reports and of any "religious experience" is closely related to distinct salvific goals, developed in specific historic circumstances within the respective religious metacultures.[3] Speaking of a "religious function" presupposes that the reports of near-death memoirs, their collection, and their redistribution will help the respective individuals to solve problems that they encounter in the realm of meaning. As "meaning" (or "making sense"), I understand the process of a continuous actualization of possibilities. Meaning ensures a continuous accessibility of the world (cf. Luhmann 1994, 93–4). Meaning making can be addressed as "religious" if narratives counter the fundamental insecurity that follows from human finitude and mortality. These narratives reduce contingency. This function—located on an individual level and present in the discourse— becomes apparent in narratives that aim to overcome the threatening annihilation of

---

[2] Ring asks (1984, 255), with reference to New Age and certain allusions to Huxley's theory of consciousness at large, if the "high rate of transcendental experience" may collectively represent "*an evolutionary thrust toward higher consciousness for humanity at large*? Could it be that the near-death experience is itself an *evolutionary mechanism* [. . .] unlocking spiritual potentials previously dormant?" Such esoteric interpretations, appreciative of Eastern religious teachings, are still influential in the 1980s (cf. Marsh 2010, 251).

[3] This does not mean that the reports or the experiences are "universal," or that their structure follows a cognitive necessity (though the presented results may be ready by Cognitive Science of Religion adepts as proving exactly this). Such claims resemble structurally other causal explanations, e.g., as impaired brain states of the dying brain. In my eyes, both fail to explain why an overwhelming majority do not have experiences near death while being in similar situations near death.

exactly the continuous actualization of embodied consciousness. Of course, speaking of the function of religion on the individual level, I do not exclude other social functions of religion on the level of respective communities or society at large. In the following, the function of near-death experiences also entails intersubjective aspects, for example, accepting "experiencers" as religious virtuosi.

In principle, my deliberation departs from the assumption that the general religious function can be exemplified by different discursive strategies. As such, they exert basically the same effect in experiencers *and* their audience. Producers of reports were, as became obvious, often well aware of earlier reported experiences. Thus, any clear distinction between individuals as experiencers on the one hand, and individuals receiving those reports—as readers or as collectors—will not do justice to the complex polyvalence of both roles. For the audience, experiences near death have served as an "invitation to a holy life" in this "Atheistical generation" (Atherton, 1680)—for almost three centuries now. The experiencers themselves encourage a religious reading of their experiences, which, taken as a quality of the reports, can be termed with Davidsen (cf. 2016, 523) the "religious affordance" of near-death narratives, promoting their religious use. I previously argued that reports of near-death experiences encompass (a) ontological (Section 5.2.1), (b) epistemic (Section 5.2.2), (c) intersubjective (Section 5.2.3), and (d) moral significance (Section 5.2.4). I take this scheme as orientation here, even if certain aspects may not be so easily assigned to one category alone.

5.2.1 ONTOLOGICAL ASPECTS

In respect to ontology, a large number of reports, and especially of the collections of reports, invigorate the belief in a death-surviving soul or consciousness. It is important to notice that only rarely the reports of respective experiences have been addressed as "proof." Mostly, and parallel to the post-Kantian critique of metaphysics and the growing self-restriction of empirical science, experiencers and collectors of the late 19th and 20th centuries have spoken more cautiously of a "strong evidence"[4] for the soul's survival. However, some more emphatically Protestant, Mormon, or Gnostic–Esoteric protagonists expressed an unshakable conviction that the experiences disclose the ultimate nature of the indestructible soul or the existence of a supra-empirical "superconsciousness." This ontological belief is not only held to reduce the fear of death. There is, so it is argued in many reports, an innermost, indestructible nature in oneself and in others, even if this soul or consciousness is often not explicitly acknowledged in the everyday life world. More specifically, protagonists of religious near-death discourse voice the opinion that the respective experiences alter attitudes toward life, integrating "death" into life. In other words, experiences near death articulate a principal suspension

---

[4] For example, Myers 1903; Barrett 1918; 1926; Scott 1931, Osis 1961; Crookall 1961; Moody 1975, 1977.

of the distinction of life–death. If near-death experiences are defined as being located beyond "clinical death," an outspoken paradox surfaces: An irreversible death is reversible. Indeed, already titles of major book contributions bear witness to this paradox—Ritchie's *Return From Tomorrow*, Moody's *Life After Life*, Rawlings's *Beyond Death's Door*, Ring's *Life at Death*, Sabom's *Recollections of Death*, Grey's *Return From Death*, or, more recently, van Lommel's *Consciousness Beyond Life*. But what follows from this? If one grants the principal possibility of a paradoxical copresence of life–death in those experiences, each side of the dichotomy is no longer seen as mutually excluding. In consequence, it can be used as an epistemically legitimate designation within the other side: a reentry of "death" in life, and "life" in death. On the "life" sides of the primary distinction, adherents of a "holistic" near-death discourse can now speak of "death in life," for example, of a real presence of the unseen reality of "death" in life. To them, an integrated awareness of this invisible presence will weaken the irreconcilability of death and dying. Furthermore, the death-in-life side of the suspended mutual exclusion of life–death is obviously present in Spiritualist–Occult protagonists of near-death discourse elaborating on practices of "astral projection." It is an intentional and reversible separation of body and soul—in short, a nonpermanent death. In contrast, the life-in-death side serves as basis for the belief that an afterworld realm can be observed and experienced by an "animated" soul or consciousness. Somehow it still possesses "life." It is still animated in the sense of being endowed with sensory organs and a body. In sum, this paradoxical copresence of life and death allows adherents to speak—while living—on how it is like to be dead. In close interaction with this paradoxical copresence, an ontological implication of near-death experiences that deserves mention is the reversal of the hierarchical values of body, mind, and soul (or consciousness). More often than not, protagonists of near-death discourse concur in their criticism of the secularizing trend to place "body" over "mind" and "mind" over "the soul." This trend, criticized as materialist or reductionist, is obvious to them in how biomedicine favors treating illness in their bodily, physiological dimension, whereas treatment of the "mind" is secondary, and of the "soul" virtually inexistent in biomedicine. To these protagonists, therefore, medico-physiological and pharmacological explanations of experiences near death are particularly problematic. They are an outcome of a general attitude they wholeheartedly reject. In sum, we could hear among them prominent voices that either adhere to a "soul-over-mind-over-matter" hierarchy or favor a "holistic" approach.[5]

Another central function of the reports and experiences refers to the ontological dimension of dying. In the large majority of the reports, dying is described as peaceful, tranquil, and free from pain. The religious function of the narrative "it would have been

---

[5] The discourse on the soul, or consciousness unbound, is dialectically tied to the body. The articulation of experiences near death always includes references to the body or bodily states. For example, diagnostics of the "clinically dead body" are indispensable if experiences beyond brain-based consciousness are articulated.

a happy death" (Montaigne), that is, interestingly, by each generation celebrated as a new discovery, seems obvious: Emotionally, the external observation of other people's often seemingly distressful dying contributes to an overall depressing picture of dying and death. It inscribes itself into the abhorrence of terminal sicknesses, impairments, and painful diseases of elderly people, the loss of beloved ones, and so forth. Any evidence to the contrary that may dampen fears of stressful dying will be wholeheartedly embraced. As we saw, the inclusion of a retrospective statement on the peaceful nature of the experience of dying (if not, of being dead) is probably the most widespread element of reported experiences near death between 1580 and 1975. Although this feature figures in many reports as a description of individual dying, it becomes, especially in collections of reports (cf. Moody and Hampe), disconnected from individual experience and ushered in as an ontological quality of dying and being dead. Although memorization of negative emotions and distressful experiences may be overridden by positive emotions brought forth by the fact of having survived a death-threatening situation, it is a crucial discursive topos of the reports. Interestingly, the topos of an immense peacefulness has also been stressed by protagonists of Naturalist metaculture. In contrast, Christian reports up to the 19th century—at least within those traditions in which the existence of hell is emphasized—include very prominent episodes of "hell" or of a "purgatory." With receding intensity, these topoi are present in 20th-century accounts as well (cf. the testimony of Welch). The religious function of "hellish" visions is, I assume, predominantly of an ethical nature and is treated in Section 5.2.2. Interestingly, it was the evangelical Christian Maurice Rawlings who in 1978 emphasized for the first time in the post-Moodian era the existence of decidedly negative, hellish, and unpleasant near-death experiences (cf. Fox 2003, 44). Rawlings (1978, 88) even went so far as to argue that the feelings of ease and the vista of beautiful environments could represent "a deceivingly pleasant situation to imply security" in order to prevent a "desire or need for changed lives."

5.2.2 EPISTEMIC ASPECTS

Analyzing the epistemic aspects of the religious function of near-death experiences, I start by defining "epistemology" for the goal pursued here as justification of knowledge engrained in a discourse on the sources of knowledge (sense experience, memory, inference, etc.). Applied to the context of the reported experiences, I proceed by outlining how experiences near death are acknowledged as sources for justifying religious knowledge. In essence, the most prominent religious function in respect to the epistemological dimension is the *reassurance of the possibility of individual religious experience as such.* Looking at the structure of reports relevant here, I may describe them as entailing different frames. As previously seen, the usual "scripts," defined as a scheme that triggers in the recipient an imagined, typical sequence of events, encompass the following elements: (1) the description of an unprepared, "lay" individual (i.e., an individual not actively searching for

"religious experience") getting into a life-threatening situation; (2) the visionary reporting a memoir—combing almost always genre-typical with idiosyncratic elements[6];
(3) the claim that the experiences happened while being clinically dead—epistemolog-
ically justified by narrative anchoring mechanisms (e.g., testimonies of doctors, family,
and friends); (4) the claim that the experiences cannot be fully expressed in language;
(5) the return into the body; and (6) the subsequent change toward more spiritual or religious attitudes. This script—canonized in Moody's synthesized "core experience" (on
the subsequent change, cf. Moody 1977, 59)—serves the epistemic function to demonstrate that even in "secular" contexts the conditions for authentic religious experiences
are always and in principle present. Reports and collections of near-death experiences not
only aim to bring back religious legitimacy of the beliefs previously described. Equally,
it is the possibility and efficacy of religious experience itself that is reinstalled, while, at
the same time, grand narratives of religion in modernity are dismissed, for example, that
religious experience will be, in an age of enlightenment, science, and secularization, no
longer possible. The script reinforces this claim by outlining the suddenness and unex-
pectedness of the "experience." It appears, as said, to be an essential part of this script
that the individual had—by the time the experience occurs—not been intentionally engaged in an active search for such experiences, and, moreover, that the experience causally initiated subsequent changes in religious life orientation. General elements of these
claims are reensured in scholarly contributions as well. In their study on the relationship
between "Near-Death Experiences and Religion," Steven A. McLaughlin and H. Newton
Malony (1984, 151, 157) present—rhetorically, as it seems—the guiding hypothesis of their
study that "intrinsic religiosity" would result in "deeper" experiences. This hypothesis,
they said, had to be dropped. Instead, they found evidence for a different correlation,
reinforcing the religious script as previously defined: Near-death experiences are "as unlikely to happen" to those with religious beliefs as to those with no such beliefs. Leaning
toward the normative religious view that "conventional religion" should be replaced by
more personal spirituality and that people are in need of "conversion or reaffirmation of
belief," the authors tell themselves: "Perhaps the slightly religious person is just as much
in need of the near-death experience as one who is very religious"—assuming that such
experiences represent "a spiritual intervention" able to change "the lives of a very diverse
group of people" (157). Religious experience should best happen unexpectedly, suddenly,
and apart from habitual, conventional religious convictions. In effect, the authors affirm
the central narrative previously mentioned, namely, that religious belief does not influence
"the depth of the NDE," but that, transformed by the experience, persons tend "to become
more religious" (159). As said, this approach reappraises the famous account of religious

---

[6] "Pre-existing belief-systems," Bettina Schmidt (2016, 6) argues, decide, "whether specific elements (e.g., seeing
a light in a near-death experience) are regarded as important and will be narrated, or unimportant and soon
forgotten." Individual idiosyncrasies may, however, underscore the credibility of the account and are therefore
key elements of near-death narratives.

experience by William James, namely, that "true" religious or mystical experience, but also conversion and so forth, can be defined and acknowledged only by its "good fruits." Key is their quality of being a "total" reaction, a thorough "transformation," a change in ethical attitudes, and so forth. In his pragmatist view, it is the effect of the experience on people's lives that matters, and this to such an extent that the actual changes in life ensure the validity, if not the sheer existence, of the experiences themselves. Although this line of thought is surely tempting and has convincing aspects, caution is advisable, because, in many cases, the change in life is an essential part of the discourse—that is, more precisely, the final part of the near-death report.

In her cognitivist model of religious experience, Ann Taves makes use of a personal testimony of an out-of-body experience by William Barnard, included in the latter's book on *William James and the Philosophy of Mysticism* (1997). As a 13 year old, Barnard (1997, 127) reports, he was "obsessed with the idea of what would happen to me after my death," and, having attempted in vain throughout the day to visualize himself "as not existing," he returned from school, and, "walking on the hot pavement next to a stand of pine trees less than a block from my home, still brooding about what it would be like to die. Suddenly, without warning, something shifted inside. I felt lifted outside of myself" (127). And, in "that exhilarating and yet peaceful moment," he had a "direct and powerful experience" of not being only a schoolboy, but that he was "a surging, boundless state of consciousness" (128). Barnard, however, explains that he is aware of the difference between the "verbal narrative" and the "experience." As a child, he had "no words with which to make sense of this experience," having experienced only "incredibly boring" Sundays in church. Much later, after practicing meditation and "studying Eastern philosophical scriptures," he could give this experience—as such a powerful, "transformative, moment"—a "viable interpretative structure" (128). Although I may note in passing that the clear description of the setting of the experience serves as a narrative "anchoring mechanism" here, this whole description of a scholar–practitioner poses unsolvable problems if directly transformed into an etic description, as it seemingly happens in Taves's discussion of the case. Adopting Barnard's perspective, Taves (2009, 98; cf. 9) argues, against the constructivist view, that the experience somehow will persist as the "same," parallel to a "thing deemed religious," and will only later—in an "attributional process"—achieve a new characterization. In consequence, she rests her argument on a solid neurophysiological basis of the "boundless state of consciousness" and out-of-body experiences, respectively. Somewhat perplexing to me, there is an "experience"—reified and taken for granted—that may be studied beyond the first-person narrative (cf. 68–71). But how can such a memoir of an experience as the one narrated by Barnard be studied physiologically? Taves suggests the study of "experiences deemed religious"—that people mark as "special" and "nonordinary" (14), and to which they "attribute" a causal relation of being meaningful (cf. 9–11, 90–118) without, however, to engage more closely with the fact that we "have" the experience only through the narrative. Barnard's—or any other's—memoir cannot be assumed to be a definite, objective description, but is liable to continuous revision. Imagine for the moment that the individual, at a later point in life attracted to psychoanalysis, uncovers a traumatic abuse that would now be held responsible for the "mystic" experience. Suddenly, it can transform into nothing less than an escapist denial of reality. In sum, Taves's theory of "attribution" and "ascription" implies that there are somehow fixed *experiences* to which certain qualities can be ascribed. However, as previously argued, the experience and its evaluation—a process of continuous reattributions and reascriptions—cannot be disentangled. Even if tried hard, the predisposed consciousness and its expectations cannot be subtracted from experience, nor can be its later (often permanent) reframing, by which the experience at hand changes, too. For that matter, an "event-cognition" model of "real-time" religious experience (cf. Asprem and Taves, 2017, 6–7) may not be the key for identifying the processes by which religious meaning is bestowed on experiences near death.

The assumed reactions in the aftermath of experiences near death are, however, an integral part of the individual's narrative and self-estimation. It is, as I argued with current narrative approaches, a "veracity mechanism" (Davidsen). It was already Moody who argued with subsequent changes in life, but most prominently, the legacy of Ring in his *Heading Towards Omega*, who saw in the aftereffects the key to their meaning. Gary Groth-Marnat and Roger Summers (cf. 1998, 114–19) published an important study on the surmised change in beliefs, attitudes, and behaviors following the respective experiences. They compared subjects with and without near-death experiences in life-threatening incidents, but included, for the first time, the testimonies of "significant others"—family, spouses—who had been requested to rate the types and intensity of changes that they had observed in the "experiencers." The study could provide evidence that, in comparison with individuals who had life-threatening experiences only, near-death experiencers scored higher in regard to strengthened afterlife beliefs, reduced fear of death, greater concern for others, and "greater transcendental feelings"—in both groups corroborated by the testimony of their peers. However, it could not find significant differences from the "non-NDE" control group in regard to changes in "traditional religious beliefs," nor in "reduced support for organized religion" (119). Moreover, in the "non-NDE" group, the life-threatening event had also considerable effects toward an increase of "religiosity," or experiences of "transcendence."[7] In sum, the "significant others" were largely in agreement with the experiencer's self-descriptions. Yet there was, the authors remark, a prominent exception. Although the experiencers rated themselves as

---

[7] Astonishingly, Groth-Marnat and Summers (1998, 119–20) summarize their result that "the extent of changes found among NDErs was consistently and significantly greater," so that being exposed to a life-threatening situation "is not the major reason why persons change following an NDE." Yet, in respect to the postincident item "religiosity" the difference of 11.6 (NDE), and 10.8 (non-NDE) on the "Life Changes Questionnaire" is less significant, whereas in the items of "transcendence" (25.1 versus 19.8) or [decrease of] "materialism" (6.3 versus 11.4), changes are more prominent. In any case, qualitative interviews, especially with significant others, would be a more revealing method to substantiate the results.

"having far greater transcendent experiences (greater purpose in life, self-understanding, inner meaning), this was not substantiated by the significant others in their lives" (cf. 120). The authors reason that this might be an outcome of the difficulty in assessing other persons' subjective experiences. This is plausible. Yet the outcome may also point to the fact that at least some experiencers did not communicate their "transcendental experiences." However, I am in general somewhat skeptical if the "significant others" can be taken as "informed controls," as Marsh holds (2010, 251), as the names of the significant others had been provided by the experiencers, and the researches had responded by sending the questionnaires to them, without further surveillance of the situation in which these questionnaires were answered. "Experiencers" will usually provide names of others by whom they feel "understood," which means that, more likely than not, these others will confer with their self-descriptions.

In any case, the postincidental interpretation of the experience as highly meaningful—relying, for the most part, solely on the experiencers' testimonies—is a crucial part of the narrative framing. It is impossible to distinguish between the experience itself, as reported in the memoir, and the postexperiential interpretations of the respective individuals. The "transformations," which are reported as an outcome, are by themselves tied to expectations, and as such influenced by former accounts. I may follow Wayne Proudfoot (1985, 123) here, arguing convincingly that "the logic" that governs the concepts by which people "interpret their experiences in different traditions shapes those experiences." Any attempt, he says, "to differentiate a core from its interpretations, then, results in the loss of the very experience one is trying to analyze. [. . .] The interpretations are themselves constitutive of the experiences." Therefore, speaking of a core experience or evaluating the depth of the experience is intricately linked to metaphors of "centrality," which, more often than not, are based on the experiencer's memoir that has been formed exactly *parallel* to changes in life orientation that took place.

As previously mentioned, reports of near-death experiences combine ubiquitous elements with idiosyncratic or culturally specific elements. It is crucial to note that both of these elements have their own epistemic functions. To declare that there is a universal, common core, or that there *is* direct, unmediated experience, yet, in the form of "interconnected universal, individual, and cultural layers" (Shushan 2016, 79), construes a core experience—a quality that we could not find in the reports. Still, a strong current within modern near-death discourse does not see the plurality of afterlife imagery or the existence of idiosyncratic elements as discouraging facts. On the contrary, it renders the reports into even more trustworthy accounts. This enactment of the reports could make use of the philosophical and psychological theory of "projection" as a mental mechanism in which the individual attributes his or her own thoughts, desires, and so forth, to the external world. In this respect, the moral "projection theory" of the *Tibetan Book of the Dead*—that the dying will experience the afterlife realm according to his or her individual karmic predispositions—could connect to earlier observations that religious diversity of afterlife imagery will depend on encultured expectations (e.g., Splittgerber

1866). Moreover, the occult and spiritualist strands experimenting with willed astral projections (training the "siddhis" of Indian yogins in a Western world of "Will Power," cf. Albanese 2007, 366) had a considerable influence on the epistemological primacy of near-death reports. In astral projections, the mind was trained in experiences out of the body that were structurally similar to experiences near death. In this metaculture, the religious function of the reports was obviously to set the soteriological goals for training— or, to make the astral projection a meaningful device that will, if mastered, play out its existential potential at the moment of death. In the Gnostic–Esoteric metaculture, the epistemic worth of experiences near death is even stronger.[8]

In addition to the moral interpretation of the life review, which is discussed in a moment, we could observe that it rendered credibility to the spirit's ability of a total recall, a full copresence of all occurrences in life—a view held by Jung-Stilling, Coleridge, du Prel, Blavatsky, and many others. Turned epistemically, the disembodied mind will at the moment of death gain full awareness of all minute details of his entire life. Therefore, it was seen as scientific evidence for the theory that the mind, in essence, never forgets a single conscious event. Dealing with a report of nearly drowning, Tuttle (1864, 63) holds that all occurrences may be "dimmed on memory's tablet, but never effaced, and the proper conditions will awake them fresh as the occurrences of the hour." Cross-fertilized by reports of cognate drug experiences, the life review and its characteristics (rapidity, mental clarity, long-lost memories as if experienced again, etc.) could now assume a new function, namely, to make plausible other paranormal claims of clairvoyance, communicating spirits, and so forth. The enhanced mental awareness in the state of "magnetic sleep" could especially be evidenced by the life review (cf. De Morgan 1863). The same function has the, in those circles, well-received narrative of a great composer's capabilities to "hear" a whole symphony "all at once" and to note it down later in an arduous process, and so forth. A special enactment of the life review for spiritualist and occult purposes, which connects to similar claims of Christian deathbed visions, is the reporting of life reviews near death in which the individual could passively retrieve lost memories or actively regain blocked memories (cf. the reports in Clark 1864; Féré 1889). A characteristic development of Western religious traditions in general, we could see how the moral interpretation of human consciousness recedes. To be confronted—in the life review, but finally in the "beyond"—with

---

[8] Surely, as Hammer (2004, 347) reminds us, the epistemic worth must always be defined in respect to background assumptions. Yet, he argues for "a sociocognitive model" that denies "the existence of religious experiences *per se*," because the experiencer tends to "adopt the culturally accepted definition of the experience if the person or group who proffers this definition is seen as authoritative." However, in concluding that "religious experience" has "little or no epistemological value, since experience and its interpretation is crucially dependent on the worldview espoused by one's reference group," he draws a problematic conclusion. Perplexingly, "religious experience" is taken for granted and, at the same time, disputed in its existence. Second, epistemic value in nonreligious discourse is in exactly the same way dependent on models of justification accepted in respective "reference groups."

one's horrid moral failures develops into a more neutral, and sometimes even optimistic, description of the "higher spiritual capacities" of the soul in Occult and Esoteric religiosity. Spokespersons of Theosophy, such as Blavatsky, Sinnett, or Yogi Ramacharaka, followed, as mentioned, the trajectory that the phenomenon attests to the perfect lucidity of the human mind. The individual should even be curious and eager to experience such a mental state—intentionally in mesmerist practice, being "forced" near death, or in death proper. In this state, the departing soul, Ramacharaka (1905, 212) argued, will discover "the reason of many things," and will see "what it all means." In the same vein, it has been made use of in substantiating the "transmission theory," namely, the idea emerging in Schiller (1891) and James (1898), that it is actually the organic restriction of the human brain that, in its filter function, is usually not capable of receiving more of a larger, "transindividual" consciousness—with the significant exemption of the life review. In sum, the life review as experienced near death or in drug use serves in the more recent religious discourse of the 1820s to the 1970s as a blueprint for mystical states—though less prominent than the spiritual practices of projecting the disembodied consciousness in other spheres justified with reference to the occurrence of "nonintentional" out-of-body experiences. Timothy Leary, reporting his life review triggered by his ingestion of psychedelic mushrooms, disclosed that he went back even to being a "one-celled organism" (Kobler 1963, 32), and Lilly (1975, 25), equally abstaining from any moral evaluation, described his experience as an "*immediate perception of the past, present, and future as if in the present moment.*"

These qualities—that the soul or consciousness will in situations near death develop higher spiritual and cognitive faculties, an unlimited awareness of objective reality, an all-encompassing memory, clairvoyance, or other telepathic powers—can be described with James's "noetic quality" of "mystical" experience. To those who experience them, they are "states of knowledge," "illuminations, revelations, full of significance and importance" (James 1922, 371; cf. Proudfoot 1985, 136–7). The religious function of this epistemology is obvious. However, it would be too narrow to focus on the "mystical" quality of these episodes only. James repeatedly stressed that as a rule these states "carry with them a curious sense of authority for after-time" (380). In addition to more encompassing experiences and reported subsequent changes in life orientation as previously discussed, it adduces further evidence on how spiritualist and occult reports in particular speak of a certain individual's higher cognitive capacities or paranormal "sensitivities" (e.g., to "see" deceased souls, or to perceive another individual's death in distant places) that surfaced for the first time in an experience near death, but were, as the reports narrate, retained in the aftermath.

5.2.3 INTERSUBJECTIVE ASPECTS

In regard to intersubjective aspects of the religious function of near-death narratives, I may distinguish two sides—intersubjective aspects within the memoir and the relationship of "experiencers" to their peers. The first aspect encompasses how they met "guides," communicated (often beyond words) with God, Jesus, angels, and other deceased, or were able to communicate with the living while being in the "otherworld." The second aspect becomes relevant in experiencers who either possess or assume through their reports an "expert status" of religious virtuosi.

Starting with the content side of the memoirs, I want to highlight the special function of "guides" in religious discourse. An escorting guide was an important element of travels into the otherworld in Antiquity and the Middle Ages. The guide, Zaleski (1987, 53) argues, is "at once an archetype, or universal motif, and a theme with a specific literary history," serving in medieval texts the function of an "instructor, protector and soul-taker." In these earlier texts, the guide explains heaven, hell, or purgatorial torments, conveys messages of God, or defends the soul approaching final judgment. Authoritative figures in experiences near death offer direct insights into how in the afterlife salvation will (finally) be achieved or punishment enacted. However, the guide may disappear while the "soul" still wanders in the otherworld. In literary terms, with the appearance of the guide the narrative assumes the form of a dialogue. Before I discuss the function of the guide in our reports more thoroughly, it should be noted that the guide still figures in some modern reports, but less often. Significantly, in a report of an intentional out-of-body experience belonging to the Spiritualist–Occult tradition, we could see a guide appearing who, like a meditation or yoga teacher, commands first to stop and, after the experience, to continue breathing (Fischer 1914, 7, 17). On the other hand, we could note a modern guide in one of Moody's reports, who, knowledgeable of processes of clinical treatment, appeases the patient's disembodied soul by instructing it how the operation, the transfer into the wake-up room, and so forth, will take place. The different states in hell are, in contrast, in the majority of more modern reports no longer part of the guided tour. Although the topography and the challenges of the otherworld explained by the guide obviously underwent changes, the function of the guide in more modern accounts is structurally analogous. Certain "evidence mechanisms" that appear in near-death discourse, such as the guide or the announcement of "having not been religiously interested before the incident," or claiming epistemic innocence by declaring "not having heard before of such experiences," are stable characteristics handed down as indispensable parts of the narrative frames and the memoirs. Of the religious functions of the reported guides, the most obvious is the nourished hope that there is (and will be) a protector and instructor, a dialogue partner, to whom the disembodied soul or consciousness may, in this precarious situation, address questions. The topos of a guide in the otherworldly realm reflects also the existence of guides in the life world. As Proudfoot (cf. 1985, 147) reminds us, guides (be it a spiritual authority, guru, or religious teacher) have an important social role in religious traditions for the preparation of, for example, mystical experience. In addition, the recipient of near-death narratives is invited to identify with the experiencer and to take the instructions given to the experiencer in the same breath as meaningful to himself or herself. The figure of the guide therefore is essential for enabling the process.

Surely, the guide being an inhabitant of the otherworld, the question of how it is possible that the guide and the disembodied consciousness speak the same language arises almost immediately. Several reports add that communication, or understanding on the side of the consciousness, has been without words or verbal articulation. The guide—or an angel, or Jesus—activates, in that respect, a complex network of expectations. From a narratological point of view, dialogues with the guide—and also with other beings such as the deceased, angels, Jesus, God, or a "being of light"—break through the monotony of a homogeneous first-person narration of the disembodied consciousness (that is in principle an entity difficult to imagine). It helps to reassure us that the otherworldly environment is a social world. As such, it can be much easier conceived of by the recipient. In consequence, the reader is invited to follow a literary account that comprises more than just a "thus have I seen." I may follow here Markus Davidsen's apt remarks on how literary accounts make use of "veracity mechanisms." These comprise, on the one hand, "evidence mechanisms" that present "the supernatural as evidently real within the story-world," and "anchoring mechanisms," that "link the story-world to the real world" (Davidsen 2016, 524). Described from this perspective, the guide (and, in certain cases, formerly deceased inhabitants, angels, Jesus, or God) represents an evidence mechanism, more specifically, what Davidsen terms "teacher discourse." It rests "on the trustworthiness of authoritative characters' claims about the reality of the supernatural." This mechanism, he holds, "comes into play when authoritative teacher figures instruct less knowledgeable characters—with whom the reader is invited to identify—about supernatural matters" (532). In that way, the recipient of near-death reports will identify with the experiencer's soul or consciousness so that all the instructions the latter receives by "teachers" will be considered as equally meaningful by the recipient.[9] The teacher discourse aims to present postmortal, supernatural encounters as a discourse with "real beings" and, which is more, the latter will become potential interaction partners of the experiencers and their audience alike—granted that the recipient concludes that the respective report(s) convey(s) information not only on what it will be like to die, but to be dead. In sum, the religious function of this narrative structure is, again, an evocative undertaking. It converges with religious expectations—drawn from written sources or oral admonition—and life-world experiences. By that, it adapts to the widespread social experience in religious communities of being instructed on religious matters by teachers, be they parents or professionals, and to perceive them as protectors (or, in the Occult and Esoteric traditions, as "spiritually

---

[9] Davidsen (2016, 528) argues that religious narratives "tell of human interaction with supernatural agents and invite their audiences to participate in the interaction with these supernatural agents in their own world." Yet, although specimens of religious narratives, religious near-death experiences cannot offer for obvious reasons a straightforward "invitation" to expose oneself to a situation near death, but offer a more modest affordance to take the visionary content of the report seriously. In addition, I should remark that the definition of religion as interaction with supernatural agents (524–5) is, in general, to narrow, as it excludes, e.g., practices of self-cultivation such as astral projection or enactments of the life review as an encounter with a higher reality—not to mention the social reality of religion.

advanced"). Guides in this life and the beyond are, to a certain extent, experts of the respective afterlife. The evidence mechanism of teacher discourse may thus lead to a second important aspect of the religious functions of near-death narratives, namely, the question of religious authority. In his extensive study of the epistemic strategies from Theosophy to the New Age, Olav Hammer (2004, 333) investigates how narratives of experience in these traditions portray the source and the recipient of "privileged insights," thereby aiming "to confer validity to the message and expert status on the experiencer." According to his deliberations, the reference to experience in Theosophy and other Occult and Esoteric traditions is "basically privileged experience, an access to higher wisdom possessed by the select few," and it is only "within the latest generation of Esoteric thought" that personal experience has "risen to the fore as a major discursive strategy—perhaps *the* major discursive strategy" (339). The narratives of experiences near death, however, show, in respect to "privileged insights," important differences. Although we must keep in mind that only a very small minority of individuals report of special experiences near death, it is nevertheless the contingent fear-of-death and near-death situations from which they are held to emerge. Those situations present themselves as a form of radical "democratization." As the proverb has it, death is the great leveler. Essentially, the reporting individuals are mostly not religious specialists *before* their experience. In fact, and almost necessarily, experiencers from around 1850 onward, but even earlier in Christian accounts of deathbed conversions, explicitly aim to avoid the impression of being religious specialists, or even being religious at all. Of course, this observation pertains to testimonies of self-ascription only. In several cases, there is conclusive evidence that the reporting individual was actually moved by matters religious and spiritual long before the near-death situation occurred. However, it would be wrong to assume that situations near death cannot be "trained" or simulated (as, we may say, in "Golden [Gate] jumps") and entail, accordingly, only revelatory insights for the "gifted," "privileged few." It became obvious how drug experiences, sensory deprivation, mediumistic states, or intentional astral travels—all, in certain respects, repeatable and susceptible of training—shared important discursive topoi with near-death memoirs. Moreover, in several instances drug experiences were reported *as* experiences near death. Therefore, and in contrast to Hammer's conclusion, the religious discourse of experiences near death does not converge with the view that only "small elites of initiates" (Marco Pasi) are capable to receive revelatory insights. Additional evidence for the "democratized" religious knowledge, encapsulated in near-death memoirs, can be seen in the overwhelming majority of lay persons who articulated such experiences in the 19th and 20th centuries—often begrudgingly noticed by religious specialists. Finally, a considerable number of women reported their experiences, among others Lydia Child, Frances Cobbe, Helena P. Blavatsky, Emily L. Fischer, Leslie G. Scott, and Gladys O. Leonard. Especially in the context of Spiritualism and Occultism (cf. Owen, 2004a; Albanese 2007, 237–44), women could claim religious authority as authors and interpreters of their own experiences (near death).

5.2.4 MORAL ASPECTS

Finally, I turn to the moral significance of the respective experiences. Obviously, a religious function can be identified in reports in which the disembodied consciousness witnesses a postmortal judgment of others. I may call this an acquisition of strategic knowledge, for example, if Thomas Say (1796) and various others within our corpus claim of having witnessed the moral fate of recently deceased. Even if uttered on the deathbed, such strategic knowledge will certainly have tremendous effects on the community of believers and bestow also retroactively plausibility on everything else that has been said by the respective individual—for example, in Say's case, a Quaker minister, on his moral admonitions. Of moral significance are also reports in which the individual reports of having achieved a higher insight into the moral law of retribution as such (e.g., Scott 1931), and, surely, also reports in which the experiencer encountered Jesus, heard a voice, or is instructed without words of the ultimate moral significance—or insignificance—of the life lived. The religious function of the survivor returning with the question "What did you do with your time on earth?," such as George Ritchie, needs no further elaboration. A telling case is the moral interpretation of the life review. Applying the "death-x-pulse" as hermeneutics sheds light on the intimate connection that the life review entertains with the idea of a postmortem judgment—even though the return into life will turn the judgment somehow into a preview, or an anticipated final judgment. In general, we could note the topos of a judgment, in which sins committed throughout a lifetime are read from a "register" or a "book of deeds," and that these long-forgotten sins are revived and remembered as if committed at the same moment (cf. Schwerdtfeger's report, 1734). As Hans Blumenberg (1981, 25–31) could demonstrate, the concept of a plurality of "books of deeds," heavenly accounts of each and every deed of each and every person, has been prominently conceptualized by St. Augustine. The latter attempted to harmonize the biblical accounts of, on the one hand, a single "book of life" (in which the names of the chosen are registered), and, on the other, the heavenly book that encompasses the total history of the world. Given that the death-x-pulse will in certain cases trigger the memory of autobiographical images, these will, in accordance with normative Christian expectations, be interpreted as moral or immoral deeds, pinned down and read from the register. As a cognitive metaphor, the register of deeds turns the maximally counterintuitive idea of an omniscient being, capable of remembering the deeds of each and every individual, into the cognitive optimum of a minimally counterintuitive idea: Now, for every individual there is a single heavenly register that had been continuously actualized. In the course of the 18th century, we can, however, witness a decisive change. Whereas in more devoted Christian deathbed visions a judgment scene is elaborately depicted, we could see in accounts of this period, for example in Binns (1842) or in Beaufort (1847), that Christian imagery of judgment is either reduced to more implicit mention (Binn's "volume of existence"), or it is only the ethical quality of the deeds that is seen and experienced as if for the first time. Interestingly, Beaufort adds that he could even reflect on the "causes" and "consequences" of right and wrong deeds. Rarely, a "hedonist" evaluation overrules the dominant moral interpretation (e.g., that the drowning "lives in an instant through all his happy and unhappy past," Eliot 1858, 151). Other reports, overflowing with gratitude, describe that the life review revealed to them all the beauty and love that they experienced (cf. the report in Heim, 1892). Nevertheless, first and foremost, there is the ethical stance engrained in the judgmental life review. As Kellehear argues, Christianity, but also other historic religions, links death with conscience, so that, Kellehear (1996, 38) notes, it is "little wonder that some kind of life review takes place in near-death circumstances." Surely, in Christian metaculture, an ethical conception of conscience prevails—a conscience that should be constantly aware of sinfulness or of the danger of transgressing the will of God. So it cannot astonish us that in early modern near-death discourse, the feature of the "book of deeds" being the basis of postmortem judgment is still a prominent feature, but assumes slowly—and parallel with the emergence of new, more soberly autobiographical accounts of experiences near death—the form of a life review without the corollary of a "judgment scene."[10] In that respect, life reviews that report a totality of each and every single deed are still within the sway of moral evaluation. Michael Marsh (2010, 156; cf. 86–8), in his attempt to explain that the life review belongs to the late phase of an experience near death, and "betokens the imminent return of consciousness," concludes that the phenomenon demonstrates "the return to earth, and the pressing need to shoulder one's responsibilities to family and workplace again" (211). Marsh, following the footsteps of Moody in reading the "life review and judgment" as correlated components, holds that it is, in the few people in which it occurs, "not a paradigmatic depiction of any realistic Christian eschatology" (211). This, of course, is not our matter to decide here. It may suffice to mention that the moral evaluation of the individual's life is a central element of Christian metaculture and as such visible in a number of near-death reports. Its centrality emerges from the fact that the "book" of *all* deeds is a perfect metaphor for a *totality of what can be experienced*. So the account of a person's biography as a heavenly "book" is a metaphor for experience as a whole. Therefore, it may not astonish us that this metaphor survives in historical circumstances in which the belief of postmortem retribution crumbles. Rephrasing H.-G. Gadamer's hermeneutic device, "being that can be understood is language," we may say this: A morally evaluated life that can be understood, is a register book of relevant deeds and their consequences.

The religious function, in this case, can also be seen in the expectation raised that at the moment of death, the recipient of such memoirs will expect that the same will happen to her or him. Although the life review has also been part of naturalist reports

---

[10] This may not exclude that the book of deeds vision itself had been conceptualized in Jewish and early Christian tradition by some individuals experiencing a death-x-pulse-triggered life review. Yet, this is a matter of speculation and cannot be substantiated, as early accounts are reigned by hagiographical and not biographical intentions.

and attracted considerable attention by naturalist psychologists, it is deeply engrained in Western conscience to evaluate one's life in moral terms. Furthermore, a predominant religious function of experiences near death has been the reinforcement, or even, as it has been reported, the "discovery" of the ethics of love and being loved, an increased concern for others, or empathy.[11] Actually, it may not astonish us that many—and especially religiously receptive—survivors of such experiences will be more aware of the precarious status of life—of their own, and that of significant others. We may assume that to express concern for others will be as important as gratefulness for having survived. "Religion," Nietzsche holds, "can be a form of thankfulness [*Dankbarkeit*]." One is simply thankful for (still) being alive, and it is for directing the gratitude to some higher instance, Nietzsche continues, "that one needs a God" (Nietzsche [1888] 1980, KSA 6, 182 [my trans.]).[12]

In general, the moral significance of experiences near death subscribes to an "ethics of listening"—for example, listening to the dying. In addition, awareness is raised that individuals in precarious situations near death, for example, in intensive care, may, on their part, still hear what others say. The ethics of listening expand also to individuals expressing their message after their return from the brink of death. An important element here has been the reported "self-censure" or "anticipated rejection" that we could see occasionally expressed in reports of the 19th century, but more frequently in reports of the 20th century. In Moody's first account, for example, there are eight responses in which the individuals said that they had negative experiences while reporting their experiences to peers, doctors, or the family, and had decided to remain silent. According to Moody ([1975] 1976, 85, cf. 84–8), they had realized "that our contemporary society is just not the sort of environment in which reports of this nature would be received with sympathy and understanding." Kellehear (1996, 64), indeed, rightly pointed out that to conclude from these cases that community reaction "is poor or unreceptive is premature." We should now go a step further. Surely a significant number of theologians of the dominant traditions were, and probably are, unreceptive in respect to religious near-death visions, if uncompromisingly offered as revelatory experiences (cf., for example, Küng's, or, more recently, Marsh's theological response). Equally, in professional settings, the majority of medical doctors might not be too willing to accept narratives of experiences straight from "the beyond." Yet reactions will vary according to the religious background assumptions of the recipients and especially in the case of significant others, though I assume that these are often in convergence. Nevertheless, "not telling others," or an often long-kept silence on the experience, fulfills again the function of a "veracity mechanism," and will grant even more plausibility because, in these cases, the individuals frame their memoirs as undisclosed "secrets." In other cases, protagonists of near-death

---

[11] Cf. the studies summarized in Groth-Marnat and Summers 1998, 111–12.

[12] One may refer to James's "grace" as a mystical experience of "union" here (see, e.g., James 1922, 260, 425, 467).

experiences are more convinced of the broader moral significance. As previously noted, in several instances experiencers were more communicative, holding to the missionary maxim "What thou seest, write in a book," and disseminate it (Revelation 1:8).

Having surveyed the religious function in its ontological, epistemic, intersubjective, and moral aspects that figure in the discourse of experiences near death, I may add a final remark. As it seems, the script of near-death experiences does not only affirm the concept of religious experience, but builds on an even more encompassing meaning of experience as transformative by surviving existential danger, a risky situation, or passing a test. The Latin (and Greek) origin, *ex-periri* ["to try," "to test"] (cf. *experimentum*),[13] with its radical *periri* ["to risk," "to cross through danger"] (cf. *periculum*, "peril"), is, significantly, mirrored also in German *Erfahrung*, etymologically from *Gefahr* [danger], Old High German *fara*, and so forth (see Lacoue-Labarthe 1999, 128). In Greek philosophy, medieval theology, and the modern configuration of science alike, experience stands in contrast to what can be learned from scripture(s). In Natural Theology, for example, evidence of experience has been set against the authoritatively proclaimed secondhand reports and the *verbum divinum* alike. Puritan theologians in early modern England especially coined the term "experimental religion," setting experimental and experiential knowledge against speculative theology.[14] Being aware of its etymology[15] may uncover one prominent meaning of experience that connects to being exposed to nonordinary situations such as traveling in unfamiliar, foreign regions; being in imminent danger; or being "tested," "having doubts," and so forth. In short, individuals learn of God's "wrath" and "mercy" exactly "through experience."[16] This is being reflected in theology too. Luther, for example, voiced in 1531 his opinion that "only experience will make a theologian."[17] I am not able here to demonstrate how prominent attempts to place experience in the center of religion (e.g., by Schleiermacher, James, Otto, or Smart) continue this earlier strand of conceptualizing experience. It may suffice to point to James who privileges "sudden" experiences, and especially those made alone in remote, solitary

---

[13] Bishop John Wilkins (1614–1672) argues in his *Principles and Duties of Natural Religion* (cf. 1675, 389–90) on the state of the blessed after death that there is only one way to know: to verify this empirically. In this spirit, he declared on his deathbed that he was "ready for the Great Experiment' " (Calloway 2014, 93 [communicated by John Brooke, Dec. 14, 1672]). "Experimentum," Harrison (cf. 2011, 413) reminds us, denotes in early modern literature often simply "experience."

[14] Cf. Harrison 2011 on the role of one's own experience as a legitimate source of knowledge besides the "word of God," or "rational deduction"; cf. also Calloway 2014, 60–63, 83.

[15] The cognate Greek terms, for example as they are used in the New Testament, e.g. *peirazō* (πειράζω), to "test," to "try," to "put to the proof," or *peira* (πεῖρα), designating an "attempt," "experience" or "to learn/know by experience" (cf. Thayer 1995, s.v.), show essentially the same spectrum of meanings.

[16] This is, however, only one strand of premodern use of experience, in contrast to "every day," "mystical," or "experimental" experience in the evolving natural sciences (cf. Harrison 2011).

[17] "Sola [. . .] experientia facit theologum," quoted in Ebeling 1975, 10. Ebeling (see 1975, 12) explains that Luther understood experience as not being in contrast to *sola scriptura*, but as an important element of securing the latter.

places. He argues that those searching first-hand individual experiences are, "for a time at least," driven "into the wilderness, often into the literal wilderness out of doors, where the Buddha, Jesus, Mohammed, St. Francis, George Fox, and so many others had to go" (James 1922, 328). This "bias toward sudden, individual experience" (Taves 2009, 5) in the conceptualization of religious experience is indeed perfectly matched within religious discourse on near-death experiences—especially if we regard those individuals who reported of respective experiences having actually survived a life-threatening danger, for example by being successfully reanimated. Against this backdrop, near-death experiences are religious experiences par excellence.

BIBLIOGRAPHY

Abraham a Sancta Clara. 1710. [. . .] *Todten-Capelle, Oder Allgemeiner Todten-Spiegel, Darinnen Alle Menschen, wes Standes sie sind, sich beschauen, an denen mannigfaltigen Sinn-reichen Gemählden das Memento Mori zu studiren.* Nuremberg, Germany: Christoph Weigel.

Albanese, Catherine L. 2007. *A Republic of Mind and Spirit. A Cultural History of American Metaphysical Religion.* New Haven, CT & London: Yale University Press.

Alexander, Eben. (2012) 2013. *Proof of Heaven: A Neurosurgeon's Journey into the Afterlife.* Waterville, ME: Thorndike Press.

Alvarado, Carlos S. 2003. "The Concept of Survival of Bodily Death and the Development of Parapsychology." *Journal of the Society for Psychical Research* 76 (2): 65–95.

Alvarado, Carlos S. 2005. "Ernesto Bozzano on the Phenomena of Bilocation." *Journal of Near-Death Studies* 23 (4): 207–38.

Alvarado, Carlos S. 2011. "Panoramic Memory, Affect, and Sensations of Detachment in the Dying: Discussions Published in France, 1889–1903." *Journal of Near-Death Studies* 30 (2): 65–82.

Alvarado, Carlos. 2012. "Explorations of the Features of Out-of-Body Experiences. An Overview and Critique of the Work of Robert Crookall." *Journal of the Society for Psychical Research* 76 (2): 65–82.

Amiel, Henri-Frédéric. (1882) 1903. *Amiel's Journal. The Journal Intime of Henri-Frédéric Amiel.* Translated by Humphrey Ward. New York & London: Macmillan.

Anonymous. 1884. [Answers by the Editors.] *The Theosophist. A Monthly Journal Devoted to Oriental Philosophy, Art, Literature and Occultism* 5 (12): 301.

Anonymous. 1714. *Levens-Loop van Hemme Hayen, op begeeren van eenige Vrinden door hem verhaalt, en door de zelven aldus opgeschreeven*, den 10 Mey, Ao. 1689. Haarlem. German translation: 1810. *Lebensgeschichte des Hemme Hayen*. Nuremberg, Germany: Steinische Buchhandlung.

Anonymous. 1847. *The book of visions. Being a transcript of the record of the secret thoughts of a variety of individuals while attending church* [...]: *Also, instances of the separation of the soul from the body— one individual being justified by faith and the other condemned* [...]. Philadelphia: J. W. Moore.

Anonymous [Beecher, Henry, et al.] 1968. Report of the Ad Hoc Committee at Harvard Medical School to Examine the Definition of Brain Death. "A definition of irreversible coma." *Journal of the American Medical Association* 205: 337–40.

Ariès, Philippe. 1977. *L'Homme devant la mort*. Paris: Seuil.

Ariès, Philippe. 1981. *The Hour of Our Death*. Translated by Helen Weaver. New York: Knopf.

Asai A., Y. Kadooka, and K. Aizawa. 2012. "Arguments Against Promoting Organ Transplants From Brain-Dead Donors, and Views of Contemporary Japanese on Life and Death." *Bioethics* 26(4): 215–23.

Asprem, Egil, and Ann Taves. 2017. "Experience as Event: Event Cognition and the Study of (Religious) Experiences." *Religion, Brain, & Behaviour*, 7 (1): 43–62.

Atherton, Henry M. D. 1680. *The Resurrection Proved: Or, the Life to Come Demonstrated*. London: T. Dawks.

Atkinson, William W. 1908. *The Inner Consciousness. A Course of Lessons*. Chicago: Advanced Thought Publishing, Masonic Temple.

Audette, John R. 1979. "Denver Cardiologist Discloses Findings After 18 Years of Near- Death Research." *Anabiosis: The Journal for Near-Death Studies* 1: 1–2.

Audette, John R. 1982. "Historical Perspectives on Near-Death Episodes and Experiences." In *A Collection of Near-Death Research Readings,* edited by Craig R. Lundahl, 21–34. Chicago: Nelson Hall.

Bagheri, A. 2007. "Individual Choice in the Definition of Death." *Journal of Medical Ethics* 33 (3): 146–9.

Baier, Karl. 2009. *Mediation und Moderne*. 2 vols. Würzburg, Germany: Königshausen und Neumann.

Baier, Karl. Forthcoming. "High Mysticism." In *Constructions of Mysticism as a Universal. Roots and Interactions Across the Borders*, edited by Annette Wilke. Wiesbaden: Harrassowitz.

Bailey, Lee W. 2001. "A 'Little Death': The Near-Death Experience and Tibetan Delogs." *Journal of Near-Death Studies* 19 (3): 139–59.

Baird, Alexander T. 1944. *One Hundred Cases for Survival After Death*. New York: Bernard Ackerman.

Baird, Alexander T. 1948. "'Out-of-the-Body' Experience." *Journal of the Society for Psychical Research* 34 (644-645): 206–11.

Baker, James. 1954. *The Exteriorization of the Mental Body. A Scientific Interpretation of the Out-of-the-Body Experience Known as Pneumakinesis*. New York: The William-Frederick Press.

Ballantyne, James R. 1852. *Yoga Philosophy, of Patanjali: With Illustrative Extracts from the Commentary by Bhoja Rājā*. Allahabad, India: Presbyterian Mission Press.

Bälz, Erwin. 1901. "Über Emotionslähmung." *Allgemeine Zeitschrift für Psychiatrie* 58: 717–27.

Barbarin, Georges. 1937. *Le livre de la mort douce*. Paris: Éditions Adyar.

Barker, A.T. [Anon.] 1923. *The Mahatma Letters to A. P. Sinnett From the Mahatmas M. & K. H.* Transcribed, compiled, and with an introduction by A.T. Barker. London: T. F. Unwin.

Bar-Levav, Avriel. 2014. "Jewish Attitudes Towards Death. A Society Between Time, Space and Texts." In *Death in Jewish Life: Burial and Mourning Customs Among Jews of Europe and Nearby Communities*, edited by Stefan C. Reif et al., 3–16. Berlin & New York: de Gruyter.

Barnard, William G. 1997. *Exploring Unseen Worlds: William James and the Philosophy of Mysticism*. Albany: State University of New York Press.

Barrett, Florence E. Perry. 1937. *Personality Survives Death. Messages From Sir William Barrett*. London: Longmans, Green.

Barrett, Justin L., E. R. Burdett, and T. J. Porter. 2009. "Counterintuitiveness in Folktales: Finding the Cognitive Optimum." *The Journal of Cognition and Culture* 9 (3): 271–87.

Barrett, William F. (1926) 1986. *Deathbed Visions: The Psychical Experiences of the Dying*. Northampton, UK: Aquarian.

Barrett, William F. 1918. *On the Threshold of the Unseen. An Examination of the Phenomena of Spiritualism and of the Evidence for Survival After Death*. New York: Dutton & Co.

Barrow, Sir John. 1847, To Dr. W. Hyde Wollaston. [Letter by Francis Beaufort]. *An Autobiographical Memoir of Sir John Barrow*. London: John Murray, 398–403.

Beaumont, John. 1705. *An Historical, Physiological and Theological Treatise of Spirits: Apparitions, Witchcrafts, and other Magical Practices*. London: Printed for D. Browne; J. Taylor et al.

Becker, Ernest. 1973. *The Denial of Death*. New York: Simon & Schuster.

Becker, Carl B. 1985. "Views From Tibet: NDEs and the Book of the Dead." *Anabiosis: The Journal for Near-Death Studies* 5 (1): 3–20.

Belkin, Gary. 2014. *Death Before Dying. History, Medicine, and Brain Death*. New York: Oxford University Press.

Bennett, John G. 1962. *Witness. The Story of a Search*. London: Hodder and Stoughton.

Benz, Maximilian. 2013. *Gesicht und Schrift: Die Erzählung von Jenseitsreisen in Antike und Mittelalter*. Berlin & New York: de Gruyter.

Benz, Ernst. 1972. "Drogen und übersinnliche Erfahrung." *Zeitschrift für Religions- und Geistesgeschichte* 24 (1): 1–12.

Berger, Peter L. 1979. *The Heretical Imperative: Contemporary Possibilities of Religious Affirmation*. New York: Anchor.

Bergson, Henri. (1896) 1911. *Matter and Memory* [*Matière et mémoire*]. Translated by Nancy Margaret Paul and W. Scott Palmer. London: George Allen and Unwin.

Besant, Annie. 1893. *Death—And After?* London, New York & Madras: Theosophical Publishing Society.

Besant, Annie. 1909. *The Seven Principles of Man*. Revised and corrected edition. London: Theosophical Publishing Society.

Binet, Alfred. 1896. "État mental des mourants." *L'Année Psychologique* 3: 629–637.

Binns, Edward. (1842) 1851. *The Anatomy of Sleep; or, the Art of Procuring Sound and Refreshing Slumber at Will*. London: John Churchill.

Birnbaum, Karl. 1920. *Psychopathologische Dokumente. Selbstbekenntnisse und Fremdzeugnisse aus dem seelischen Grenzlande*. Berlin: Springer.

Blackmore, Susan. 1993. *Dying to Live*. Buffalo & New York: Prometheus.

Bland, Betty. 1996. "The Near-Death Experience: A Theosophical Perspective." *The Messenger* (March): 1–3.

Blavatsky, Helena P. (1882) 1991. "Death and Immortality." In *Blavatsky: Collected Writings*, Vol. IV, edited by Boris de Zirkoff, 250–6. Wheaton, IL: Theosophical Publishing House. [Originally published in *The Theosophist*, 4, 2 (1882): 28–40].

Blavatsky, Helena P. 1877. *Isis Unveiled. A Master-Key to the Mysteries of Ancient and Modern Science and Theology*. Vol. I, *Science*/ Vol. II, *Theology*. New York: J. W. Bouton.

Blavatsky, Helena P. 1889a. "Memory in the Dying." *Lucifer* 5 (26): 125–9.

Blavatsky, Helena P. 1889b. *The Key to Theosophy*. London: The Theosophical Publishing House and New York: W. Q. Judge.

Bloch, Oscar. 1903. *Vom Tode. Eine gemeinverständliche Darstellung*. 2 vols. Berlin: Juncker. [Danish: 1903. *Om Døden. En almenfattelig Fremstilling*. 2 vols. Copenhagen: Bojesen.]

Blumenberg, Hans. 1981. *Die Lesbarkeit der Welt*. Frankfurt: Suhrkamp.

Blumenberg, Hans. (1960) 2010. *Paradigms for a Metaphorology*. Translated by Robert Savage. Ithaca, NY: Cornell University Press.

Bolzoni, Lina. 2006. "Mnemonics." In *Dictionary of Gnosis & Western Esotericism*, edited by Wouter J. Hanegraaff et al., 793–800. Leiden: Brill.

Bondeson, Jan. 2001. *Buried Alive. The Terrifying History of Our Most Primal Fear*. New York & London: Norton.

Borjigin, Jimo, UnCheol Lee et al. 2013. Surge of Neurophysiological Coherence and Connectivity in the Dying Brain. PNAS www.pnas.org/cgi/doi/10.1073/pnas.1308285110 (accessed Oct. 21, 2017).

Boudinot, Elias. 1828. *Memoirs of the Rev. Wm. Tennent: Formerly of Freehold, New-Jersey*. Philadelphia: A. Claxton.

Boyer, Pascal. 2001. *Religion Explained. The Evolutionary Origins of Religious Thought*. New York: Basic Books.

Bozzano, Ernesto. 1923. *Phénomènes psychiques au moment de la mort*. Paris: Édition de la B. P. S.

Bozzano, Ernesto. 1931. "Della 'Visione panoramica' o 'Memoria sintetica' nell'imminenza della Morte." In *Indagini sulle manifestazioni supernormali*. Vol. 1, 50–97. Città della Pieve: Dante.

Bozzano, Ernesto. (1934) 1937. *The Phenomena of Bilocation*. Translated by G. Gobron. Paris: Jean Meyer.

Bremmer, Jan N. 2002. *The Rise and Fall of the Afterlife*. London & New York: Routledge.

Broad, Charlie D. 1953. *Religion, Philosophy and Psychical Research*. London: Routledge and Keagan Paul.

Broad, Charlie D. 1962. *Lectures on Psychical Research*. London: Routledge and Keagan Paul.

Brockmann-Jerosch, Marie, Arnold Heim, and Helene Heim. 1952. *Albert Heim. Leben und Forschung*. Basel, Switzerland: Wepf & Co.

Bromberg, Walter, and Paul Schilder. 1933. "Death and Dying." *The Psychoanalytic Review* 20 (2): 133–85.

Brown, H. F. 1895. *J. A. Symonds. A Biography*. 2 vols. New York: Scribner's.

Bulmer, Joseph B. [J. B. B.]. 1833. *An Account of the Infancy, Religious and Literary Life of Adam Clarke*. New York: D. Appleton.

Byrd, Richard E. 1939. *Alone*. New York: G. P. Putnam's Sons.

Cahagnet, Louis-Alphonse. 1848. *Magnétisme: Arcanes de la vie future dévoilé*. Paris: Chez l'auteur. (Translation in *The Celestial Telegraph*. 2 vols. New York, 1851).

Cahagnet, Louis-Alphonse. 1850. *Sanctuaire au spiritualisme*. Paris: Germer Baillière.

Cahagnet, Louis-Alphonse. 1851. *The Sanctuary of Spiritualism: A Study of the Human Soul and of Its Relation With the Universe Through Somnambulism and Ecstasy*. N.p., 1851.

Calloway, Katherine. 2014. *Natural Theology in the Scientific Revolution: God's Scientists*. London: Pickering & Chatto.

Carrington, Hereward. 1912. *Death: Its Causes and Phenomena. With Special Reference to Immortality*. New York: Funk & Wagnalls.

Carrington, Hereward. 1920. *Higher Psychical Development (Yoga Philosophy). An Outline of the Secret Hindu Teachings*. New York: Dodd, Mead & Co.

Carrington, Hereward. 1937. *The Psychic World*. New York: G. P. Putnam's Sons.

Carus, Carl G. 1846. *Psyche. Zur Entwicklungsgeschichte der Seele*. Pforzheim, Germany: Flammer und Hoffmann.

Charlier, Philippe. 2014. "Oldest Medical Description of a Near-Death Experience (NDE). France, 18th Century." *Resuscitation* 85 (9) (September): e155.

Child, Lydia M. 1843. *Letters from New York*. New York: Charles S. Francis, and Boston: James Munroe.

Ciccarese, Maria P. 1984/1985. "Le visioni di S. Fursa." *Romanobarbarica* 8: 231–303.

Clark, Davis W. 1852. *Death-Bed Scenes: or Dying with and without Religion: Designed to Illustrate the Truth and Power of Christianity*. New York: Lane & Scott.

Clark, Davis W. 1864. *Man All Immortal: Or, the Nature and Destination of Man as Taught by Reason and Revelation*. Cincinnati, OH: Poe & Hitchcock.

Clarke, Edward H. 1878. *Visions: A Study of False Sight (Pseudopia)*. Boston: Houghton, Osgood.

Clarke, J. J. 1994. *Jung and Eastern Thought: A Dialogue With the Orient*. London & New York: Routledge.

Clavigero, Francesco S. 1787. *History of Mexico*. Vol. I. London: G. G. J. Robinson.

Cobbe, Frances P. 1877. "The Peak in Darien: The Riddle of Death." *Littell's Living Age and New Quarterly Review* 8 (July): 283–93.

Cobbe, Frances P. 1882. *The Peak in Darien. With Some Other Inquiries Touching Concerns of the Soul and the Body. An Octave of Essays*. London: Williams and Norgate, and Boston: George H. Ellis.

Coleridge, S. T. 1817. *Biographie Literaria; or Biographical Sketches of My Literary Life and Opinions*. 2 vols. London & Camberwell: S. Curtis.

[Colerus, Johann Christoph]. 1734. *Bericht von dem verstorbenen Manne in Hornhausen, welchen Pastor Kern an der Preuss. Regierung und Consist. in Halberstadt abgestattet. It. Prophetische Prüfung einer Hornhausischen Begebenheit nach dem Lichte der Heil. Schrifft*, Acta historico-ecclesiastica. Vol. I, 30–47. Weimar, Germany.

Collier, Barbara B. 1972. "Ketamine and the Conscious Mind." *Anaesthesia* 27 (2) (April): 120–34.

Collongues, Léon. 1862. *Traité de dynamoscopie, ou appréciation de la nature et de la gravité des maladies par l'auscultation des doigts*. Paris: P. Asselin, Gendre et successeur de Labé.

Corazza, Ornella. 2008. *Near-Death Experiences: Exploring the Mind-Body Connection*, London & New York: Routledge.

Corazza Ornella, and F. Schifano. 2010. "Near-Death States Reported in a Sample of 50 Misusers." *Substance Use and Misuse* 45 (6): 916–24.

Couliano, I. P. 1991. *Out of This World. Otherworldly Journeys from Gilgamesh to Albert Einstein*. Boston & London: Shambhala.

Cozzens, Samuel W. [ca. 1874]. *The Marvelous Country: Three Years in Arizona and New Mexico.* Boston: Shepard and Gill.

Crookall, Robert. 1960. *The Study and Practice of Astral Projection.* London: Aquarian.

Crookall, Robert. 1961. *The Supreme Adventure: Analyses of Psychic Communications.* London: James Clarke.

Crookall, Robert. 1964. *More Astral Projections. Analyses of Case Histories.* London: Aquarian.

Crookall, Robert. 1965. *Intimations of Immortality.* London: James Clarke.

Crow, John L. 2013. "Accessing the Astral With a Monitor and Mouse: Esoteric Religion and the Astral Located in Three Dimensional Virtual Realms." In *Contemporary Esotericism,* edited by Egil Asprem and Kenneth Granholm, 159–80. Durham, NC: Equinox.

Dass, Ram, and Ralph Metzner. 2010. *Birth of a Psychedelic Culture. Conversations About Leary, the Harvard Experiments, Millbrook and the Sixties.* Santa Fe, NM: Synergetic Press.

David-Néel, Alexandra. (1931) 1937. *With Mystics and Magicians in Tibet.* London: Penguin Books.

David-Néel, Alexandra. (1961) 1978. *Immortalité et réincarnation. Doctrines et pratiques. Chine— Tibet—Inde.* Monaco: Editions Rocher. [Engl. trans. 1997. *Immortality and Reincarnation. Wisdom from the Forbidden Journey.* Rochester, NY: Inner Traditions.]

Davidsen, Markus A. 2016. "The Religious Affordance of Fiction: A Semiotic Approach." *Religion* 46 (4): 521–49.

Davis, Andrew J. 1853a. *The Great Harmonia Concerning the Seven Mental States.* Vol. III: *Seer.* Boston: Benjamin B. Mussey.

Davis, Andrew J. 1853b. *The Present Age and Inner Life. A Sequel to Spiritual Intercourse.* New York: Partridge and Brittan.

Davis, Andrew J. 1866. *Death and the After-Life. Three Lectures.* New York: A. J. Davis & Co.

Davis, Andrew J. 1867. *A Stellar Key to the Summer Land* (5th ed.). Boston: Colby & Rich.

Davis, Lloyd. 2006. "Critical Debates and Early Modern Autobiography." In *Early Modern Autobiography: Theories, Genres, Practices,* edited by Ronald Bedford et al., 19–34. Ann Arbor: University of Michigan Press.

Dawkins, Richard. 2006. *God Delusion.* London: Black Swan.

de Benneville, George. 1791. *A True and Most Remarkable Account of Some Passages in the Life of Mr. George de Benneville.* [Translation of the French manuscript]. London: Sold by the Editor.

Delacour, Jean-Baptiste. 1973. *Aus dem Jenseits zurück. Berichte von Totgeglaubten.* Düsseldorf & Vienna: Econ. Translated as *Glimpses of the Beyond. The Extraordinary Experiences of People Who Crossed the Brinks of Death and Returned.* New York: Delacorte Press.

Delanne, Gabriel. 1909; 1911. *Les apparitions matérialisées de vivants et des morts* 2 vols. Paris: Librairie Spirite Leymarie.

Deleuze, Joseph P. F. 1843. *Practical Instruction in Animal Magnetism.* Revised Edition, With an Appendix of Notes by the Translator, and Letters. New York: D. Appleton.

De Morgan, Augustus and E. Sophia [C. D. and A. B., pseud.]. 1863. *From Matter to Spirit. The Result of Ten Year's Experience in Spirit Manifestations.* London: Longman, Green.

Dendy, Walter C. 1841. *The Philosophy of Mystery.* London: Longman.

Denton, William. (1871) 1874. *Is Spiritualism True?* Boston: William Denton.

Denton, William and Elizabeth M.F. Denton. 1871. *The Soul of Things. Or, Psychometric Researches and Discoveries.* Boston: William Denton.

de Quincey, Thomas. (1821) 2013. *Confessions of an English Opium-Eater and Other Writings.* Oxford: Oxford University Press.

de Quincey, Thomas. (1821/1845) 1851. *Confessions of an English Opium-Eater and Suspiria de profundis*. Boston: Ticknor, Reed, and Fields.

Deveney, John P. 1997. *Astral Projection or Liberation of the Double and the Work of the Early Theosophical Society* (Occasional Papers, Vol. 6). Fullerton, CA: Theosophical History.

Deveney, John P. 2004. "An 1876 Lecture by W. Q. Judge on His Magical Progress in the Theosophical Society." *Theosophical History* 9 (3): 12–20 [German translation of Judge 1876: see Judge 1877].

Dieguez, Sebastian. 2010. "'A Man Can Be Destroyed but Not Defeated': Ernest Hemingway's Near-Death Experience and Declining Health." *Frontiers of Neurology and Neuroscience* 27: 174–206.

Dieguez, Sebastian. 2013. "Doubles Everywhere: Literary Contributions to the Study of the Bodily Self." *Frontiers of Neurology and Neuroscience* 31: 77–115.

Dinzelbacher, Peter. 1989. *An der Schwelle zum Jenseits. Sterbevisionen im interkulturellen Vergleich*. Freiburg, Germany: Herder.

Dostoevsky, Fyodor. 2011. *The Eternal Husband and Other Stories*. Translated by Richard Pevear and Larissa Volokhonsky. New York: Random House.

Duerr, Hans P. 2015. *Die dunkle Nacht der Seele. Nahtod-Erfahrungen und Jenseitsreisen*. Berlin: Insel.

Dugas, Ludovic. 1898. "Un cas de depersonnalisation." *Revue Philosophique de la France et l'Étranger* 45: 500–7.

Du Monchaux, Pierre-Jean. 1766. *Anecdotes de médecine ou choix de faits singuliers qui ont rapport à l'anatomie [. . .] et auxquelles on a joint des anecdotes concernant les médecins les plus célèbres*. Lille, France: J. B. Henry.

Dunbar, Ernest. 1905. "The Light Thrown on Psychological Processes by the Action of Drugs." *Proceedings of the Society for Psychical Research* 19: 62–77.

Dupotet de Sennevoy, Baron. 1838. *An Introduction to the Study of Animal Magnetism*. London: Saunders & Otley.

du Prel, Carl. 1869. "Oneirokritikon. Der Traum vom Standpunkt des transcendentalen Idealismus." *Deutsche Vierteljahrsschrift* 126: 188–241.

du Prel, Carl. (1884) 1885. *Die Philosophie der Mystik*. Leipzig: Ernst Günthers Verlag.

du Prel, Carl. (1884) 1889. *The Philosophy of Mysticism*. 2 vols. London: Keagan Paul.

Durville, Hector. 1909. *Le fantôme des vivants. Anatomie et physiologie de l'ame. Recherches expérimentales sur le dédoublement des corps de l'homme*. Paris: Librairie du Magnétisme.

Durville, Hector. 1910. "Projection of the Human Double." *Annals of Psychical Science* 9: 477–9.

Easting, Robert. 2006. "Access to Heaven in Medieval Visions of the Otherworld." In *Envisaging Heaven in the Middle Ages*, edited by Carolyn Muessig and Ad Putter, 75–90. London & New York: Routledge.

Ebeling, Gerhard. (1974) 1975. *Die Klage über das Erfahrungsdefizit in der Theologie als Frage nach ihrer Sache. Wort und Glaube*, Vol. III. Tübingen, Germany: Mohr, 3–28.

Edmonds, Judge John W. (1874) 1875. *Letters and Tracts on Spiritualism. Also Two Inspirational Orations by Cora L. V. Tappan*. London: J. Burns.

Egger, Victor. 1895. "La durée apparente des rêves." *Revue philosophique de la France et de l'Étranger* 40: 41–59.

Egger, Victor. 1896a. "Le moi des mourants." *Revue philosophique de la France et de l'Étranger* 41: 26–38.

Egger, Victor. (1896b). Le moi des mourants: Nouveaux faits. *Revue philosophique de la France et de l'Étranger* 21: 337–368.

Ehrenwald, Jan. 1974. "Out-of-the-Body Experiences and the Denial of Death." *Journal of Nervous and Mental Disease* 159 (4): 227–33.

Eliot, George. 1858. *Scenes of Clerical Life.* New York: Harper & Brothers.

Ellwood, Robert. 1992. "How New is the New Age?" In *Perspectives on the New Age,* edited by Jane R Lewis and J. Gordon Melton, 59–67. Albany: State University of New York Press.

Engmann, Birk. 2014. *Near-Death Experiences: Heavenly Insight or Human Illusion?* Cham & Heidelberg: Springer.

Evans-Wentz, W. Y. 1911. *The Fairy-Faith in Celtic Countries.* London, New York [. . .]: Oxford University Press.

Evans-Wentz, W. Y., ed. (1927) 2000. *The Tibetan Book of the Dead or the After-Death Experiences on the Bardo Plane, according to Lāma Kazi Dawa-Samdup's English Rendering.* [Text of the 3rd edition 1957.] With a new Foreword and Afterword by Donald S. Lopez. Oxford: Oxford University Press.

Evans-Wentz, W. Y. 1935. *Das tibetanische Totenbuch. Aus der englischen Fassung des Lama Kazi Dawa Samdup.* Mit einem psychologischen Kommentar von C. G. Jung. Zurich: Rascher.

Evans-Wentz, W. Y. 1935. *Tibetan Yoga and Secret Doctrines.* London: Oxford University Press.

Fechner, Gustav T. (1835) 1906. *On Life After Death.* Chicago: The Open Court Publishing Co.

Fechner, Gustav T. 1853a. "Zwei Fälle eines merkwürdigen Wiedererwachens der Erinnerung an das gesammte frühere Leben im Augenblicke drohenden Ertrinkens." *Centralblatt für Naturwissenschaften und Anthropologie* 3: 43–7.

Fechner, Gustav T. 1853b. "Vergleichspunkte zwischen den Träumen, den Hallucinationen und dem Wahnsinn." *Centralblatt für Naturwissenschaften und Anthropologie* 40: 770–5.

Féré, Charles. 1889. "Note pour servir a l'histoire de l'état mental des mourants." *Compte Rendu des Séances de la Société de Biologie,* 9: 108–10.

Féré, Charles. 1898. "L'état mental des mourants." *Revue philosophique de la France et de l'Étranger* 45: 296–302.

Féré, Charles. 1892. *La pathologie des émotions. Études physiologiques et cliniques.* Paris: Félix Alcan.

Ferenczi, Sandór. 1912. "Zur Begriffsbestimmung der Introjektion." *Zentralblatt für Psychoanalyse* 2: 198–200.

Field, Clive. D. 2017. *Secularization in the Long 1960s. Numerating Religion in Britain.* Oxford: Oxford University Press.

Flammarion, Camille. 1920, 1921, 1922. *La mort et son mystère. Tome I: Avant la mort. Tome II: Autour la mort. Tome III: Après la mort.* Paris: Flammarion.

Flammarion, Camille. 1922. *Death and Its Mystery. Vol. I. Before Death. Proofs of the Existence of the Soul. Vol. II. At the Moment of Death. Manifestations and Apparitions of the Dying; "Doubles"; Phenomena of Occultism. Vol. III. After Death. Manifestations and Apparitions of the Dead; The Soul After Death.* New York & London: The Century, and London: T. Fisher Unwin.

Fischer, Emily L. 1914. *A Visit to the Astral Plane or Another Proof of Life Beyond the Grave.* Philadelphia: E. Fischer.

Fischer, John M., and Benjamin Mitchell-Yellin. 2016. *Near-Death Experiences. Understanding Visions of the Afterlife.* New York: Oxford University Press.

Fischer, Roland. 1967. "The Biological Fabric of Time." *Annals of New York Academy of Sciences* 138: 440–88.

Fox, Mark. 2003. *Religion, Spirituality, and the Near-Death Experience*. London & New York: Routledge.

Fox, Oliver [Hugh G. Calloway]. 1920a. "The Pineal Doorway. A Record of Research." *Occult Review* 31 (4): 190–8.

Fox, Oliver. 1920b. "Beyond the Pineal Door." *Occult Review* 31 (5): 251–61.

Fox, Oliver. 1939. *Astral Projection: A Record of Out-of-the-Body Experiences*. London: Rider.

Francis, John R. (1894) 1900. *The Encyclopaedia of Death and Life in the Spirit-World. Opinions and Experiences From Eminent Sources*. Chicago: The Progressive Thinker Publishing House.

Frankl, Viktor, and Otto Pötzl. 1952. "Über die seelischen Zustände während des Absturzes." *Monatsschrift für Psychiatrie und Neurologie* 123: 362–80.

Freud, Sigmund. 1918. *Our Attitude Towards Death*. Standard Edition. Vol. 14. New York: Norton, 289–300.

Freud, Sigmund. (1900) 1921. *The Interpretation of Dreams* (3rd edition, 1913). Translated by A. A. Brill. New York: The Macmillan Company.

Friedman, David M. 2008. *The Immortalists: Charles Lindbergh, Dr. Alexis Carrel, and Their Daring Quest to Live Forever*. New York: HarperCollins.

Fuller, Henry H. 1898. *The Art of Memory: Being a Comprehensive and Practical System, of Memory Culture*. St. Paul, MN: National Publishing Co.

Funk, Isaac K. 1907. *The Psychic Riddle*. New York & London: Funk & Wagnalls.

Gebauer, Christian. 2013. *Visionskompilationen. Eine bislang unbekannte Textsorte des Hoch- und Spätmittelalters*. Münster, Germany: Lit.

Geddes, Sir Auckland. 1937a. "A Voice From the Grandstand." *The Edinburgh Medical Journal* 44 (6): 365–84.

Geddes, Sir Auckland. 1937b. "'A Voice From the Grandstand.' Reviewed by W. H. S." *Journal of the Society for Psychical Research* 30: 103–5.

Glaser, Barney G., and Anselm L. Strauss. 1965. *Awareness of Dying*. New York: Aldine.

Goodrick-Clarke, Nicholas. 2008. *The Western Esoteric Traditions. A Historical Introduction*. New York: Oxford University Press.

Govinda, Lama Anagarika. (1957) 1977a. *Foundations of Tibetan Mysticism*. Bombay: B. I. Publications.

Govinda, Lama Anagarika. (1957) 1977b. *The Way of the White Clouds. A Buddhist Pilgrim in Tibet*. Bombay: B. I. Publications.

Graham, John W. 1933. *Psychical Experiences of Quaker Ministers*. London: Journal of the Friends' Historical Society.

Green, Celia E. 1968. *Out-of-the-Body Experiences*. London: Hamish Hamilton.

Greyson, Bruce. 1983. "The Near-Death Experience Scale: Construction, Reliability, and Validity." *Journal of Nervous & Mental Disease* 171: 369–75.

Greyson, Bruce. 2006. "Near-Death Experiences and Spirituality." *Zygon* 41 (2): 393–414.

Greyson, Bruce. 2010. "Seeing Dead People Not Known to Have Died: 'Peak in Darien' Experiences." *Anthropology and Humanism* 35 (2): 159–71.

Grinspoon, Lester, and James Bakalar. 1979. *Psychedelic Drugs Reconsidered*. New York: The Lindesmith Center.

Grof, Stanislav, and Joan Halifax-Grof. 1976. "Psychedelics and the Experience of Death." In *Life After Death*, edited by Arnold Toynbee and Arthur Koestler, 182–202. London: Weidenfeld and Nicolson.

Grof, Stanislav, and Joan Halifax-Grof. 1977 [1978]. *The Human Encounter With Death*. With a Foreword by Elisabeth Kübler-Ross. New York: Dutton.

Grof, Stanislav, and C. Grof. 1980. *Beyond Death*. London: Thames and Hudson.

Groth-Marnat, Gary, and Roger Summers. 1998. "Altered Beliefs, Attitudes, and Behaviors Following Near-Death Experiences." *Journal of Humanistic Psychology* 38: 110–25.

Grube, G. M. A. 2002. *Plato: Five Dialogues* (2nd ed.). Translated by G. M. A. Grube. Indianapolis, IN: Hackett.

Grutschnig-Kieser, Konstanze. 2006. *Der 'Geistliche Würtz = Kräuter = und Blumen = Garten' des Christoph Schütz. Ein radikalpietistisches UNIVERSAL-Gesang = Buch*. Göttingen: Vandenhoeck & Ruprecht.

Gunn, Susan. 1995. "Pearl: Medieval Dream Vision and Modern Near-Death Experiences." *Journal of Religion and Psychical Research* 18: 132–40.

Gurney, Edmund, Frederic W. H. Myers, and Frank Podmore. 1886. *Phantasms of the Living*. 2 vols. London: Trübner & Co.

Haage, Bernard D. 2006. "Alchemy II: Antiquity–12th Century." In *Dictionary of Gnosis & Western Esotericism*, edited by Wouter J. Hanegraaff et al., 16–34. Leiden: Brill.

Habermas, Gary, and J. P. Moreland. 2004. *Beyond Death. Exploring the Evidence for Immortality*. Eugene, OR: Wipf & Stock.

Haddock, Joseph W. (2nd ed.) 1851. *Somnolism & Psycheism; Or, The Science of the Soul and the Phenomena of Nervation, as Revealed by Vital Magnetism or Mesmerism*. London: J. S. Hodson.

Haddock, Joseph W. 1852. *Somnolismus und Psycheismus oder die Erscheinungen und Gesetze des Lebens-Magnetismus oder Mesmerismus. Nach eignen Beobachtungen und Versuchen*. Leipzig: Verlag Ambr. Abel.

Hammer, Olav. 2004. *Claiming Knowledge. Strategies of Epistemology From Theosophy to the New Age*. Leiden & Boston: Brill.

Hammer, Olav, and Mikael Rothstein, eds. 2013. *Handbook of the Theosophical Current*. Leiden & Boston: Brill.

Hampe, Johann C. (1975) 1979. *To Die Is to Gain. The Experience of One's Own Death*. London: Darton, Longman, and Todd; Atlanta, GA: John Knox Press.

Hanegraaff, Wouter J. 1996. *New Age Religion and Western Culture: Esotericism in the Mirror of Secular Thought*. Leiden: Brill.

Hanegraaff, Wouter J. 2012. *Esotericism and the Academy: Rejected Knowledge in Western Culture*. Cambridge: Cambridge University Press.

Hanegraaff, Wouter J. 2013. "Entheogenic Esotericism." In *Contemporary Esotericism,* edited by Egil Asprem and Kennet Granholm, 392–409. Sheffield, UK: Equinox.

Hanegraaff, Wouter J. 2016. "The First Psychonaut? Louis-Alphonse Cahagnet's Experiments with Narcotics." *International Journal for the Study of New Religions* 7 (2): 105–23.

Hanegraaff, Wouter J. 2017. The Theosophical Imagination. *Correspondences* 5, 3–39.

Hanegraaff, Wouter J. et al., eds. 2006. *Dictionary of Gnosis & Western Esotericism*. Leiden: Brill.

Hardinge, Emma. 1860. "On Living Spirits and Dying Spiritualism." *Banner of Light* 7 (18), 2.

Hardinge, Emma. 1870. *Modern American Spiritualism*. Third Edition. New York: The Author.

Hardinge Britten, Emma. 1876. *Ghost Land; Or, Researches in the Mysteries of Occultism. Illustrated in a Series of Autobiographical Sketches*. Boston: Hardinge Britten.

Hariot, Thomas. (1588) 1903. *A Briefe and True Report of the New Found Land Of Virginia*. Reproduced in Facsimile from the First Edition of 1588. New York: Dodd, Mead & Co.

Harrison, Peter. 2011. "Experimental Religion and Experimental Science in Early Modern England." *Intellectual History Review* 21 (4): 413–33.

Hart, Hornell. 1954. "ESP Projection: Spontaneous Cases and the Experimental Method." *Journal of the American Society for Psychical Research* 48: 121–46.

Heim, Albert. 1892. "Notizen über den Tod durch Absturz." *Jahrbuch des Schweizer Alpenclub* [Bern: Zentralkomitee des Schweizer Alpenclub], 327–37.

Hemreck, Arlo. 1988. "The History of Cardiopulmonary Resuscitation." *The American Journal of Surgery* 156 (6): 430–36.

Heywood, Oliver. 1685. *A Narrative of the Holy Life and Happy Death of That Reverend* [. . .] *Mr. John Angier*. London: Tho. Parkburst.

Hibbert, Samuel. 1825. *Sketches of the Philosophy of Apparitions*. Edinburgh: Oliver & Boyd.

Hickok, Guy. 1927. "Hemingway Vows His Soul Flew Out of His Body During the Rout On Piave, but Came Back Again." *The Brooklyn Daily Eagle*, April 13, 1927: 16.

Hill, John A. 1911. *New Evidences in Psychical Research; A Record of Investigations, With Selected Examples of Recent S. P. R. Results*. London: William Rider.

Hill, John A. 1918. *Man Is a Spirit. A Collection of Spontaneous Cases of Dream, Vision and Ecstasy*. New York: George H. Doran Co.

Hoffmann, Matthias. 2011. *Sterben? Am Liebsten plötzlich und unerwartet. Die Angst vor dem sozialen Sterben*. Wiesbaden: Springer.

Hofmann, Albert. 1979a. *LSD—Mein Sorgenkind*. Stuttgart: Klett Cotta.

Hofmann, Albert. 1979b. "How LSD Originated." *Journal of Psychedelic Drugs* 11 (1-2): 53–60.

Hofmann, Albert (1980) 2013. *LSD. My Problem Child. And Insights/Outlooks*. Oxford: Oxford University Press.

Horowitz, Mardi. 1969. "Flashbacks: Recurrent Intrusive Images After the Use of LSD." *American Journal of Psychiatry* 126 (4): 565–9.

Horst, Georg C. 1830. *Deuteroskopie oder merkwürdige psychische und physiologische Erscheinungen* [. . .]. *Für Religionsphilosophen, Psychologen und denkende Aerzte: eine nöthige Beilage zur Dämonomagie, wie zur Zauber-Bibliothek*. 2 vols. Frankfurt: Wilmans.

Hunter, R. C. A. 1967. "On the Experience of Nearly Dying." *American Journal of Psychiatry* 124: 84–8.

Huxley, Aldous. (1946) 1947. *The Perennial Philosophy*. London: Chatto & Windus.

Huxley, Aldous. 1954. *The Doors of Perception and Heaven and Hell*. London: Chatto & Windus.

Hyslop, James H. 1898. "The Consciousness of Dying." *Journal of the Society for Psychical Research*, 8 (June): 250–5.

Hyslop, James H. 1907. "Vision of the Dying." *Journal of the American Society for Psychical Research* 1: 45–55.

Hyslop, James H. 1918a. *Life After Death. Problems of the Future Life and Its Nature*. New York: E. P. Dutton.

Hyslop, James H. 1918b. "Visions of the Dying." *Journal of the American Society for Psychical Research*, 10 (Oct.): 585–645.

Illich, Ivan. 1974. *Medical Nemesis*. London: Calder & Boyars.

Illich, Ivan. 1976. *Limits to Medicine—Medical Nemesis: The Expropriation of Health*. London: Marion Boyars.

James, William. 1898. *Human Immortality. Two Supposed Objections to the Doctrine*. Boston & New York: Riverside Press.

James, William. (1902) 1922. *The Varieties of Religious Experience. A Study in Human Nature.* New York: Longmans, Green & Co.

Jaspers, Karl (1946). *Allgemeine Psychopathologie* (4th ed.). Berlin & Heidelberg: Springer.

Johnson, Raynor C. 1953. *The Imprisoned Splendour: An Approach to Reality Based Upon the Significance of Data.* New York: Harper & Row.

Johnstone, Robert E. 1973. "A Ketamine Trip." *Anesthesiology* 39: 460.

Jonas, Hans. 1969. "Philosophical Reflections on Experimenting with Human Subjects." *Daedalus* 98: 219–47.

Jonas, Hans. 1974. "Against the Stream." In *Philosophical Essays: From Ancient Creed to Technological Man*, 132–40. Englewood Cliffs, NJ: Prentice-Hall.

Jonas, Hans. (1970) 1987. "Gehirntod und menschliche Organbank: Zur pragmatischen Umdefinierung des Todes." In *Technik, Medizin und Ethik: Zur Praxis des Prinzips Verantwortung*, 219–41.Frankfurt: Suhrkamp.

Jonsen, Albert R. 1998. *The Birth of Bioethics.* New York: Oxford University Press.

Judge, William Q. 1877. Gibt es eine Magie und Zauberer? *Psychische Studien* 4 (5): 193–201.

Judge, Willliam Q. (1889) 1890. *The Yoga Aphorisms of Patanjali. An Interpretation.* Assisted by James Henderson Connelly. New York: The Path.

Jung, Carl G. (1935) 2000. "Psychological Commentary." In *The Tibetan Book of the Dead*, edited by W. Y. Evans-Wentz, xxxv–lii. Oxford: Oxford University Press.

Jung, Carl G. 1963. *Memories, Dreams, Reflections.* New York: Random House [German: 1962. *Erinnerungen, Träume, Gedanken von C. G. Jung.* Aufgezeichnet und herausgegeben von Aniela Jaffé. Zurich & Stuttgart: Rascher].

Jung, Carl G., and Wolfgang Pauli. 1952. *Naturerklärung und Psyche.* Zurich: Rascher [*The Interpretation of Nature and Psyche.* New York: Pantheon Books].

Jung-Stilling, Johann H. (1808) 1834. *Theory of Pneumatology.* London, England: Longman, Rees, Orme et al.

Jung-Stilling, Johann H. (1808) 1832. *Theorie der Geisterkunde in einer Natur-, Vernunft- und Bibelmäßigen Beantwortung der Frage: Was von Ahnungen, Gesichten und Geistererscheinungen geglaubt und nicht geglaubt werden müße.* Stuttgart: Wolters.

Kanne, Johann A. (1815) 1842. *Leben und aus dem Leben merkwürdiger und erweckter Christen aus der protestantischen Kirche. I. Theil.* Leipzig: F. A. Brockhaus.

Kant, Immanuel. (1766) 1899. *Dreams of a Spirit-Seer: Illustrated by Dreams of Metaphysics.* London: Swan Sonnenschein, and New York: Macmillan.

Kant, Immanuel. 1974. *Anthropology From a Pragmatic Point of View.* Translated by Mary J. Gregor. The Hague: Martinus Nijhoff.

Kastenbaum, Robert, ed. 1979. *Between Life and Death.* New York: Springer.

Kastenbaum, Robert. 1984. *Is There Life After Death? The Latest Evidence Analysed.* London: Rider.

Kastenbaum, Robert. 1996. "Near Death Reports. Evidence for Survival of Death?" In *The Near-Death Experience. A Reader*, edited by Lee W. Bailey and Jenny Yates, 245–64. New York & London: Routledge.

Keen, Suzanne. 2007. *Empathy and the Novel.* Oxford: Oxford University Press.

Kellehear, Allan. 1996. *Experiences Near Death: Beyond Medicine and Religion.* New York: Oxford University Press.

Kellehear, Allan. 2007. *A Social History of Dying.* Cambridge: Cambridge University Press.

Kellehear, Allan. 2009. "Introduction." In Elisabeth Kübler-Ross, *On Death and Dying*, vii–xviii. London & New York: Routledge.

Kern, Gottfried. 1734a. "II. Beylage / In einem wahrhafften und umständlichen Bericht von dem verstorbenen Mann in Hornhausen, namens Johann Schwerdtfeger" *Geistliche Fama*, 13: 105–10.

Kern, Gottfried. 1734b. *Nachdenklicher Bericht, was sich mit Johann Schwer[d]tfeger, in Hornhausen, nahe bei Oschersleben: zwei Tage vor seinem Abschied aus dieser Welt Merkwürdiges zugetragen. Auf Verlangen Eines vornehmen Herrn aufgesetzet vom dasigen PASTOR Kern* . No publisher given.

Kinsella, Michael. 2016. "Near-Death Experiences and Networked Spirituality: The Emergence of an Afterlife Movement." *Journal of the American Academy of Religion* 85 (1): 168–98.

Knoblauch, Hubert, Ina Schmied, and Bernt Schnettler. 2001. "Different Kinds of Near-Death Experience: A Report on a Survey of Near-Death Experiences in Germany." *Journal of Near-Death Studies* 20 (1): 15–28.

Knoblauch, Hubert. 1999. *Berichte aus dem Jenseits. Mythos und Realität der Nahtod-Erfahrung.* Freiburg: Herder.

Knoblauch, Hubert, and Hans G. Soeffner, eds. 1999. *Todesnähe: Wissenschaftliche Zugänge zu einem außergewöhnlichen Phänomen.* Konstanz, Germany: UVK.

Kobler, John. 1963. "Dangerous Magic of LSD." *Saturday Evening Post*, Nov. 2, 1963; Vol. 236, Issue 38, 31–40.

Kripal, Jeffrey K. 2010. *Authors of the Impossible. The Paranormal and the Sacred.* Chicago & London: University of Chicago Press.

Kübler-Ross, Elisabeth. 1972. "The Experience of Death." In *The Vestibule,* edited by Jess E. Weiss, 47–53. Port Washington, NY: Ashley Books.

Kübler-Ross, Elisabeth. (1970) 2009. *On Death and Dying. What the Dying Have to Teach Doctors, Nurses, Clergy and Their Own Families* (40th Anniversary Ed.). London & New York: Routledge.

Kuchynka, Karel. 1931. "Das Sehen seiner Selbst (Autoskopie)." *Zeitschrift für metapsychische Forschung* 2 (6): 169–72.

Küng, Hans. 1984. *Eternal Life?* London: Collins.

Lacan, Jacques. (1953) 2004. "The Function and Field of Speech and Language in Psychoanalysis." In *Ecrits*, translated by Bruce Fink. New York: Norton.

Lacoue-Labarthe, Philippe. 1999. *Poetry as Experience.* Translated by Andrea Tarnowski. Stanford, CA: Stanford University Press.

Lamont, John. 1894. "Striking Spiritual Experience." *The Two Worlds* 371 (7): 633.

Lancelin, Charles. [1913]. *Méthode de Dédoublement personnel. Extérioration de la neuricité. Sorties en Astral.* Paris: Hector et Henri Durville.

Landis, Robert W. [Robert Wharton]. 1859. *The Immortality of the Soul and the Final Condition of the Wicked Carefully Considered.* New York: Carlton & Porter.

Larsen, C. D. 1927. *My Travels in the Spirit World.* Rutland, VT: Tuttle.

Leadbeater, Charles W. 1896. *The Devachanic Plane: Its Characteristics and Inhabitants.* London: Theosophical Publishing Society.

Leadbeater, Charles W. 1911. *The Inner Life.* 2 vols. London: Theosophical Publishing Society.

Leary, Timothy. 1967. *Start Your Own Religion.* Millbrook, NY: Kriya Press of the Sri Ram Ashrama.

Leary, Timothy. (1968) 1995. *High Priest*. Berkeley, CA: Ronin.

Leary, Timothy. 1977. *Exo-Psychology. A Manual on the Use of the Human Nervous System According to the Instructions of the Manufacturers*. Los Angeles: Starseed/Peace Press.

Leary, Timothy, Ralph Metzner, and Richard Alpert. 1964. *The Psychedelic Experience. A Manual Based on the Tibetan Book of the Dead*. Secaucus, NJ: Citadel Press.

Le Maléfan, Pascal. 1995. "Vécu de mort imminente et onirisme: un chapitre inattendu de l'histoire de la psychologie dynamique." *Information psychiatrique* 71 (8): 773–80.

Leonard, Gladys O. 1931. *My Life in the Two Worlds*. London: Cassell.

Leonard, Gladys O. 1937. *The Last Crossing*. London: Cassell.

Lévi, Éliphas. 1860. *Histoire de la magie*. Paris: Germer Baillière.

Lévi, Éliphas. (1856) 1861. *Dogme et rituel de la haute magie. Tome 1: Dogme*. Paris: Germer Baillière.

Lévi, Éliphas. 1861. *La clef des grands mystères suivant Hénoch, Hermès Trismégiste, et Salomon*. Paris: Germer Baillière.

Lévi, Éliphas. (1860) 1922. *The History of Magic* (2nd ed.). Translated by Arthur Edward Waite. London: Rider.

Lévi, Éliphas. 1959. *The Key of the Mysteries*. Translated by Aleister Crowley. London: Rider. Reprint, New York: Samuel Weiser, 1970.

Lilly, John C. 1972. *The Center of the Cyclone: An Autobiography of Inner Space*. New York: Julian Press.

Lilly, John C. 1975. *Simulations of God. The Science of Belief*. Toronto, New York & London: Bantam Book.

Lindbergh, Charles A. 1927. *We*. New York & London: G. P. Putnam's Sons.

Lindbergh, Charles A. (1953) 2003. *The Spirit of St. Louis*. New York: Scribner.

Lock, Margret. 1996. "Death in Technological Time: Locating the End of Meaningful Life." *Medical Anthropology Quarterly* 10 (4): 575–600.

Lock, Margret. 2002. *Twice Dead. Organ Transplants and the Reinvention of Death*. Berkeley, Los Angeles & London: University of California Press.

Lommel, Pim van. 2010. *Consciousness Beyond Life: The Science of the Near-Death Experience*. New York: HarperOne.

Lommel, Pim van, and R. Wees et al. 2001. "Near-Death Experience in Survivors of Cardiac Arrest: A Prospective Study in the Netherlands." *The Lancet* 358 (9298): 2039–45.

Long, Jeffrey P., and Jody A. Long. 2003. "A Comparison of Near-Death Experiences Occurring Before and After 1975: Results From an Internet Survey." *Journal of Near Death Studies* 22: 21–32.

Lopez, Donald S. Jr. 2011. *The Tibetan Book of the Dead. A Biography*. Oxford & Princeton, NJ: Princeton University Press.

L'Orne, Asa. 1894. "The Evidence of Anæsthetics." *Borderland* 1 (6): 564–5.

Ludlow, Fitz H. 1857. *The Hasheesh Eater. Being Passages from the Life of a Pythagorean*. New York: Harper & Bros.

Luhmann, Niklas. 1994. *Soziale Systeme, Grundriß einer allgemeinen Theorie*. Frankfurt: Suhrkamp.

Luhmann, Niklas. 1995. *Social Systems*. Stanford, CA: Stanford University Press.

Luhmann, Niklas. 2000. *Religion der Gesellschaft*. Frankfurt: Suhrkamp.

Luhmann, Niklas. 2013. *A Systems Theory of Religion*. Stanford, CA: Stanford University Press.

Lundahl, Craig R., and Harold A. Widdison. 1983. "The Mormon Explanation of Near-Death Experiences." *Anabiosis: The Journal for Near-Death Studies* 3 (1) (June): 97–106.

Lutz, Antoine, et al. 2004. "Long-Term Meditators Self-Induce High-Amplitude Gamma Synchrony During Mental Practice." In *Proceedings of the National Academy of Sciences [PNAS] of the USA.* http://www.pnas.org/content/101/46/16369.full (accessed Oct. 21, 2017).

Macario, Maurice M. A. 1857. *Du sommeil des rêves et du somnambulisme dans l'état de santé et de maladie.* Paris: Perisse frères.

Manson, Deborah K. 2013. "The Male Body as Medium in Poe's Mesmeric Fiction." In *The Spiritualist Movement: Speaking With the Dead in America and Around the World,* edited by Christopher M. Moreman, 140–53. Santa Barbara, CA: ABC-CLIO, LLC.

Marsh, Michael N. 2010. *Out-of-Body and Near-Death Experiences. Brain-State Phenomena or Glimpses of Immortality?* New York: Oxford University Press.

Marsh, Richard L., and Gordon H. Bower. 1993. "Eliciting Cryptomnesia: Unconscious Plagiarism in a Puzzle Task." *Journal of Experimental Psychology: Learning, Memory, and Cognition* 19 (3): 673–88.

Martensen-Larsen, Hans. 1925-27. *Om Døden og de Døde.* Copenhagen: Frimodts Forlag. [German translation: 1931. *An der Pforte des Todes. Eine Wanderung zwischen zwei Welten.* Berlin: Furche Verlag].

Martinović, Jelena. 2012. "Aus dem historischen Rahmen fallend. Stürzende Alpinisten aus den 1890er Jahren." *Figurationen* 1: 28–43.

Martinović, Jelena. 2015. "Experiencing Death to Improve Life." *The Psychologist* 28 (2): 166–7.

Martinović, Jelena. 2017. *Mort imminente. Genèse d'un phénomène scientifique et culture.* Lausanne, Switzerland: MetisPresses.

Mascuch, Michael. 1997. *Origins of the Individualist Self. Autobiography and Self-Identity in England, 1591–1791.* Cambridge, UK: Polity Press.

Mattiesen, Emil. 1925 [1987]. *Der Jenseitige Mensch: Eine Einführung in die Metapsychologie der mystischen Erfahrung.* Berlin & New York: de Gruyter.

Mattiesen, Emil. 1931. "Der Austritt des Ich als spiritistisches Argument." *Zeitschrift für Parapsychologie* 6: 413–37, 481–94.

Mattiesen, Emil. 1936–1939. *Das persönliche Überleben des Todes. Eine Darstellung der Erfahrungsbeweise* (3 vols.). Berlin: de Gruyter.

Maury, Alfred. (1861) 1878. (4th ed.). *Le sommeil et les rêves. Études psychologiques sur ces phénomènes et les divers états qui s'y rattachent, suivies de recherches sur le développement de l'instinct et de l'intelligence avec le phénomène du sommeil.* Paris: Didier.

McLaughlin, Steven A., and H. Newton Malony. 1984. "Near-Death Experiences and Religion: A Further Investigation." *Journal of Religion and Health* 23 (2): 149–59.

McLeod, Hugh. 2007. *The Religious Crisis of the 1960s.* Oxford: Oxford University Press.

Melton, Gordon J., ed. 2001. *Encyclopedia of Occultism & Parapsychology* (5th ed). 2 vols. Farmington Hills, MI: Gale.

Metzinger, Thomas. 2009. *The Ego Tunnel: The Science of the Mind and the Myth of the Self.* New York: Basic Books.

Mikorey, Max. 1960. "Das Zeitparadoxon der Lebensbilderschau in Katastrophensituationen." *Zentralblatt Neurologie Psychiatrie,* 159, 4; reprinted in G. Schaltenbrand, ed. *Zeit in nervenärztlicher Sicht.* Stuttgart: Enke 1963, 32.

Mitra, Rájendralála. 1883. *The Yoga Aphorisms of Patanjali. With the Commentary of Bhoja Rájá and an English Translation*. Calcutta: J. W. Thomas.

Monroe, Robert A. 1971. *Journeys Out of the Body*. Garden City, NY: Doubleday.

Monroe, Robert A. 1982. *Far Journeys*. New York: Doubleday.

Montaigne, Michel de. (1580) 1827. *Essais*. Edited by Amaury Duval. Paris: Rapilly.

Montaigne, Michel de. 1849. *The Complete Works of Michel de Montaigne, Comprising His Essays*. Translated by Charles Cotton, edited by William Carew Hazilitt. London: John Templeman.

Moody, Raymond A. (1975) 1976. *Life After Life: The Investigation of a Phenomenon-Survival of Bodily Death*. New York: Bantam.

Moody, Raymond A. 1977a. *Reflections on Life After Life*. Harrisburg, PA: Stackpole Books.

Moody, Raymond A. 1977b. "Near-Death Experience: Dilemma for the Clinician." *Virginia Medical* 104 (10): 687–90.

Moody, Raymond A. 2012. *Paranormal. My Life in Pursuit of the Afterlife*. New York: HarperOne.

Moreau, Jacques J. 1845. *Du hachisch et de l'aliénation mentale: Études psychologiques*. Paris: Fortin, Masson et Cie.

Morioka, Masahiro. 2005. Painless Civilization and Fundamental Sense of Security. A Philosophical Challenge in the Age of Human Biotechnology. *polylog: Forum for Intercultural Philosophy* 6. https://them.polylog.org/6/fmm-en.htm (accessed Oct. 31, 2017).

Morse, Donald R. 2008a. "An Old NDE." *Journal of Spirituality and Paranormal Studies* 31 (3): 121–3.

Morse, Donald R. 2008b. "Another Even Older NDE." *Journal of Spirituality and Paranormal Studies* 31 (4): 181–2.

Muldoon, Sylvan J. 1936. *The Case for Astral Projection*. Chicago: Aries Press.

Muldoon, Sylvan J., and Hereward Carrington. 1929. *The Projection of the Astral Body*. London: Rider and Co.

Muldoon, Sylvan J., and Hereward Carrington. 1951. *The Phenomena of Astral Projection*. London: Rider and Co.

Munk, William. 1887. *Euthanasia: Or, Medical Treatment in Aid of an Easy Death*. London: Longmans, Green, and Co.

Murphy, Gardner. 1945. "An Outline of Survival Evidence." *Journal of the American Society for Psychical Research* 39 (1): 2–34.

Myers, Frederic W. H. 1893. *Science and a Future Life. With other Essays*. London, New York: Macmillan.

Myers, Frederic W. H. 1903, 1904. *Human Personality and Its Survival of Bodily Death*. 2 vols. London: Longmans, Green, & Co.

Nagel, Thomas. 1974. "What Is It Like to Be a Bat?" *Philosophical Review* 83 (4): 435–50.

Nagel, Thomas. 1986. *The View from Nowhere*. Oxford: Oxford University Press.

Nahm, Michael. 2009. "Terminal Lucidity in People with Mental Illness and Other Mental Disability: An Overview and Implications for Possible Explanatory Models." *Journal of Near-Death Studies* 28 (2): 87–106.

Nahm, Michael. 2011. "The *Tibetan Book of the Dead*: Its History and Controversial Aspects of Its Contents." *Journal of Near-Death Studies*, 29 (3): 373–98.

Neugebauer-Wölk, Monika. 2013. "Historische Esoterikforschung, oder: Der lange Weg der Esoterik zur Moderne." In M. Neugebauer-Wölk et al., eds. *Aufklärung und Esoterik: Wege in die Moderne*, 37–72. Berlin & Boston: de Gruyter.

Niemand, Jasper. (1891) 1920. *Letters That Have Helped Me*. Compiled by Jasper Niemand. Reprinted from the *Path* [1890–1891]. Los Angeles: United Lodge of Theosophists.

Nietzsche, Friedrich. 1977. "Twilight of the Idols." In *The Portable Nietzsche*, translated by Walter Kaufmann. New York: Viking, 463–564.

Nietzsche, Friedrich. 1980. *Sämtliche Werke, Kritische Studienausgabe in 15 Bänden*. Edited by G. Colli and M. Montinari. (15 vols.). Munich & New York: Dtv (cited as KSA).

Noyes, Russell Jr. 1971. "Dying and Mystical Consciousness." *Journal of Thanatology* 1 (1): 25–41.

Noyes, Russell Jr. 1972. "The Experience of Dying." *Psychiatry* 35: 174–84.

Noyes, Russell Jr., and Roy Kletti. 1972. "The Experience of Dying From Falls" [translation of Heim 1892]. *Omega* 3: 45–52.

Noyes, Russell Jr., and Roy Kletti. 1976a. "Depersonalization in the Face of Life-Threatening Danger: A Description." *Psychiatry Interpersonal & Biological Processes* 39 (1): 19–27.

Noyes, Russell Jr., and Roy Kletti. 1976b. "Depersonalization in the Face of Life-Threatening Danger: An Interpretation." *Omega* 7: 103–14.

Noyes, Russell Jr., and Roy Kletti. 1977a. "Panoramic Memory: A Response to the Threat of Death." *Omega* 8: 181–94.

Noyes, Russell Jr., and Roy Kletti. 1977b. "Depersonalization in Response to Life Threatening Danger." *Comparative Psychiatry* 18: 375–84.

Noyes, Russell Jr., and D. Slymen. 1979. "The Subjective Response to Life-Threatening Danger." *Omega* 9: 313–21.

Obeyesekere, Gananath. 2012. *The Awakened Ones: Phenomenology of Visionary Experience*. New York & Chichester, UK: Columbia University Press.

Ogston, Sir Alexander. 1919. *Reminiscences of Three Campaigns*. London: Hodder and Stoughton.

Olcott, Henry Steel. 1880. "The Occult Sciences." *The Theosophist* 1 (11) (August): 264–7.

Ong, Walter J. (1982) 2002. *Orality and Literacy. The Technologizing of the Word*. London & New York: Routledge.

Osis, Karlis. 1961. *Deathbed Observations by Physicians and Nurses*. New York: Parapsychology Foundation. http://babel.hathitrust.org/cgi/pt?id=mdp.39015001033722;view=1up;seq=6 (accessed Oct. 21, 2017).

Osis, Karlis, and Erlendur Haraldsson. (1977) 1997. *At the Hour of Death. A New Look at Evidence for Life After Death*. New York: Avon Books [2012: White Crow Productions].

Owen, Alex. 2004a. *The Darkened Room: Women, Power and Spiritualism in Late Victorian England*. Chicago: University of Chicago Press.

Owen, Alex. 2004b. *The Place of Enchantment. British Occultism and the Culture of the Modern*. Chicago: University of Chicago Press.

Owen, Robert D. 1860. *Footfalls on the Boundary of Another World: With Narrative Illustrations*. London: Trübner & Co.

Oxenham, John, and Erica Oxenham. 1941. *Out of the Body. A Plain Man's Parable of the Life to Come, etc*. London: Longmans, Green.

Oxon, M. A. [William Stainton Moses]. 1876. "On the Trans-Corporeal Action of Spirit. Part I." *Human Nature* 10 (3): 97–125.

Oxon, M. A. 1877. "On the Trans-Corporeal Action of Spirit. Part II." *Human Nature* 11 (1): 245–57.

Pahnke, Walter. 1963. "Drugs and Mysticism. An Analysis of the Relationship between Psychedelic Drugs and the Mystical Consciousness." PhD dissertation. Cambridge, MA: Harvard University.

Pahnke, Walter. 1964. *First Impressions of First LSD Experience of March 30, 1964*. (Purdue University, Psychoactive Substances Collection, http://earchives.lib.purdue.edu/cdm/singleitem/collection/psyc/id/7) (accessed Oct. 21,2017).

Pahnke, Walter. 1969. "The Psychedelic Mystical Experience in the Human Encounter With Death." *Harvard Theological Review* 62: 1–21.

Pahnke, Walter N., and William A. Richards. "Implications of LSD and Experimental Mysticism." *Journal of Religion and Health* 25 (1966): 64–72. [reprint in Tart 1969].

Paist, Samuel H. 1861. *A Narrative of the Experience of Horace Abraham Ackley, M. D., Late of Cleveland, Ohio, since his Entrance into Spirit-life: received through the mediumship of Samuel H. Paist of Philadelphia*. Philadelphia: Lippincott & Co.

Parnia, Sam, et al. 2014. "AWARE—AWAreness during REsuscitation—A Prospective Study." *Resuscitation* 85 (12): 1799–805.

Pascal, Blaise. (1660) 1910. *Pascal's Pensées*. Translated by W. F. Trotter. New York: Collier & Son.

Passavant, Johann C. 1821 [revised ed. 1837]. *Untersuchungen über den Lebensmagnetismus und das Hellsehen*. Frankfurt: H. L. Brönner.

Pearce-Higgins, John D. 1973. *Life, Death and Psychical Research: Studies on Behalf of the Churches' Fellowship for Psychical and Spiritual Studies*. London: Rider.

Pelley, William D. 1929. *'Seven Minutes in Eternity' With Their Aftermath, Together With a Biographical Sketch*. New York: Robert Collier Inc.

Perty, Maximilian. 1861/1872. *Die mystischen Erscheinungen der menschlichen Natur: dargestellt und gedeutet*. Leipzig & Heidelberg: Winter [enlarged ed., 2 vols., 1872].

Pfister, Oskar. 1930. "Schockdenken und Schockphantasien bei höchster Todesgefahr." *Zeitschrift für Psychoanalyse* 16: 430–55.

Pfister, Oskar. 1931. *Schock und Schockphantasien bei höchster Todesgefahr. Eine psychoanalytische Studie*. Vienna: Internationaler psychoanalytischer Verlag.

Pfister, Oskar. 1981. *Shock Thoughts and Fantasies in Extreme Mortal Danger*. Translated by Roy Kletti and Russell Noyes, Jr. in "Mental States in Mortal Danger," *Essence* 5: 5–20.

Phelps, Elizabeth Stuart. 1883. *Beyond the Gates*. Boston: Houghton Mifflin.

Piéron, Henri. 1901. Sur l'interpretation des faits de rapidité anormale dans le processus d'évocation des images. In *IVe Congrès International de Psychologie*, edited by P. Janet, 439–48. Paris: Félix Alcan.

Piéron, Henri. 1902. "Contribution a la psychologie des mourants." *Revue philosophique de la France et de l'Étranger* 27: 615–16.

Piéron, Henri. 1903. "La rapidité des processus psychiques." *Revue philosophique de la France et de l'Étranger* 28: 69–95.

Pike, Sarah M. 2004. *New Age and Neopagan Religions in America*. New York: Columbia University Press.

Pötzl, Otto. 1939. "Physiologisches und Pathologisches über das persönliche Tempo." *Wiener Klinische Wochenschrift* 52 (24): 569–73.

Powell, Arthur E. 1925. *The Etheric Double. The Health Aura of Man*. Wheaton, IL: Theosophical Publishing House.

Powell, Arthur E. 1927. *The Astral Body and Other Astral Phenomena*. London: Theosophical Publishing House.

Poulet, Georges. 2011. "Bergson: The Theme of the Panoramic Vision of the Dying and Juxtaposition." Introduction and translation by Mark Cirino and William J. Hemminge. *PMLA* 126 (2): 483–99.

Pratt, Orson. 1850. *Divine Authenticity of the Book of Mormon*. Liverpool, UK: R. James.

Price, Henry H. 1953. "Survival and the Idea of 'Another World.'" *Proceedings of the Society for Psychical Research* 50 (182): 1–25.

Price, Henry H. 1968. "The Problem of Life After Death." *Religious Studies* 3 (2): 447–59.

Proudfoot, Wayne. 1985. *Religious Experience*. Berkeley: University of California Press.

Ramacharaka, Yogi [William W. Atkinson]. 1905. *Fourteen Lessons in Yogi Philosophy and Oriental Occultism*. Chicago: Yogi Publication Society.

Ramacharaka, Yogi. 1906. *A Series of Lessons in Raja Yoga*. Chicago: Yogi Publication Society.

Randolph, Paschal B. 1860. Boston Spiritual Conference. *Banner of Light* 8, 13 (Dec. 22): 8.

Randolph, Paschal B. 1861. *Dealings With the Dead. The Human Soul, Its Migrations and Its Transmigrations*. Utica, NY: M. J. Randolph.

Randolph, Paschal B. 1863. *The Rosicrucian's Story. Or, the Little Window at the Foot of the Bed*. New York: Sinclair Tousey.

Randolph, Paschal B. (1866) 1868. *After Death, The Disembodiment of Man*. Boston: Published by the author.

Randolph, Paschal B. 1867. *The Guide to Clairvoyance, and Clairvoyant's Guide* [. . .]. *Also A Special Paper Concerning Hashish*. Boston: Rockwell & Rollins.

Rau, Reinhold, ed. 1968. *Briefe des Bonifatius, Willibalds Leben des Bonifatius*. Edited in Latin with German translation. Darmstadt, Germany: Wissenschaftliche Buchgesellschaft.

Rawlings, Maurice. 1978. *Beyond Death's Door*. London: Sheldon.

Reitz, Johann H. 1717. *Historie der Wiedergebohrnen*. Idstein, Germany: Haug.

Rhodes, Leon S. 1982. "The Near-Death Experience Enlarged by Swedenborg's Vision." *Anabiosis: The Journal for Near-Death Studies* 2 (1) (June): 15–35.

Rhodes, Leon S. 1996. *Tunnel to Eternity. Swedenborgians Look Beyond the Near-Death Experience*. Bryn Athyn, PA: Published by the author.

Richmond, Cora L. V. 1915. *My Experiences While Out of My Body and My Return After Many Days*. Boston: Christopher Press.

Ring, Kenneth. 1980. *Life at Death. A Scientific Investigation of the Near-Death Experience*. New York: Coward, McCann &. Geoghegan.

Ring, Kenneth. 1984. *Heading Toward Omega: In Search of the Meaning of the Near-Death Experience*. New York: Morrow.

Ring, Kenneth. 2000. "Religious Wars in the NDE Movement: Some Personal Reflections on Michael Sabom's Light & Death." *Journal of Near-Death Studies*, 18: 215–44.

Ritchie, George G. 1963. "Return From Tomorrow." *Guideposts*, June 1963 [reprinted in Jess E. Weiss. 1972. *The Vestibule*. Port Washington NY: Ashley Books, 63–7].

Ritchie, George G. 1991. *My Life After Dying—Becoming Alive to Universal Love*. Norfolk, VA: Hampton Roads Publishing.

Ritchie, George G., and E. Sherrill. 1978. *Return From Tomorrow*. London: Kingsway.

Rose, Seraphim. 1980. *The Soul After Death: Contemporary 'After-Death' Experiences in the Light of the Orthodox Teaching on the Afterlife*. Platina, CA: St. Herman of Alaska Brotherhood.

Rosen, David H. 1975. "Suicide Survivors. A Follow-Up Study of Persons Who Survived Jumping From the Golden Gate and San Francisco-Oakland Bay Bridges." *Western Journal of Medicine* 122 (April): 289–94.

Roszak, Theodore. 1969. *The Making of a Counter Culture: Reflections on the Technocratic Society and Its Youthful Opposition.* Berkeley: University of California Press.

Royle, Nicholas. 2003. *The Uncanny.* Manchester, UK: Manchester University Press.

Sabom, Michael B. 1982. *Recollections of Death: A Medical Investigation.* London: Corgi.

Sabom, Michael B. 1998. *Light and Death. One Doctor's Fascinating Account of Near-Death Experiences.* Grand Rapids, MI: Zondervan.

Sabom, Michael B. 2003. The Shadow of Death. Two Parts. *Christian Research Journal* 26, 2 and 3 (http://www.equip.org/article/the-shadow-of-death/, accessed Oct. 23, 2017).

Sabom, Michael B., and Sarah Kreutziger. 1977. "The Experience of Near Death." *Death Education* 1: 195–203.

Sabom, Michael B., and Sarah Kreutziger. 1978. "Physicians Evaluate the Near-Death Experience." *Theta* 6: 1–6.

Sawicki, Diethard. 2002. *Leben mit den Toten. Geisterglaube und die Entstehung des Spiritismus in Deuschland 1770–1900.* Paderborn & Munich: Schönigh.

Say, Thomas. (1796) 1805. *Short Compilation of the Extraordinary Life and Writings of Thomas Say: In Which is Faithfully Copied* [. . .] *the Uncommon Vision, Which He Had When a Young Man.* New York: John Langdon.

Schacter, Daniel L. 2001. *The Seven Sins of Memory. How the Mind Forgets and Remembers.* New York: Houghton Mifflin.

Schiller, Ferdinand C. S. 1891. *Riddles of the Sphinx: A Study in the Philosophy of Evolution.* London: Swan Sonnenschein.

Schlieter, Jens. 2013. "Checking the Heavenly 'Bank Account of Karma': Cognitive Metaphors for Karma in Western Scholarship and Early Theravāda Buddhism." *Religion* 13 (4): 463–86.

Schlieter, Jens 2018. "'Death-x-pulse.' A Hermeneutics for the 'Panoramic Life Review' in Near-Death Experiences." In *Imaginations of Death and the Beyond in India and Europe,* edited by Günter Blamberger and Sudhir Kakar. Singapore: Springer, 145–69.

Schmeidler, Gertrude Raffel, and R. A. McConnell. 1958. *ESP and Personality Patterns.* New Haven, CT: Yale University Press, and London: Oxford University Press.

Schmidt, Bettina E., ed. 2016. *The Study of Religious Experience. Approaches and Methodologies.* Durham, NC: Equinox.

Schmithausen, Lambert. 2001. "Aldous Huxley's View of Nature." In *Aldous Huxley Between East and West,* edited by C. C. Barfoot, 151–73. Amsterdam & New York: Rodopi.

Scott, Leslie G. 1931. "Dying as a Liberation of Consciousness: Record of a Personal Experience." *Journal of the American Society for Psychical Research* 25: 113–17.

Seelbach, C. 1864. *Fingerzeige der göttlichen Weltregierung in wunderbaren Ahnungen und Vorhersagungen, Träumen und Gesichten, sowie Gebetserhörungen.* 2 vols. Stuttgart: Steinkopf.

Shantz, Douglas H. 2008. *Between Sardis and Philadelphia: The Life and World of Pietist Court Preacher Conrad Bröske.* Leiden: Brill.

Shaw, Jane. 2006. *Miracles in Enlightenment England.* New Haven, CT: Yale University Press.

Sheils, Dean. 1978. "A Cross Cultural Study of Beliefs in Out of the Body Experiences, Waking and Sleeping." *Journal of the Society for Psychical Research* 49: 697–741.

Shipley, Morgan. 2015. *Psychedelic Mysticism. Transforming Consciousness, Religious Experience, and Voluntary Peasants in Postwar America*. Lanham, MD & Boulder, CO: Lexington Books.

Shushan, Gregory. 2009. *Conceptions of the Afterlife in Early Civilizations. Universalism, Constructivism, and Near-Death Experience*. London & New York: Continuum.

Shushan, Gregory. 2016. "Cultural-Linguistic Constructivism and the Challenge of Near-Death and Out-of-Body Experiences." In *The Study of Religious Experience*, edited by Bettina E. Schmidt, 71–87. Durham, NC: Equinox.

Siegel, Ronald K. 1983. "Bozzano and the First Classification of Deathbed Visions: A Historical Note and Translation." *Anabiosis: The Journal for Near-Death Studies* 3 (2) (December): 195–201.

Siegel, Ronald K. (1989) 2005. *Intoxication. The Universal Drive for Mind-Altering Substances*. Rochester, VT: Park Street Press.

Siegel, Ronald K., and A. E. Hirschman. 1984. "Hashish Near-Death Experiences." *Anabiosis: The Journal for Near-Death Studies* 4 (1) (Spring): 69–86.

Siémons, Jean-Louis. 1889. *A Nineteenth Century Explanatory Scheme for the Interpretation of Near-Death Experience: The Transpersonal Model of Death as Presented in Madame Blavatsky's Theosophy*. Paris [publisher not given], http://www.blavatsky.net/index.php/near-death-experiences (accessed Oct. 23, 2017).

Simeon, Daphne, and Jeffrey Abugel. 2008. *Feeling Unreal: Depersonalization Disorder and the Loss of the Self*. Oxford: Oxford University Press.

Sinnett, Alfred P. 1881. *The Occult World*. London: Trübner and Company.

Sinnett, Alfred P. (1883) 1885. *Esoteric Buddhism* (5th enlarged ed.). London: Chapman and Hall.

Sinnett, Alfred P. 1914. *In the Next World. Actual Narratives of Personal Experiences by Some Who Have Passed On*. London: Theosophical Publishing Society.

Sinnett, Alfred P. (1896) 1918. *The Growth of the Soul. A Sequel to 'Esoteric Buddhism'*. London: Theosophical Publishing House.

Slingerland, Edward. 2004. "Conceptual Metaphor Theory as Methodology for Comparative Religion." *Journal of the American Academy of Religion* 72 (1): 1–31.

Smith, Seraphina G., ed. 1893. *Recollections of the Pioneers of Lee County*. Dixon, IL: Inez A. Kennedy.

Snyder, Mark, Elizabeth D. Tanke, and Ellen Berscheid. 1977. "Social Perception and Interpersonal Behavior: On the Self-Fulfilling Nature of Social Stereotypes." *Journal of Personality and Social Psychology* 35 (9): 656–66.

Sogyal Rinpoche. 1992. *The Tibetan Book of Living and Dying*. London: Rider.

Sollier, Paul. 1896. "L'état mental des mourants." *Revue philosophique de la France et de l'Étranger* 21: 303–7.

Sollier, Paul. 1903. *Les phénomènes d'autoscopie*. Paris: Alcan.

Solow, Victor D. 1974. "I Died at 10:52 A.M." *Readers Digest* 105 (630; October): 178–82.

Sperber, Michael. 2012. "Traumatic Brain Injury and Therapeutic Creativity." *Neurology Times*, http://www.neurologytimes.com/ptsd/traumatic-brain-injury-and-therapeutic-creativity (accessed Oct. 23, 2017).

Splittgerber, Franz. 1866. *Schlaf und Tod*. Halle/Saale: Julius Fricke.

Stasulane, Anita. 2013. "The Theosophy of the Roerichs. Agni Yoga or Living Ethics." In *Handbook of the Theosophical Current*, edited by Olav Hammer and Mikael Rothstein, 193–216. Leiden: Brill.

Steiner, Rudolf. (1909) 1910. *Die Geheimwissenschaft im Umriss*. Leipzig: Max Altmann.

Steiner, Rudolf. 1922. *An Outline of Occult Science.* (authorized translation from the 4th ed.). New York: Anthroposophic Press.

Steiner, Rudolf. 1987. *Rudolf Steiner Gesamtausgabe. Vorträge vor Mitgliedern der Anthroposophischen Gesellschaft. 1904–1914.* Dornach, Switzerland: Rudolf Steiner Verlag.

Steiner, Rudolf. 1994. *Anthroposophische Menschenerkenntnis und Medizin. Elf Vorträge* [1923–1924]. Dornach, Switzerland: Rudolf Steiner Verlag.

Stengel, Friedemann. 2011. *Aufklärung bis zum Himmel: Emanuel Swedenborg im Kontext der Theologie und Philosophie des 18. Jahrhunderts.* Tübingen: Mohr.

Stevens, Jay. 1987. *Storming Heaven. LSD and the American Dream.* New York: Grove.

Stevenson, Ian. (1966) 1974. *Twenty Cases Suggestive of Reincarnation* (2nd revised and enlarged ed.). Charlottesville: University of Virginia Press.

Stevenson, Ian. 1977. "Research Into the Evidence of Man's Survival After Death." *Journal of Nervous and Mental Disease* 165: 152–70.

Stevenson, Ian, and E. W. Cook. 1995. "Involuntary Memories During Severe Physical Illness or Injury." *Journal of Nervous and Mental Disease* 183 (7): 452–8.

Stevenson, Ian, and Bruce Greyson. 1979. "Near-death Experiences: Relevance to the Question of Survival after Death." *Journal of the American Medical Association* 242 (3): 265–7.

Stratton, F. J. M. 1957. "An Out-of-Body Experience Combined With ESP." *Journal of the Society for Psychical Research* 39 (692): 92–7.

Strube, Julian. 2016. *Sozialismus, Katholizismus und Okkultismus im Frankreich des 19. Jahrhunderts. Die Genealogie der Schriften von Eliphas Lévi.* Berlin & New York: de Gruyter.

Sudduth, Michael. 2016. *A Philosophical Critique of Empirical Arguments for Postmortem Survival.* Basingstoke, UK: Palgrave Macmillan.

Swedenborg, Emanuel. 1758. *De coelo et ejus mirabilibus, et de inferno: Ex auditis & visis.* London: John Lewis.

Swedenborg, Emanuel. 1778. *A Treatise Concerning Heaven and Hell, Containing A Relation of many Wonderful Things therein, as heard and seen by the Author, the Honourable Emanuel Swedenborg* [.....] *Now First Translated from the Original Latin.* London: James Phillips.

Swedenborg, Emanuel. 1854. *A Compendium of the Theological and Spiritual Writings of Emanuel Swedenborg.* Boston: Crosby and Nichols.

Tanne, Janice Hopkins. 2004. "Humphrey Osmond." *British Medical Journal* 328 (7441): 713.

Tart, Charles T. 1967. "A Second Psychophysiological Study of Out of the Body Experiences in a Gifted Subject." *International Journal of Parapsychology* 9: 251–8.

Tart, Charles T. 1968. "A Psychophysiological Study of Out of the Body Experiences in a Selected Subject." *Journal of the American Society for Psychical Research* 62: 3–27.

Tart, Charles T., ed. 1969. *Altered States of Consciousness. A Book of Readings.* New York & London: Wiley.

Taves, Ann. 2009. *Religious Experience Reconsidered. A Building-Block Approach to the Study of Religion and Other Special Things.* Princeton, NJ: Princeton University Press.

Taylor, Charles. 2007. *A Secular Age.* Cambridge, MA & London: Belknap.

Taylor, Thomas. 1825. *The Fragments That Remain of the Lost Writings of Proclus.* London: Black, Young, and Young.

Thayer, Joseph. 1995. *Greek–English Lexicon of the New Testament: Coded with Strong's Concordance Numbers.* Peabody, MA: Hendrickson Publishers.

Thonnard, Marie, et al. 2013. "Characteristics of Near-Death Experiences Memories as Compared to Real and Imagined Events Memories." *PLoS One* 8 (3): e57620. doi: 10.1371/journal. pone.0057620 (accessed Oct. 23, 2017).

Thurston, Herbert. 1935. "Memory at Imminent Death." *The Month. A Publication of the English Provenance of the Society of Jesus*, 165 (Jan.): 49–60 [published by Longmans, Green, & Co.].

Tiryakian, Edward A. 1996. "Three Metacultures of Modernity. Christian, Gnostic, Chthonic." *Theory, Culture and Society* 13 (1): 99–118.

Top, Brent L. 1997. "Thought Communication, Speed of Movement, and the Spirit's Ability to Absorb Knowledge: Near-Death Experiences and Early Mormon Thought." *Journal of Near-Death Studies* 15 (3): 203–16.

Tucker, Louis. 1943. *Clerical Errors*. New York: Harper & Row.

Tudor Pole, Wellesley. 1917. *Private Dowding. The Personal Story of a Soldier Killed in Battle*. London: Watkins.

Turvey, Vincent. 1909. *The Beginnings of Seership; Or, Super-Normal Mental Activity*. London: Stead's Publishing House.

Tuttle, Hudson. 1864. *Arcana of Nature; Or the Philosophy of Spiritual Existence and of the Spirit World*. Vol. II. Boston: William White.

Tuttle, Hudson. 1871. *Arcana of Spiritualism. A Manual of Spiritual Science and Philosophy, or, the History and Laws of Creation*. Boston: Adams & Co.

Tyrrell, George N. M. 1943. *Apparitions*, London: Gerald Duckworth and Co.

Tyrrell, George N. M. (1947) 1954. *The Personality of Man. New Facts and Their Significance*. Middlesex, UK: Penguin Books.

Ulmer, Bernd. 1988. "Konversionserzählungen als rekonstruktive Gattung. Erzählerische Mittel und Strategien bei der Rekonstruktion eines Bekehrungserlebnisses." *Zeitschrift für Soziologie* 17, 19–33.

Uxkull, C. 1934. *My Death and Revival. (An Entirely True Revelation of a Man's Experience)*. Trans. from the Russian by Basil Doudine. Arrochar, NY: Emerald Pocket Library. [repr. as Uexküll, K. 1961. *Unbelievable for Many, but Actually a True Occurrence*. Jordanville, NY: Holy Trinity Russian Orthodox Monastery; and again 1976. *Orthodox Life* 26 (4): 1–36.].

van Uytfanghe, Marc. 1991; 1992–1993. "Les visions du très haut Moyen Âge et les récentes 'expériences de mort temporaire'. Sens ou non-sens d'une comparaison. Première partie." *Instrumenta Patristica* 23: 447–81; Seconde partie, *Sacris Erudiri* 33: 135–82.

Veatch, Robert M. 1977. *Death, Dying and the Biological Revolution: Our Last Quest for Responsibility*. New Haven, CT: Yale University Press.

Veatch, Robert M. 1978. "The Definition of Death: Ethical, Philosophical and Policy Confusion." In *Brain Death*, edited by Julius Korein, 307–18. New York: New York Academy of Sciences.

Veith, Frank J., et al. 1977. "Special Communication: Brain Death I: A Status Report of Medical and Ethical Considerations." *Journal of the American Medical Association*, 238 (15): 1651–5.

Vincent, Ken R., and John C. Morgan. 2006. "An 18th Century Near-Death Experience: The Case of George de Benneville." *Journal of Near-Death Studies* 25 (1): 35–48.

von Stuckrad, Kocku. 2014. "Esoteric Discourse and the European History of Religion: In Search of a New Interpretational Framework." *Scripta Instituti Donneriani Aboensis* 20: 217–36.

Walker, Barbara A., and William J. Serdahely. 1990. "Historical Perspectives on Near-Death Phenomena." *Journal of Near-Death Studies* 9 (2): 105–21.

Webster, John. 1677. *The Displaying of Supposed Witchcraft: Wherein is Affirmed that there are Many Sorts of Deceivers and Impostors*. London: J. M.

Weiss, Jess E., ed. 1972. *The Vestibule*. Port Washington, NY: Ashley Books.

Welch, Thomas. 1976 [1950s or 1960s; before 1968]. *Oregon's Amazing Miracle*. Introduction by Gordon Lindsay [Reprint]. Dallas, TX: Christ for the Nations.

Wharton, Francis. 1859. *A Treatise on Theism, and on the Modern Skeptical Theories*, Philadelphia: J.B. Lippincott & Co., London: Trübner & Co.

Whipple, Guy Montrose. 1909. "The Observer as Reporter: A Survey of the 'Psychology of Testimony'." *Psychological Bulletin* 6 (5): 153–70.

Whymper, Edward. 1880. *The Ascent of the Matterhorn*. London: John Murray.

Wiesenhütter, Eckart. 1977 [1974]. *Blick nach Drüben: Selbsterfahrungen im Sterben*. Hamburg: Gütersloher Taschenbuch.

Wilkins, John. 1675. *Of the Principles and Duties of Natural Religion* [. . .]. London: Printed by A. Maxwell for T. Bassert et al.

Wiltse, A. S. 1889. "A Case of Typhoid Fever with Subnormal Temperature and Pulse." *St. Louis Medical and Surgical Journal* 57: 355–64 [reprinted in *Proceedings of the Society for Psychical Research* 8 (1892): 180–7].

Winslow, Forbes B. 1860. *On Obscure Diseases of the Brain, and Disorders of the Mind: Their Incipient Symptoms, Pathology, Diagnosis, Treatment, and Prophylaxis*. Philadelphia: Blanchard & Lea.

Wittgenstein, Ludwig. (1953) 1986. *Philosophical Investigations*. Translated by G. E. M. Anscombe. Oxford: Basil Blackwell.

Wittgenstein, Ludwig. 1969–75. *On Certainty (Über Gewißheit)*. Edited by G. E. M. Anscombe and George Henrik von Wright. Oxford: Basil Blackwell.

Wolfe, Napoleon Bonaparte. 1875. *Startling Facts in Modern Spiritualism*. Chicago: Religio-Philosophical Publishing House.

Woodrooffe, John G. (1927) 2000. "Foreword: The Science of Death." In *The Tibetan Book of the Dead*, edited by W. Y. Evans-Wentz, lxv–lxxxiv. Oxford: Oxford University Press.

Yalom, Irvin D. 2008. *Staring at the Sun: Overcoming the Terror of Death*. San Francisco: Jossey-Bass.

Zaleski, Carol. 1987. *Otherworld Journeys: Accounts of Near-Death Experiences in Medieval and Modern Times*. New York: Oxford University Press.

Zander, Helmut. 2007. *Anthroposophie in Deutschland. Theosophische Weltanschauung und gesellschaftliche Praxis 1884–1945*. 2 vols. Göttingen: Vandenhoeck & Ruprecht.

NAME INDEX

Albanese, Catherine L., xix, 126, 129, 132, 302, 306
Alexander, Eben, ix–xi, xvi, 34–35
Alpert, Richard, 201–203
Alvarado, Carlos S., 70, 88, 107, 111, 113, 119, 136, 145, 171, 178, 186, 189, 247
Amiel, Henri-Frédéric, 113–114
Aries, Philippe, 231–234
Asprem, Egil, 41, 259, 300
Atherton, Anna, 57–59, 286, 295
Atkinson, William W. *See*
   Ramacharaka, Yogi
Audette, John R., 7, 9, 51, 173, 175
Augustine, St., 182, 307

Baier, Karl, 39, 120, 123, 202, 218
Baird, Alexander T., 146
Bälz, Erwin, 114, 198
Barnard, William G., 299
Barrett, William F., 145–146, 176, 196, 295
Becker, Ernest, 28
Belkin, Gary, 239, 241–242
Bennett, John G., 13–14

Benneville, George de, 67, 286, 289
Benz, Ernst, 202
Berger, Peter L., 33, 222, 253
Bergson, Henri, 13, 15, 112, 171, 183
Besant, Annie, 88, 125
Binns, Edward, 83–84, 86, 288, 307
Birnbaum, Karl, 111, 169
Blackmore, Susan, 12, 275
Blake, William, x
Blavatsky, Helena P., xxiv, 39, 81, 120, 122–128, 130, 154, 160, 289, 302–303
Bloch, Oscar, 113
Blumenberg, Hans, xxxi, 307
Bondeson, Jan, 59, 242
Bosch, Hieronymus, xxv, 6, 288
Boyer, Pascal, 34–35
Bozzano, Ernesto, 111, 145, 171, 172
Bremmer, Jan N., 48–49, 85, 286
Broad, Charlie D., 5, 144, 183
Buddha, xix, 103, 124–125, 130–131, 160, 161, 197, 311
Bulwer-Lytton, Edward G., 126
Byrd, Richard E., 176–177

SUBJECT INDEX